Policewomen

A History

SECOND EDITION

KERRY SEGRAVE

McFarland & Company, Inc., Publishers

Jefferson, North Carolina

LIBRARY OF CONGRESS CATALOGUING-IN-PUBLICATION DATA

Segrave, Kerry, 1944–
    Policewomen : a history / Kerry Segrave. — Second edition.
        p.   cm.
    Includes bibliographical references and index.

    ISBN 978-0-7864-7705-0 (softcover : acid free paper) ∞

    ISBN 978-1-4766-1210-2 (ebook)

    1. Policewomen—History.   2. Policewomen—United
States—History.   I. Title.

HV8023.S44 2014
363.2082—dc23   2013044306

BRITISH LIBRARY CATALOGUING DATA ARE AVAILABLE

On the cover: Policewomen Pitkin, Schroeder, Stevenat, Elder &
Wilson, Bain News Service (Library of Congress); police badge
(Stockbyte/Thinkstock); brick texture (iStockphoto/Thinkstock)

Manufactured in the United States of America

*McFarland & Company, Inc., Publishers
    Box 611, Jefferson, North Carolina 28640
    www.mcfarlandpub.com*

Contents

Preface

This book is a review of the history of policewomen from the inception of the profession up through 2012. In tracing the entry of females into police work I have begun with the movement of women first into the occupation of matron, which became relatively common in the 1870s and 1880s. The societal forces that paved the way for females to become matrons continued to exist, resulting in women moving into police officer jobs in the early twentieth century.

I examine the occupation of policewomen to determine how they entered law enforcement; the duties they held; the view held of policewomen by their peers, superiors, and by the general public; the pressures that brought about their appointment; what changes took place over time; the discrimination and harassment they faced; and how they later came to be integrated into policing as they were assigned interchangeably with male officers—a change that started at the end of the 1960s.

About two-thirds of the material in this book is based on U.S. experiences, with that from other countries, especially from the United Kingdom, making up the remainder.

Research for this book was conducted in the UCLA library system and at the Los Angeles Public Library. Social science and history databases were searched, along with newspaper indexes and books on law enforcement and police history. In addition, the memoirs of a few of the earliest policewomen were most helpful. Online databases were used for the material included in the revised edition.

Introduction

Women entered law enforcement work in the late nineteenth and early twentieth centuries. This was a time when a strong feminist movement was altering the position of females in society. Women agitated for a variety of measures to move them toward equality with men. One area of concern was that of the imprisonment and detention of women by the police. In dozens of cities throughout America and other parts of the world, women's groups lobbied for protection of female detainees, who were subjected to sexual and other abuses by the all-male law enforcement system. Initial victories came in the prison system and police station lockups where females were gradually hired as matrons to supervise and oversee women detainees. It was a move strongly resisted by much of the male police establishment.

As feminists lobbied for equality and as people became increasingly urbanized, the place of women in society did alter. It became more common and acceptable for females to be out on city streets at any time, unaccompanied by a male escort. In turn this led to women more frequently interacting with the police, as, for example, when they would report an incident of harassment to an officer, or be themselves harassed by the police. This period marked the beginning of the era when nice women were out alone or in pairs or groups at night. Previously women in such circumstances had been prostitutes, alcoholics, or homeless, or perhaps all three. They were treated accordingly by the male police. But respectable middle-class females started interacting with the police — such as when suffragettes were moved along or detained at demonstrations — and they were often appalled by these interactions. This led to further feminist activism in the early twentieth century in pursuit of hiring policewomen to deal with females away from prisons and station lockups.

Despite objections, the activists succeeded in getting a token number of policewomen hired by many big city police departments in the early decades of the 20th century. Those early policewomen had a limited and narrow range of duties: their mandate was to protect women and children, and they functioned largely as social workers with police badges. They supervised public entertainment areas such as dance halls and amusement arcades where they worked to keep young females from engaging in sexual activities. In addition, they dealt with prostitutes and rape victims. European policewomen had precisely the same duties, although they often had greater dealings with prostitutes since that occupation was legal in parts of Europe. Resistance to the concept of women in the police force was perhaps greatest in England. It took the impetus of World War I to initiate their entry into police work, when many women were taken on to help protect soldiers from venereal disease, which was then described as a rampant problem by the military authorities.

This early role of policewomen remained constant until the late 1960s and early 1970s. Despite widespread male opposition, a few male police officials were willing to tolerate policewomen in token numbers and in limited roles. Male officials who remained hostile often took revenge by limiting policewomen to matron-only duty or to clerical work. Policewomen themselves never challenged their early limitations. The narrow role was the only one they sought or felt competent to perform. Indeed, at the time it was the only role they would have been allowed. It was in many ways an extension of the stereotypical view of women: protectors of youth, guardians of morals, nurturers, caregivers, and mothers. Not one of the early policewomen felt a woman could or should function as a general duty patrol officer. Policemen broke up fights, handled guns, and arrested people. Policewomen did not arrest. Whenever possible they talked and used moral persuasion, and their very presence as mothers convinced most people to be good, just as social workers attempted to do. Policewomen helped usher in the era of proactive policing, compared to the strictly reactive law enforcement in existence at the turn of the twentieth century.

A change in status for women to the general duty police officer began with agitation in the 1960s, which brought a few breakthroughs and then major advances in the 1970s. Once again a notable force was a strong feminist lobby then fighting for various issues. Despite the fact that hostile males trained them, gave them assignments, observed them, rated them, discriminated against them, harassed them, and sometimes deliberately put the female officers' lives at risk, policewomen acquitted themselves well — always being rated the equal of males as efficient, capable police officers, sometimes even exceeding males. Crucial to women making this advance — besides feminist lobbying — was a sympathetic political administration, with the result that dozens of court orders were imposed and consent decrees signed that caused many city police departments to hire females in sufficient numbers so they could be assigned to general patrol duty.

While they have already proven themselves as capable, policewomen still face much discrimination and harassment at the hands of the male police. In spite of this, the public has always been and still remains far more supportive of policewomen than the male officers. Today policewomen amount to around 14 percent of total police strength, even exceeding 20 percent in a few large cities. With the general weakening of affirmative action in the 1980s, 1990s, and beyond, it is unlikely that this percentage will significantly and permanently increase in the foreseeable future. Harassment and discrimination against policewomen remains rampant well into the 21st century.

Cities and their citizens are the losers in this battle, since policewomen don't brutalize the public the way policemen often do. Complaints by citizens are far more frequently concerning male officers, while policewomen receive far more compliments. Lawsuits and settlements for excessive use of force by the police cost cities tens of millions of dollars yearly. The user of excessive force is almost always a policeman, not a policewoman.

1

U.S. (Police Matrons),
to 1910

Before females were able to assume their early and limited role as police officers, they entered law enforcement as matrons, both in prisons and in police station lockups. Fueling the drive by women to have females employed as matrons and police officers was the desire to protect women from the potential abuses they were exposed to when they were thrust into the all-male world of prisons and police. Appointments of women to these roles came about only after intense pressure and lobbying by various women's groups, moves that created a great deal of resistance in the all-male establishment.

Indiana reportedly was the first place in America to open a prison solely to house women. That was in 1873. In the absence of such institutions female detainees were held in the same prison as men, sometimes located on a separate floor or wing of the building, but sometimes in sex-segregated cells, within sight of the incarcerated opposite sex. All tending to both male and female detainees—including searches—was performed by male guards. Not surprisingly, in those years under such conditions, female detainees were subjected to sexual abuse by male guards and by male detainees. From the establishment point of view this arrangement of mixed prisons was useful, since the females could be put to work in a traditional role of performing cleaning duties throughout the facility. Of course, that put them at even greater risk of assault since they had to move through the entire complex.[1]

A second such institution was the Women's Prison in Sherborn, Massachusetts, which opened in September 1877. Reportedly, it came into being due "to the efforts of women who have worked long and faithfully, if unknown and silently, for the amelioration of the condition of women in prisons and when released from them." According to this article the writer knew of only two other prisons in the world that housed females exclusively and wherein the inmates were under the immediate control of women. One of them was in England while the other was the aforementioned institution in Indianapolis. About a year after it opened it was pronounced to be such a success that "we wonder it has been so long delayed." In another report the Women's Prison was described as "more like a charitable home" or "a reformatory institution" than a penitentiary. Some six months after it opened it contained 355 inmates ranging in age from 16 to 68 and not more than one-half of those inmates were foreign born, although a large number of the American born detainees were said to have foreign-born parents. There were a few African-American women in the facility. As well there were 43 babies in the facility's nursery with 14 of those having been born at the prison in the six months since it had opened. Such a baby or infant was allowed to stay at the prison with its mother up to the age of 18 months. At that early date the facility, built for a maximum of 297 inmates, was over its capacity. Reportedly, a large proportion of the inmates could neither read nor write.[2]

When the four-story New York City Prison (the Tombs) opened in 1838, female detainees were initially held on the top floor with males incarcerated on the lower floors. This arrangement lasted only briefly due to a "brutal outrage" (a rape or attempted rape) by one of the male detainees. Because of this, female detainees were removed to a smaller building on the compound which was for them exclusively. Vigorous lobbying by a group called the American Female Society led to the appointment in 1845 in New York City of six police matrons; two were assigned to the Tombs, with the other four assigned to the detention facility on Blackwell's Island. They were the first appointed in the United States. Ten years later a small apartment was constructed on-site at the Tombs for the matrons. By 1870 the Tombs employed one matron, Flora Foster, who was paid $600 per year and three assistant matrons who each received $425 per year. However, this was in stark contrast to the 11 male deputy keepers who were each paid $1,000 a year. A brief newspaper piece in 1870 stated that Foster had been a matron at the Tombs for 21 years and that she was wealthy, "but she holds the place from love of the excitement it brings."[3]

Outside of New York City no other official matron appointments were made for several decades after 1845. Lobbying efforts by women's groups increased in the 1860s, becoming particularly intense in the 1870s through the 1890s. This lobbying was directed toward having females appointed as matrons in prisons and also in the police lockups attached to various station houses. The idea of matrons at police stations became the focus of the pressure as this was the point in the law enforcement system where a female first made contact with the authorities. A major driving force behind the pressure was the sexual abuse female detainees were often subjected to. In New York City in 1890 a police officer pleaded guilty to the attempted assault of a 15-year-old girl being detained in a station house lockup. Another report noted that in the 1880s and 1890s cities like Chicago, New York and Jersey City started to hire matrons "in the wake of a series of assaults on female felons by their arresting officers." When the *New York Times* described the lack of privacy female detainees had — how cells for men were often directly across from cells for women — the newspaper hinted at the assault situation by writing, "In a few cities real abuses were reported before the law securing police matrons could be passed." In addition New York reporter Nellie Bly of *The World* was credited with "exposing the methods used by mustached policemen in handling women prisoners." Bly was the pen name of an American pioneer female journalist, Elizabeth Jane Cochrane (1864–1922), who was a huge media star in her day. Another article said her description of the treatment of female prisoners in the police stations was a major achievement and "the appointment of police matrons to care for female prisoners was the result of that piece." That was an exaggeration but Bly and others like her were all crucial in advancing the concept of women being an active part of the police service.[4]

By the 1870s groups involved in pressing for police matrons included the national Woman's Christian Temperance Union (WCTU), the Federation of Women's Clubs, the National League of Women Voters, local associations and clubs including social agencies operating in the protective field, and by social hygiene groups. Also active in lobbying efforts were the Men's City Clubs of Philadelphia and Chicago. It was the WCTU that was considered the major lobbying organization. Early demands to have a matron at the station lockups during daytime hours to see that detainees were properly dressed for court appearances, changed to a demand that a matron have total charge of female detainees 24 hours a day for as long as they were in custody. The WCTU got involved around 1875, or even a bit earlier, during its temperance crusade. WCTU members first began visiting the prisons with the one thought of helping those female detainees who had fallen through the influence of strong drink. From there they moved into agitation for prison reform with respect to women and to similar reforms in the police lockups around the country.

The first police matron (outside of the Tombs in New York) was appointed in Portland, Maine, in 1878. Earlier that decade a female physician had been in court and saw sights (not specified) that so appalled her she reported the matter to the WCTU. Prominent members of that group began to visit female detainees and to attend court sessions. Due to the pressure applied by the WCTU, and others, city officials agreed to appoint a matron to attend the police court and care for the female detainees, or act as their friend in the county jails. But there were no appropriations to meet the expense so the WCTU paid the matron's salary for the first year out of its own treasury (another source stated that only half of her salary was paid by the WCTU). That was in 1877. The next year, 1878, she was a fully paid Portland employee. She worked only daytime hours. Providence, Rhode Island, was the next city to follow this lead and the first to institute 24-hour-a-day matrons.[5]

Through the efforts of the WCTU and other groups, police matrons were appointed in Jersey City, New Jersey, in 1880; Chicago in 1881; Boston in 1883; Baltimore, St. Louis, and Milwaukee in 1884; Detroit, Denver, and San Francisco in 1885; and Cleveland and Philadelphia in 1886. The WCTU's program at the time was, "Push the matter of police matrons in every city; commence at once and continue until successful." In Philadelphia during the spring and summer of 1886, a number of that city's "charitably disposed and benevolent women" met with the mayor to agitate for the hiring of matrons. After much consideration and resistance, this was done with the hiring of four in October of that year. While the four were appointed by the mayor, their names had been submitted by the United Women's Charities of that city.[6]

Generally, this experiment of employing matrons was considered a success wherever it was tried. The odd failure was felt to be the result of appointing an unsuitable woman to the post for political or other inappropriate reasons. To guard against this, the organizations pressing for matrons often put forward the names of individuals who were then appointed by city mayors. For example, in 1887 the State of Massachusetts passed a law directing the appointment of police matrons in all cities with a population of 20,000 or more. The bill contained a clause which mandated that the appointment of such matrons be put in the hands of a committee of women drawn from the different groups agitating for those appointments. Reportedly, over 5,000 women were arrested in Boston every year. Its population in 1890 was 448,477. An account published in 1904 declared that Mrs. Abbie Jackson of Boston was about to take her first vacation from her job as police matron in 30 years. She was said to be highly successful in managing "refractory prisoners" and to have had 20,000 women under her care throughout that 30-year career (likely an inaccurate number).[7]

During the 1888 meeting of the National Conference of Charities and Corrections Bishop Ireland gave "personal testimony to the imperative need for such help and protection for women" that matrons could provide. Mrs. J. K. Barney, a WCTU executive, described the ideal matron as "a middle-aged woman, scrupulously clean in person and dress, with a face to commend her and a manner to compel respect; quiet, calm, observant, with faith in God and hope for humanity." One year earlier the 13th annual National Conference of Charities and Corrections adjourned in July 1886 in St. Paul, Minnesota. With 472 delegates attending it had been the largest such conference every held to that time. One speaker was Barney of Rhode Island whose official title was superintendent of prison, jail, police and almshouse work for the national WCTU. She made an earnest appeal in favor of women matrons at police stations saying that "within twenty-four hours revelations had been made to her that would make the women of St. Paul blush if they heard it." However, no details were provided. It was reported that "her speech was rapid, earnest, full of pathos and truth, and had a marked effect on the audience." Mrs. M. A. Warner of Minnesota, connected with the prison work of the WCTU, spoke also and said it was an "outrage on humanity" to have things conducted as they were then. Mrs. Elizabeth B. Fairbanks of Milwaukee, member of the State Board of Charity told how any community could have a police matron if they wanted to. In Milwaukee a request for a police matron had been refused on the ground that the community would not approve it. Faced with that refusal her group had then put their hands in their own pockets and paid her salary for two years, and any city could give itself a matron by responding in that fashion.[8]

Barney spent some 20 years agitating in New York City for the appointment of police matrons. Progress was slow and unsatisfactory, and it always "met with opposition." By the 1880s the best she and others had accomplished was in providing occasional voluntary services for detainees. Pressure was intensified during that decade. On the night of March 2, 1882, a mass meeting was held for the purpose of having matrons appointed at all of New York City's 31 police stations. Many speeches were made and resolutions were passed, declaring that "the cause of mercy and morality alike demands the presence of police matrons." During the quarter ending September 30, 1881, 20,000 females were detained in station lockups; of those, 5,000 were arrested for being drunk and disorderly; and those females detained were searched by males. At that meeting, "Instances were cited when want of treatment of female prisoners by suitable Matrons had resulted in death of the prisoners." However, no specific details were reported. Mrs. Lillie Devereaux Blake (an American suffragist and reformer) presided over that meeting. Blake said legislation was needed for establishing police matrons in police cells. She cited recent cases of arrests of women and said it might be the lot of any woman to be taken to a police station if an accident befell her in the street. Resolutions were adopted at that meeting setting forth that in police stations of the city from 10 to 500 women were every night consigned either on criminal charges or from homelessness and were in the charge of men who were their only attendants in case of illness. "The cause of mercy and morality demanded that there should be police matrons," she thundered. At the request of New York City Police Commissioner Mason, all of the police captains sent to him their opinions regarding the employment of matrons in the police stations in 1883. With the exception of Captain Leary of the City Hall Police, all the captains were opposed to it. It was said by them that few female prisoners were searched in the stations and none by men. No "respectable woman," it was declared, would consent to serve as a matron and submit to "the abuse and vile language of the depraved women who were prisoners in the stations."[9]

An experiment took place in Brooklyn, New York, when it was reported in May 1882 that the police magistrates had thrown open the courts in Brooklyn to the work of police matrons and the matrons, "who are maintained at private expense, [and] are working with zeal." One editor noted there was an air of practical benevolence about the work of the "good women who are to act as missionaries" in the unceasing procession of sad and unfortunate human beings that pass through the police courts. The number of such women involved in the matron work was not given, but it was said that they were to try to rescue from "further degradation" the women who ended up in the system and to care for them in a facility they ran called the Wayside House (or Home) and to set the faces of those unfortunates "toward a life of temperance, industry and virtue." A different editor called the experiment a new movement afoot in New York to "reclaim fallen women." With the police courts and prisons in Brooklyn being thrown open to them the matrons were to "seek out the young women who have begun to tread the downhill path — the intemperate women, the abandoned, and like characters—and seek to turn them into the paths of honesty and virtue." This editor concluded, with respect to the project, "It is practical charity, and not encumbered with any 'ism.'"[10]

Later in 1882 it was reported that Mrs. H. F. Crocker and Mrs. H. A. Johns had been appointed as police matrons in Brooklyn through the action of the First Brooklyn WCTU, which furnished the money for that purpose. The influence of such matrons could be seen in the following example. On July 15, 1882, Ella Larrabee, a 17-year-old girl who committed several burglaries in Brooklyn to get finery to wear to Coney Island, was before Justice Moore in the Kings County Court of Sessions, on a charge of burglary in the first degree and on a charge of grand larceny. In view of the influence of Matron Crocker, who told Moore earlier that she believed the girl would ultimately reform, the prisoner was allowed to plead guilty to a charge of burglary in the third degree. However, at the court appearance Crocker told Moore she had about given up hope for reform on the part of the prisoner. Nevertheless, Moore was lenient and sentenced Larrabee to 15 months in the penitentiary, stating if her behavior was good she could be out in 12 months. Larrabee gave her occupation as "hair comber." By 1887 these matrons seemed to have disappeared without a trace. In June of that year the Brooklyn Board of Aldermen appointed 13 police matrons. Mayor Whitney vetoed the resolution on the grounds that three or four were enough and that the appointments should be made by the police commissioner instead of by the aldermen. A resolution to override the mayor's veto passed by a vote of 13 to two. However, as no provision had been made in the budget for the payment of the matrons, regardless of their number, the action of the aldermen was without effect.[11]

Finally, in 1888 New York State passed legislation allowing New York City to appoint two matrons to each of its police stations. As well, the bill allowed all cities with a population of over 20,000 to appoint police matrons. On May 29 Governor David B. Hill signed that bill into law. It provided that within three months after the passage of the act the mayors of all cities in the state, except New York and Brooklyn (where the police commissioners had the authority), should designate one or more station houses in their cities for the detention and confinement of all women under arrest. For each of those police station houses, "there shall be appointed not more than two respectable women, who shall be known as police matrons." Women thus appointed were to be recommended by at least 20 women of "good standing" in their communities. Where only one matron was to be attached to a police station she had to reside within the station, or within a reasonable distance from it, and was to hold herself in readiness to respond to any call from the station at any hour, day or night. As well, the act stipulated that sufficient accommodation for women under arrest was to be provided separate and apart from the accommodations for males, and each station was to be so arranged that no communication could be had between the men and women therein confined, except with the consent of the matron.[12]

One newspaper editorial stated that Hill deserved praise for signing the bill that provided for matrons. He felt that the idea that women who got arrested should be locked up in the same stations with men and should be without the care of attendants of their own sex "is not consonant with the finer instincts of humanity." A different editor in another part of America also praised the New York State bill saying, "This is simply an act of decency and humanity and it is to be hoped that similar laws will be passed by all states of the union." Similar sentiments were expressed on the West Coast from where an editor wrote, "A similar reform is surely needed in San Francisco."[13]

A report in October 1888 observed that neither in New York nor Brooklyn had the law to appoint matrons been put into effect with the reason given in both cases being a lack of money. The New York City police commissioner had made a nominal compliance with the law some time earlier by designating the specific police station in which women would be confined, while the Brooklyn police commissioner selected five stations, and to those designated stations all female detainees were taken. However, there was no gain in that because there were no matrons to care for them. In some ways it was worse because it meant that sometimes females were transported (usually in open wagons even in bad weather) a greater distance to reach one of the five designated facilities. A New York City editor observed, with respect to the noncompliance, "It is not credible to the authorities of the two cities that they refuse to provide money for an object which commends itself to the best judgment of all humane and benevolent minds." A week or so later a piece appeared briefly profiling Mrs. Emma Beckwith, Brooklyn's woman candidate for mayor. Her chief reason for running, she said, was so that women could be employed as inspectors of factories and as police matrons, "and I intend to devote my entire salary to paying the police matrons, for whose appointment there has been a law passed, but for whose salaries no provision has been made. I do not need the salary, for my husband will continue to support me, as he always has done." She lost that election a few days later.[14]

However, over a year later this bill still had not been implemented in New York City as no actual appropriation of money was made by the politicians to fund the positions. An angry Mrs. I. J. Howard of the WCTU complained that "the mayor and the city officials are Roman Catholic and most of them foreigners; they have very little in common with and very little regard for American Christian women." Reportedly, 20,000 women and girls, on average, were arrested in New York City every year. The great majority were guilty of no serious offense, according to an editor on a New York daily. Fully 80 percent of those females were charged with "turbulent or disorderly conduct, intoxication, vagrancy or quarrelling." The number of convictions for felonious offenses committed by women amounted to about 1,000 per year. Thus, the other 19,000 arrested were either discharged before or after trial, or given bonds to keep the peace. "Fully three-quarters of the number of those arrested are therefore guilty of no real offence against the laws," declared the editor. To him it meant women should be in charge of those arrested females and thereby "many abuses to which the women moving in this reform have called attention, and of which they complain with great reason, would be abated." He added further that in this matter a board of intelligent public servants would need no prompting.[15]

The matter remained awash in controversy into the 1890s. Authorities argued that the appointment of matrons involved extra expense and was really unnecessary. The police "did not want women bothering around, and women, when asked to arouse themselves in the matter, said that no decent women could be found who would be willing to expose themselves to the scenes at a police station." After noting the "real abuses" that were forced on female detainees, the *New York Times* stated that females were sometimes housed in cells directly opposite males and that female detainees often had to give birth without a woman being present. In one unnamed city, police claimed the scrub-woman was available to be called in when necessary at births, but the police had never deemed it necessary. Overall, the *New York Times* was in favor of matrons, although it put a reverse spin on just who was being corrupted when it expressed fears for the male population of station house lockups (from female detainees): "The effect upon comparatively innocent men and boys is not to be ignored, and these are often exposed to corrupting manners."[16]

By the summer of 1890 the state law authorizing the appointment of police matrons had been on the books for two years, but New York City still refused to act. The law was permissive but not mandatory, meaning that a city was authorized to make such appointments but not legally compelled to do so. During 1889 a state law mandating the appointment of matrons made it all the way through the legislature to the governor's desk, but there it was vetoed. The governor reasoned that the matter should be left to the discretion of local authorities until it appeared obvious they would not do their duty. If faced with such a refusal by local authorities to comply with the existing permissive statute, the governor indicated a willingness to then sign a measure mandating compliance. And that was what had to be done to bring New York City into compliance. In March 1892 Governor Hill signed into law the bill making it mandatory on the police commissioners to appoint matrons and, under the act, to do so within three months. A number of smaller New York State cities had already appointed police matrons. However, as the New York police commission was obdurate and the law was only permissive the only remedy was an amendment to the act making it mandatory.[17]

Pressure on New York City's officials continued to be applied by various groups. Sometimes they took the same stance as the *New York Times*— blame the female detainees themselves. Josephine Shaw Lowell of the New York State Board of Charities wrote to the Board of Police explaining her group's desire for matrons, saying the group based its argument "upon the ground that common decency demanded that drunk and degraded women should be removed from the sight and hearing of the men and boys who for various reasons are held in station houses." Being careful to avoid offending, she continued, "We said that we deemed it a great wrong that such women should be allowed to contaminate by their evil conduct and language men and boys, arrested perhaps for some trivial offense, or perhaps entirely innocent. We did not say that we thought the women in the station houses unsafe while under the care of officers appointed by you, for although we had heard such accusations, personally I could not, I confess, believe them." Lowell then closed her letter by mentioning the 15-year-old girl who was the victim of an attempted assault by a police officer. Perhaps this letter could be viewed as an indirect attack by a woman who knew her position was weak and took a pragmatic approach — a woman who felt a direct attack on the police as sexual abusers would only raise their resistance to the employment of matrons. While her letter made it clear Lowell was aware of sexual victimization, she brought it up in the context of blaming females and pointing out the usefulness of matrons in protecting men. The Board of Police continued to drag its feet, claiming a lack of funds made it impossible to hire any matrons.[18]

Harpers' Weekly agreed that matrons were needed in New York. This was in part a class issue for them as women were out more and more on their own in cities, with the result that "innocent women" from sudden illnesses or other causes could find themselves suddenly brought to a police station. This contrasted with the other women who traditionally interacted with the police — the homeless, alcohol abusers, prostitutes, and petty thieves. *Harper's* was less concerned about what happened to these lower-class detainees, writing of the "innocents": "Humanity, civilization, common decency, demand that they shall not needlessly be exposed to frightful outrage"; while humanity and decency also required that the same segregation "shall be extended to other women, however degraded, in order that the station houses shall not become in ways which are entirely avoidable, dens and schools of vice."[19]

Toward the end of 1890 a *New York Times* editorial stated, giving no specifics, "Recent experience has given new force to the demand for matrons," urging the authorities to comply in order to save the police department from scandal. Most likely this was a reference to more sexual abuse of detainees. Still resisting, the police commissioners refused to appoint matrons, offering as one reason that "a police matron would not be safe from insult by the policemen of the station houses." As the word "insult" like "outrage" was a code for rape or assault, this was a not so subtle threat.[20]

The New York City Police Commissioner most notably against the proposal of matrons for his city was John Richard Voorhis who said there were two reasons why women and girls arrested by the NYPD should be subjected to the indignity and indecency of search by male officers and should be deprived of the presence and guardianship of a matron while in custody. The first reason was expense — estimated to be $30,000 a year for the matrons. The second reason, said Voorhis, was because "fully 90 per cent. of the females arrested are of the very lowest and most depraved strata of human life and society." A newspaper editor noted the city was about to spend $35,000 for a new entrance into Central Park and "The city can certainly afford to pay for a year the sum of $30,000 for the employment of matrons in those police stations to which girls and women may be brought — seeing that these women are, of all others, the most helpless."[21]

In response to those comments from Voorhis, Josephine Shaw Lowell wrote a long letter to the editor of the *Sun* newspaper. Lowell (1843–1905) was a progressive reform leader in the United States. She was perhaps best known for creating the New York Consumers League in 1890. In her letter she summarized many of the objections to matrons noting that many argued a more complete separation of the sexes was not necessary as they were practically kept separate at that time. However, she rebutted, in all cells every word said by a female could be heard by every man and boy in any station house and in some station houses every man and boy could see every woman in it, depending on where she stood in the cell. Lowell noted that many argued it would "demoralize the force" to have matrons on duty at the station houses. And that the commissioners said that no evil resulted from the present system. Pointing out reports of assaults were pervasive she observed that the defenders of the status quo "ignore the constant moral injury to all men and boys brought within sight and hearing of degraded women in the station houses." Commissioners also argued matrons were not needed by saying there were women employed in the station houses to do many things which matrons would be called on to do. The women referred to were those hired by the policemen themselves to make their beds in the station houses (in was a regular practice for policemen to sleep at their station houses). However, these women, noted Lowell, were not under the control of the Police Board and they were not selected by any process of examination. As well their character was not investigated. They had no recognized position in the NYPD, yet rule 526 of the Police Board directed that these women shall be called upon to search women prisoners and to care for them under certain circumstances. Commissioners often argued, continued Lowell, the female prisoners were often too bad to be cared for by women. The only counter to that, said the reformer was by the counterargument "that the worse they are the more horrible it is that they should degrade themselves in the presence of men." An experienced officer was quoted as having said that matrons could never manage the fighting drunks they sometimes got and it took sometimes as many as three or four men to get one such woman into a cell and that they objected very much to being handled by the officers—which, of course, was Lowell's point and an argument for matrons. In conclusion Lowell declared the demand for police matrons "is made in the name of common decency to protect the women prisoners from further self-degradation, to protect the men and boys from contamination, to protect the police force from temptation. It is made because women prisoners in the station houses are usually degraded and irresponsible, not because they are sometimes merely unfortunate." She worried that thousands of drunken women should each year be left for hours under the care of men and practically in company with men and boys and called such a system "an outrage against common decency which should not be continued in this city."[22]

All the pressure paid off when the first civil service examination for matrons in New York City was held in May 1891. The 28 women tested had to answer questions such as what to do in the case of childbirth and what to do with a drunken woman. In addition, the candidates were required to do simple problems in arithmetic and read from the newspaper (aloud to an examiner). One of the math problems required candidates to show that 10 women could not be put in nine single cells. Salary for the post of matron could be no less than the lowest salary paid to a policeman, then $1,000 per year. Some 140 applications had been initially received by the police board but the board whittled the number down when it decided not to appoint any woman to a matron's place if she was less than 30 years old or more than 45. Since 20 of the initial applicants had ranged in age from 21 to 29 and 20 others ranged from 46 to 70, they were all eliminated. Several eminent women had been invited to help the Civil Service Board out in administering the exam. One was Josephine Shaw Lowell (one of the State Charity Commissioners) who assisted the examiners "and gave advice and good cheer to the nervous and frightened candidates." Doctor Vosburgh, the medical man of the Civil Service Commission, was present to give a physical examination to each of the applicants but it consisted only of questioning the candidates regarding their general health. Eventually a list of the 20 highest candidates on the exam would be certified and the police board would select its police matrons from that list. For a start eight stations were to be designated to receive females— meaning the first target was to hire eight matrons. The first four matrons started work in New York City police stations on October 5, 1891, much later than in many other cities, and by 1899 the city employed 61 police matrons. Civil service exams in Brooklyn early in 1892 resulted in 48 names on the eligible list. A total of eight matrons were to be appointed but only two of them "at once." They were to be assigned to the new Eighteenth Precinct Station with the matron salary set at $800 per year.[23]

Less than three weeks after the first four matrons started work, Josephine Lowell wrote to the police commissioners complaining that the work expected of the matrons was excessive. On the day shift matrons worked ten-hour days; on the night shift they worked 14 hours, including a period from six P.M. Saturday through eight A.M. Monday. In addition, these women were obliged to climb the stairs around 30 times a day. Lowell urged the hiring of more matrons. In reply to the letter Commissioner Voorhis stated that matrons were not expected to do any more work than the doormen of the station houses and that Lowell's letter "bore out the position taken by the board at the beginning that the work was too hard for women."[24]

As of March 1, 1899, the NYPD had a total strength of 7,364 officers and men, of whom 91 were in the bicycle squad, 89 were in the tenement house squad, 164 were detectives, 33 were in the sanitary corps, and nine were detailed for service in the House of Detention. There were also 38 police matrons, bringing the total force to over 7,400. A little over six months later, on October 16, 1899, more matrons were added to the force, bringing the total to 59. They had new uniforms and shields that, said a news account indicated "their elevation to full membership in the force. Henceforth they are subject to all the discipline of the regular policemen and will also benefit from the pension fund." Their uniform was a tailor made blue serge with a tight fitting waist and a skirt to the shoe tops. Their shield was smaller than a patrolman's and rather more circular. It contained the inscription "Police Department City of New York" and "Matron."[25]

A large turnout appeared in July 1886 for the annual meeting of the Hennepin County (Minn.) WCTU, "most of whom were ladies." Mrs. Van Cleve spoke of the importance of employing police matrons for station houses and jails. Through the instrumentality of good women, she said, accommodations for women had been provided at the city lockup and jail in Minneapolis. But while it was a great improvement upon the old plan of shutting these women up in common cells, the new arrangement fell far short of what should be done on behalf of the female prisoners. She illustrated the need for matrons by incidents in her experience in visiting the lockup and jail and said a movement should be started in Minneapolis to secure matrons for these institutions. The matrons, she urged, "should be kind, Christian ladies, who would attempt the reform of the female prisoners by instilling the love of God in their hearts, as only in this way could permanent reform be accomplished."[26]

Some seven months later in March 1887 a county commissioners' meeting was held in Minneapolis at which a communication was received in person from Harriet G. Walker and Abby G. Mendenhall of the Sisterhood of Bethany, Lydia W. Hoblit and C. A. B. Merriam of the WCTU, and Annie L. Stuart of the Woman's Christian Association. As well it was endorsed by Judges Lochren, Rea, and Young of the district court, and Judges Bailey and Mahoney of the municipal court, in relation to the case of female prisoners. The petition set forth that the ladies mentioned (and others) had visited the county jail and police stations and made the following complaints: bad sanitary conditions, bad ventilation, insufficient heat for cold weather, and "foul-tongued women of sin, insane women and young girls of 15" perhaps only awaiting trials on charges of which they would be found innocent were herded into one common room "to their great bodily danger and moral hurt." The petition also complained about the constant possibility of intrusion into the one woman's cell where women were confined, at any hour of the day or night, by "persons of the other sex, as jailers, turnkeys, sheriff, or whoever they may bring into the room, either on errands of business or curiosity." The petitioners argued such an arrangement was "immodest, indecent and degrading to the morals even of prisoners." All of this led, said the petitioners, to the female prisoners being made much worse and not better by being detained in any of those facilities. It also caused them to be "injured in bodily health, hardened in sin and degraded in morals by such imprisonment. Many young and practically innocent girls have thus been led astray." As a remedy the petitioners urged the construction of a jail for women only, and that all detainees therein be placed under the care of police matrons. As to the argument they felt likely to be made that the small number of female prisoners did not justify a dedicated facility it was said that in 1885 police in Minneapolis alone arrested 454 females. It was also argued that it was the testimony of many judges of all municipal courts in America that many more sentences to confinement in prison or jail would be passed on women if a "right and proper" place of detention for them was in operation. Therefore the peace and welfare of the community in general would be enhanced.[27]

By the middle of 1888 both Minneapolis and St. Paul had police matrons on the job. In municipal court in St. Paul in June of that year three women arrested a few days earlier were arraigned on the charge of being "occupants of a house of ill-fame." The case of Annie Craig was continued while Mattie Lynn was fined $10. Nellie Ellsworth was sentenced to 20 days at the work-house, but the sentence was suspended upon the recommendation of the police matron (unnamed), who had secured work for the girl. Ellsworth had professed a desire to lead a better life. Sometime around June 1888, at the request of various charitable and benevolent institutions in the city, the police commission had created the post of police matron, and Mrs. Rice was appointed to the position.[28]

A female reporter with a St. Paul newspaper wrote about her experiences in the Minneapolis police lockup in March 1889, after causing herself to be arrested and confined therein. Miss Brooks (and her companion Miss Mamie Morris) arrived in St. Paul on a Tuesday on the 9 P.M. train from Manitoba. At the station while the pair were waiting for a connecting train, Brooks discovered money was missing from her satchel and eventually accused Morris. Police were called and Morris was taken away to the station house where the police matron was called in. She was described by Morris as "a middle-aged woman with a pleasant countenance." According to the story the matron said to Morris, "Now, dear, don't cry. I haven't a doubt but you're innocent. Your face doesn't look like that of a thief. But the law requires that I search you." While waiting alone in a room at the station Morris rifled through the contents of the matron's table. One thing she found was the matron's account book. On the first page was the following affirmation; "I, the police matron, pledge myself to honor God in the keeping of the records and all that I do." Of the eight or 10 cases recorded therein Morris noted that three women had been detained overnight and released, so she supposed they had been innocent. Mrs. S. E. Paine was identified as the police matron. Eventually Morris was taken to the corridor where the women were kept. It contained the matron's room and the common cell. Within that common cell were the individual cells, each measuring about six feet in height and length, and four feet in width. They were open to view and provided no privacy. Paine had been employed there for about one month. Morris reflected on the "utterly unprotected condition" of women who had been brought there prior to the time a matron was in charge and found it was easy to believe that there was some foundation for the stories of brutality and ill-treatment which had been heard in the past. Within the cell room Morris was made uneasy by a strong odor of sewer gas and found vermin of all sorts running about the walls and floors. She concluded that a matron at the police station was a necessity.[29]

A piece on the duties of Mrs. Louise Paine, matron at Minneapolis' central police station, appeared in March 1890. She was the only matron in Minneapolis and could be called upon at any hour of the day or night. In her annual report Paine said that during the year 1889 she had charge of 383 women (of these 103 were arrested for drunkenness, 79 for being found in houses of ill-fame, 70 were charged with disorderly conduct, 37 were common prostitutes, 27 were keepers of houses of ill-fame, 35 were charged with fornication, eight were charged with larceny, six with using abusive language, six with incorrigibility, four with vagrancy, three with assault and battery, three with adultery, two with violating the liquor laws, one for the destruction of property, and one for fast driving. Besides that she also had charge of 11 insane women and 94 lost children. Minneapolis had a population of 164,738 in 1890. When a female was arrested by the police in Minneapolis she was taken to central and turned over to the matron. The second floor of the station was given over to the matron and her detainees. The only furniture in each cell was a mattress placed on a narrow shelf. When the matron received a prisoner she was said to have a double duty to perform. She acted both as the friend of the prisoner and the jailer. She had a duty to search her prisoner and, said a reporter, "while she is doing this she talks to the prisoner in the way that only a woman who pities another can."[30]

Mrs. E. Louise Paine returned to the news in the fall of 1891 when it was reported that an opposition to her had sprung up among the various charitable organizations, which were said to pay half of her $60 a month salary. Women who represented the Bethany Home, the WCTU, and several other organizations, appeared to think that Paine was more independent than was becoming under the circumstances. It was also alleged that Paine discriminated in favor of the Home of the Friendless as against the Bethany Home.[31]

The situation with respect to police matrons in Washington, D.C., did not look very promising in February 1888 when it was reported the commissioners did not favor a House bill (H. R. Bill 6172) for the appointment of matrons. It would have required two police matrons at each station and at the time there was said to be no suitable accommodations for them. (In these early days probably about half of all matrons lived in an apartment or some accommodation on the site of the lockup. This was especially true when a station had only one matron who was on call 24 hours a day.) Commissioners grumbled that if the bill passed it would be necessary to make extensive modifications to the police stations in order to provide suitable accommodations for those matrons and for those who would require their services. No such money was in the police budget for the coming fiscal year, it was said. Somehow money was found because by June 1889 the nation's capital had some police matrons at work. On June 30 of that year the Washington police force consisted of 376 men (one major, one captain, two inspectors, nine lieutenants, 28 sergeants, 185 privates (class 1), and 150 privates (class 2). Of that total 56 had been added in the previous year. The records and property of the department were cared for by three clerks, 19 station keepers (jailers), eight laborers, two messengers, three ambulance drivers, and seven patrol-wagon drivers. As well, three police matrons, for the examination and care of female prisoners under detention at the station houses, were employed in the department.[32]

At a Police Commission meeting on August 2, 1888, in Los Angeles, after some discussion, Mrs. M. A. Watson was appointed police matron at a salary of $60 per month. Police Chief Cuddy opposed the appointment, said a reporter, "tooth and nail." Mayor Workman defended her remarking that he knew of the good work she had done in charity work in the community and that he would rather have her on the force than many policemen he knew of. Within a few weeks of her appointment two of the major newspapers in the city were attacking each other over Watson. The *Los Angeles Herald* said in its August 31 edition there had been a print attack a day earlier in the pages of the *Los Angeles Times*. It was said therein that since Watson had been appointed matron she had never darkened the door of that facility in her official capacity. In reply the *Herald* stated that it went without saying the assertion was willfully and maliciously false. Motivation for the attack was reported to be that a woman in custody knew something about an important case and when a *Times* reporter spoke to Watson the matron refused to tell him anything for publication. That so angered the reporter that he swore he would get even with her. In the opinion of the *Herald* he had carried out that threat by maligning her ability as a police matron. A different account stated that in Los Angeles up to around 1895 all women arrested were put in one small cell. It measured about eight feet by 14 feet, was cold and damp, and had scarcely any daylight in it. They were not cared for by a woman but by the male jailer or some male trusty. Through urgent and repeated appeals by the WCTU better accommodations were furnished by the city for female prisoners, no later than the end of 1895. Sometime in that period a matron was placed in charge of them through the day, but not at night. During 1894 in Los Angeles 258 women had been under arrest at the police station. A new jail was then under construction; it would have a separate ward for female prisoners. As well there was supposed to be a room and office for a matron in the new facility.[33]

An official ordinance creating the position of police matron in Los Angeles and providing for her appointment was finally published in full in June 1889. Ordinance 123 was signed by Freeman G. Teed, city clerk, and approved by Mayor Henry T. Hazard. Said matron was to be appointed by the Police Commissioners of Los Angeles and to hold office for one year, or during the pleasure of said Police Commission, at a salary of $60. Policemen appointed in this time period had a certain amount of job security and often were part of a pension plan. When someone was appointed at the pleasure of someone else it meant that person could be fired without cause and without notice. That did not happen to a policeman. The matron created by this ordinance was under the immediate supervision and control of the chief of police "and shall perform such duties in connection with the ordinary duties of Police Matron as said Chief of Police may from time to time direct."[34]

An act of the Pennsylvania Legislature in 1889 mandated the employment of police matrons in cities within the state. As a result of that act Pittsburgh police chief Brown picked two women from a large number of applicants and the pair commenced their duties at Central station in June 1889. Both women were widows "of mature age." Mrs. Sadie Earley (widow of bricklayer William, who died two years earlier) was the day matron and Mrs. Runie Brennen (widow of policeman Pierce and mother of policeman Pierce Junior) was the night matron. They would alternate day and night shift on a monthly basis. Their duties were said to consist of controlling and caring for female prisoners, searching them when they were brought in, and attending them when they were sick. They were also expected to make the beds and to keep the rooms tidy of the emergency police (that is, the beds of policemen who slept in the stations). By the end of 1889 the salaries for the year for matrons in Pittsburgh were reported to total $4,500 with the appropriations for the Police Bureau falling $3,000 short. Chief Brown requested the transfer of $3,000 from the Bureau of Health appropriation to the Bureau of Police.[35]

Also in Pennsylvania, matrons were first employed by Philadelphia in the early months of 1899. In their first five months on the job those matrons, probably six in number, had under their care 1,129 women and 183 children. A later news account stated that through the efforts of the "associated committee of women on police matrons" of the New Century Club, six police matrons had been placed in the police stations in Philadelphia. A report from that committee asserted that the monthly reports of those matrons had demonstrated the necessity for their existence, and "the personal supervision of our members confirms all that has been written, and demonstrated that this department of municipal government is one which no city can afford to neglect."[36]

As of the end of 1893 Chicago had, reportedly, 30 police matrons with a head matron in charge of the others. During 1893 they had cared for 35,119 women and girls. In 1898 an article profiled Chicago police matron Mrs. Sarah Jane Littell, who rode in a police patrol wagon every day of the week except Sunday. She was court matron at the Harrison Street station and was required to accompany all female prisoners to the county jail. For years she rode in open wagons but an order requiring covered wagons was enacted, "thus saving prisoners from the elements and the humiliation of a public ride through the city streets." In those wagons men and women were transported together, all handcuffed. Women were loaded in first, followed by Littell, and then the male prisoners were loaded into the wagon. On March 9, 1898, Littell was to celebrate her 15th year on the job. And when appointed, said the account erroneously, she was "the only police matron in the world." Back when Littell was hired in 1883 the abuses of female prisoners at the police stations "were so revolting" that the WCTU petitioned Mayor Carter H. Harrison to appoint a police matron. He declined on the ground that no reputable woman would accept the position but finally allowed the WCTU to experiment at its own expense. Littell was hired for $30 a month, which was paid by a woman named Mrs. Carse. Little was an immediate success and at the end of the year was regularly employed by the city. She was given a room at the station which she occupied for seven years. Before her appointment the women complained bitterly that the men jeered and openly insulted them while they were in the wagon on route to jail. "But from the beginning Mrs. Littell commanded the respect of the most hardened criminals, and her charges are unmolested either by look or gesture," declared a reporter. Littell spent 13 years on duty in the police lockup. Then, two years earlier, she was appointed court matron and was in the courtroom from 9 A.M. to 3 P.M. and was on call until 10 P.M. When the court adjourned she rode over to the jail with the female prisoners. By this time there were 31 matrons on the Chicago police force, including Miss L. L. Waller, the chief matron, but Littell still wore "Star No. 1."[37]

Early in 1894 the Martha Washington assembly, Knights of Labor, of Leadville, Colorado, composed entirely of women, passed a resolution at one of their meetings thanking the police board of Denver for making it the duty of police matrons to give directions and needed assistance to women who arrived at the Union transportation depot.[38]

A few months later in 1894 an account related that the "long struggle" of the woman's council to secure police matrons for the city of Cleveland had finally met with success. Mrs. Harriet Garfield and Mrs. Emma Essinger had been appointed matrons by the mayor of Cleveland. Those women received $666.66 a year, or two-thirds of the $1,000 salary of a patrolman. Essinger was the widow of a mail clerk and since the death of her husband had supported her two children and her aged mother.[39]

A letter to the editor of a Fort Worth, Texas, newspaper from the WCTU was published in February 1895. It said that the ladies of the WCTU had been trying for some time to get a police matron in Fort Worth "and securing the names of over a hundred of the heaviest taxpayers, we petitioned the city council in the name of justice, decency and right" to pass an ordinance creating a police matron position. That petition was turned over to the police committee, which decided a matron was not a necessary position. According to the letter 1,500 arrests of women were made in 1892 in Fort Worth: "Most of these women are very low, but we do not think them past the consideration of our Christian people. To have these women searched and handled by police officers does not look well for the fair name of our city." The letter went on to point out that all large cities in America then had police matrons on staff and 20 states had compulsory laws on the subject. One of the objections the police committee made to the WCTU petition was that "the women arrested were so low and vile that no good woman could act as matron." The organization wondered if they were lower in Fort Worth than in all the other cities that had matrons. In conclusion the WCTU asserted, "It is not a desirable position for a lady to assume, and there will be no scramble for the place, but a good, Christian matron can be found who will take the place, and the good a good matron will do for the poor, misguided female outcasts who are arrested in our city every day God alone knows."[40]

San Francisco had no police matrons early in 1896, complained Mrs. Booth of the Salvation Army that year. She pointed out that women from her organization, in the absence of matrons, were regularly called for and sent out to the police lockups to tend to women and children who ended up being detainees.[41]

Mrs. Lydia A. Dennison was appointed police matron in Kansas City, Missouri, on February 5, 1896. She was not the first matron in the city but there had been none on the job for the previous year. Her duties were the usual ones of performing searches and tending to the females detained in the lockup but she was also expected, said a journalist, "to have a motherly supervision over all indiscreet young girls in the city." Whenever the police noticed a young girl who was "acting indiscreet" Matron Dennison was to be notified and she would then confer with the girl's parents "with a view of correcting the girl." It was a new duty for a matron in Kansas City. Just five months later a terse news story reported Dennison had been discharged by the police commissioners. No reason was reported. The vacancy was not filled and it was reported that it was not the intention of the police board to employ a matron.[42]

As the twentieth century began the census of 1900 showed the city of Council Bluffs, Iowa, to have passed the 25,000 figure for its population. That meant it had to comply with an Iowa State law that required cities having a population of 25,000 and over to provide for female detainees by appointing two or more police matrons for each station house in the city that provided for the detention of females. As a result of those census numbers members of a Council Bluffs committee for police matrons called on Mayor Jennings and Police Chief Albro urging the appointment of matrons in Council Bluffs.

From the start, though, the mayor had refused to entertain requests for a matron. His excuse had always been the expense. When he was approached again in September 1900 he told the committee women he held out no hope for that year and that there would be no money to pay a matron salary until after next year, with the advent of a new fiscal year. Yet just a few days earlier Jennings had bragged that he expected to save at least $1,000 out of the police appropriations for that year. The committee of women was willing to compromise in the sense of accepting only one matron, instead of the two required by law. After being rebuffed the women vowed to continue the matter and to look at other options to enforce the law.[43]

The number of police matrons in America was not great by 1900 but it was growing rapidly and by that time most of the country's major cities had one or more matrons on their police forces. Opposition to the idea was certainly not dead or absent but it was a shadow of what it once was. Back in 1892 a newspaper story listed matrons in the U.S. that were known to the writer. Chicago then had 23, Buffalo had 2, and Philadelphia had 11. Manchester and Nashua in New Hampshire had one each while New Orleans had one. Massachusetts had 22 with 10 being in Boston, two each in Cambridge and Fall River, and one each in Lawrence, Lynn, Lowell, New Bedford, Worcester, Springfield, and Holyoke. San Francisco also had one but, reportedly, "she never attends to the most degraded." The police chief there said he "will allow no woman to be humiliated by such association."[44]

Not that it was all smooth sailing for police matrons from 1900 onward. When a new city administration took the reins in Minneapolis in January 1901 the previously mentioned matron, Mrs. Paine, was summarily ousted from her post and replaced by Mrs. Sarah B. Schaeffer. The incoming Albert Alonzo Ames had announced after winning the election but before being sworn in that he would make a change in the office of police matron, among other changes. Friends and supporters of the former matron were said to have expressed their full approval of the change "so long as it was certain that a change was to be made." Doc Ames (as Albert was known) also fired the city's police chief, replacing him with his brother Fred. It was Fred Ames who fired Paine and installed Schaeffer, described as the widow of a soldier. Doc Ames was reported to have gone on to create one of the most corrupt governments in the city's history.[45]

An attempt to roll back some of the benefits matrons received was launched in 1901 but was apparently unsuccessful. During March of that year Russell Sage (very wealthy financier, railroad executive and Whig politician) and several other well-known New York men petitioned the legislature at Albany in behalf of New York City police matrons. The petitioners asked that the recommendations of the Charter Revision Commission excluding the police matrons from the uniformed police force and from the benefits of the

Police Pension Fund should not be adopted. Assemblymen Davis and Henry had accordingly drawn up a measure to be incorporated into the revised charter, which would continue the present status of the matrons. It was apparently adopted.[46]

A police report for Lincoln, Nebraska, for the year ending March 31, 1901, revealed in detail the work of police matron Hyde. It was reported, "She is employed to steady feet which stagger, to inspire vicious women with a desire to reform. The task is a very difficult one." During that year the police arrested 222 women. Lincoln's population in 1900 was 40,169. That same year 1,612 men were arrested. Hyde visited most of those arrested women in jail to find out what they intended to do when released and encouraged them to return to their homes "and employ themselves decently." She had secured 15 places of employment for such women, sent seven to the convent of the Good Shepherd, one to Bancroft Rescue Home, two to Milford Home, and one to the Salvation Army Home. Hyde also placed five babies in homes, made 70 calls on behalf of neglected children, solicited charity for eight "worthy" poor people, secured entrance for four women to the YWCA, secured railroad transportation for seven destitute women, taken seven women and children to the Home of the Friendless, returned three runaway girls to friends and sent three women (through her recommendation) to the insane asylum. In addition, Hyde made 1,120 calls on or for the "destitute and desperate."[47]

The first police matron in the St. Louis jail, or Four Courts building, was Mrs. Harris, who held the position for 15 years until her death. Mrs. M. L. Kintzing held the position as of 1902. Once a woman was placed in a holding cell the only attention the detainee received from the matron was a supply of towels, soap and combs, taken to her every morning during her stay behind bars. As of January 1902 she had four girls in one detention room. One had left home because she was unhappy and had come straight from De Soto, Missouri, to the office of the chief of police to tell him she would no longer remain at home and would find work in the city, although she had a total of three cents and nowhere to go. A city merchant heard her story and said he would give her employment in his store. Another one of the girls was awaiting the arrival of her parents (who had alerted the police to find her) to pick her up. Kintzing also had charge of an 11-year-old boy named Ike Crosby who had stolen shovels and sold them. He was waiting for the police to transport him to the House of Refuge. Additionally, the matron had temporary charge of a three-year-old girl while her mother was held downstairs as a drunk. In August 1901 45 girls and boys were placed for one or more days in her care with the same number in September, 55 in October, and 60 in November. Kintzing's apartment in the Four Courts consisted of six rooms. She was one of many women who were the sole matrons in their facility. Since they were on call 24 hours a day (to deal a female who was brought to the lockup at any time) most of them were required to live within the jail complex, with a separate room or apartment for living. As well they usually had a room used as a working office, a room separate from the common cell room, which in turn contained a number of individual cells for detainees.[48]

Mrs. Sarah B. Schaeffer, matron at Minneapolis, 1901.

Mrs. Bridget Cummings was the matron in charge at police headquarters in St. Paul, Minnesota, in 1902. The women's room in that lockup was on the second floor and consisted of one long, well-lighted room. Within that were four individual cells. Cummings said she usually did not lock women into the cells but gave them the freedom of the larger room, except for drunks whom she did lock up into the individual cells until they sobered up. All the food her charges ate was prepared by the matron, who had an apartment of her own next to the jail. Cummings was allowed 14 cents for each meal "which consists, as a rule, of coffee and bread and butter." The arrests of women in St. Paul were said to hardly average one a day. Arrests of women during the day were mostly for shoplifting, stealing, and disorderly conduct. Arrests of women at night were mostly for "street strolling" and disorderly conduct.[49]

A description of the duties of a police matron in New York City in 1904 was given by Alice C. Woodbridge, a visitor for the Woman's Prison Association. She said New York then had 80 police precincts and that about 35 of the stations had matrons, 70 in number. In 1902 10,000 lost children were brought to New York station houses, and 247 foundlings had to be cared for. Woodbridge said that in Brooklyn women were often transported miles (by the police) before reaching a station with a women's department. Sometimes they were driven miles in open wagons (mostly gone by 1904) even in rainstorms. A police matron's salary was then $1,000 a year; she wore the uniform of the service and she remained eligible for a pension. In stations where there were two matrons they alternated between 14 hours night duty and 10 hours day duty, week about. Also, on alternate Sundays they were on duty for 24 consecutive hours. The private rooms of most matrons were up a long flight of stairs with the prisoners being kept on a different floor. As it was the rule that a police matron in New York City must "visit" each detainee once every half hour it meant the matron had to go up and down those stairs 28 times a night.[50]

Los Angeles had two police matrons as of the summer of 1906, Mrs. Aletha Gilbert and her assistant, Mrs. Loretta McPeak. Gilert would go on to become a Los Angeles policewoman in 1910 or 1911 and was not the only matron in the U.S. who made such a transition. At the time the city was considering adding a third as the two then worked 12-hour shifts. They were paid $75 a month. In addition to caring for all women prisoners, one of the matrons was required to be present at all operations on women patients in the receiving hospital. Whenever a woman was injured on the street, or fell in a faint, or was brought into the hospital with a gaping wound, a policewoman was summoned at once. Mrs. Gilbert had then been connected with the LAPD women's department for about 15 years. She was an assistant to her mother, Mrs. Lucy Gray, who for years was matron. Gilbert had held her post as head police matron for about two years, since the death of her mother. Gilbert argued the two matrons that on staff could do the increasing work (from a rapidly growing population) but should get a pay increase. An extra matron would be $75 a month. Gilbert argued it was cheaper for the city to increase the salary of the current pair up to $100 a month.[51]

When a lengthy article about police matrons in New York City was published in 1909 the author of the piece mentioned that the days of "pull" for women interested in the job had ended some 10 years or so earlier when the matrons became "regular" members of the force, eligible for the pension plan, and so forth. Before that the level of education of applicants was often not asked and the fitness of the candidates was ignored, to mention a few things. If a candidate seemed to have a grasp of the duties of a police matron and came "well recommended" that was enough. And, of course, that last item was true all over America. Usually it meant an applicant had to be well connected to one or another of the women's organizations in the community, such as the WCTU. Usually no other standard was applied to the candidate. New rules introduced in New York, and elsewhere, meant women had to pass a civil service examination and only applicants within a certain age range, such as 30 to 50, were considered. Pay for the position was raised to $1,000 a year in New York.[52]

An idea of how desirable the police matron's position had become in New York City could be seen in the number of applicants. In March 1904, when a civil service exam for the position was held, 905 applications were filed, including ones from school teachers, trained nurses and "women of mental attainments who had never worked for a living." A total of 375 passed the exams and of that number perhaps 35 had since been hired by the city to fill matron vacancies in the NYPD. The names remaining on the 1904 eligible list were all cancelled in June 1909 when a new civil service examination was announced. For that exam in June 466 applications were filed with the decrease said to be due to new rules for the position. The age limit was cut to women aged 30 to 40 and "a woman's word was not taken on this point, either." Apparently in the past the examiners took the lady's word as to her age. Further, the medical examination was much more careful in 1909 with all candidates being required to do certain physical tasks such as lifting weights, running, jumping and stooping. No woman under 5'0" (without shoes) was allowed to apply. As a result of the changes 156 of the 466 applicants failed to pass the medical and physical tests. Fourteen more backed out before the mental examination was administered, leaving 296 to take the final test. At the time this piece was written that test had not been run but officials thought about 40 percent would pass. Candidates were given questions to answer such as what means would they take to maintain discipline and quiet among women who were under the influence of liquor; how they would proceed to search a woman accused of thievery. They were given a hypothetical situation wherein a girl of 15, a drunken woman, and an injured or helpless woman were brought in and turned over to their care. What would they do with each one? A new question introduced for the first time to matron exams in 1909 was, "Write a complaint of not less than 250 words to the captain of your precinct concerning a patrolman who persists in coming to your office on various pretexts, although you have warned him repeatedly that his action is a violation of the rules of the department and exceedingly annoying to you." It was a very rare allusion in this era to sexual harassment. After an applicant had passed both the physical and mental tests she was "required to submit certificates of good character from twenty women of good social standing living in New York, none of whom was a relative." So much for the idea that pull was then absent from the process. After a woman was appointed as a police matron in New York City she was on probation for three months.[53]

At this time, 1909, the NYPD had 69 police matrons spread among 35 precincts and Bellevue Hospital, which had two matrons all the time guarding prisoners under observation in the psychopath ward. The number of matrons was regulated by what the appropriations for the police board allowed with the current sum permitting a total of 70 matrons. In the Tenderloin district of the city three matrons worked eight-hour shifts. In most other precincts two were assigned to each station. In 1903 12 new matrons were installed but that year was an exception as the turnover in all other years since 1901 had ranged from two to five. A matron could retire on half pay after 20 years on the job. Reportedly, the higher pay had led to more highly qualified women applying. According to the reporter, "Once the matron was a nondescript looking person because of her clothing, which was made in any old style and of any sort and color of fabric. For the last five years the police matrons when on duty have worn a uniform corresponding to that of a policeman, shield and all." All women and children arrested were brought to the station house and put in the matrons' care as soon as they left the lieutenant's desk in the reception area. "The police matron of today is not easily discouraged even though she does find that perhaps 90 per cent or so of the women put in her care are morally oblique and past help," declared the journalist. An unidentified matron told the reporter, "A matron gets very little encouragement in her missionary attempts with women arrested for intoxication, and

"Drunken Woman" in NYPD Tenderloin police station cell showing cot, toilet bowl, and sink with running water, 1909.

after a few years' experience most of us agree that perhaps all of these, with the exception of 2 per cent will go lower instead of reforming. The same is true of women rounded up as vagrants." Hours of work for the New York matrons remained at 10 hours on day shift (8 A.M. to 6 P.M.) and 14 hours on night shift (6 P.M. to 8 A.M.), week about. Every other week she worked from 8 A.M. Sunday to 8 A.M. Monday with no relief. That was true in all but one or two of the busiest precincts where three matrons assigned to a single station worked eight hour shifts. A recently instituted rule forbade policemen from visiting a police matron's office for any reason at all, except police business. It was, reportedly, a strictly enforced rule with, in the event of a violation, the policeman involved being fined five days' pay while the matron was fined three days' pay.[54]

As of June 1910 the police matrons in Los Angeles were paid $75 a month while at the end of 1910 those in San Francisco received $85 a month. That same year the NYPD comprised 87 captains, 621 lieutenants, 583 sergeants, 8,562 patrolmen, and 193 doormen for a total of 10,046. They continued to employ 70 police matrons. As of 1911 Kansas City, Missouri, had eight matrons while Buffalo (twice the size of Kansas City) had four. Cleveland employed three police matrons, Omaha one, Milwaukee one, and Seattle had four.[55]

An editorial piece back in 1896 wondered why was it that females and males on police departments were not paid the same salary or thereabouts: "How is it that the lady who acts as police, jailer, matron, cook, housekeeper, etc., for twelve hours a day is paid but $40 a month, while the men on the force doing eight hours' work get twice that salary?" Of course, no answer was provided. However, outside of this piece that question never seems to have arisen in the era of matron-only titles for women in the police service. Later, from 1910 onward when women with the title of policewoman did exist, the question did arise, at least from time to time. (Some early policewomen were paid the same as starting male officers, but not often.) And that illustrated "what's in a name." Distance the title from the comparison job and one tends to decrease the number of awkward questions.[56]

When Elmer Graper published his book on police administration in 1921, he observed that the use of police matrons was a successful experiment, "although there was much opposition on the part of authorities as there has been to the more recent agitation for the employment of policewomen." Graper noted that nearly all cities of importance then had police matrons. However, there were still some metropolitan areas that did not employ any police matrons by the 1920s.[57]

2

U.S., 1880–1909

During this period agitation for police matrons continued, peaked, and was successful. By 1910 the position and the need for it was well established. Hostility to the idea and movement against the idea were by no means dead but they were receding quickly. As that battle continued and was won some of the focus and attention shifted to the idea that policewomen were needed. It would be 1910 before a female could be hired and officially given the title of policewoman by her employer (the media sometimes used the term to describe somebody who was officially called something else). When matrons began to be hired in many parts of the country in the beginning of the 1880s they could have easily have been given the official designation of policewomen, albeit with very limited and circumscribed duties. But society was not ready to accept such a jump in the role of women. So the women who entered the police service in the period 1880 to 1909 were called matrons to disassociate them from real police officers. For example, if one had both policemen and policewomen one might be tempted to ask questions as to whether they had more or less equal duties, equal pay, and so forth. Since society refused to accept such concepts it — society — labeled these early women in the police service by what was clearly a pejorative term. Matron conjured up images of weakness, impotence, lethargy, inactivity, and so on, while the word policeman conjured up images of strength, vibrancy, decisiveness, power, and so forth. When women called policewomen finally were hired it was with very limited and circumscribed duties and the title could have easily been used in 1880 and applied to the matrons. But it took 30 years of agitation and lobbying by women before society would, not without great reluctance, concede and use the term that should have been first applied back around 1880. "What's in a name?" Shakespeare famously queried. And the answer was indeed a lot. When San Francisco was in the process of getting its first policewomen the city officials debated and struggled with that dilemma for quite awhile, delaying the appointment for months after finally deciding not to call them policewomen but to call them "women protective officers." However, it was too

33

late. If the powers that be were reluctant to use the term the media, and Hollywood, were quicker to adopt it and from 1910 onward women taken into the police service (not specifically to tend to detainees in the lockups) were called policewomen.

How the establishment felt about the idea of female police could be seen in this very brief, and very snide, comment published in 1881 in a South Carolina newspaper: "Some Milwaukee people ask the appointment of female police officers. Well, a pretty woman could capture almost anybody."[1]

Agitation for female police officers overlapped that for police matrons and was also evident in the late 1800s. In early 1880 a *New York Times* editorial drew attention to a letter from a Mrs. Blake, who wrote about the "systematic outrages on the sacredness of womanhood which are constantly perpetuated by the Police." She was referring to the fact that women were arrested by men, confronted by male sergeants at the stations, and then locked up by males. Blake suggested female police be hired to "take charge of women who are arrested." The newspaper editor mocked the idea by pointing out that the sacredness mustn't be outraged in the street either, necessitating a "double and bisexual Police force" with as many females as males, a member of each gender on patrol together, and with members of each sex forbidden to arrest members of the opposite sex. In a more serious vein the editor attacked the idea of female police by saying their addition to the force would be an expensive and doubtful experiment for which there was no reason. "Respect for the sex is a very pretty thing," noted the account "but when the sex is drunken, foul-mouthed and riotous, the policeman who has to perform the duty of arrest is to be pitied more than the wretch who has long since discarded the last remnant of womanhood."[2]

A couple of years later the newspaper published a letter critical of the idea wherein the writer envisioned women "armed with silk umbrellas instead of clubs" and derided their ability to make arrests, wondering if they would substitute "politely worded notes of invitation to attend supper at the station house instead of making a regular arrest."[3]

A similar black-humored sentiment was expressed by the editor of a California newspaper published in March 1886. In that account it was reported the suffrage women in New York advocated the employment of policewomen. "That is a reform we favor. It will furnish employment for many of the gentle sex who are not gentle, and will occupy that surplus muscle which now wreaks itself via the rolling pin within the domestic circle. How delightful to have a petticoated fly cop brandish a club and make you move on."[4]

And still more, from an editor on a Minnesota newspaper, published in April 1887. Mrs. Isabella Beecher Hooker, it was reported, proposed a "novel" police reform plan. It was to put women on the police force: "A knobby little policewoman in vivandiere [French name for women attached to military regiments as canteen keepers] dress would be a pretty sight on the streets to be sure. But will Mrs. Hooker kindly inform us what is the policewoman to do when a mouse makes its appearance on her beat?"[5]

Yet another quip, this one from the *Boston Courier* and reprinted in other newspapers, including one in St. Paul, Minnesota. When female police officers were appointed an encounter between one and a tipsy individual might go like this, speculated an editor. The female officer takes his arm to lead him to a streetcar. "Try and keep yourself up. There! I thought you would do it. My back hair is all coming down. Here, hold my club until I put up my hair.... There, you've dropped my club." The conductor of the streetcar told the female officer he did not stop for drunks. She began to weep, "Whatever in the world can I do with him."[6]

Then a woman by the number of Lily A. Thompson surfaced in the nation's capital and soon became a media star as she apparently experienced her 15 minutes of fame. It began with a story in the *Washington Times* on November 21, 1894, that observed there was a woman in Washington, D.C., who wanted to be a police officer. It started by saying, "A dainty little policewoman, twirling her highly-polished locust and strutting jauntily down the street with her helmet tilted coquettishly backward until it rests on the top of her collar, while the front rim is fringed by her waving fringes, is a possible picture on the broad thoroughfares of the Capital City in these fin de siecle days." It went on to explain that "a scented little missive, written in a feminine hand, but couched in business terms" was received in the office of the district commissioners on November 20. It was signed Mrs. Lily A. Thompson and made a formal application for her appointment on the police force "as an all-around 'copper' and patrolman — or woman." In her letter Thompson cited the last WCTU national session wherein a report was made and favorably received urging the appointment of women as police officers "with the view of elevating the different forces by the commingling of women of respectability with the male guardians and the minimizing of some of the brutal practices now employed by policemen in making arrests." Thompson informed the district commissioners that in her opinion moral suasion could be made a more potent factor in arresting culprits than the club, blackjack or pistol. A reporter for the newspaper met Thompson for an interview and declared, "She is a natty little widow with a well-rounded form and pleasant face.... Mrs. Thompson is a believer in dress reform and is considered quite an athlete in gymnastic circles." She was 23 and had been a widow for a short while. She admitted to the reporter that she had applied for the job, saying, "Why not? I feel that I could do more with an obstreperous prisoner than one of your big, gruff policemen." It seems that Thompson was not provided with any privacy by the commissioners who, apparently, turned her entire letter over to the newspaper. They regarded it as that much of a joke. The contempt in which the woman was held could be seen in the title of the piece, "Lily Pines for a Billy."[7]

On the same day the article appeared an editorial on the topic appeared in another part of the newspaper. The editor wondered, sarcastically, why should there not be a policewoman. He wrote, "Would her skirts offer any objection to the twirling of a club. Are feminine fingers any less capable than male digits when it comes to subduing a refractory 'drunk and disorderly' by grabbing a handful of hirsute and yanking it with a gentle insistence. The *Times* thinks not."[8]

Mrs. Lily A. Thompson, 1895. One of the earliest women to formally apply for a position as a policewoman. Her application was met with hostility and ridicule.

One day later, in the same newspaper, Thompson was reported to be "the talk of the town." Even then "many intelligent and influential ladies" had been enlisted in her behalf. At the Wimodaughis Club the women members offered the thought that since Thompson was "nervy" enough to apply and "face public opinion" she would not be found wanting in courage if she was appointed. Mrs. Dr. Caroline Winslow (at the above club) said she favored Thompson's appointment because "as police officers women could do much to elevate and give tone to the force. To do that is woman's province." Mrs. Caroline Kent, wife of Reverend Alexander Kent, pastor of the People's Church, said the position of a policewoman was not a desirable one but a very necessary one. Mrs. Kent could not understand on general principles why a woman should want to be a police officer with all the attendant hardships and exposure. She believed in "co-labor" but "there are certain positions we have no desire to fill. I do believe, however, that a strong, magnetic woman would make a good police officer." Mrs. E. M. S. Marble (described as a leader "in nearly every movement for woman's advancement") thought Thompson should get the opportunity, assuming she was bright and intelligent. "Ladies have entered so many new fields during the last few years and worked so acceptably that we have hardly any cause now to fear innovations as we once had," she explained. "The elevating influence of women has been illustrated in every avenue in which she has been employed." At the end of this article was attached a letter to the editor (from an unnamed female subscriber to the newspaper). It was entirely out of place and not on the usual page with the other letters to the editor printed that day. It read, in part, "Being a woman myself, of ordinary female delicacy, I am shocked at the request of a woman for a position which would place her in contact with the low and brutal elements which pervade the lowest strata of a city." She suggested Thompson would be better off in the household duties of her own circle, as a volunteer, for example, steering adults away from liquor and giving moral guidance to orphan boys. Her last remark to Thompson was, "I trust that she will not so unsex herself as to accept the baton and buttons of a policeman, even if it should be unwisely tendered."[9]

A few days later, on November 25, it was reported that Thompson had been so besieged by curiosity seekers, newspaper reporters, and so on, that she had gone into hiding for the time being. She had received many letters, some requesting a photograph from her. One letter from August Vogel made Thompson an offer of $15 a week if she would place herself on exhibition in a Bowery Dime Museum clad in a full policeman's uniform with baton and badge. She quickly replied, "Nothing can ever induce me to go on a dime museum or any other stage and figure as a freak." (Dime museums were very popular at this time and designed as centers for entertainment and moral education for the working classes. Distinctly lowbrow they had more in common with carnival sideshows of a later time. A dime museum was where one might go to see a six-legged dog or a two-headed baby). The owner of an unnamed "big business house" in Washington offered to pay her a "fair salary" and furnish a complete police uniform for her use if she would consent to patrol the interior of his establishment from December 1 until the holidays ended.[10]

Some 10 days later Thompson was in Judge Kimball's police court to observe and to take "my first lesson in police work," she said. Reportedly she was the center of attention while she was there. Thompson was accompanied by a female journalist from Baltimore who was said to have proposed to write a long feature story about Lily for one of the big magazines.[11]

By this time interest in Thompson was lagging. Late in January 1895 it was reported she had received an offer of employment. It came to her through the efforts of Detective Maurice Quinlan of Washington police headquarters. The offer came to her as a letter from the American Detective Agency of Concord, New Hampshire, offering her a job as "fly cop" to represent that agency in Washington, D.C. Supposedly Thompson had taken the offer under advisement and she considered whether to become a "sleuth instead of a uniformed policewoman."[12]

A few days later a little more background of Thompson appeared, in a

West Coast newspaper. She was described as weighing not much more than 100 pounds. Her original application letter to the district commissioners read, in part, "As it is the purpose of the Woman's Christian Temperance Union to urge the experiment in this city of placing women on the police force, as was decided at the recent convention of that organization, I desire to have my name entered upon your record as the first applicant for the appointment as a female police officer. I believe, with the leaders of the W.C.T.U. that more can be accomplished while making arrest by the use of moral suasion than by the use of club, pistols and brute force. The experiment of female police officers is worth trying." Thompson was 23, a native of Charleston and admitted "there were not many women suffragists in that section of the country." She had acquired her ideas on the subject since coming to Washington about four years earlier. When she was three her parents moved to eastern Tennessee and in that mountain region she grew to womanhood. It was there she developed a fondness for outdoor exercise and became an accomplished horsewoman and, according to her friends, a splendid rifle shot. She acquired a taste for athletics of all sorts and was an expert with Indian clubs and dumbbells. From her home near Knoxville, Thompson came to Washington, and since the death of her husband a short time earlier she had supported herself by sewing and by occasional work at copying. But the interest in Lily Thompson was over and after February 1895 no more mentions of her appeared in print. Whatever her intentions she was treated badly by the media and the establishment, reduced to little more than a freak and a bad joke. Today, Thompson probably would have no trouble becoming a police officer. But her time was 1894 and it would be sixteen more years before a police agency could and would hire a woman with the title "policewoman" albeit with very, very, very limited duties. Thompson seemed to be intelligent, active, ambitious and with a strong desire to make something of herself and her life. But like so many other women with similar qualities she would be treated with contempt, reduced to the level of a joke and then dismissed from view.[13]

At a meeting of the WCTU in a Washington, D.C., church on December 4, 1894, Mrs. Ruth G. D. Haven told the audience: "If you really cannot find any other work to do you ought to amuse yourself for a while by organizing for the one object to get an appointment for women as policemen, and if you fail in that raise money to pay them yourselves." That idea was contained in her lecture "A Nation's Suicide, the Sacrifice of our Girls. What shall we do about it?" Haven wanted to see women out patrolling streets, not alone but in pairs. "But if a woman were on such now dangerous routes [the 'worst' streets] the locality would soon be purified and it would be as safe to patrol alone as those in the most respectable sections of the city. There ought to be a woman policeman on every beat in Washington," she explained.[14]

Even if there were no policewomen in America that did not mean someone could not use the concept as an advertising gimmick. An ad in a Kansas City, Missouri, newspaper on May 8, 1895, contained the bold headline in large type "Female Police." That ad began by stating, "Why not? They can arrest a man's attention with the minimum of exertion; capture a man with a smile, He will succumb to a glancing shot from her eyes." That ad continued in the same vein for a bit more before it turned to its main purpose — that of selling hats at the store of A. A. Pearson, 1006 Main Street, Kansas City.[15]

When the National American Woman Suffrage Association and the Chicago Political Equity League held a joint two-day conference in Chicago in November 1897 the Reverend Anna H. Shaw declared from the rostrum that she wanted to be a "policeman." She said she had been fired up for ten years to hold an office in a large municipality and the office she wanted most was that of "a common policeman." Shaw asserted that the mayor of Chicago should realize the importance of having women represented on the police force. She thought he could get such recruits from the ranks of the Salvation Army and the American Volunteers. As well, she believed he could obtain from those organizations on short notice "2000 women whose presence on the streets of Chicago in uniform would do more toward elimination of crime than many times that number of men." She thought arrests made up only a small part of a cop's job and "it ought to be just as much his duty to prevent people from becoming criminals as to take them into custody after they have gone wrong." Shaw added, "It is in this direction that the presence of women on the police department would be a benefit. I would rather be a police officer in Chicago or New York than mayor of either city."[16]

Mulling over Shaw's words a couple of days later a newspaper editor recapped them in print and then said, "The idea of a woman being a policeman runs counter to all American political and social notions, and no doubt it will be a long while before such an idea can even be tolerated." He added that it was not quite certain that there wasn't something in Shaw's suggestion about women on a police force: "They certainly could not be bigger failures in many respects than the ordinary policeman is, who often can't or won't see when wrongdoing is going on." In conclusion the editor declared, "Miss Shaw is either far in advance of her time, or sadly out of joint with it."[17]

Elizabeth Cady Stanton, one of America's best known and loved women's leaders, said in 1900, "There ought to be about fifty women police on the New York City force. They ought to be of discreet age and a principal part of their duties should be the looking out for young girls coming to the city as strangers. And some of them ought to patrol the streets at night, to look after women going home from work or the theatres."[18]

A number of false starts made it into print in this period with a number of announcements of the imminent arrival of one or more policewomen in one or other cities around the nation. None of them came to fruition, at least not at the time announced. One example took place on December 4, 1902, when the city council in Norfolk, Virginia, was reported as having authorized the employment of a female police officer who would receive the same salary as a patrolman and would wear an appropriate uniform. The duty of that officer would be to care for all the female prisoners at police headquarters and to meet the boats and trains that arrived in Norfolk and take care of all the women coming from them into the city who may have had need of police protection.[19]

If the members of the Intermunicipal Committee on Household Research had their way there would be women police within New York in the coming few weeks, or so it was reported in April 1905. New York City police commissioner McAdoo had been asked by representatives of that group to appoint a "sufficient number of females preservers of the peace to cope with the refractory girl servants who decline to accept a discharge and, with skillet armed, defy the world." The society women behind the household research movement declared their purpose was to "protect" the servant and employer alike "and assert that a woman policeman can better accomplish the result than a rude man who chews tobacco and knows naught of diplomacy." McAdoo, it was said, was not reconciled to the idea and "fears the complication that might ensue should a mild-mannered and highly refined policewoman be called into a kitchen to eject a six-foot girl who was simply asking for a scrap. To say the least, he is skeptical of the powers of persuasion under the circumstances."[20]

The most publicized and reported false start in this period took place in Bayonne, New Jersey, starting in March 1906. Mrs. Julia Goldzier, who was prominent in many women's clubs in Bayonne, wanted women appointed to the Bayonne police force. She had written to Mayor Pierre Garven. It was a needed measure she told him, to save the children. In her letter to Garven she said, "I desire to call your attention to the pathetic degeneration of our youth, especially our boys. Even those of refined parents are loutish, sickly, sunken chested, slouchy in gait, and have a general rundown appearance." She thought men's clubs were bad for men and children as these were places for "holding smoking and drinking bouts, gambling and general licentiousness." On the other hand, women's clubs, argued Goldzier, were places for moral, mental and spiritual improvement. "It would be a small extension of authority to organize a police system to protect our children," she exclaimed. Since society already employed women to teach the children she reasoned it would be no startling innovation to employ women as guardians over those same children. When the children were at home or in school they were safe. All the mischief was done in the streets. "Policemen patrol our streets to protect property. Why shall not policewomen patrol the streets for the protection of our boys?" she wondered. If her reform was adopted, she concluded, "Better citizens would result and the standard of living would be raised."[21]

Newspaper attacks on Goldzier's idea began the next day when someone wrote, "Mrs. Goldzier conceives her lady cop as something of a composite truant officer, teacher, nurse, playmate, vice-mother and city disciplinarian." In reply Goldzier stated, "I don't intend that my lady patrolmen shall supersede the men." She wanted regularly paid women, with authority over all citizens in the interests of the young. "I plead for my policewomen that they may keep our children from saloon corners, the haunts of the gross." She envisioned two shifts with one working 6 A.M. to 2 P.M. and the second shift on duty from 12 noon to 8 P.M. As well she proposed to make it obligatory for every child to be in its home by that hour in the evening. Her policewomen, she speculated, "could suggest amusement to loafing boys—stop quarrels and all kinds of naughtiness. They would be empowered to reprove men who were setting the children bad examples." She thought men were often not fit for their own boy's society. What are men like? she queried. Her answer was, "They swear and drink and smoke and are so vulgar and disgusting that children ought to be kept away from them." She added, "I have a husband who's a real gentleman but most are too vile to be called by that name." But, on the contrary, she stated women "are helpful companions for children. They are sweet and have no bad habits." If her reform were adopted Goldzier confidently declared, "Police women would set Bayonne aloft on a pedestal as the most progressive spot in all our glorious country."[22]

A couple of months later Goldzier and her supporters were ready to present petitions for female officers to Mayor Garven and the city council of Bayonne. "Policewomen are bound to become an institution in the whole civilized world," she enthused. Garven claimed he was not opposed to the concept but "uncertain" as to whether Bayonne would support the idea. The reformer had given a lot of thought to what type of uniform her proposed officers should wear, bearing in mind how important first impressions could be. She believed it would be "natty but not gaudy" and feature a "becoming" helmet and a divided skirt, which would allow for women to do physical things such as climbing fences more easily. Also, her women would wear knee boots and would carry "a small but serviceable club." Goldzier reiterated that what inspired her for the idea were "drinking, smoking and spitting men."[23]

Some 10 days after that an editor recapped Goldzier's idea before remarking, "There is the germ of a great idea in it. But is there any practical way to apply it?" He worried that the question of uniform could cause trouble because one of woman's primary instincts is to dress according to her own tastes. Therefore, one of these proposed policewomen, call her Policewoman Smith, "would die rather than be seen on the street with a hat just like that worn by the hateful Policewoman Jones. The difficulty is so fundamental that it seems to block the whole project."[24]

Later in May 1906 it was reported that Goldzier was still circulating petitions "for the appointment of women police to guard the morals of boys and girls while at play out of doors" in Bayonne. Her petition declared, "We, the undersigned mothers, wives and daughters of the voters of Bayonne, who, though not represented are yet taxed not withstanding it is contrary to the cause of the revolution of 1776 and the Constitution of the United States today, do hereby demand that the Mayor and Council take some definite action to provide women police." Mayor Garven exclaimed that he did not know what to think and "I want time to think it over."[25]

A few days later a newspaper piece was run under the byline of Owen Langdon. It read like an editorial or what today would be called an op-ed piece. Many newspapers printed the piece. Langdon started out by saying: "It was only a joke, of course — though this is denied — that so many citizens of Bayonne should sign a petition asking for the appointment of women policemen, but the proposition has occasioned a good deal of talk." Langdon suggested the proposition was not entirely new and that every time local conditions became unbearable somebody suggested that if women had the management of things they would be different: "Women police have been seriously and not merely sarcastically proposed in many parts of the west." He went on to say that the difficulty of the division of labor between policemen and policewomen was said to be not impossible and that "women's clubs have taken up the question by declaring that an auxiliary police force of women is quite possible with a view to improving municipal housekeeping." Women police need not be asked to arrest 300-pound men who were violent "though they would expect to tap spitters on the shoulder and order them to the station." They would report or arrest statute violators of many kinds, "and in various ways help keep city streets decent." In conclusion Langdon stated, "One reformer suggests that women police could in no way be more serviceable than in looking after the men policemen. They need a lot of watching."[26]

Almost a full year passed before Goldzier was heard from again. At the end of March 1907 she said that about 500 people had signed her petitions (the population of Bayonne was 32,722 in 1900 and 55,545 in 1910). It was said that "most" of those signers were women. When it was finally submitted the mayor and council of Bayonne tabled the petition "and some jokes were cracked over it." Goldzier had spent more time thinking about a proper uniform for her hypothetical force and this time she had settled on dark blue blouses and bloomers, with or without skirts, military caps with gold braid, and patent leather boots. Double rows of gold buttons were to adorn the blouses. Instead of clubs the policewomen would carry switches (a slender flexible rod used especially in whipping or administering discipline — something perhaps like a riding crop). In order to arouse more interest in her reform Goldzier had issued a pamphlet which had been heavily circulated in the city. In it she said, "Would not only immoral women accept positions on the police force?" Her answer was that the question surprised her as much as the idea that only immoral women would take positions as wives, school teachers or nurses. "It is the old tyranny in man, fearing to give liberty to woman lest she misuse it as he misuses it."

In her pamphlet she asserted that her critics and "the horrified public shouts that policewomen would encourage race suicide" (meaning that working women would not be home producing babies). In conclusion the reformer declared, "The healthful outdoor exercise as a policewoman, with its limited hours and easy work, will soon make our women strong and free as men." Her pamphlet was titled, "Policewomen: An Appeal to the People of Bayonne" in which she set forward her arguments on the issue. To those who worried that policewomen would drag women into politics, Goldzier stated this was an argument for policewomen not against, because "women purify the home, the street, business, and camps and women in politics would purify politics. Those who cannot realize this should be in the lunatic asylum." With regard to the idea that a woman's place was in the home, she dismissed that as "senseless twaddle."

Also addressed was the idea that "the horrified public shouts that policewomen would encourage race suicide." Goldzier said that was nonsense, since one child saved equaled one child born, arguing how the "unwedded lady cop" could save a child from being trampled to death by a runaway horse or stop a child bully from killing another child with a "tossed missile." Under Goldzier's plan female police would be appointed to patrol the streets for the protection, assistance, and entertainment of our children while they are out of their parents' sight." Finally, she presented her petition and arguments to city officials. However, the Bayonne City Council could barely contain its snickers as it "jocosely pigeonholed her request."[27]

Near the end of 1908 Goldzier had spent well over two years in letter writing, agitating and lobbying the Bayonne Common Council and had failed to secure the appointment of policewomen. So she appeared personally before a committee of that body in December "and made a stirring but ineffectual argument and plea." She was assisted by her husband, who also was said to be an advocate for women police.[28]

Two years passed without any results but a seemingly unfazed Goldzier declared, in February 1909, "I am the dominant mind. I am here to show others their duty." She added that "anyone who doesn't agree with me is a pinhead." (At that point in the article the reporter, Ethel Patterson, admitted she substituted in the last word of the quote but claimed it was what Goldzier meant). If it was even "mildly" suggested to Goldzier that it was a policeman's duty to protect our children as much as to protect property she explained it would be the duty of her policewomen not only to protect but to "assist" and "entertain" as well.[29]

Yet just two months later an article appeared that declared "Policewomen are to be a reality here" in Bayonne. However, the fine print was a killer. Having been authorized by the city council at the suggestion of Goldzier, it was reported, nine volunteers would do duty policing the park during the summer only. Those women were not to be called "policewomen" but were to be known as "guardian mothers" and would not wear uniforms at all. They duty would not be to make arrests "but to instill a spirit of politeness in the youngsters of Bayonne. They will urge the children not to make noise, to be gentle and rise always and give their seats to elders." Those "guardian mothers" would do duty on alternate afternoons and would serve without pay. They do not seem to have ever come into existence.[30]

Jokes continued and even Hollywood took up the concept. The joke came in the midst of the Bayonne coverage. It is the future and the dream of suffrage has arrived. There are female cops. After a struggle a policewoman has arrested two porch climbers. They ask her not to shoot them as she holds them at gunpoint. Then one of the pair points out to the policewoman that during the chase and capture her hair got messed up and her hat was no longer on straight. Panicking, she said she would never think of going along the street like that and dashes off to find a mirror. The two felons escape into the shadows. Now to the movie. While the idea of policewomen had not been officially accepted in any jurisdiction nor any woman hired with that title the capitalist system had noticed and was already starting to use the idea for marketing—meaning the ad for the hat store.

Now Hollywood, hardly more than a baby, took notice. If one had wandered into the Elite Picture Show in Alexandria, Virginia, in January 1909 (after paying the five cent admission fee) one would have seen the live headliner Chrissie Waltham, described as a "Favorite Irish and Coon Singer." As well, the patron would have seen a program of four film shorts, one of which was *Female Police Force*. It was produced by Pathe Freres and released in the US on May 8, 1908. No other information about this production seems to have survived.[31]

Another false start occurred in April 1907 when it was announced in the press that Toledo, Ohio, was to have "a staff of women policemen." Reportedly that had been decided by the board of public service with the women police to be detailed to the various city parks to look after wayward children who frequented those places at night. While the women were to be vested with full police authority "they will be under the control of the Juvenile Court."[32]

During February 1908 an editorial about a New York City club that passed a resolution advocating the institution of a "female police force" appeared in several US papers. Those club women argued the time for such a force was then and the city had to have women's help to "lead its future citizens [boys] away from the door of the saloon and induce him to throw away his half smoked cigarette." That caused the editor to ask, rhetorically, "Is it not apparent upon a little reflection that it is in the power of womankind to accomplish the results aimed at without having to don an unbecoming helmet and sport a tailor-made coat of blue with brass buttons?" That is, women should stay home and supervise their children there. "When all the mothers of America strive to become the police of their families as well as the judges, ministers and guardian angels thereof — a surprising and protean variety of accomplishments, not, however, beyond the womanly range — then will the necessity for that neophytic apparition, the public policewoman, disappear, and madam will throw away her unnatural baton and resume her rightful rolling-pin," he concluded.[33]

Another editorial about the above cited New York club appeared about six weeks later. This one said that club had recently discussed the clothing suitable for their proposed new force. But when the meeting adjourned "several vital matters were still unsettled. For example, what is the proper angle at which the helmet should be perched above the pompadour and whether a veil should be adjusted over the aforementioned helmet?"[34]

At the first meeting of the season of the Woman's Democratic Club of New York City, on September 25, 1908, it was decided to bring before the City Federation of Women's Clubs, at its next meeting, a resolution calling attention to the work being done then in Bayonne, New Jersey, and suggested efforts in the same direction in New York City and elsewhere. Said Florence Adams, secretary of the club, "Let us have policewomen as soon as we can get them. They, much better than men, could deal with children who commit small offenses." She added, "Many children are afraid of policemen and run away at the sight of them, whereas a policewoman could make friends with them and lead them to substitute innocent play for their mischief." Adams added, "Too many small boys take up smoking. Policemen are too grand in their uniforms to notice things like that. Policewomen would." As she sat down she remarked, "I wouldn't have them wear the man's uniform."[35]

Around 1909 a women's group in Grand Forks, North Dakota, called the Florence Crittenton Circle advocated the need for women police to cope with social conditions leading to delinquency. Acting on this pressure, in May 1910, the city council passed an ordinance creating the position of police matron. Despite the name of the position, duties of the job were considered to be in the realm of policewomen. But apparently no one was hired for that position for some time.[36]

In a March 1909 editorial in the *Los Angeles Herald* about women's rights in general, and women's place in the world, the editor stated, "We do not propose that women should become members of the police force, although if some one were to ask why there should not be policewomen as well as matrons, the question might be difficult to answer."[37]

At a national probation officers' convention the delegates suggest that all civilized communities should have policewomen as well as policemen: "Public sentiment in favor of the appointment of women police officers is growing rapidly."[38]

During this period there were a number of articles and profiles on women identified as policewomen. These were all females connected in some way with the police service, but not as matrons. Nor were any of them officially called policewomen. It was the media that labeled them that way. Some were policewomen in all but name, more or less, but many were not even close, just press exaggerations. However, they did illustrate that the media had an increasing interest in the subject.

According to a September 1896 report, St. Paul, Minnesota, had just got a "female policeman" in the person of Mrs. Edwin T. Root of that city, who had recently been appointed to the position by the mayor of St. Paul. He had done so, said the story, to achieve "more effectual work in rescuing young girls who have fallen into evil ways." While she was said to have authority to make arrests, it was not expected that she would do so, except in cases of emergency.[39]

A couple of weeks later the Root story was covered in another newspaper (just one more of many) with a lead paragraph that declared, "The first woman to be made a member of a police force and the only one in the world authorized to wear a police star, lives in St. Paul, Minn." The article headline was "The First Policewoman." Continuing on the article said that Root had just been created "a full-fledged officer of the law" by the mayor of the city. "Mrs. Root may not walk a beat, but no representative of the law in the city has any more authority to make arrests than she." Reportedly, "Hers is not a 'special' appointment but the same as that of the man who wears blue and swings a club. The cause of Mrs. Root's ambition is not a desire for notoriety but to enable her to better aid young girls who have fallen into evil ways." She was said to have long been engaged in that type of work but found herself seriously handicapped by lack of authority to investigate. So she applied to the mayor for the appointment she received. Root was president of the Hamline WCTU, had doubled the group's membership and made "persistent war" on a saloon where young girls were in the habit of assembling. It was in connection with her "rescue work" that she needed the police star. Mrs. Root was 46 years old.[40]

One of the more bizarre exaggerations came in a story under the headline "A Constable in Petticoats," which appeared in August 1897. It was said that Allegheny, Pennsylvania, could claim the honor of having "the first female constable in the Eastern States if not the entire country." The woman in question was Florence Klotz, the 18-year-old daughter of Alderman Edward Klotz of Allegheny. "She serves warrants, summonses and subpoenas with all the authority and determination of a male minion of the law," the reader was told. Florence was described as a "bloomer brigade girl" who thought her advanced ideas regarding women's rights were fostered through a study of the bloomer question and attendant subjects. She secured her position through the illness of her father's regular constable. His absence placed Alderman Klotz in embarrassing positions several times and it was on one of those occasions that Florence was pressed into service, that being some two months earlier, about January 1897. Since then she had done nearly all of her father's work. After she was sworn in as a constable

Mrs. E. T. Root, 1896. One of many women called "first policewoman" during the period 1890 through 1909. She was not.

her first task had been to serve three subpoenas in a civil suit. Florence rode her bicycle four miles to serve one of them. A "little jeweled revolver" was reported to be her only defense against possible assault. It was presented to her by a constable from another ward.[41]

Another article on Florence Klotz related that before she joined the police she wheeled her bike through Allegheny County getting trade for her father's candy factory. She planned to do the same thing in the coming summer. One of her cases involved a butcher who had kicked in the door of his house when he found himself locked out of his premises by the landlord. Florence brought him to court to face a suit for malicious mischief. In a separate case, when a

14-year-old boy refused to go with her when she arrived to take him to court she roughed him up and brought him in crying.[42]

As of May 1899, it was reported, Helen Wilder wore the star of the Hawaiian police on her breast and "she is probably the only woman police officer in the world." She was also described as wealthy, heiress of a vast Hawaiian estate, and prominent in Hawaiian society.[43]

In a different account it was related that the 23-year-old Wilder was "a regularly appointed special officer" of the Hawaiian police force, who wore a silver star. Wilder had solicited the job. It was said she loved animals and children and it was to protect "her small and lowly friends" that she asked for an appointment on the police force. And when the powerful, wealthy and well connected ask they almost always receive. In one of her first tasks she came to believe the captain of a steamship that had recently arrived in port had mistreated his children. Wilder investigated and marched him down the gangplank of the ship to jail. She arrested another man for mistreating a horse he was driving (it was attached to a street car). Helen Wilder carried handcuffs.[44]

Just two or three months later it was reported that Mrs. Horace J. Craft (neé Helen Wilder), after an extended honeymoon on the mainland, was again in evidence "in her credible work as a police-commissioned officer of the local society for suppression of cruelty to animals."[45]

As of June 1901 Sergeant Mary E. Owens had been with the Chicago police force for 12 years and was described as "the only woman in the world holding such an office." She worked in connection with the Chicago Board of Education. The school law required that children under 14 were not allowed to work in stores, factories, and so on, and that they must attend school. Owens was required to keep a constant supervision over those places, rescuing children illegally employed therein and she also roamed the streets hunting up truants. She was the only officer detailed for that work.[46]

The twelve years of service credited to Owens in the above account actually included time not spent on the police force. As of 1901 she was on the regular police payroll, wore sergeant's badge No. 97 and reported daily to Chief Colleran of the detectives. Owens began her official career in 1889, soon after the death of her husband. She had four young children to support but no trade and no training. Her husband's friends brought enough pressure to bear to have her chosen one of the five women health officers appointed by Mayor DeWitt Cregier. When the women were all dropped by the Health Department Mrs. Owens had made herself "so conspicuously useful" to the police that Mayor Carter Harrison Sr. told Police Chief McClaughry, in 1893, to appoint her "patrolwoman," with a special assignment in the sweatshops, department stores and shopping district where most of the violations of the child labor and compulsory education laws were being violated. When Owens was interviewed in 1901 and asked about her work as a cop she laughed and said, "I never arrest anybody and it is mean to say that I am 'the shoplifting sleuth.' I have nothing to do with general detective work and never had." She added, "For years I have been attached to the board of education as a special officer. Of course I have full police power, but I find myself more than busy rounding up truants, looking after cruel parents and preventing violations of the child labor law." Owens was 34 and had four children aged 12 to 18. City officials agreed in stating that, aside from her police work, she had accomplished great good in the cause of charity:

Mrs. Mary E. Owens in a 1901 sketch.

"Every factory employer, manager and owner of a store in the business district of Chicago knows Mrs. Owens and she has made most of them her friends."[47]

When the headline of a January 1907 article declared "Portland has a Lady Cop" and the story went on to declare the Oregon city "has a female police officer, and claims to be the first municipality in the United States to be able to so boast" it turned out to be somewhat of an exaggeration. She was Mrs. Sarah A. Evans and she had obtained her star from Mayor Lane so that her work as "city market inspector" could be performed more efficiently. For a year Evans had occupied her post as market inspector, having been appointed at the request of the Domestic Science Circle, an organization of housewives who desired to trade in clean shops. Evans worked hard and her friends and associates patronized those stores she had placed on Portland's "clean list" of retailers. Because one storekeeper refused to let her take samples of goods from his premises and resisted her when she attempted to place him under arrest, Evans appealed to Mayor Lane and was awarded the star "and the necessary papers that go along with it, in all sufficient to make her a 'policeman in skirts.'"[48]

One of the more egregious examples of exaggeration could be found in the December 1907 article that profiled, according to the title, "America's First Policewoman Sports Dainty Kerchief Instead of Club." The reference was to Chicago's Miss Dorothy Stewart, who had just donned her official uniform and star in that city as "America's first policewoman." As it turned out Stewart had been sworn in as a "special policeman to guard the ticket line at the Auditorium Theater. Her particular mission was to care for the women and children." Stewart wore a regulation police coat, a service cap and a blue skirt trimmed with much gold braid. Reportedly, she had refused to carry a club; "Instead a lace handkerchief enforces her orders," although no details as to how that happened were published. "I like the work," said Stewart. "It would be a suitable occupation for any woman. My duties are to keep the women and children in line at the ticket window. Of course, women never like to stand in line. I never saw one that did, and when a man grabs them by their arms it only make them angry. So I just speak kindly, and I find it has a better effect than a club."[49]

An article that appeared at the beginning of 1909 was part story and part editorial about Miss Fannie Bixby, who was called a deputy of a Long Beach, California, constable who "has been sworn into office and is wearing her special policeman's star." That article was headlined "Policewoman." Bixby was described as wealthy but did not see that as any incentive to lead a "social butterfly" life. So, she was interesting herself in poor young girls whose poverty had cost them dearly and, "in the language of the Bible, has verily been their destruction." According to the article, "The example of a woman like Fannie Bixby is worth whole volumes of moralizing. With a few fearless missionaries like Miss Bixby actively at work, society will soon be reformed." A couple of weeks later another article related that a girl was transported by the police from Long Beach to Los Angeles under the control of Fannie Bixby, "police matron."[50]

Another story from Chicago, this one in May 1909, told the reader that Miss Josie (Josephine) E. Sullivan was Chicago's first policewoman. She was described as a "special" but had all the powers, privileges and duties of a "regular." Her beat was limited to the State Street department stores. Sullivan received her commission from Police Chief Shippy after he had received a legal opinion from Corporation Counsel Brundage that her appointment was all right. Her principal duty was to catch shoplifters and pickpockets in those department stores. She was provided with a star, whistle and a patrol box key. When Shippy asked Brundage for an opinion on the appointment of a woman as a member of the Chicago police department he received a reply that should have been appreciated by every suffragist. Some of the points decided were that in construction of statutes and ordinances words imputing masculine gender could be applied to females, and that no person would be precluded or debarred from any occupation, profession or employment (except military) on account of sex, provided that it did not affect the eligibility of any person to an elective office. Thus the City of Chicago legal advisor determined there was no express disqualification in law and nothing in the duties imposed by statue law or city ordinance upon a police officer that would imply the necessity or intended exclusion of either sex. A different article also declared she had been sworn in as a "policewoman" and was "the only one of her sex engaged in such work." On her first day on the job Sullivan was robbed of her pocketbook. According to this account she wore a star and "carries a tiny pistol in her pocket."[51]

Later in 1909 a Seattle newspaper reported on Dr. Mary Martin, described in at least two accounts as a "special police officer" working with the Young Women's Christian Association (YWCA). She spoke out publicly about the dangers of baby farms (the care of infants in private homes) and on another occasion she warned young women of a scam involving a fake trade school that took money from people promising they could learn a trade and promising to get them jobs in the trade. They delivered on none of their promises. That phony school promised to train young women in the art of decorating china. As it turned out Martin had, whatever she may have been, a temporary appointment during the Alaska Yukon Exposition (a world's fair) held in Seattle in 1909.[52]

One woman who was a policewoman in all but name in this period was at work in Portland, Oregon. In July 1909 it was reported that Mrs. Lola G. Baldwin was under full municipal pay as a police officer and also held a record for arrests, having, with her assistant, made 488 arrests in nine months, against 375 arrests by 152 men on the Portland force, covering a period of 12 months.[53]

At one time Baldwin was the secretary of the National Travelers Aid Association. When Portland hosted the Lewis and Clark Exposition in 1905, many citizens saw a need for protective work to be performed on behalf of women who would be coming to the city. These young women were seen as potential victims of poor social conditions and undesirable influences. To this end, travelers aid work was organized by the YWCA. Baldwin was put in charge of this with two assistants. When the fair ended that year this protective work was considered so successful that it was continued, and many women visitors decided to stay in Portland. For three years the YWCA carried the financial responsibility. Baldwin was given police power and sent for by the police every time a female was brought into court. Because her work brought her into contact with the police so often, the suggestion was made to turn Baldwin's appointment (and that of her assistants) over to the city and ask for an appropriation. Immediately there was opposition, but when it was pointed out that the requested sum of $6,000 was just half of what Portland spent on its dog pound, the financial side of the case was won. As Baldwin worked at shutting down "side doors" (code for brothels) to saloons and dance halls, she was twice threatened with shooting and once received a package of poisoned tea. When the city became Baldwin's employer it organized a Department of Public Safety for the Protection of Young Girls and Women. Later

Above and opposite page: Suffragette posed in police uniform at Cincinnati on September 23, 1909, to illustrate the concept of women police. This was part of the agitation for such a reform.

this department became a division of the police bureau by charter. As first director of the department, Baldwin stayed long enough on the job to outlast six chiefs of police and five mayors. Baldwin and her assistants were never officially designated as "police" but merely as "workers" or "operatives."[54]

One of the almost policewomen from this era did start her professional life as a matron, and she came closer to the mark than anyone else.

In New York City one of the early matrons was Isabella Goodwin, whose patrolman husband had died in 1895. Having an interest in police work,

Goodwin took the civil service exam, achieved the acceptance list, and was appointed matron at the Mercer Street Station in 1896. There she stayed until 1910, still making $1,000 a year, when the police began to use her more and more in detective functions. Among other things she helped gather evidence against fortune-tellers bilking citizens, broke up various banking scams and extortion rackets, and exposed fake medical practitioners. The case that brought her the most fame came in 1912 when she solved the Trinity Place robbery that had netted thieves $25,000. The then-47-year-old mother of four disguised herself as a down-and-outer to get a job as a live-in domestic for a pair of females believed to have connections to the main suspects in the robbery. Goodwin soon learned they were indeed the robbers and ascertained their location, leading to their arrest. A contemporary newspaper account described her as having "a kind motherly face. Her dark hair is not yet streaked with gray. And her gray eyes are full of expression and sympathy. A broad forehead denotes intelligence and her whole manner would lead one to take her for a married woman of the well-to-do class." On her move into more interesting work Goodwin commented, "After so many years at what you might call the drudgery of the profession, I was glad enough to be put on the special investigation work." Under the law the city's police chief had the right to appoint any member of the police force to the position of first-grade detective — bypassing civil service rules. Taking advantage of that proviso, Goodwin was appointed to the rank in 1912 with an annual salary of $2,250, finally shedding the title matron that she had carried to that day.[55]

There was no other way for Goodwin to become a police officer and no other promotions possible. Goodwin was the world's first female detective, although she had already worked as such for two years but at a matron's salary. The use of matrons in other capacities by police departments was not uncommon. Any time a female was needed a matron was a likely draftee, and if none was available a policeman's wife or girlfriend might be pressed into service. Goodwin was unusual in that she got recognition with a formal promotion and a salary increase, albeit delayed. Most matrons received none of these. While matrons were sometimes used as police officers, the opposite was much more common. Females hired as police officers were given only matron-type duties if a hostile hierarchy was determined to make life unpleasant for them. This method has been in continual use right into the modern era.[56]

And that set the stage for the appointment of the first policewoman in America, Alice Stebbins Wells, in Los Angeles in 1910. She was the first in the sense of being officially hired by a police agency as a policewoman. All the above women were set apart by being named to their position by one person (usually a mayor or police chief), a position arbitrarily created by that one person as compared to a body such as a city council acting in concert to officially create and officially fill a new position (after a period of expected and publicly aired opposition)—that of policewoman. Wells was the first female to meet all of those criteria. As well her personality and tireless efforts to secure more female police meant she remained a strong media presence for years to come. Unlike, say Goodwin, who did not seem to ever seek out public attention and the limelight, Wells, conversely, thrived on it. Wells' appointment ushered in a frantic period of activity from 1910 to 1916 when policewomen were ever in the news and appointed in many different cities.

3

U.S., 1910–1916

Although she was preceded by many other women who were called policewomen in various media accounts, Alice Stebbins Wells was the first female to be hired with the designation policewoman applied to her officially by the employing police force. Her appointment was also the first instance of a woman officer being hired as a direct result of pressure by groups brought to bear on a city administration. Many accounts listed her as the first female cop, and in many ways she was. Her ambition, drive, and sense of mission also set her apart from the few who had gone before her. That made her a major organizer and public figure in the movement for female police. Traveling across the country making speeches on a rigorous schedule, Wells was a natural for media attention. While some earlier women had done similar work, none of the others had the personality or sense of purpose to play a major role in the push for policewomen, nor had they any apparent desire to be media figures. Wells might have spent less actual time on the job as a policewoman than someone like Baldwin or Goodwin, yet she became generally known and accepted as the country's first policewoman.

Little has been recorded of her early background. Having worked as a social worker in Brooklyn and having studied criminology for two years at Hartford Theological Seminary, Wells moved to Los Angeles sometime before 1910. She did social work in Los Angeles and perhaps was an assistant pastor at a church. Other, often sketchy, accounts of her early life indicate she may have once been an assistant pastor at the Plymouth Church in Brooklyn and that she later spent two years as pastor of a church in Oklahoma. While doing her voluntary work with young people, Wells found she could be effective only by visiting saloons, poolrooms, and dance halls—places where the youth congregated. One problem she had was that as a volunteer worker she had little clout. A second problem was that a decent woman rarely, if ever, ventured into one of these venues with or without an escort. The proper handling of youth, she thought, was one of the greatest fields of applied Christianity. Wells decided to become a member of the police force. It seemed to be the answer to her problems as it would cloak her with the dignity and authority of the law. It also struck her as logical and reasonable to have female offenders and young people handled by female police officers. Wells' first attempt to join the force met with a resounding no. Wells then sought community support before making another attempt. Canvassing influential citizens, Wells got 100 or so leading residents to sign a petition pushing for her appointment to the police force. Fearing a hostile reaction from the press and the public, Wells kept her petition secret until its actual presentation to the mayor. Quickly the city council granted

Alice Stebbins Wells, 1910

her request, with Wells becoming a police officer in September 1910. One year later the position of policewoman became classified under the civil service in Los Angeles. Said Wells, "Women and children have a right to a representative in the police department."[1]

Mrs. Alice Wells apparently first came to media attention in Los Angeles as a representative of the Prison Reform League, which criticized the methods of the LAPD, on the night of February 11, 1910, in an address on "Prison Reform" delivered by her at the Third Presbyterian Church. She described the police system as "lawless" and scored officers for being overzealous in making arrests. She urged the public to become aroused. That appeared to be the only time she styled herself as Alice Wells. Thereafter she was always known as Mrs. Alice Stebbins Wells. A few days later in a letter to the editor she continued her attack on the police department and called again for reform.[2]

Wells spoke again on the evening of March 15, 1910, on the subject "A Trust Betrayed." It was, once again, an attack on the Los Angeles police system and was delivered at a meeting of the Los Angeles Improvement Association. On the afternoon of May 1, 1910, the tireless Wells addressed a mass meeting on the same topic of police reform at the First Baptist Church in Long Beach, California, at 3 P.M. On the same evening, at 7:30, she spoke on the topic at the Mount Hollywood Congregational Church in Hollywood.[3]

Activity to get Wells on the police force intensified that summer in Los

Angeles. On June 9, 50 people "prominent" in the city presented a petition to the city's police commission asking it to appoint a woman to the police force "to be employed in ferreting out law breaking on the part of café and amusement hall proprietors in permitting minors to frequent such places." The petition was handed in by Mrs. Hester Griffith, state president of the WCTU. Wells, around the same time, filed an application for appointment to the office which the petition hoped to create, stating she had worked in other cities in an effort to prevent and check the spread of crime among juveniles. That petition read, in part, "We further request that in appointing such officer you consider the application of Mrs. Alice Stebbins Wells whose wide experience and sincere interest in the welfare of our children particularly fit her for the position." The Friday Morning Club (described as an "influential" Los Angeles women's group) added its own communication to the demand to create the position of policewoman and appoint Wells to fill it. It declared that one of the most active agencies in the prevention of juvenile crime had been the appointment of a woman police officer, "one whose duty it is to watch doubtful places of amusement and to aid and care for such young people as come under her observation, to the end that useful lives may be lived by many who drift into ways of crime and carelessness through friendlessness and loneliness." The club added, "Denver and many eastern cities have found this addition to their regular police department of great value, and we earnestly request your honorable body to appoint a woman as special police officer to enforce such ordinances prohibiting minors from frequenting undesirable cafes and places of amusement."[4]

A few days later the police commission of Los Angeles discussed the petition at its regularly scheduled meeting and reportedly it was "looked on with favor." It was passed on to the city council with a recommendation that the position of policewoman be created. A similar recommendation accompanied the application of Wells. Police Chief Galloway wanted to be assured that in the event of her appointment Wells would report directly to him "and not to any club or charitable organization and that she would be under the rules and regulations governing the patrolmen in the department." Police Commissioner Topham assured the chief that the answer to his concerns was yes, that she would be treated "as any patrolman in the department." Remarked Police Commissioner Wellborn, "I realize that a woman would be a valuable adjunct to the department in handling juvenile cases. I am heartily in favor of this office being created, for there are certain infractions of the law that can best be ferreted out by a woman."[5]

Due to the fact that Wells was an educated woman, a social worker, and had deliberately sought and secured the opportunity to work as a policewoman, Wells' appointment generated a good deal of media attention. Much of it was less than complimentary, such as, "many journalists presented the situation in a half-comic matter and pictured the woman police officer in caricature as a bony, muscular, masculine person, grasping a revolver, dressed in anything but feminine apparel, hair drawn tightly into a hard little knot at the back of the head, huge unbecoming spectacles, small stiff round disfiguring hat, the whole presenting the idea in a most repellant and unlovely guise."[6]

When he handed Wells her police badge the Los Angeles chief of police said he was sorry to offer a woman an insignia of office so plain, but "that when he had a squad of amazons he would ask the police commission to design a star edged with lace ruffles." Continuing, the chief noted Wells wore no uniform, carried no weapon, "and as often as possible keeps her star in her handbag ... she has no idea of using physical force in the discharge of her duties, which are no less varied than those of her brother officers, and often identical with them." Wells was, said the chief, to apply preventive rather than punitive methods, and to particularly zero in on "the social evil." On the job Wells was charged with the supervision and enforcement of laws concerning dance halls, skating rinks, penny arcades, picture shows, the parks on Sundays, and similar places of public recreation. In addition, she searched for missing persons, maintained an information bureau for women, and monitored "unwholesome bill-board displays." Her salary was said to be $75 a month, compared to a patrolman who started at $102.[7]

Regarding her decision to become a police officer Wells said, "The police department represents the strategic point at which virtue can meet vice, strength can meet weakness, and guide them into preventive and redemptive channels." Asked about the causes of crime, Wells replied that many causes arose from improper conditions in the home, because "in many homes, deferential treatment toward all womankind is not insisted upon. A girl accustomed to easy familiarity within the home is not quickly affronted by undue freedom from the chance acquaintance." Women themselves had to be directly and indirectly involved in the remedy for this; for example, by insisting "upon a single standard of morality, the elevation of domestic service to a place equal to other respected occupations ... will do much toward stemming the tide" of females running afoul of the law. In making her rounds Wells found scarcely any penny arcade "whose pictures are not suggestive of evil." She favored censorship of bawdy humor, violence, sex, and "scenes of gilded sex," insisting this was all for the "ultimate good of the public." Wells was there, she said, "to find the needs and point the way."[8]

Wells' first day on the job was September 13, 1910. *The Los Angeles Times* reported she would be "the first woman policeman, if such an anomaly is possible, in Los Angeles." On the job, according to the paper, "she is not to wear a uniform or carry a baton, but to discover places and people with immoral tendencies, and bring to her aid the operation of agencies of reclamation."

She was to perform preventive work against immorality. Groups named as instrumental in backing her application to become a police officer were the WCTU and the Friday Morning Club. In a September 14 article the *Los Angeles Times* openly mocked her by referring to her in print as the "little woman" and "Officer Wells— maybe it should be Officeress Wells." Said Wells, prior to that story, "This is serious work, and I do hope the newspapers will not try to make fun of it." After Chief Galloway spoke to her on her first day on the job Wells was sent out with Patrolman Marden who was to show her through the different penny arcades, skating rinks, dance halls, picture theaters and other places frequented by minors, keeping tabs on which was to be the most important part of her job. She was to report to Sergeant George Curtin, the same as other patrolmen, and would not act in conjunction with the so-called "purity squad."[9]

Just six weeks into her job Wells was still lobbying. At the end of October 1910 she declared, "Six more patrolwomen are needed for the city of Los Angeles." She appealed to the clubwomen interested in civic reform to volunteer as her assistants. It was said Chief Galloway would swear in those deputies to Mrs. Wells with full power to act as special officers. Wells added "As there is no provision at the present time for more than one salaried policewoman, my assistants will have to give their services without hope of remuneration. I do not consider this a serious feature, however, as it will eliminate any person from entering the work from a purely mercenary standpoint." She had been sworn into office under the same oath of office as men took, including the chief. Her deputies, she said, would have the same official powers that she herself possessed. Wells hoped to make a personal appeal for assistants to the Friday Morning Club "as I wish the women of brains and leisure. The hysterical woman who goes into the work merely for a fad will be of no service, as the position requires hard work and cool judgment. I can use as many women as will volunteer." She added that any who came forward need not devote an entire day to the task as any hours from morning to midnight that the candidate was willing to work would be useful to her. However, no assistants were ever used or employed by Wells.[10]

During her first year, Wells made 13 arrests. In addition to patrolling amusement places she noted, "I have regular office hours, and women come for help and advice for which they would not go to the regular police department." By the latter part of 1912 the Los Angeles Police Department had three female officers and three police matrons.[11]

If the media mocked the appointment of Wells as a police officer, women in general applauded the move with Wells soon being flooded with requests for advice and lectures. Within two years of her appointment she was given a six-month leave of absence from the force to go on a speaking tour. During 1912 to 1914 Wells delivered 136 lectures in 73 cities throughout the United

States and Canada. Sponsors included religious groups of all kinds, civic groups, men's clubs, and every kind of woman's group — ranging from the Evanston, Illinois, Current Event Class to the Women Taxpayer's League of Cincinnati. On one tour Wells delivered lectures in 31 cities in 30 days. In many of the cities where she spoke the municipality was considering hiring female police. In at least some of these she had a positive effect. After hearing her speak the director of public safety in Philadelphia announced he would at once request the necessary appropriations to employ female officers.[12]

Alice Stebbins Wells, 1915

One audience openly hostile to Wells confronted her in Grand Rapids, Michigan, in 1914 when she addressed the International Association of Chiefs of Police. One heckler yelled, "Call the patrol wagon, another nut gone wrong." Nor was the rest of the group much less hostile, for "in fact they all but put Mrs. Wells out of the meeting."[13]

According to Wikipedia Alice Stebbins Wells was born in Manhattan, Kansas, on June 13, 1873, and died in Los Angeles on August 17, 1957. She served with the LAPD from 1910 until she retired in 1940, having attained the rank of sergeant in 1934. While she was 37 years old when she became a Los Angeles policewoman next to nothing was known or published about her life to that point. Not so much as a word seemed to have made it into print about her husband, who certainly was out of the picture by the time Wells arrived in Los Angeles.[14]

False starts were also regularly reported in this period. A March 1910 report indicated that Indianapolis might soon place women on that city's police force. Mayor Shank had submitted such a plan to the board of public safety. A newspaper editor added the thought that "possibly they may be called policewomen, be supplied with baton, pistol, helmet and star and be selected from the 180-pound applicants who are expected to rally to the enlistment office. The experiment may be worth trying, though it is a novel one."[15]

A news story later in 1910 carried the headline "Work of the Policewomen of Chicago." However, the brief piece was actually about a group of some ten women — then on the job for about a year — who monitored the activities of children at amusement places, and so on. It was the Juvenile Protective Association.[16]

An example of an exaggeration also could be found in 1910 with an article titled "Policewoman is a Sphinx." This was also from Chicago and told the tale of Miss Kate Adams, secretary to Leroy T. Steward, chief of police of the city. According to the story Adams became "actual head" of the police department the other day when the chief took a week's vacation, "and for the first time in history 3,000 bluecoats fell under the rule of a woman." It was, of course, all nonsense. Not that Adams herself cooperated in the piece. When a reporter asked her, "How does it feel to be chief of police?" she replied, "How should I know?" Adams was a young woman who had worked as a clerical for a few months for the chief, and that was all. Even the article added, far down in the piece, "Assistant Chief Schuettler is, of course, officially the acting chief." It all illustrated how enamored the media was becoming to the idea of policewomen.[17]

Reportedly, Miss Nan Stevens, who had charge of the quarantine department of the Board of Health, "is a policewoman — a real officer of the law. And she has the same rights that all policemen have. She has been sworn in as a special policeman and wears her star, a badge of authority." That was in May 1911 in Omaha, Nebraska. Early in that year Stevens, a trained nurse, was added to the health department and given charge of people suffering from contagious diseases. During the epidemics of scarlet fever, smallpox, diphtheria and other disease Stevens was frequently refused admission to houses throughout the city. That lack of authority led the health department to provide that Stevens would not be handicapped in her work and had the power to impose on people during the course of her duties.[18]

During the fall of 1911 it was announced that Lucy Page Gaston had been appointed to the Chicago police force "with the power to arrest minors who smoke cigarettes— provided, of course, that she can catch them." That article was headlined "Chicago's Policewoman."[19]

It was reported that Mrs. John S. Crosby, president of the Women's Democratic Club of New York had accepted the badge of deputy sheriff from Sheriff Harburger. "My club has always advocated policewomen. I will do anything I am expected to do in the preservation of peace and morality," she said after getting her badge. "I am a suffragist but that will have no bearing on my work as deputy sheriff," she added. "I would arrest a suffragette just as soon as any other person if she were breaking the law. If they try breaking windows, I'll pull them in." According the story's headline Crosby was "New York's First Policewoman."[20]

Out west in San Jose, California, Mrs. William F. Curry, wife of William

F. Curry, clerk of the justice court of San Jose township, reportedly had been sworn in as a deputy constable, to serve without pay. The appointment was made by Constable F. M. Marshall. It was also said that interesting stories were told of Mrs. Curry's physical prowess and, although she had yet to make her first arrest, "it is expected that she will give a good account of herself should she have occasion." Every morning she donned boxing gloves with her husband and they sparred for "3 lively rounds." Recently she had taken a hand in a domestic quarrel in her neighborhood and "administered a beating" to a husband who was abusing his wife. It was unclear whether Mrs. Curry did that before or after her appointment.[21]

Agitation and lobbying for policewomen took place in many cities all over America with the intensity and number of such efforts increasing in the wake of the publicity attendant to the Wells appointment. In Sacramento, California, the question of having a policewoman had been discussed freely at various meetings of the Retail Members Association, as of March 1910, and "what was at first considered a joke has become a real live question." It was thought the association might soon recommend to the trustees that a woman be named as special detective with police powers. It was further added there were "numerous violations of the law which can not be checked by policemen, and for this reason a woman is wanted," although no details were provided.[22]

A story appeared in July 1910 that Baltimore was considering the advisability of adding women cops to its regular force. With respect to that idea Mrs. Katherine Waugh, vice president of the National Suffrage Association, said, "It would be a great thing for the women of this city to have a member of their own sex in authority in case they need help and I think the idea of women police might be an excellent one, until we can get the more powerful protection of the ballot and the right to serve on juries." The Woman's Suffrage Club of Baltimore and its president, Mrs. Maddox Funk, also advanced the idea of having women on the police force "to break up flirting and ogling."[23]

Just one day later, however, it became apparent there would be no women police in Baltimore unless the next sitting of the Maryland Legislature passed a bill providing for such an innovation. Miss Edna Beveridge, chair of the auxiliary committee on women police of the Suffrage Club, had a final interview on the issue on the afternoon of July 11, 1910, with Maryland attorney general Straus. He assured her the appointment of women as auxiliary police would be unconstitutional and without precedent. Beveridge protested, arguing that Baltimore already had police matrons. That was true, admitted Straus, "but provisions were made for them by special legislation and the best thing you can do is to start a campaign with the object of dragging the matter before the Legislature." Beveridge declared she would carry the message to the General Assembly.[24]

If Dr. Anna Shaw could have had her way, at the start of 1911, there would have been 100 women police in New York City as quickly as they could be hired. Her theory, outlined to members of the Political Equality Association, was that none but "policemen of their own sex" could successfully cope with certain conditions in New York. She elaborated, "If you want to stop the white slave traffic and keep boys and girls away from vicious moving pictures, restaurants and dance halls, you must have women policemen." Shaw would select her female cops from the ranks of the Salvation Army and would make Maud Ballington Booth chief of the female squad (she was a leader of the Salvation Army, having married the second son of that organization's founder, and a co-founder of the Volunteers of America).[25]

Shaw added, a little later, that not so long ago she saw a man in a Chicago court who, in one of the cheap moving picture shows there, in the course of three months, had taken "twenty-three young women and little girls and shipped them off to Texas." She was talking, of course, of supposed white slave traffic and went on to declare, "That thing could never happen if capable women, as the Salvation Army women would be, were acting as police in cheap moving picture shows, cheap theaters and restaurants." Although she had only recently asked the mayor of New York for 100 policewomen she asserted, "Now I ask for a thousand in New York City and hundreds of thousands for the other cities and town in the United States that need them."[26]

In a 1909 address at the University of Minnesota in Minneapolis, Dr. Anna Howard Shaw, president of the National Women's Suffrage Association, called for 100 policewomen to be hired in every big city in America, stating that they "would make for improved civic conditions. The criminal needs mothering. If women were on the police force, their watchfulness, care and attention to people who need their wholesome influence, backed up by authority, would prove a most useful and uplifting measure." Shaw's idea provoked a sarcastic editorial the very next day in the *New York Times*, which was particularly incensed at the idea of "mothering," noting that "criminals will generally applaud the suggestion," and deriding the "spectacle of one hundred policewomen mothering them ... it is hopeless for them to try and infuse more sentiment in police methods." Equating real female intelligence with the unintelligent image of them found in popular entertainment, the newspaper sneered that the police should hire some females as detectives to work on unsolved crimes for their "alertness" and because they "are so effective in farce, romance and the service of the Custom House."[27]

Eighteen months later Shaw gave a lecture in New York City in which she called on that city to hire 1,000 female police. When she had been lobbying for just 100 Shaw wrote to the mayor of New York City, telling him that when he hired women officers he should "have them all Salvation Army women, and to have Mrs. Booth pick out just the kind that could do the work."[28]

At around the same time an article stated that a committee of women had declared that every man who had held the office of police commissioner in Boston had been a failure, and that group of women had petitioned Massachusetts governor Foss to appoint a female commissioner. Heading that committee was Mrs. Charlotte Smith, president of the Women's Homestead Association. It claimed to represent some 50,000 women. If the appointment of a female commissioner was impossible then the committee wanted women police inspectors. If that was impossible then they wanted the present police force increased, reformed and regulated. If that was impossible the women declared Foss should at once take steps to call out the militia to "suppress wickedness in Boston."[29]

Still in the first few months of 1911, a Seattle, Washington, newspaper stated, "The idea of policewomen, which at first was regarded as shocking and absurd, is growing in favor." The report added that the first woman police officer had just been appointed at Sapulpa, Oklahoma. Mrs. Mabel Bassett had been provided with a star and a regular salary and had the same powers as any member of the town's police force. She had been assigned to look after the juveniles and keep those under 16 years of age off the streets after 8 P.M. Also, it was said the authorities in Milwaukee were planning to have their first policewoman. Miss Edna Finch, a trained nurse, who stood highest in the competitive examination was expected to be appointed soon. She was to be on duty around factories to ensure that sanitary conditions were in compliance with the law.[30]

Commenting on Foss in Boston and the petition by women for a female police commissioner a well known female journalist of the era, Nixola Greeley-Smith (the granddaughter of Horace Greeley) said in her column that she could not see the "peculiar efficiency" that would attach to a woman police official. As to a police "captainette" she joked about many a wife who could administer the third degree (to her husband). She added; "Seriously considered, a woman Police Commissioner belongs to comic opera and a woman policeman would be a joke to the most timid criminal in the city." Some time earlier one of the advocates of a "feminine finest" in urging the argument upon Nixola made the remark, she continued, that the "woman policeman" could enter a saloon whenever she suspected liquor was being sold to minors, show her badge and enforce the law. Said Nixola, "But obedience to the law is not enforced by the mere showing of a badge. It is the force behind the badge that cows the criminal." And what woman of normal sympathies, she argued, "would want to use the only efficient force possible to her — that of firearms? A group of small boys shooting craps would laugh at the attempts of a woman police officer to break up their game, and laugh not only at her, but at every principle of government she might feebly endeavor to represent."[31]

Suffragette arrested in London, UK, during a protest in 1913. Such handling of upper- and middle-class women in America by policemen led to pressure and lobbying for the appointment of police matrons and then policewomen.

Considerable speculation was aroused in April 1911 in Tacoma, Washington, following the assertion of Clarence Parker (a prominent politician) that he favored women policemen. "Some of the speculation has been mingled with mirth," said a newspaper editor. Noting that women in Tacoma had taken a strong interest in the city's vice district the editor wondered why women should not be appointed to the police force to aid in regulating things that women had determined to keep watch over: "There is no more reason why they should be kept off the police force than that they should not vote. Mr. Parker's determination to put women on the force will doubtless gain him many votes."[32]

Never long out of the newspapers Alice Stebbins Wells was profiled in the September 1911 issue of *Sunset* magazine. According to that piece Wells was practically on duty all the time "and most of her Sunday is spent in the various parks of the city watching over the welfare of girls" (that was, presumably, her one day off in the week). Wells was said to have concluded that "an alarming increase in the delinquency of girls is due to economic conditions that are thrusting vast number into underpaid, overworked positions." In the story Wells was quoted as saying that the solution for girl delinquency lay in "the dignifying of domestic service to a profession. It must be made just as honorable as that of the teacher, the stenographer or the clerk."[33]

Miss Mary E. Brown became the first regular commissioned woman police officer appointed in Seattle, in September 1911. Mayor Dilling selected her. Brown had been national superintendent of the curfew for the WCTU and was in charge of the purity department of the Washington State WCTU.[34]

Los Angeles policewoman Wells, "attired in a blue suit adorned with brass buttons and trimmed with braid," announced in February 1912 that she would tour California delivering lectures. She had been granted 15 days of unpaid leave, in addition to her regular vacation of equal duration and she expected to visit about 25 California cities. The subjects she intended to lecture upon were described as "social hygiene and the possibilities that lie in the path of the police woman in the moral uplift of unfortunate women."[35]

An article published on March 3, 1912, presented a roundup of what had happened in the field of policewomen. In Sapulpa, Oklahoma, Miss Vivian Carter, Miss Mabel Burton, and Miss Gertrude Mack were appointed detectives by Mayor Denton and the selections were confirmed by the city commissioners. The women had brought about the arrest of a "notorious burglar and highwayman" and the appointments as detectives were in the manner of reward and recognition of their "good work for the community." In the same city it was reported that Mrs. Mabel Bassett was the "animate curfew bell" for children who were on the streets after 8 P.M. Miss Edna Finch was given police power in Milwaukee and assigned to the duty of visiting factories to see that the legal requirements as to sanitary conditions were fulfilled. Miss

Lucy Johns became a deputy sheriff of Fayette County, Virginia, and was given a gold star, accepted an ivory-handled revolver and was "assured an official status in the community" of Staunton, Virginia. In the community of Evansville, Indiana, Miss Lydia Metz had the distinction of becoming (a few months earlier) the first policewoman in Indiana. She was a trained nurse and, it was reported, "Her badge of authority aids in giving her immunity from harm in her night missions of mercy."[36]

On March 18, 1912, Alice Stebbins Wells was on her California lecture tour and spoke twice that day in Cabot Hall in Oakland, once in the afternoon and once at night. "Mrs. Wells is a tiny woman and does not wear the blue cloth and brass buttons that usually go with her office, but a distinctly feminine garb, lace trimmed, albeit most simple and in her hair is a girlish bow of black ribbon," said a reporter. Wells, it was reported, insisted on femininity for women. She believed the work of wifehood and motherhood was the "highest and most sacred profession in the world." As the remedy for much of the social evil (for boys and girls) she prescribed training in social hygiene. Said Wells, "The preservation of our social fabric depends on getting a large number of our women back into lines that are distinctly feminine. Home making, home keeping, motherhood, these things we must guard jealously and the way to do it is to keep our girls in the home, keep them from the office and the store." She added, "They are being weaned away from their home instincts for a few clothes or the price of their small pleasures.... They merely bring down the work and wage of men." At 9 A.M. the next morning Wells delivered an address to the girls of Oakland High School at that institution.[37]

After Wells' lectures in Oakland a committee was appointed within a short period of time. Its purpose was to work toward having appropriations for policewomen included in the next budget of the City of Oakland. Groups represented on that committee included the WCTU, the Child's Welfare League, the YWCA, and the Public Service Club.[38]

Continuing on her tour, Wells spoke in San Francisco on March 20 where she said women police officers placed emphasis on prevention in their work. Her California lecture tour was under the auspices of the WCTU. Her San Francisco talk was titled "The Need for the Police Woman and Her Work." As far as she was concerned, "The woman police officer is a perfectly natural, logical step for our advancement in civilization." Some of her duties included giving advice to mothers as to how to keep their daughters under control, and listening to the woes of unhappily married women or deserted wives. An the end of her lecture the audience passed a resolution urging the San Francisco Board of Police Commissioners to appoint policewomen in their city. On June 30 that year Wells was back in Oakland where she delivered a talk at the Plymouth Congregational Church on the topic "Side Lights on the Girl Question."[39]

In April 1912 Mrs. Louis de Keeven Bowen, president of the Juvenile Protective Association of Chicago, suggested policewomen in plainclothes and in uniforms would be an effective means of lessening crime. Bowen declared the number of wayward girls would be reduced and the attitude of boys toward authority would be changed.[40]

On July 11, 1912, a total of 75 women were slated to take the civil service examination for the position of policewoman, a position recently created by the Seattle City Council through the efforts of Councilman Austin E. Griffiths. Up to that date the police chief of the city had the authority to employ four policewomen. Those women taking the test ranged in age from 30 to 61.[41]

One month later in Topeka, Kansas, Mayor Billard appointed Mrs. Lillian A. King a member of the Topeka police force. King formerly published a newspaper. She was president of the Kansas State Temperance Union. As to her duties, it was reported, "Mrs. King will be detailed to arrest wayward young girls."[42]

The problem of prostitution was often a crucial reason behind the push to hire female police. Agitation for these new officers in Boston began at least as early as 1912. At that time the Massachusetts White Slave Traffic Commission, in a report to the state legislature, called attention to increasingly large numbers of young girls aged 12 to 18 who could be found each night roaming city streets. To remedy this, the report recommended the appointing of "well qualified women — as adjuncts of the police system." Other groups, such as the Massachusetts State Federation of Women's Clubs, joined the lobbying efforts, with the result that in May 1914 the state enacted a general law which provided for the appointment of females as special police officers. The first city to take advantage of this statue was Haverhill, which in 1915 appointed the first woman officer in Massachusetts. Other cities followed this example.[43]

Prostitution was also a problem in Detroit where in 1914 the Girls' Protective League was advocating the need for women police to deal with prostitutes. In some cases the league was being called in for consultation by an apparently bewildered police force. However, progress was slow, for in 1917 they were still lobbying, and they brought in Alice Wells to lecture and help exert pressure.[44]

In many areas laws were being passed and female police were being hired. Reportedly, Minneapolis appointed one in 1911. A Maryland law of 1912 provided for up to five, calling them "matrons to the police force" to distinguish them from "station-house matrons." Baltimore had three that year with Mary S. Harvey, associated for ten years with the Federated Charities, being the first. Later were added Elizabeth Faber, fluent in four languages, and Margaret Eagleton, also associated with Federated Charities. These three looked after minors of both sexes, patrolled amusement facilities, and visited prostitutes at brothels.[45]

When the Kansas City Board of Police Commissioners appointed a woman police officer in 1913 they announced that she was to be "the city's mother to the motherless."[46]

No sooner had Wells finished her California tour than she was off again. In the middle of September 1912 it was announced she had left on a six months' tour (unpaid leave) of investigation of conditions in other cities. Of course, while doing that she also found the time to deliver lectures. On September 26 she addressed a meeting of the Woman's Union in Kansas City, Missouri. "Every city needs women police officers. Strangers would prefer to appeal to them," she told her audience. "The only weapon I carry is a key to patrol boxes." As well, she discussed her personal experiences with the crowd.[47]

Some evidence for the growing presence and importance of policewomen could be seen in the events that took place in Portland, Oregon at the end of October 1912. A policewomen's conference, the first of its kind, began there on October 25 with representatives present from San Francisco, Oakland, Sacramento, Seattle, Spokane, and other West Coast cities. The delegates to the conference were described as "women actually engaged in doing police officer work." The purpose of the conference was for "exchanging ideas on the subject of police protection for young women." That conference came to an end on the night of October 26 after a two-day session. These were women "in charge of woman and girl protection from every city of importance on the Pacific coast." A second conference was scheduled for a year later, to be held in Seattle in July 1913. Officers selected at the Portland conference were Mrs. Lola G. Baldwin from Portland (president), Mrs. Winnifred Covell from Tacoma (vice president), and Mrs. Albert Johnson from North Yakima (secretary and treasurer).[48]

A movement had been set in motion for policewomen in Washington, D.C., as of November 12, 1912. The opening shot was to be fired a week later on November 19 at the Unitarian Church when Wells was slated to deliver her much anticipated lecture. To give the lecture "added strength" and "to attract the city's most representative and influential men," a social betterment committee had been formed. The names of about two dozen people, many of them men, were listed in the account. "I am in favor of a woman officer for social betterment," said Justice Stafford. The idea that there was a great amount of work connected with the police department that a woman officer could do better than a man was said to be prevalent. "If a policeman in uniform goes into a dance hall the dancers are placed on guard because they can spot him by his uniform, but if a woman in plain clothes goes into one of the local dance halls where conditions should be investigated she will not be detected and as a result a great work for social and moral betterment can be done," explained committee member Mrs. Helen Gardener. It was also noted in this account that Baltimore had only recently began this "experiment" of having policewomen with three of them employed out of five authorized by an act of the Maryland Legislature.[49]

A couple days before Wells spoke in Washington a news account observed, "As the first policewoman in the United States, Mrs. Wells has had to bear the brunt of much ridicule, but she claims that wherever her 'experiment' has been tried the ridicule has given way to praise."[50]

Before her lecture in Washington on November 19, the Los Angeles policewoman gave a talk in Baltimore on November 18 under the auspices of a committee there headed by Cardinal Gibbons. Meanwhile, Helen Gardener, in charge of the lecture in the nation's capital stated that many young girls came to Washington looking for work. When they arrived, though, they very seldom had a great deal of money. Thus, "they usually are objects of attack by unscrupulous men. They know not who to go to with their troubles, because they hesitate in pouring out their hearts to policemen. But with women officers things would be different. Good advice and a motherly protection would be offered them."[51]

During her Washington lecture Wells declared one or more policewomen should be connected with every police department "for the sole purpose of receiving complaints from women, if for nothing else." She added, "Women hesitate to go to a policeman for information and advice. This is easily understood and, as a result, it behooves every municipality to provide women officers who can render help in many ways where a man is entirely powerless." She argued the policewoman was particularly adapted to preventive work and was the best fitted to handle juvenile offenders, "for a woman has the motherly instincts that enable her to accomplish wonderful tasks." As well, she believed that women were of great value in tracing missing persons. Wells told of her experiences in Los Angeles in preventing the sale of tickets to cinemas or any other places of public amusement to children under the age of 14 unless accompanied by adults. She noted that many arrests were made as the result of her investigations. The tireless Wells also lectured in Philadelphia around this time and on November 20 Director of Public Safety Porter of Philadelphia announced he would request at once an adequate appropriation from his city council for the employment of "women detectives." This was apparently a result of the Wells talk.

Speaking in general terms of the "strays" (children) that could be found in any American city, Wells said, with respect to women in general and policewomen specifically, "We have guided their feet since the world began and why shouldn't we do it now in the day of their greatest need?"[52]

Even though Wells was on the road lecturing life went on for the remaining policewomen in Los Angeles as they tended to their duties near the close of 1912. On a morning late in November a woman attired in a trim blue suit walked into the offices of Captain of Detectives Mooney in San Francisco and announced she had come to take two runaway girls caught in San Francisco back to Los Angeles. A perplexed Mooney said that he was expecting an Officer Shatto. She was. Her card read, "Mrs. Rachel D. Shatto, policewoman, Los Angeles City." She showed her star bearing No. 140. A bemused Mooney turned over the girls to the Los Angeles officer. Shatto had been an LAPD officer since July, some four months earlier. She was one of three policewomen on the force. Shatto's work was with the juvenile bureau. In response to a reporter's question, Shatto said she never revealed where she carried her revolver and handcuffs. A couple of weeks later Mrs. Ola Taylor, also an LAPD officer, told a reporter there were four policewomen on the force, all of whom were connected with the juvenile department. It was her duty to take charge of all women who were arrested, to search them, and take care of all girls. She said the policewomen were not sent out on the streets to make arrests although they were provided with stars, keys to the patrol boxes, and police whistles. In speaking of women voting, as all could do in California, Taylor said she was not a suffragette and was not in favor of women voting unless they owned property or had a business.[53]

As 1912 drew to a close an editor on a Honolulu newspaper declared that many cities had found one effective method of crime prevention was in the appointment of policewomen. He said six cities had women regularly employed and many other cities were demanding them. Seattle, he said, had just appointed five at a salary of $85 a month and "they are patrolwomen who cover definite beats." Elsewhere, however, they were usually detailed to theaters, skating rinks, dance halls, city parks, and amusement places. No uniforms were worn nor any clubs carried by any of them. Their work, he continued, was preventive rather than punitive, although when the occasion demanded they made arrests. "The policewoman is a sociologist. She relies on a cultivated brain rather than on muscular brawn to cope with the tasks that she meets," he explained. In Minneapolis the policewoman position was created on the recommendation of the grand jury and the vice commission, he said, who urged that there should be a woman officer to look after the young girls on the streets at night, in the dance halls and cafes. Miss Emilie L. Glorieu was appointed to that post. According to the editor, people in Honolulu had a movement agitating for the appointment of policewomen to give young women the protection demanded and "conditions here demand specialized effort to protect females from the pitfalls of the streets and coffee-saloons and low-class eating houses."[54]

On December 17, 1912, Wells, continuing with her speaking tour, delivered a talk at noon before a hundred members of the Woman's Municipal League in New York City who were assembled in the home of Mrs. Lincoln Cromwell, 711 Park Avenue. Declared Wells, "A woman police platoon assigned to the white light district is the solution of the white slave problem." She was described in this article as "the only municipal police officer in the United States assigned to the regular police duty" who was then on a leave of absence from the LAPD to tour the country "advocating the establishment of a woman police force to watch over the morals of girls." Officer Wells added, "Woman is the natural protector of morality and wields the larger influence over young girls on the downward path." If women police officers were assigned to watch the sources of danger to girls "and uproot the evil, there would be immediate relief. It is impossible to determine the character of certain sources of evil unless women find out in the way that women alone can, the chances of girls being led astray." She explained that when she was assigned to report on conditions in picture theaters she found it easy to circulate among the young girls and find out exactly what was taking place in those theaters, and "several of the moving picture shows which I had closed in Los Angeles would still be running to the ruin of many exposed children if any other course had been adopted. A woman police officer questioning girls in the neighborhood can find out where liquor is being sold to minors and who are agents of vice by winning the confidence of the victims."[55]

A couple of days later a New York newspaper ran a lengthy letter to the editor from Helen Kendrick Johnson (writer, poet and prominent actress who opposed the women's suffrage movement). It was a comment on the Wells lectures. Johnson deplored "the desertion of womanly ways of working." She wrote of a delicate looking relief worker who did outreach work each evening on the streets of New York City for the Florence Crittenton Rescue House for women and girls. That relief worker was on the streets in the dark "to save the girls and women from evil men or their own depraved selves. She needs no policeman's badge. Her womanly modesty and simple hearted love for humanity and her sex are her safeguard." There was testimony, Johnson continued, that when woman attempted the kind of work that society "naturally lays upon men she loses something of man's respect." Springing from civilization was man's belief that woman, being essentially different from him, "is better than he and has natural tastes and duties that he cannot know or do, but should help to keep sweet and separate." Suffrage, to its discredit, argued Johnson "has always aimed to break down this God given barrier of sex difference." The Salvation Army woman needed nothing but her bonnet with the red band to safeguard her in a saloon where the roughest men were gathered: "They do not and dare not to molest her, because they know that she comes as a Christ lover to bring his soul saving message. A policeman's uniform or badge would go far to destroy the effect of her work; her attitude toward the men would be entirely changed."[56]

A day or two later Alice Stebbins Wells was interviewed in New York City at the home of a friend after arriving back in that city from a Philadelphia lecture. Times had changed, said Wells, and police conditions had not changed with them. With a great deal of insight she captured in a few sentences just what had happened between the time matrons arrived on the scene in 1880 (in any numbers) and her own appointment in 1910 as an official policewoman to generate the need for such a position. "Thirty years ago the police dealt with a public composed chiefly of men, and it was all right to have the force composed entirely of men. But now we have a public consisting of men, women and children — women and children are out in the world more and more each year," she explained. "While I don't for a minute think police-women should be appointed for street duty — men are better fitted for that, and most policemen are very kind to little children and quite capable of pro-tecting them in most instance, though, perhaps, in sections where there are many girls and children women patrolmen might be of special use." She firmly believed there should be women on the police force of every city to aid in the preventive work. Wells told the reporter some stories about herself and the other two policewomen on the job in Los Angeles. Along with her other duties Wells had regular office hours when any woman in the city was welcome to come to her and tell the policewoman her troubles, and she tried to help her. She spoke of abused women who told her about bad husbands— women, Wells insisted, who would never go to a police station and tell those same troubles to the desk sergeant, "and sometimes, by just going and talking to an ugly husband, letting him know that his wife had spunk enough to come and talk to me, I have been able to effect quite a change in the household." At that time Wells had been a policewoman for a little over two years. During her first year she made 13 arrests, chiefly for infringement of the law in dance halls and moving picture shows. Of late her work had been mostly in tracing up people for relatives who wrote to the LAPD to say that Uncle John had not been heard from in two years and was supposed to be in Los Angeles. Could you please find him? Yes they could, or at least try. Apparently, in this time period the police service in most places undertook such tasks. When asked why women should be on a police force the LAPD officer said there were two reasons. In the first place, she replied, was detail work, for which women had a greater capacity for than did men and "women care for the pro-tection of children more, probably than men do. That is the chief reason why they are needed on the force."[57]

The socially very prominent Mrs. William K. Vanderbilt sent a letter on March 1, 1913, to the New York legislative committee for remedial police leg-islation. In that letter she urged that a squad of policewomen be appointed to deal with vice in New York.[58]

Another lobbyist before that committee was Mrs. O. H. P. Belmont (Alva Belmont, rich and powerful socially, who fought for women's rights issues). In a statement she delivered in person to that committee (the Wagner committee) she declared an effective way to reduce the "white slave evil" was to appoint women to the police force. The suffrage champion had delivered her views on March 5 after the committee had asked Belmont to give her views as to what would be the best in the way of remedial legislation for the police departments. Said Belmont, "In the light of recent developments and the appallingly increasing traffic in girls for immoral purposes I have come to believe that we are urgently in need of women on the police force." She envisioned some sort of cooperative effort with, perhaps, a male officer and a female officer on the streets together. "I believe that when a man accosts a woman in the street the policewoman should be empowered to compel the policeman to arrest the offender and the policewoman's testimony accepted." She continued, "It is rarely that we hear of a man being brought into court on a charge brought against him by a woman while we constantly hear of women who are condemned for soliciting simply on the word of a man who is usually more guilty than the woman." She was trying to find a way to deal with the real problem of second-class personhood for women who were sexually harassed on the street (the terms used then were "flirting"—sometimes—but more usually "masher") with the woman's word never accepted (he said—she said) while a man accusing a woman of sexual harassment (soliciting) often had his word alone accepted. Belmont mentioned, as an example, a recent factory strike when the factory girls who were brought into court for participating in the various conflicts between strikers and strikebreakers and then dismissed by the magistrate at night. As they left the court building, Belmont explained, they were surrounded by procurers "who were actively engaged in a vigorous effort to lure them into houses of prostitution. Were women authorized to protect girls under such conditions this nefarious practice would at least prove less prosperous." At the end of her appearance before the committee Belmont asserted, "My contention that we need women on the police force because men do not understand the woman's point of view is proved almost every day in the leniency shown by the courts throughout the Union toward the men charged with criminally assaulting defenseless women."[59]

One month later a bill in the New York State Assembly that provided for the appointment of 20 or more women to the NYPD (the Lewis bill) was said to be getting more and more support from women. Almost without exception, it was reported, the women's clubs favor the bill while suffrage organizations and charitable and reform societies were also all united in support of the measure.[60]

Later in April 1913 it was reported that two plainclothes patrol women would walk beats in the downtown district of Los Angeles at night, beginning May 1. That innovation was announced on April 28 by Police Chief Sebastian, who added that the policewomen so engaged would devote most of their efforts to the protection of girls. Of course, he explained, if they happened upon a holdup their prescribed duties did not preclude them from capturing the bandits. Wells and Rachel Shatto were named as the pioneer patrol women. They were to visit dance halls, skating rinks, movies and other places of amusement, as well as cafes frequented by young women. This was a strange article since the policewomen there had, in essence, been doing just that from the start.[61]

San Francisco moved closer to appointing its own policewomen in May 1913 when the city's board of supervisors appropriated the necessary finds in the new budget for the appointment of three women to the police force. However, a barrier still existed for City Attorney Long advised city officials that it would be necessary for the board of supervisors to create the position of policewoman in accordance with the terms of the city charter. The money for the three positions had been side aside at least partly as a result of the lobbying effort by Mrs. Lillian Harris Coffin, president of the New Era League (said to represent 9,000 women in San Francisco) and other civic leaders. If those three women tried to enter the police force under the existing civil service rules for policemen they would find it necessary to undergo and pass, as specified by the charter, the same examinations as passed by recruits of the United States Army, explained Long.[62]

A brief report in newspapers around May 6, 1913, noted the Arnold city administration of Denver had fired Josephine Roche (described as "public amusement inspector") because she went before the grand jury with testimony "about intoxicated boys and girls doing dirty rag dances in public." Roche had been appointed to her post probably in March 1913.[63]

Several weeks after that a longer account observed that Roche (Vassar '08) had just been appointed deputy sheriff of Denver, supposedly the first female deputy sheriff in America. Her appointment, though, was only a temporary one, given to her by a sympathetic sheriff while she fought to get her old position back in the police department. Jacqueline Roche was studying sociology at Columbia University and doing settlement work in New York City when the Denver City Council passed an ordinance providing for a policewoman to censor city amusements. Judge Ben Lindsey of Denver wrote to her to come to his city and take the job. She passed the civil service examination with "top notch honors" and took the job. She turned her attention to dance halls violating liquor laws. When she reported those matters to the police board they listened but never acted. They began hiding dance permits from her, so she would not know where to go to check on compliance with the laws. Then Roche turned her attention to cafes that were also believed to be violating the liquor laws. "Many of these places were nothing but wine rooms where young girls were allowed to come without escort. That is against the law in Denver," said Roche. She reported those violations to the police board only to have it refuse, again, to act. Then the police board did act — it discharged Roche. That action led to a mass meeting where 600 men and women showed up to demand she be reinstated. All over the city organizations of various sorts protested against the firing of Roche. In the meantime the police board had ordered the cafes in question to stop selling liquor at midnight, and to stop selling it without meals.[64]

Denver also acquired its first female officer in 1912 when Josephine Roche was appointed inspector of amusements in the Department of Safety, after the city passed an ordinance establishing its right to regulate and control such places. Roche patrolled dance halls, cinemas, skating rinks, and other places of commercialized amusement. When she started work she tried to avoid the necessity of making arrests. Instead, she talked "earnestly" to those she dealt with and "appealed to their sense of decency and love of family." When dealing with gang youths she appealed to their "better nature." One story had it that a policeman went to a dance hall in the course of his duties, whereupon a male juvenile began to beat up the policeman. Roche happened on the scene and stopped the fight with a "few stern words," then escorted the policeman to a place of safety. Roche felt females were naturally better suited to deal with children and juvenile delinquency; "We no longer believe in the old theory that law must be enforced by the club or by the revolver. You cannot force people to do right. You cannot beat goodness into them. You have to show them why they should obey the law. Just because a woman is a woman and disassociated from the idea of force, she can frequently enforce the law with more ease than a man," she explained.[65]

On July 8, 1913, the district court in Denver ordered the reinstatement of Roche to her job on the Denver police force. She argued she was under civil service and could not be discharged except on formal charges and after a hearing. Roche had received no formal hearing nor were any charges filed against her formally. The district court concurred with Roche's arguments. However, her stay back on the force was brief. In August 1913 she resigned, stating only that she spent much time investigating and, while not making many arrests, when she did make arrests her cases were not prosecuted.[66]

When Newport, Rhode Island, appointed policewomen to patrol its beaches in the summer of 1913 it prompted Second Deputy Police Commissioner George S. Dougherty of New York City to declare that he did not expect policewomen at Coney Island anytime soon. Said a reporter, "There seems to be no immediate danger that the department will be swept off its feet in a mad frenzy to follow Newport's example." Dougherty was described by the reporter as having a "conservative view on the whole woman police question." Explained Dougherty, "Women are useful in the Police Department as matrons and to handle women prisoners and lost children. They are useful sometimes too, as detectives to secure evidence that a man could not secure,

Policewoman at work at Newport, Rhode Island, circa 1913.

by testing fortune tellers or getting in close contact with women criminals or associates of male criminals."[67]

San Francisco continued to struggle as 1913 moved along. In June the board of supervisors wavered for some time as to whether it should allow $1,200 or $1,464 as the yearly salary for each of the policewomen to be appointed. After a lengthy debate the sum of $1,200 was set as the salary. Policemen received $1,464.[68]

New York City was not making much headway in establishing policewomen in its municipality, but other cities in the state were. As of June 1913, the first policewoman "in the vicinity" of New York City had entered into her duties, said a news story. Mrs. Joseph S. Wood was appointed to that position in Mount Vernon, New York, on June 21. As her first duty she was to settle a domestic dispute wherein both parties had appealed to her. Wood was a prominent anti-suffragist of Westchester County. Reporter Marguerite Marshall thought that was an inconsistency on Wood's part for to want to be a police officer "is surely a much more aggressive and 'unfeminine' desire than to want to drop a little piece of paper into a ballot box." Wood explained to Marshall that she always believed women should interest themselves in civic affairs, and she thought every town should have a policewoman with those people devoting themselves to seeing the laws against cruelty to animals were enforced, to compel obedience to the sanitary ordinances and the regulations of the board of health. And in the larger cities, such women should endeavor to help and protect young girls. Wood added she felt policewomen should not be asked to join in the raids on gambling houses and saloons or do other work in which great physical strength was necessary. "There are many things that must always be left to men, because men are naturally best fitted for them. But I do feel that women might help in the social side of police work," she asserted. She had lived in Mount Vernon for 48 years and knew Mayor Edwin W. Fiske and Police Commissioner James D. Connor. She was a member of many clubs and badgered city politicians for various improvements. "It simply seemed to me that I could do better work in my own little field with just the extra touch of authority given by the police badge. When I spoke to the Mayor he said, 'certainly, if you wish it.' That's how it happened." By that she meant that was how she got the job; she simply asked (badgered) for it and it was given to her. Wood told the reporter she planned to rarely, if ever, wear her badge but it was there if she needed it. "If I tell a man not to throw his refuse on the sidewalk and he continues to do so, I can show him that I have the power to compel him to obey me," she explained. Asked if she would arrest such a miscreant Wood said if an arrest was necessary "I should try to detain the person in question until a policeman arrived." High on her list of items to investigate was "spooning in the park" and "also I shall set my face against the turkey trot and kindred dances. I believe that young people should have a good time and I like to help them. But it must be in the right way."[69]

Oakland, California, clubwomen had begun to agitate in order to obtain policewomen for their community a year earlier when Wells had visited and lectured in their city. They were still at it in June 1913. That month representatives of many of the civic and welfare organizations of the city asked again that city officials appoint female police. However, the petitioners were stalled off as no definite answer was given to the women.[70]

At the same time, late June 1913, more than 200 applications had been submitted to the San Francisco Police Commission for the positions created by the board of supervisors for the job of policewoman. The hurdles apparently had all been cleared. Applicants for the jobs had to be between 21 and 35 years of age, stand 5'9" and weigh 150 pounds (it was not stated whether these were maximums or minimums). Salary remained fixed at $100 per month, compared to the starting pay of $122 for a policeman. Many of the women who had applied had the endorsement of the various women's clubs in the area. Twenty were to be selected to form an eligible list.[71]

A couple of days later it was announced that three policewomen were to be named that night, June 30, in San Francisco. According to the article "they will be set at large to catch and to protect the young girl in the strange city and in other ways to be the Harriet Beecher Stowe of the white slave abolition movement." That reporter added "The constitutional club women of San

Francisco are responsible for the plan of the police commission to appoint three" female police. They had appeared before the board of supervisors and petitioned for the reform citing Los Angeles and declaring San Francisco must have some women police too. Those new recruits were to be appointed from month to month, instead of for life or during good behavior, as were the conditions under which policemen were hired. It was reported that one of the three would be assigned to the ferry building, another to the Third and Townsend streets transit depot and the third one would "roam."[72]

Then a new snag appeared. It was over the question, "What is a policewoman and what shall her title be?" Until the police commission could answer that question the civil service commission, it was reported, could not certify eligible candidates for positions on the force. The civil service declared it must know what the women would do before it could establish what qualifications they should have. When the civil service sent the question to Police Chief White about the duties of these women the chief acknowledged that he was "stumped" when it came to determining what a policewoman's duties would be.[73]

Meanwhile, in Chicago it was announced on July 7 that 10 policewomen would be appointed "at once" in accordance with a special message sent to the council on that day by Mayor Harrison. They were to be assigned to the bathing beaches and parks. The civil service commission was to arrange for physical examinations of the candidates. Local suffragist leaders in Chicago thought that a policewoman should have the following qualities: she must be husky; she must have nerve; she must have had experience in social service; she must understand young people; she must have common sense; she must have ideals. All of those suffragists agreed those appointed must have a star while the more militant among them felt they should carry a revolver but "none took kindly to the idea of a policewoman swinging a club."[74]

John P. Irish (a powerful newspaper owner in Oakland, California) took issue with the women of Oakland who desired a policewomen's bureau for their city. He had sent to Mayor Mott and the city council, in the middle of July 1913, a protest against the proposed auxiliary police system. He called the plan "fantastic." That proposal had been approved by Mott and Commissioner F. C. Turner of the department of public health and safety, following a conference held a day earlier and attended "by a number of women who are active in social service work in this city." Details of the proposed policewomen's bureau had yet to be fixed. Miss Bessie Wood, one of the leaders in the drive for the bureau, said the necessity for such supervision was evident to those who had to deal with problems concerning girls' and young women's protection.[75]

A reporter by the name of Arthur Brinton wrote a roundup article, published in July 1913, about the phenomenon of the policewoman which was abroad in the land. From Los Angeles to Newport, Rhode Island, she was catching on and making good "even in the eyes of those critics who scoffed at the idea of female shield and star bearers," he enthused. He mentioned Isabella Goodwin, the New York City female detective, and cited her as saying, "Most women have a natural interest in people and a natural instinct to set things right, where a man might simply keep out of trouble and wait for a real infraction of the law. A man is always a man first even if he is a policeman, and he might laugh at a girl when what she needed was a good talking to." As well, he mentioned Miss Minnie Smith and Miss Janet Buchanan as newly hired patrollers of the beach at Newport, and Mrs. J. J. Farley of Dallas, Texas, who was Captain Farley, although he added that Farley was really only a police matron but had the rank of captain. Other policewomen he named were Wells; Mrs. Margaret Kelly and Mrs. William Moore of St. Paul, Minnesota; Mrs. Sue Hudkins of Chanute, Kansas; Mrs. Joseph S. Wood of Mount Vernon, New York; Miss Ora Matthews of Kalamazoo, Michigan; Miss Josephine Roche of Denver; and Miss Eva L. Vanhoesen of Somerville, New Jersey, as some of those then in police service.[76]

San Francisco continued to struggle on and by the end of July 1913 the city had appropriated $3,600 for the coming fiscal year to pay the salaries of three policewomen for the full year. To that point 22 women have applied and the article went so far as the list all 22 of them publishing their full names and addresses.[77]

On August 2, 1913, Mrs. Nannie Melvin began her first day on the job in Asbury Park, New Jersey, as that city's first policewoman, armed, said a news story "with motherly advice instead of a nightstick." She was 46 years old and told a journalist, "I suppose one of my duties will be to see that exaggerated split skirts and translucent gowns are not worn at Asbury. I also expect to act as censor for bathing suits. I intend to be broad-minded about it. Bloomers are better than some skirts and anyone who wants to bathe in the right kind of bloomers can do so. If it was up to me I'd make the men wear shirts." Melvin went on to say, "I expect to be particularly useful in those phases of misdemeanors which a woman recognizes more easily than a man — when a man and woman get too close together, for instance." Officer Melvin was on duty from 9 A.M. to 1 P.M. and from 8 P.M. to 1 A.M. daily.[78]

On August 1 Mayor Harrison of Chicago appointed 10 policewomen just before leaving for his summer home. They were to be assigned to bathing beaches, small parks, playgrounds, and juvenile court. They had full power to "make arrests, call patrol wagons, censor bathers, and make men move along the street." They would not wear uniforms at least at present as they could be replaced in two or three months after the civil service commission held an examination. Those women were Mrs. Alice Clement (perhaps Clements), Miss Emma Nukom, Mrs. F. Woodman Willsey, Mrs. Madge

Chicago's 10 policewomen on August 5, 1913, left to right (note the first named is mostly out of the photo) Mrs. Anna Loucks, Miss Clara Olsen, Miss Fannie Willsey, Miss Margaret Wilson, Mrs. L. C. Parks, Mrs. Margaret Butler, Mrs. Alice Clement, Mrs. Emma F. Neukon, Mrs. T. D. Meder (supervisor), Gertrude Howe Britton (supervisor).

(Margaret) Wilson, Mrs. Lulu Parks, Mrs. Anna Loucks, Mrs. Mary Boyd, Mrs. Margaret F. Butler, Clara Olson, and Mrs. Nora Lewis.[79]

    Those 10 women in Chicago went on duty for the first time on August 4, 1913, wearing small silver stars and wearing blue tailor-made suits. The police chief refused to furnish them with guns or clubs "and they will use hatpins in case of emergency." Like regular detectives, said a news account, "the coperines will walk the beat in pairs" being assigned to the amusement parks and bathing beaches. During the winter they would patrol the dance halls. (This was one of the earliest news accounts that mocked the idea of policewomen by giving them a humorous name. It quickly caught on in newspapers all over the country. For the next several years a term such as copette, and numerous variations, would abound). At the end of this particular piece the reporter remarked that a policeman not wearing a uniform was called a plainclothes man but "don't call the coperines 'plain clothes' women."[80]

    On August 6 a nattily dressed young man stood on State Street in Chicago tipping his hat and smiling at passing women shoppers. Then someone touched him on the shoulder. "Say, you beat it," ordered a voice at his side. He asked who she was. "I am a member of the Chicago police department — a police woman to be exact. You are a masher, I take it, and have no business here. Now you just move on as fast as you can." The youth disappeared; the officer was Mrs. Alice Clements.[81]

A couple of days after the Chicago policewomen made their appearance on the streets of the city an editorial writer in the nation's capital stated they did so "despite funmaking and frivolous attacks" and were "the pioneers in a very momentous experiment, which should be treated very seriously by the police department of that city, even if the public refuses to do so." He also observed there seemed to be no cut and dried policy concerning the duties of the new officers. He thought there were various duties in police work for which women officers seemed to be especially fitting. At bathing beaches and in the parks there was work to be done "that they should be better able to do than the men. They are likely to show better taste in the supervision of those places, also a higher regard for social morals." Some of those women, he added, had expressed a willingness to be sent in pursuit of the masher. Their real value to the police department, the editor thought, was that they should not be given routine duties or special duties, but that they should be ready to perform any and all duties "wherein women would be more effective than men." Those women had an exceptional opportunity to disprove two accusations persistently made against their sex, the editor concluded: "that women cannot obey orders and that they cannot keep a closed mouth." If they were to be of service to the Chicago Police Department they would have to do both.[82]

On the evening of August 7 Mrs. Nellie Cameron, actress, was arrested by Officers Margaret Butler and Margaret Wilson in Chicago, on a charge of disorderly conduct. When she appeared before Municipal Judge Rafferty Butler told the judge that she saw Cameron accost three or four men in the street, individually, and that to all appearances she had been drinking. Reportedly, the charges were dismissed because Cameron turned on the tears and got Rafferty's sympathy.[83]

In those early years the biggest media coverage on the appointment of women officers took place in Chicago perhaps due to the large number hired at the same time. For at least several years women in Chicago had petitioned again and again for female police but always met with refusal. Wells lent her support when she lectured there in 1912. A little progress had been made in 1910 when Chief Justice Olson of the Municipal Court of Chicago appointed a committee of women trained in social work to study the functions of the Municipal Court and to make recommendations. One was that the city should appoint female officers to take statements from women and minors who came to the attention of the department and to be in attendance at court when their cases were heard. The following year a woman social worker was placed on duty at the Chicago police station. Many people came to the station house to air their real or imagined grievances; the social worker was assigned to do away "with petty, degrading litigation and adjust the less serious complaints." Chicago passed an enabling ordinance in December 1912, which authorized the hiring of female police. The number to be hired was not fixed by law but was to be determined by the amount of appropriations voted by the city council for salaries.[84]

Mayor Carter Harrison urged the city council to hire 10 women for the police department "as an integral part of the city's police force, to be assigned to bathing beaches, parks, and juvenile court work." An order was passed, with Harrison appointing 10 women on August 1, 1913. Their first day on the job was August 5. A police superintendent wagered with a reporter covering the event that the "copettes" would be late for the 10 A.M. roll call. Apparently he won his bet for reportedly "most" of these women were indeed late.[85]

In making his plea for this reform Harrison argued that certain classes of police work, such as the supervision of amusement places, beaches, parks, and playgrounds and duties connected with the Juvenile Court, could be handled better by females because "greater care and appreciative attention to the morals and physical requirements of girls may be expected from policewomen than from ordinary policemen, who necessarily become hardened to some extent by reason of the character of the services they are called upon daily to perform."[86]

Of these 10 women hired, eight were widows, all had social work experience, and they ranged in age from 25 to 50. Police training consisted of two hours of instruction that morning of August 5 delivered by Chief McWeeny in his office. Some of the rules he gave them included, "Don't stretch the truth. Don't be too strenuous, have compassion. Present all cases fairly and squarely. Don't be nosy. Don't use too much force in making arrests. Don't complain about long hours. Don't talk more than necessary; let your commanding officer do most of the talking." One of these women told a reporter, "The park is just full of spooners, who should make love at home." After the instructions from the chief and swearing in, each female received a police whistle, fire and patrol box key, a book of rules, and a regulation police badge.

Details as to the women's apparel and powers had been decided by Chief McWeeny and a committee of female social workers. The chief had considered assigning them to stations in the red light districts, but it was decided in the end they would be of greater service in the public parks and places of amusement. Whether they would wear uniforms and carry revolvers were then still undecided. They were to visit public dance halls, excursion boats, beaches, and train stations, and try and keep young people off the street at night. Said

Arming the policewomen of Chicago, April 1914. The caption of the photo noted "they seem to be handling the revolvers in the gingerly manner characteristic of most women."

the department, "They will obtain information rather than make arrests, although on occasions they may be called upon to arrest some one."[87]

Later on August 5 they were assigned in pairs to five police stations. At one of these, the pair was taken outside the station by an officer to be shown how to use a call box, "but they came back in a hurry," reported another male officer from that station. "It seems that when they stepped up to the patrol box a crowd got around them, and I guess it was a little too rank for the women," he explained. "Anyway, they got back to the station safely."[88]

While the *Literary Digest* called this reform "Chicago's latest novelty," some elements of the media accepted women in a limited police role. Many of those who approved pointed to the experience of some European countries where the policewoman was viewed as the best and most effective agent in the fight against "the monster of modern society known as the white slaver." The *Charleston News and Courier* endorsed the idea of women police on this basis. The *Chicago Daily News* offered the opinion that Chicago's policewomen marked the end of the idea that "any officer of the law must be a heavy-footed and more or less slow-witted male person armed with a formidable club and a revolver." It added that appointing female police went even further and placed "the emphasis upon sympathy and understanding instead of upon mere muscle." Less enthusiastic was the *New York World*, which felt the only place for women was "as sanitary police, as special officers of the Health Department" where they would not "prove more inefficient or careless than men." Raising an issue that would be used consistently over the coming years, the *New York World* wondered about the physical strength of women. It wondered what would happen if one of these women was confronted by a killer, or an armed robber or rowdy: "Will she seize the murderer red-handed, wrest his smoking pistol from him, and march him off to the corner, bruised and subdued, to wait for the wagon, while a mob clamors for his life?" This newspaper thought that less progressive communities could get along without female officers until women had proven they could handle the physical aspects of the rougher parts of duty.[89]

Some type of unofficial media watch seemed to have been mounted over these Chicago women to detail the first arrest. Each of the 10 were reportedly eager to have that honor, despite their orders from the chief to "instruct and persuade" in lieu of arresting. On the evening of August 7, two of the female officers arrested Nellie Cameron on a disorderly conduct charge. From the crowd that had gathered to observe the arrest someone yelled, "Three cheers for the women cops and their first arrest."[90]

If the Chicago Police Department had deliberately set out to create a situation in which females were shown to be physically incapable of being police officers, they couldn't have done it better than the way events unfolded during an incident in 1914. Early in March of that year, Police Chief Gleason assigned some of the female officers to oversee a waitress boycott of a downtown restaurant. Scuffles occasionally broke out between pickets and police. The crowd that gathered to view these female interactions was so large that mounted male police had to move in to disperse the onlookers. Gleason soon removed the females from this duty, claiming their failure was due to lack of physical strength, but he grudgingly admitted that the situation was "complicated by the hampering of onlooking crowds." A reporter covering the dispute offered his opinion that because of this incident, "it was shown that women will resist strenuously being arrested by a sister in uniform." Gleason concluded, "Policewomen are failures at handling disorderly persons of their own sex." That was how the *New York Times* covered the story. But it was not quite like that.[91]

A few days later, on March 7, Gleason swore in nine more female officers. These women were ordered to report for jujitsu instruction so that, according to Gleason, they would be fit for emergency encounters. The *New York Times* headlined its report simply, "Policewomen to Wrestle."[92]

On August 8, 1913, Major Richard Sylvester, the chief of the Washington, D. C., police force, told a newspaper reporter that for the past 10 or 12 years his department had female employees who had been called upon from time to time to engage in police and detective duties. Sylvester then came out in favor of policewomen. He praised the usefulness of police matrons, a development he thought that had long passed the experimental stage. As well, he added, in New York, Los Angeles, and Chicago a sphere of criminal work had been found for women. In Washington, matrons had for many years been employed along detective lines. But, Sylvester observed, "It could be impractical, for instance, to arm a woman with a revolver or a club, or ask her to patrol a beat in some of the quarters of the District. This, to my mind would be bad judgment and might lead to disastrous results." Sylvester's opinion was, therefore, that while "Washington does not need, and probably will never have, women in uniform patrolling the streets and alleys, for the purpose of preserving the peace, there will be women members of the police force who will have jurisdiction over matters more closely pertaining to the morals and apathy of her own sex, and to the children of both sexes."[93]

Also on August 8, the situation in San Francisco surfaced, once again. They found themselves with yet another snag. This time it was literally about Shakespeare's famous question as to what was in a name. Apparently, it was indeed a whole lot, at least in the eyes of the San Francisco Civil Service Commission in their formal demand to the city's board of supervisors that the city amend the recent ordinance that had created the position of policewoman so that they shall be known by the "more ladylike appellation of social service inspector." Civil Service Commissioner Matthew Brady stated, "Policewomen should be gentle and tactful. They should not be called policewomen at all. It is not dignified nor womanly. The term is too athletic, too suggestive of the vigorous work performed by policemen."[94]

A week later the police commissioners in San Francisco sent a memo to the supervisors to remind them that when they drafted the new ordinance recreating the position of policewoman they included the following qualifications: applicants be between the ages of 21 and 35, citizens and residents of San Francisco for the previous five years, and be able to pass a medical examination. They further recommended that the females be give the title of "Women Protective Officers."[95]

That latest snag in San Francisco prompted an editorial from an area newspaper. That editor thought the most recent suggestion for the job title was a "dignified and appropriate appellation" as the chief duties of the women who held such positions would be exactly as the title indicated — the protection of women. Then the editor took to calling them policewomen for short as he argued, "Any beginning is better than none, and it is high time the beginning is to be made." He added, "The light minded, the frivolous, the unintelligent and the hostile may laugh or sneer at the woman protective officer and may nickname her 'copette,' but she will prove her value to the city and will earn her salary just as soon as she and her sister officers go to work."[96]

A couple of days later it was reported that officials in San Francisco were still arguing over the official name for the position — women protective officers, social service inspectors, or as one political commentator had suggested, coppette. It was said that "all agree that 'policewoman' is a harsh, undignified term."[97]

Things then went quiet for several weeks until it was announced on September 26 that three policewomen were to be appointed by the police commission on Monday, September 29. They were to be known officially as women protective officers. More than 500 applications for the jobs had been filed. As the civil service list of eligible applicants had not then been drawn up, the women appointed would be made temporary employees. It was rumored that Mrs. Kate O'Connor, a social worker at the hall of justice, would be one of the appointees. On the day the names were to be released a San Francisco newspaper, in its early edition before the names were known, ran a strange headline over a picture of a woman modeling a policewoman's uniform, alongside a uniformed male officer. That headline read, "See Copper Watch Coppette; Watch Coppette Cop Jobette."[98]

O'Connor was named as one of the three, along with Miss Katherine Eisenhart. The third position was left vacant with a promise from the city that she would be named before the end of the week. Eisenhart had been an active worker in the recent municipal railway campaign and had been active in many civic movements. O'Connor had been identified with women's reform and welfare work. It was reported that one of the policewomen would be assigned to the ferry building with the other two being assigned to "special cases." Meanwhile the civil service commissioners were still studying the scope of the examination to be soon held for the creation of an eligible list for the position. It had been decided, though, that there would be no severe physical tests such as climbing a ladder, vaulting over a wooden horse, wrestling with a stuffed dummy or toying with 150-pound weights, as was the case for men taking the exam for policeman. All had been eliminated from the "copettes" exam, wrote a journalist. "Good health will be practically the only physical requirement." The *San Francisco Call* newspaper fell in love with the term "copette" (and its many spelling variations) and would go on to use it excessively for a few years. While being superficially in favor of the reform in its editorials and articles its real attitude could perhaps be more easily seen in its not so subtle denigration of the job through its demeaning name-calling.[99]

A fledgling advertising industry even moved in to try and turn the media attention to a profit. An ad for the Tait-Zinkard Café appeared in the paper on October 2, asking how a policewoman should be dressed. The café management invited the mayor, supervisors, police commissioners, and the general public to view its idea of a policewoman's uniform with an exhibition of same held from 11:30 A.M. to 2 P.M., from 6 P.M. to 8 P.M., and from 10:30 to midnight, daily. Given the specific hours of the exhibit the implication seemed to be that a live person would be modeling the uniform, but that was unstated. The café was located at 168 O'Farrell Street, opposite the Orpheum Theatre.[100]

Miss Viola Miller, barely out of her teens, was appointed by the City Council of Ottawa, Illinois, as a member of its police force. The headline of the article called her "America's Second Policewoman," but she was a long way from that. For two years she had worked as a deaconess in the Epworth Home for Delinquent Girls in St. Louis. "Of course I shan't wear a police uniform. I will wear my deaconess uniform and quite a large, shiny, silver star — to impress my importance and official position on all beholders," she explained. She added that there was "nothing in the world I would rather do than work for girls and with girls." Miller saw a broader field for herself in Ottawa. She planned to meet the trains arriving in Ottawa and direct girls coming to the city to boarding houses and to secure work for them, "I shan't carry a stick; that would be foolish — because I could never use one like I am told policemen do — striking people over the head with them and that sort of thing." But what would she do in case she had to make an arrest, a journalist asked her. She replied, "I can't imagine the man or woman so hardened by misfortune, drink or evil ways who would resist arrest at my hands." Miller did not believe in using force, convinced that kindness would conquer anyone. However, she admitted she had never dealt with bad men or even bad boys. After she finished high school Miller entered the Training School for Methodist Deaconesses at Cincinnati. Following two years there she went to the Chicago Training School and studied for one year. She spent most of her early life growing up in a small town in southeastern Ohio. Next she took up social settlement work in Quincy, Illinois, staying there for one year. Two years earlier she had gone on to St. Louis. The City of Ottawa was to pay Miller $50 a month as a policewoman. A deaconess of the Methodist Church received, besides her current expenses, $10 to $12 a month. Miller started her duties on April 1, apparently in the coming year of 1914. Miller had not taken any competitive examination for the job. The appointment came through the Woman's Club of Ottawa. Her fame from Quincy and St. Louis had, reportedly, spread to Ottawa and with the passing of the ordinance for a policewoman by the City of Ottawa, Miller was mentioned for the job by the members of that club.[101]

Alice Stebbins Wells was in the news less often but she was still busy. At the end of October 1913 it was reported that she was on her way to attend the National Purity Congress at Minneapolis and hoped to secure the next session of that body for San Francisco in 1915.[102]

Things continued to advance in San Francisco, slowly. On the morning of October 21, 1913, the three policewomen were sworn in. They were Mrs.

Kate O'Connor, Mrs. Katherine (Katheryene) C. Eisenhart, and Mrs. Margaret Victoria Higgins. While they were sworn in by Police Chief White their duties were said to still be unclear. Those three professed themselves ignorant of what they would do but thought it probable their work would be principally among women and children and both preventive and protective in nature. There was, however, "no question of a uniform" and they would be no patrolling of a beat. White said the date of the swearing in was unexpected to him and as he would be busy over the next week at the least he would, therefore, have no time to outline the duties of his new recruits. "I shall be glad," said Chief White, "if they will take a vacation for the next week." The oath sworn before Police Chief D. A. White went as follows: "I, Kate O'Connor, do solemnly swear that I will support the constitution of the United States and the constitution of California, and that I will faithfully discharge the duties of a woman protective officer for the city of San Francisco according to the best of my ability. So help me God."[103]

On October 30 one of the three San Francisco policewomen spent the day on watch in the police courts. Cases involving women were to be her study. According to the story there was no uniform for the "copette" as "she is facetiously termed by the public at large." (Well, no. It was the newspaper that incessantly used the phrase, which may have then been picked up by the public.) Another one of the three devoted her day to a search for "blind pigs" (places dispensing liquor without a license)—such as at a grocer's store, at a confectioners, and so forth. The third policewoman spent that working day "as sort of traveling aid" at the ferry terminal and the Third and Townsend streets station. Women arriving at those transit centers were approached by the policewoman, offered aid, warned, or given some other kind of help. It was proactive behavior with the woman approaching travelers rather than waiting for travelers to approach her. A day later it was reported that the "coppettes" had been detailed to watch Mrs. Mary Vaughn, indicted by the grand jury for an alleged attempt to extort money from Judge Robert Widney. When the case was called in court that morning it was reported that Vaughn was too ill to attend. At that point the "coppettes" were assigned, on eight hour watches, to guard the woman.[104]

Another example of the type of duties policewomen performed could be seen in the November 1, 1913, report that came out of Chicago. On that day Mrs. Emmeline Pankhurst (famed British political activist and suffragette leader) arrived in that city to find an "entire battery" of policewomen there who had formed her body guard to escort her from the station to the LaSalle Hotel. Since Chicago had only 10 policewomen the entire battery was limited to that number, unless matrons had been pressed into service.[105]

Mrs. H. J. Platts was appointed a "special policewoman" in Alameda, California, in November 1913. She explained, in an article listing her as the author, that her duties were to work among the boys and girls of Alameda and "to endeavor to keep them clean, sweet and wholesome in mind, body and spirit." It was also her work to make life a little less gray for the poor, a little less burdensome to the sick and a little less hopeless to the despondent, "by interesting not only myself but other charitably inclined people in their cases. To correct the steps of the young who are inclined to be wayward, by pointing out to them the better forms of amusement and occupation, as part of my duty." Platts thought her work in Alameda could best be designated as that of a city probation officer, although she did not have that title. She planned to keep a watchful eye on public playgrounds and parks so that boys and girls could "be made to see the advantage" of having for companions children of the same age. She also would watch for cafes selling liquor to young girls. Since this piece was published in the *San Francisco Call*, the editor thought it necessary to add a line right below Platts' name in the author byline — "Alameda Coppette."[106]

Mrs. Mary Boyd, one of Chicago's policewomen, was described as "not a large woman, but she is muscular," in a news account. On December 25, 1913, she boarded a streetcar as Tessel Wendt, a "powerfully built man," was engaged in a fight with the conductor over a transfer. Boyd separated them, telling Wendt he was under arrest. When the man resisted the officer she pulled him from the streetcar, stood him against a post and rang for the patrol wagon. Boyd rode to the station with her prisoner. When the *San Francisco Call* picked this story up off the wire the newspaper added its own title to the piece, as all newspapers did. That title started off "Muscular Coppette."[107]

Near the end of 1913 Chicago police chief John McWeeny suddenly resigned from the force without warning, after a dispute with Mayor Carter H. Harrison. Then for the first time in the history of Chicago, a news story would have the reader believe "a woman was reckoned in the running for the office which had been vacated — and her name was Mrs. Gertrude Howe Britton." However, John Gleason, a Chicago police captain for a number of years was selected for the post. According to the journalist "the fact still remains that a woman was considered as a possible incumbent for the position of chief." Britton was one of "the most prominent" social workers in America and at the time of the article was described as the head of Chicago's new force of policewomen. The article was, of course, nonsense. No policewoman in America to that date had been allowed any supervision or direction, however minor, of policemen, nor would one for a long time to come.[108]

If things had advanced slowly in San Francisco, and they had, it was nothing compared to the snail's pace with which the idea of having police-women on the local force was moving along in New York City. Early in 1914 New York City mayor John P. Mitchel reportedly had three candidates already

Three San Francisco policewomen sworn in by Police Chief White on October 21, 1913, (left to right) Mrs. Katheryene Eisenhart, Mrs. Margaret Higgins, Mrs. Kate O'Connor.

for policewomen and one of them wanted to carry a gun. They were three suffragists—"enthusiastic and active suffragists." According to the report it was not settled that New York City would have policewomen but a bill to allow them had been introduced into the legislature at Albany, and that was enough to justify a hope, thought a reporter. One candidate was Mrs. A. M. Wilkinson, who wanted to start off by going after bad boys aged from 12 to 18. Mrs. Sophie Kremer was a second candidate, and she was more anxious to do something for the girls to keep them out of saloons. Third on the list was Mrs. Winter Russell. However, she declined to tell the reporter what she would do if she ever got to be sworn in as a policewoman. That bill in Albany provided for 20 policewomen in New York.[109]

Lobbying pressure in New York City seemed to bear fruit in 1914 when state Assemblyman Mark Eisner introduced a bill in Albany that inserted a clause into the greater New York charter requiring the police commission to appoint 20 or more female police. They were to be regular uniformed members of the force assigned to patrol various places of amusement in the city.[110]

Generally, this bill was strongly supported by women's clubs and suffragettes. Appearing before the assembly's Cities Committee, which was investigating the bill, was Mary Wood, representing 90,000 clubwomen who felt policewomen would substantially reduce the amount of money needed to reform wayward girls. Joseph McMahon argued before the committee that women on the force "could successfully take on work which the men should not be expected to do." Another who appeared before the committee urging passage of the measure was Alice Wells, who was described as

Miss Alvina McLaughlin, in one of the new "Coppette" uniforms, meets Policeman N. R. Norton of the park playground detail

Three weeks before the San Francisco women were sworn in an area newspaper published this posed shot with a real policeman and a woman who had applied for one of the first three spots. She did not get it. Note the "humorous" caption.

wearing "a khaki uniform and a large shield. Her brown hat, with an attractive plume, was distinctly feminine." Police Commissioner Waldo argued against the measure, claiming the police had nothing to do with the morals of the

city, and declaring that "the force was only for the protection of life and property." In March 1914 the Cities Committee killed the bill on the ground that
the city had the authority to hire female police if it wished to do so. The committee also declared that, as a mandatory measure, the bill grossly violated
the principle of home rule.[111]

Agitation continued in New York City, where in 1916 the New York City
Federation of Women's Clubs passed a resolution calling for the city to hire
female police officers. That resolution was proposed by the indomitable Julia
Goldzier, who frequently lobbied in New York when not doing the same in
Bayonne, Goldzier's resolution proposal was an annual affair that she had
begun a number of years earlier and, "since then she has lived down a great
deal of ridicule. The women have come to agree with her, and the resolution
went through with enthusiasm yesterday."[112]

Mrs. Corinne Carter, wife of the Reverend W. D. Carter, living in Seattle,
Washington, was reported in January 1914 as having the distinction of being
the only African American policewoman on the West Coast. In fact it was
said there was only one other in the United States, and that was a woman
located in New Orleans. Carter had been appointed to the post that month
by Chief of Police Claude J. Bannick and had been issued with star No. 430.
She was 34 years of age and her appointment made her "a full-fledged police
officer in every detail except salary, as she has consented to forego this item
until she has demonstrated her necessity to the force." Reverend Carter was
pastor of Mount Zion Baptist Church in Seattle. Mrs. Carter worked with the
juvenile division of the police department and with the juvenile court in keeping "colored children in order." She weighed 160 pounds and stood about 6'
tall.[113]

Wells was back in the news early in February 1914 when she spoke in
New York City, coincident with the bill for 20 policewomen then trying to
work its way through the legislature in Albany. The Los Angeles officer said
she believed the policewoman would have a deterrent effect on the masher
(sexual harasser). She went on to explain that she had been herself approached
by a masher. Wells told reporters she had stopped for a moment to look at a
cinema poster when a man came up and "ingratiatingly" asked her if she
wanted to see the film, and he offered to take her. Said Wells, "Now I can
readily imagine that if I had been a poor young girl without a nickel and worse
yet, with the knowledge that I never would have a nickel to spare for such a
treat, I might have accepted the man's offer and so possibly have taken the
first step to ruin." She explained that she was in New York City when it all
happened and if the incident had occurred in Los Angeles she would have
watched that man and that cinema to see he did not do a repeat "with a
younger and more innocent woman." Officer Wells reported another incident
to her audience. In Los Angeles she once saw a young girl walking along by

herself at night, and Wells thought from her manner the girl needed her attention. So she followed the girl, who stopped at a dime museum and asked for work. The manager said he didn't need her there but could use her in another branch of his museum in the area. They walked off together. Wells continued to follow. After a distance he asked the young girl into a drugstore to have an ice cream. The pair did so and Wells continued to tag along behind. When they reached the door of their destination Wells walked up to them, touched the girl on the shoulder and told the blustering man she would take charge of the girl and look after her. Without another word he walked away.[114]

One of the more controversial issues involving policewomen took place in Chicago at the end of February 1914 and involved a labor strike at a restaurant. This was the labor dispute covered differently in the *New York Times*, as mentioned earlier. The eatery involved was Henrici's on Randolph Street. A reporter sympathetic to labor noted if you went there with visiting guests you could have "a glimpse into 'Darkest Russia's' methods of dealing with women who had dared to protest against starvation wages and unfair conditions." The workers on strike apparently were females, employees of the restaurant. On Wednesday, February 25, a band of society women and social workers called on Chicago chief of police Gleason to protest against the officers stationed in front of Henrici's where the strike was in progress "and where two girls have been so brutally man-handled that they are in the hospital." Those women protestors demanded that female officers be stationed at the restaurant, seemingly believing that policewomen would be less physical with the strikers. Dispatched to the scene that same day to keep the peace were Mrs. Mary Boyd and Mrs. Marie Loucks, two of the Chicago policewomen, but differences existed between the band of women protestors and Gleason as to the duties of the policewomen. When Loucks and Boyd arrived there the remaining policemen (still in a majority at the site) continued to taunt, insult and harass the strikers. Minnie Meyer, one of the strikers, sick and tired of this type of treatment from the policemen (this was a common treatment of strikers by policemen anywhere in the country in this time period — and often it was much worse) and asked Boyd if she was not there to protect the females from such insult. "I am here to protect Henrici's from annoyance by you girls," Boyd was said to reply. Boyd and Meyer, and other striking females, got involved in some type of physical altercation and it ended with Boyd taking Meyer and some other girls into custody. Those striking employees were, reportedly, doing nothing other than telling people approaching the restaurant that there was a strike on at the eatery. Eventually six females were arrested and taken in. Reporter Jane Whitaker, disappointed at the remarks of Boyd, declared "the police department [was] supported by each and every citizen, but pledged to protect, apparently, only the monied interests." Whitaker wondered if those society women who protested initially would ponder "whether they improved or hurt the situation when they relied on women police to protect working girls." Mentioned here but not in other accounts was that policemen had been abusing, attacking, harassing, and arresting the striking women. The two policewomen dispatched were no real improvement but not worse, either. While they abused the strikers they did so to a lesser degree than had the policemen, and as the men would continue to do as the strike dragged on.[115]

A few days later it was announced in Chicago in the media that policewomen were considered to be a failure when it came to handling disorderly people of their own sex, or crowds. It was a matter of lack of physical strength on the part of women police coupled with the inordinate curiosity their presence caused, explained Police Chief Gleason, who removed the policewomen who had been attempting to handle the waitress strike at the restaurant. In replacing the policewomen with policemen Gleason said the presence of the women officers drew such a crowd as to create a dangerous condition. On the day Gleason issued his remarks a total of four women and three men were arrested for loitering and picketing in front of the restaurant. The idea that the policewomen lacked the physical strength to deal with the situation was disproved by the fact the Boyd manhandled and arrested half a dozen women.[116]

Miss Annie Foresythe, Aurora, Illinois, policewoman, was planning a vigorous crusade, in March 1914, against flirting in Aurora streets every night, with the arrival of milder weather. As soon as the warmer weather returned, the flirts will be out, she asserted.[117]

Chicago's policewomen became among the first to be armed and received a fair amount of attention in the media as the group of now 15 received instruction in the use of firearms. A March 23, 1914, photo showed a picture of three of them being trained. According to the article, "From the way in which they hold their revolvers before the camera it is evident that they don't know much about revolvers. For example, Mrs. Clement in this photo is shooting with her right hand while she sights with her left eye, a method which is absolutely de trop in the best gunmen's circle." In that photo the trainees were Mrs. Marion Wrightman, Mrs. Lulu B. Parks and Mrs. Alice Clement. The trainer was Lieutenant W. H. Westbrook.[118]

A few days later one of the Chicago 15, Lulu Parks, was in New York City on official business to pick up a suspect who had fled Chicago to that city. A reporter asked Parks about guns and the visiting officer said she carried two of them — a regular .32 caliber police revolver with the other one being a shorter weapon. However, when the journalist asked her where she carried her weapons Parks declined to comment. With respect to the progress of Chicago's policewomen, Parks stated, "The policewomen of Chicago have investigated dance halls, wine rooms and restaurants and the police officials have said that the results were much better than could have been obtained by men or stool pigeons."[119]

Just a day or two after that, shop talk took place in the common area of a New York City hotel. The participants were Lulu Parks and Alice Wells, who was once again on the road. Parks said to a reporter in reply to a question, "Of course there is some excitement when we make arrests, but we have never had any trouble in bringing in a prisoner. You see, we count the men on the force as our protectors as well as our friends, and they are quick to respond to a call for assistance." Wells was in the summer uniform of the Los Angeles policewomen while Parks was dressed in plainclothes. Officer Wells explained to the reporter that she was taking a long leave of absence on her own account to investigate police conditions in various parts of the country and in the hope of advancing the appointment of women in cities where only men were employed on the police force. Parks told this reporter she carried her revolver in her handbag. With respect to selection, Wells commented that in Los Angeles women applicants to the force were required to undergo a severe physical as well as mental examination.[120]

At the end of March 1914, the academic world weighed in with a long newspaper piece purported to deliver great intellectual truths, or something, about the failure of the Chicago policewomen to handle the recent strike of women in that city. It came from David Edgar Rice, a professor at Columbia. As part of his byline, under his name, it read "the Famous Psychologist." Under the title of "Why Women would rather be arrested by Men" the piece went on to call attention to "some of the most fundamental principles of the psychology of sex." The thought was that the women would be gentler and more tactful and lock up a striker "just as a mother would take a daughter home. As a matter of fact, the policewomen used more violence with their sex than an ordinary policeman would have done," said Rice. Actually they used less violence than did the policemen. As well, Rice continued, the idea the strikers would yield more peaceably to officers of their own sex than to men was wrong; "As a matter of fact they resisted the policewomen more fiercely than if they had been policemen." No, over the course of a long dispute they resisted the harassment from the policemen vigorously. When it was over the police chief said, according to Rice, that the two female officers, Loucks and Boyd, would be transferred "and let it be understood that the system of female policemen was a failure." No, Gleason said, they were a failure on the picket line and with crowds, no more. Rice then declared that the woman was instinctively accustomed to seeing a man in the place of public power and authority and resented seeing a woman in such a place. "It is an instinct as old as the race, and arguments cannot remove it. I know that many enthusiastic suffragists even would never tolerate the idea of a woman President," he brayed. In the second place, he continued, a woman put in the place of public power lacked the physical superiority that belonged to a strong man but went on to say later, "The two women alone charging into a crowd of striking waitresses Henrici's and, after a hot fight, arrested six of them." Then Rice added another reason why they were a failure, a reason that probably was hoary even then: "her greater emotional excitability also plays an important part." He then added the bizarre thought that female offenders were likely to fare better at the hands of policemen: "This is to be found in the instinctive respect that men, on the whole, have for members of the opposite sex." No, it was the wholesale lack of respect that caused women around the nation to lobby for police matrons and then for policewomen. Rice concluded by stating, "For these reasons, then, Chicago's experiment seems destined to result in failure."[121]

Another article, in April 1914, discussed the prowess of Chicago's policewomen on the firing range. They were still undergoing training and it was reported that 12 of them made a revolver shot average of 88.48 percent. Said M. L. C. Funkhouser, second deputy police superintendent, "Chicago policewomen are better marksmen than the men. Twelve policemen taken from the ranks, not the experts, but the average patrolman, cannot make a better record than the women did." One of the policewomen, Marie Crot, made a score of 96 percent and nine of the 12 were rated as expert shots with averages of 84 percent or higher. In a separate article a photo was published showing four policewomen receiving their service revolvers. An unnamed captain declared, "Despite their general fearlessness, they seem to be handling the revolvers in the gingerly manner characteristic of most women."[122]

When Pittsburgh hired its first four policewomen in 1914, their assignments were to visit hotels and all other places of public amusement frequented by girls and women as well as being in attendance at court sessions to assist all charged females. Their badges were marked Pittsburgh Auxiliary Police.[123]

While Goldzier had failed for years in Bayonne, New Jersey, Ruth McAdie succeeded on the first try. She was secretary of the Playground Commission in Bayonne when she wrote to the mayor in April 1914 asking him to give members of her commission police powers in parks and playgrounds. The mayor did so, not realized that the R. McAdie who wrote the letter was a woman. On June 3 Ruth announced that hereafter spooning in the parks had to stop. She had electric lights installed in the darker areas and stated she intended to keep the benches clear of lovers in the future. This aroused a certain amount of controversy. Just one week later, on June 10, McAdie announced she would resign, and she turned in her shield on July 7. Her resignation was prompted by her dislike of the notoriety she had generated. In addition, she said she became convinced "that keeping an eye open for spooners was not a dignified occupation."[124]

Prior to 1910 Cleveland's city administration maintained a policy of sup-

Policewoman Lulu Parks of Chicago, circa 1913–1915. The caption of the photograph noted "they seem to be handling the revolvers in the gingerly manner characteristic of most women."

pression of vice. A change of administration led to a period of about two years during which vice activities were openly tolerated within a specific segregated district. Another change of administration in 1912 resulted in a policy of increasing suppression of vice, which in 1915 resulted in the abolition of the segregated district. Of course, vice didn't stop; it meant that prostitutes, among others, were arrested by the police instead of being left alone. With more females coming in contact with the police, churches and civic groups agitated for preventive and protective work to be done with females. A committee of women formed a group to undertake raising funds for the salary of a trained social worker to deal with girls and women coming to the attention of the police. The chief of police consented to the employment of Sabina Marshall, so long as she was paid by private funds. Later in 1915 a second group of women began to agitate strongly for the appointment of female police. A major catalyst was the murder of a 16-year-old girl in a vice situation. These two groups joined forces in 1916 and became known as the Women's Protective Association of Cleveland (WPA). That same year, after six months as a social worker, Marshall was appointed to the police department with the title of Special Investigator. She was given a police badge but no power of arrest. The WPA — of which Marshall was executive secretary — had to continue to pay her salary. Marshall's job title was chosen carefully: "This title was used as there seemed to be a popular prejudice against the word 'policewoman' and it was feared the work might be hampered by the name." The WPA continued to agitate for regular police by giving talks around the city. In 1917 the group endorsed a plan for a policewoman's bureau with 29 officers, two at each station, under a woman director. As might have been expected, such an ambitious proposal had no chance of being passed by the city council.[125]

A recurrent duty for female police was to pick up and transport fugitives from one jurisdiction to another. Miss Helene Young, accused of having cashed forged checks in Los Angeles, fled to Chicago in May 1914. Policewoman Mrs. D. T. Anderson of Los Angeles was dispatched to Chicago to escort the fugitive back to the California city.[126]

In a lighter vein were movies, a comic strip and a joke on the topic. In a brief description of four films on the bill in a February 1913 listing for the Imperial Theater in San Francisco was one called *The Masher Cop*, described as satirizing policewomen in Southern California. It was produced by Biograph and released in the US on January 30, 1913. A 1914 film was *The Policewoman*, supposedly based on the life of Alice Stebbins Wells. It was produced by the Balboa Amusement Company in Long Beach, California, and was said to have starred Alice Wells as herself. No other information about this film seems to have survived. A review published in October 1914 briefly looked at the film *Oh! Look Who's Here!* a recently released comedy. Mr. Hawkins was a tired businessman who gave the world of commerce up to live and work on a farm. Mrs. Hawkins was a militant suffragette who got a job as a policewoman "and proceeds to act the part." Hawkins had adventures with a cow while trying to milk her and, meanwhile, Officer Hawkins managed to help a burglar to escape while locking up innocent victims, and so on. An ad for the Page Theater in a Medford, Oregon, newspaper in October 1914 featured a three film bill. Leading the program was Ethel Barrymore appearing in *The Nightingale*. One of the two supporting films was from Vitagraph, called *Officer Kate*. The description in the ad read, "She becomes a policewoman. Her husband gets a good-looking hired girl to run the home. Kate resigns from the force."[127]

Diana Dillpickles was the name of a four-panel comic strip that appeared in various newspapers in this period. On several days in September 1914, as found in the pages of a Tacoma, Washington, newspaper (and also appearing in other papers) the strip concerned itself with a policewoman. In the September 30 installment a uniformed policewoman was placed in a department store to watch for shoplifters. She spotted a woman walking around suspiciously for a long period of time, and not buying anything. She seized the woman and took her to the police station only to have the desk sergeant tell her that the woman arrested was the store detective. And finally, a joke from January 1915. "Yegg" is an old slang term for a safecracker. The first yegg says to his pal that Handsome Hal had broken away from many a policeman but they had landed him at last. The second yegg asked if it was because they had overpowered him. Not exactly, replied the first yegg: "The department sent a handsome policewoman after him and he couldn't resist her."[128]

Another example of the loose usage of the term policewoman and the equally loose way police powers were sometimes distributed in this era could be seen in the story of Marie McGlone (Mamie McGlona), a story that was published in January 1915. She lived in Philadelphia was called a policewoman in the headline of the story. She wore a regular uniform on duty at the Bellevue Theatre in Philadelphia, located at Front Street and Susquehanna Avenue. It was reported she knew when an audience should laugh or weep during a film showing and when some smart character decided to "kid" the picture by laughing at the sad scenes or expressing an opinion out loud a gentle tap on the head reminded them "the first woman cop in Philadelphia is on the job." When two youths got smart one night the "fair coppess" caught them by their necks and banged their heads together. McGlona weighed 175 pounds. She was sworn into her office by Philadelphia director of public safety Porter on January 2. She was said to realize that pleasure in life was a necessity, and she was glad to be in a position to keep the element from spoiling the movies.[129]

At about the same time a letter to the editor of a Chicago newspaper, signed "Anti-Policewoman" perhaps summed up the thinking of those in the general public who still resisted the reform. The letter writer declared the female police were not worth what they were paid. "In the first place, they are not physically qualified. They can't run, they can't fight, and I cannot imagine one of them stopping a runaway, grappling with a thug or making a fire rescue," he wrote. "I do not think any woman of refinement or culture would aspire to the job." Adding, perhaps, his own opinion, the headline writer for this letter to the editor titled it "Against the Copettes."[130]

Chicago policewomen continued to be profiled for their duties more than the women in any other city. But, of course, that city had more policewomen on its force than any other city in the country. In February 1915 a woman in Chicago named Anna Safen, had six agents who sold her tamales. She had two of those agents with her one day that month when she tracked down two other agents, men who had failed to bring back the money they owed her. One thing led to another and a fight broke out involving all five of the people. Policewoman Alice Clement happened along and subdued all five with her revolver and took all into a patrol wagon she had summoned. At the station the two rogue agents were booked. With respect to Clement and her work, the news account stated, "She has arrested mashers, she has arrested bogus policewomen, she had caught shoplifters and pickpockets, and she has captured at least one escaped lunatic. The quelling of a little street corner riot was merely a part of the day's work."[131]

Meanwhile, the situation in New York crept along as slowly as ever. On April 3, 1915, a bill was introduced into the New York State Legislature in Albany that would provide for the appointment of policewomen in New York City. That bill was introduced by Senator Samuel Jones (R). Under the terms of the bill as many women could be placed on the force as the Board of Estimate and Appropriations would appropriate salaries for, but they could not be put in a position of authority over men.[132]

On April 20 the New York State Senate, by a vote of 28 to 17, passed the Jones bill. According to a reporter, "The Senate had a good time during discussion on the measure, which was reported from committee more as a joke than anything else, and there was surprise when it was found that the bill had been passed." Jones argued that a few policewomen could watch over the many young and innocent women who came to New York. Senator Walker (D) joked that Jones should find a way to save some of the boys who came from upstate New York to visit New York City. Senator Boylan (D) said that New York City did not need policewomen and, anyway, "The bill fixes the [minimum] age limit at 30 years and no woman of that age will admit it," joked the politician. In any event, it was widely believed the Assembly would kill the Jones bill. It did.[133]

The trend to demean the job of policewomen and the women who filled those roles through the use of a term such as "copette" spread to more and more newspapers during this period. It did eventually die out but not for several years. One egregious example could be found in the title of a story published on March 6, 1915: "Enter the Copperette to jolt Jersey violators of law with night stickette." In this example the headline writer had followed along from the example of reporter Marguerite Marshall's text. She wrote, "And now it's the policewoman, the copperette, that's going to give the naughtiness of New Jersey its next jolt." In that state Governor Fielder had just signed into law the bill introduced by Senator Colgate that authorized the appointment of women police officers. Every municipality could appoint women as police officers with the same rights and powers as policemen. According to the law those policewomen were to perform such duty as the authority in charge of police matters directed, although physical examinations and physical requirements for the positions could be waived.[134]

Alice Stebbins Wells, on the road yet again, spoke on May 18, 1915, in Baltimore before the National Conference of Charities and Correction. For a long time, she said, "the woman policeman has been a figment of the imagination, held up to ridicule as the acme of the absurd and impossible, but though the last echo of derision still reverberates," the policewoman movement has grown. According to the figures she then recited to her audience, Chicago had 20; Los Angeles, Baltimore, and Seattle had five each; San Francisco and St. Paul had three each; Topeka, Minneapolis, Dayton and Toronto had two each, while Vancouver, Fargo, Grand Forks, Rochester (New York), Ottawa, Aurora, San Antonio, Syracuse, Muncie, Denver, Colorado Springs, Superior, Jamestown (New York), Fort Wayne (Indiana), Racine (Wisconsin), and Phoenix (Arizona) had one each. She added that she believed Sioux City (Iowa), Beatrice and Omaha (Nebraska), Boston and Salem, (Massachusetts), Bellingham (Washington), and Ithaca (New York) were to be included in the list (but was apparently unsure). She also named Poughkeepsie, New York, and Des Moines, Iowa, as places where a policewoman was paid from private funds, with the approval of the police chief. In addition, Wells continued, there were numerous cities that employed police matrons. The need of women on the police force had arisen, she explained, from the fact that industrial and social energy no longer centered in the home "but has given us an age in which men, women and children, eat, sleep, work and play together as never before in the world's history."[135]

When she delivered that talk Wells was four months short of five years of police service. When a reporter asked her why she began the career she replied, "I just couldn't stand seeing and knowing how much women needed women to look after them! It is nothing short of criminal for women to have to submit to verbal examination by men. Of course, there are police matrons, but no one can deal with women or with a young girl as efficiently as another woman. In every instance it is more successful, and far better for the girl, that she be handled by women." As far as Wells was concerned the idea that the moment a woman laid herself liable to arrest and was caught, she was immediately "shriven of all that ever qualified her as a gentlewoman is a monstrous idea. She is just as human, just as worthy of being saved and just as due consideration as is the girl who is in the home." Wells concluded, "Chaperonage should not cease with the entrance of the girl into civil life. Indeed, it should continue there just as in her own home, for when the state takes charge of her it holds her in loco parentis."[136]

A glimpse into the attitude of the police chiefs of American cities toward policewomen was seen in May 1915 when a meeting of the International Association of Police Chiefs was being held in Cincinnati. Wells happened to be in that city when the conference was in session. She was on her way home to Los Angeles after attending a Baltimore conference. She approached the chiefs and asked if the annual report of her organization, the International Association of Policewomen, could be included as part of the International Association of Police Chiefs' annual report. Those chiefs, said a reporter, did not "take kindly" to the idea and turned down Wells' proposal.[137]

A reporter by the name of Mrs. Marshall McLean lamented, at the end of May 1915, the fact that New York City was one of the few big cities in America without policewomen. She noted some of the failed attempts to have enabling legislation passed at Albany. In April 1913 a bill was introduced into the New York State Legislature authorizing the appointment of policewomen, but it did not pass. Assemblyman Eisner introduced a bill in January 1914 for the appointment of policewomen. That measure was voted down on the grounds that city authorities already had to power to appoint as many police-women as they liked. Then the Jones bill was introduced in the last session of the Legislature but it too failed. Acting on the above cited privilege to appoint without a specific bill being passed at Albany, two New York State cities had acted on their on and, as of May 1915, had appointed policewomen. On June 21, 1913, Mrs. Joseph S. Wood was appointed to the police force of Mount Vernon. Wood was supplied with a star and an "electric flashlight." When she was appointed Wood said, "My particular duty will be so see that the health, pure food and anti-cruelty laws [with respect to animals] are observed and to prevent the spooning of couples in Hartley Park. I frequently take walks through the park at night and I have observed deplorable condi-tions. I propose to stop all that even if it is necessary to make arrests and lock the spooners in cells." Only a few days before the appointment of Wood, the City of Poughkeepsie engaged a policewoman in the person of Mrs. Vincent Charles Meyerhoffer with "her salary being paid by a number of well to do women." Like Mrs. Wood, Meyerhoffer would not don a uniform. Her work was described as consisting mainly of "guarding the morals of the young and patrolling amusement places." Some of the other cities McLean listed as hav-ing female police included Oakland, Philadelphia, Cleveland, and Asbury Park, New Jersey. Cleveland, she said, boasted the only mounted police-woman. In those cities some of the women wore uniforms, some did not, some carried revolvers, some carried clubs, and some were armed with switches. She also mentioned a Viola Goetchius in New Jersey and that Lon-don, England's first policewoman was Mrs. Hughes, a 36-year-old who was appointed in March 1914. She also wrote at length about Chicago and the fact that city had sworn in 10 policewomen on August 5, 1913. On October 25, 1913, because of the large number of applicants for positions on the Chicago police force a new rule prohibited women under 30 from being appointed to the department. Those seeking the $900-a-year jobs had to be between 30 and 40, 5'9" in height, and weigh between 115 and 180 pounds. With respect to arguments that women police were too physically weak for the demands of the job, McLean pointed out those Chicago policewomen were perfectly capable of taking care of themselves and the job, and that was shown in Feb-ruary 1914 when two of them arrested six striking waitresses at Henrici's Restaurant and brought them to Central Station.[138]

In July 1915 Mrs. Grace Headifin became the first woman appointed a member of the Paterson, New Jersey, police force. She was described as about 40 years of age, 5'10" and weighed 140 pounds. She said she was proud to be a policewoman: "I feel I can help boys and girls—perhaps save them from much unhappiness. My work is the supervision of public dance halls. While my experience is brief, and my remuneration nothing, I will feel repaid in knowing I am helping to serve the young folks." Being in charge of the dance halls she meant to see the patrons of those places "keep to the conventional waltzes and two-steps, and do not wander into the 'kitchen sink' and others of the new dances." Headifin was formerly police matron at the Passaic County Jail. She wore no uniform but a small "gold detective's badge." In the summer she had only one dance hall to look after but when the cool weather returned all 30 of Paterson's public dance halls would be in operation.[139]

When Alice Stebbins Wells had been in Baltimore in the summer of 1915 she was elected president at the National Conference of Policewomen that was in session there. It met as part of and during the National Conference of Charities and Correction. In forming that new organization, Wells outlined a new system of police work. She urged that policewomen be mutually exchanged between cities so that by going about incognito they might be better able to discover in strange cities conditions hitherto unexpected. Other officers elected at the National Conference of Policewomen session were Miss Mary Steele Harvey (Baltimore policewoman — vice president), Mrs. Georgiana Sherrot (Minneapolis policewoman — secretary), and Miss Anna McCully (Dayton, Ohio, policewoman — treasurer).[140]

Another article appeared in a New York City paper in September 1915 pointing out the lack of progress in getting policewomen appointed in New York City, the nation's largest urban area. Despite the increasing appointments of women to police departments around the country, this reporter observed that despite success elsewhere it was not likely they would appear in New York "for some time to come." Police Commissioner Woods was described as not being against them, "but owing to the conditions in the city he does not deem it wise to extend their activities." Woods saw a slight value for women, in fields such as white slavery, but not much else. Yet, the reporter observed, in most cities with policewomen the experiment and its results had been praised. One exception was reported to be Mayor Jay E. House (1915–1919) of Topeka, Kansas, who had no hesitation in asserting the experiment there had been a failure: "My personal experience with policewomen was brief. I fired the two attached to the Topeka police force as one of my first official acts." Topeka first employed policewomen two years earlier, around about May 1913. They drew a patrolman's pay of $75 a month. "I never was able to discover what their duties were or to discover that they had duties," complained House. "They had no effect on conditions one way or another." He added, "If I have any sense of humor the policewoman is the biggest joke in the world. As I understand it, the duty of a policeman is to protect property and to preserve order. A woman can do neither. To decorate her with a star and send her out to do patrol duty merely is to give her license to meddle with her neighbors' business." Over in Salem, Massachusetts, Mayor M. J. O'Keefe explained his predecessor appointed a policewoman about two years earlier and that she was the only one on the force. "She has no particular duties assigned her," said O'Keefe, "she wears no uniform, she receives no salary, she simply wears a badge. Her name is Miss Ethel Osborne and she was appointed principally for the purpose of censoring dances and picture houses." He added that his city was comparatively free of crime by women with only three or four locked up in a year, mainly for drunkenness. In Jamestown, New York, one police-woman had been employed for a year and Mayor S. A. Carlson declared he had no hesitancy in asserting that "the plan has been a success." He explained that the services of a woman had proved very helpful in the prevention of excessive drinking and other "demoralizing influences." Racine, Wisconsin, then had one policewoman while St. Paul, Minnesota, had three, who were paid a salary of $900 a year, which was the same salary as a starting patrolman. Minneapolis was reported as having two female police.[141]

Just how tenuous a hold these early women had in their pioneering role can be seen from Roche and the experience in Topeka, Kansas. In that city the Good Government Club lobbied the city administration for female police. In recognition for the club's services to Topeka, Mayor R. L. Colfran appointed an advisory council from the Good Government Club to work with the city administration. This led to the council recommending the hiring of female police, so in 1913 the mayor appointed Eva Corning as Topeka's first policewoman. Armed with a badge and a whistle, but no other uniform or insignia, Corning hit the theaters, cafes, train stations, and dance halls. During her two years on the force she made just 20 arrests, mainly of boys violating the anti-smoking law. She mostly sent kids home for curfew violations. Then Jay E. House was elected mayor in 1915, a man who had never been in favor of police reform. He immediately abolished the female police positions in Topeka.[142]

An article published in October 1915 looked at the duties of two Chicago policewomen in dealing with flirts; they watched for those flirts [sexual harassers] at the Dearborn Street transit station. Miss Marie Crot and Miss Marian Wrightman were the two officers and the reader was told "neither would be taken for an officer. Either would be as much at home pouring an afternoon tea as overpowering a pickpocket. Both have made high averages at revolver practice, but still are equally proficient in handling darning nee-dles." Crot explained to the reporter about the "Obvious Flirt." He sat down in the station beside a likely looking woman and tried to strike up a conver-sation with her. Crot watched him, approached him, and told him if he didn't have a train ticket "or something to prove that you are not simply an obnox-ious pest about the station I'll lock you up." After that dressing down he ran away outside the station, but Crot shouted to a policeman on the corner who collared him. The flirt had no ticket in his possession and was taken to the police station. The next morning in police court he was fined $100 and solemnly vowed he would "never again accost any member of the opposite sex without proper introductions." Crot pointed out to the reporter there were two other categories; one was the "Seductive Flirt" (not really explained) with the other being the "Professional Flirt, otherwise known as the white slaver."[143]

In Aurora, Illinois, Ann Forsyth had been on the job for a year or so. In the past year she had made just 13 arrests, as her focus was on prevention. She dealt with a lot of domestic troubles. One night she found a woman on the streets crying. She told the officer her husband put her out of the house when he was drunk. Forsyth found the woman work in the country where she could take her two boys. "If I weren't any account at all it would be worth while just to have the girls know there is a policewoman. I have no beat. I just walk around town and go to the dance halls. They know I'm on the street and I know practically all the girls," she told a reporter. "The danger of the dance halls lies not in the dancing nor in the management, but in the bar. Nine times out of ten the girl who falls, falls first through drink." Forsyth had a hard time getting a city ordinance passed prohibiting girls, or boys under 12, from selling newspapers on the street, but she succeeded. "I also enforce a curfew law at 9 o'clock, although we don't have the law. I just go ahead and clear the streets of children at 9," said Forsyth. When she was off on vacation "the little rascals knew it, and mere babies had a lovely time selling papers as long as I was away." She also told the journalist of the high number of "mental deficients" on the streets and said, "The value of the policewoman is in straightening out tangles for women and girls, and even men, which would never be brought to the policeman." Social workers tried to raise people from a low level to a higher level, said Forsyth, "to make a scholar out of a hod carrier. We don't. We try to adjust him to his level, to find out what is wrong and right it. That is more reasonable and therefore more satisfactory."[144]

As of November 1915 it was reported that the women of Columbia, Missouri, were divided in their attitude toward a petition to be presented to the city council asking that a policewoman be appointed in Columbia. Said Mrs. John T. Esrey, one of the leaders of the petition, "The position of the woman would be more that of a probation officer than a policewoman. We need such an officer to supervise the welfare of our youth, especially at such places as the fairgrounds, Chautauqua grounds, the stations and the rest room at the courthouse." Mrs. C. W. Greene remarked, "With the present attitude of the men on the subject the installation of such an officer would be a difficult task." A state law had recently been enacted that said that cities with a population of 5,000 or more could have policewomen.[145]

Another example of a policewoman on duty came in the story of Miss

Florence Kopp, a special policewoman of Hackensack, New Jersey (perhaps Constance Kopp of Wyckoff, New Jersey), at the end of 1915. She arrested Reverend Herman A. Von Matthesius, a fugitive from justice, after a struggle on the stairs of a subway station in Brooklyn. Von Matthesius, a practicing physician as well as a minister, was convicted two months earlier of assaulting two boys in Hackensack. Feigning illness he was placed in the prison ward of the Hackensack hospital and escaped on November 6. Kopp received a tip that the fugitive was to meet a friend at the subway station. Heavily veiled she waited for him to arrive and then put her hand on his shoulder and placed him under arrest. He began to struggle; holding him with one hand she reached into her handbag with the other and extracted a pair of handcuffs, which she then strapped on his wrists. He was returned to Hackensack. Kopp weighed 180 pounds.[146]

When Ann Forsythe, the policewoman of Aurora, Illinois, was asked at the beginning of 1916 how the policemen on the force treated her she replied, "Very nicely. They're mostly a good-natured, warm-hearted lot of men, though not particularly intelligent. The policeman looks upon his work as a job, and his chief asset in performing his duties is his physical force. The policewoman is a welfare worker, usually well educated and specially trained for social service." Forsythe added that as soon as it was publicly announced that she was to serve as a policewoman crowds began to pour into her office: "I was asked to quell incorrigible children and brutal husbands, even to hunt up deserting ones. Many a shirker of conjugal duties I've trotted back to the bosom of his family!"[147]

Later in 1916 policewomen were added to the "dry squad" of the Tacoma, Washington, Police Department. Their identity was known to only three or four officers on the force and they were not listed as regular members of the department. Two women "specials" had been doing efficient work for some days by the time this report surfaced, attacking the illicit sale of liquor in Tacoma. One of the women trapped the chef of a prominent Pacific Avenue hotel by ordering a quart of whiskey from him through a hotel bellboy. That chef was then served a 30-day sentence at the city jail. Bootleggers in Tacoma had become so suspicious because of frequent arrests recently that it was almost impossible for the male investigators to purchase drinks from suspected illegal sites, leading the force to turn to policewomen.[148]

In the middle of 1916 a report issued by the US Bureau of the Census revealed that policewomen were then employed in 26 cities. However, the early burst of media attention to the topic and the relative flurry of appointments had peaked and ended, the years 1910 to 1915 were indeed good years and productive years for the cause of policewomen. Very little happened in 1916, nor were many media accounts about policewomen published. The one city that notably had not embraced the idea of policewomen was New York

City; the nation's largest and most diverse. It might logically have been expected to be at the forefront of the movement; it was not.[149]

Writing in the summer of 1917, reporter Mary Sumner Boyd said that Mrs. Hannah D. Long of Trenton, New Jersey, began her duties as the first policewoman in New Jersey in January 1916. She looked after dance halls, places where liquor was supposedly being sold to minors, and it was also her duty to look after girls who were in the street after dark. She also stated that as of December 1916 there were somewhere between 115 and 125 policewomen serving in American cities and that Chicago had 40 of those serving women.[150]

The appointment of females to police departments was most intense and most successful in the period 1910 to 1916, when women became police officers in a number of American communities. Behind the lobbying there were women's groups always bringing pressure. Rapid industrialization in the late eighteenth century and into the nineteenth century increased the factory workforce. Young women and men left rural areas for the cities to seek work which was becoming more and more scarce in the rural areas. These new factory hands were often cut off from families and left on their own. While these young women didn't have a lot of leisure time, they did have some, and so they could be found by themselves or in groups of females out on the streets. This was a violation of cultural norms in that "respectable" women did not go anywhere without a male escort. In addition, they were in cities full of strangers, compared to a rural environment where people knew most of their neighbors and other townspeople. In response to this urbanization commercialized places of amusements sprang up to cater to these people who had time on their hands. In turn they became magnets to lure more people to the cities. Facilities such as dance halls, arcades, and cinemas offered cheap entertainment to lonely young women. Women became much more visible, more public, and much more likely to be without a male escort at most times.

The women's movement had been growing for decades and was very strong and vocal during the early twentieth century seeking the vote, among many other reforms. Agitation included demonstrations and picketing. Police were often summoned to move the women along, and sometimes to take them into custody. These mostly middle- and upper-class women were horrified to be touched by men, even when no violence, excessive force, or sexual assault threat was present. For example, when a policeman simply took a female picket by the arm and led her from the road to the sidewalk it violated another social norm; with the exception of a spouse or immediate family member, a male did not touch a female. This was not true for the bulk of the population —for the lower class often lived in cramped quarters in crowded tenements— but the ideas of the ruling class were indeed the ruling ideas. If a picketing suffragette was taken to a police station and held for even just a few hours or longer, it was a deep shock to her sensibilities of gender and class that she was so exposed and vulnerable to males. All of these things helped fuel and drive the pressure for female police. For the first time females were coming into contact with the police on an increasingly frequent basis. Therefore, female police were needed to deal with them, or so the reformist women were convinced.

This period was marked also by much media attention to the problem of white slavery — young females spirited away somewhere and forced to be prostitutes. White slavery was a major media issue worldwide from the 1880s or so through the 1910s. Prior to this period, prostitutes were dismissed as "fallen" women, victims of their own inadequacies. Yet some observers knew of far too many exceptions to that stereotype. Thus it was convenient to exaggerate and focus on white slavery, whereby responsibility could still be affixed to individuals — the slave traffickers. This was easier than focusing on the social factors of prostitution: that a brutal and exploitative society which paid females a wage which could barely be lived on, provided no social welfare programs whatsoever, and often provided no work at all was largely responsible for the rise in prostitution, whether the rise was real or perceived. Women had no other options in many cases — either prostitute themselves or die. Prior to this increased visibility of women, most females who came into contact with the police were detained for alcohol or prostitution offenses, with the odd petty thief or shoplifter, and, of course, the homeless — practically all from the lower classes. The female reformers agitating for policewomen weren't really interested in these women. It was a class difference, with the reformers accepting male ideology that the hardened prostitute or alcoholic or homeless woman was indeed beyond redemption. Therefore, these reformers urged policewomen to do preventive and protective work, to save the innocent; the others were hopeless. Since virtually all of the early policewomen were drawn from the ranks of the reformers that was what happened. And that was why there was a seeming contradiction in reasons for agitation for police station matrons. The long-term fallen prostitutes (lower class) were a threat to the innocent male police and inmates, while the innocent young girls (middle or upper class) suddenly in contact with the police for the first time were at risk of assault by these very same males.

Alice Wells declared that the impetus for women to become police came from a desire to care for young people who needed help, that "the power of the policewoman to counsel and protect fills a real need." To her, many troubled women who had been able to confide in policewomen would have had difficulty relating to a policeman. Writing in 1914, Maud Darwin noted that more men and women were in the workforce with more and more females to be found in amusement places. This resulted in the general public in cities no longer being composed "mostly of males." Darwin added, "This increased publicity of their lives has made the establishment of the woman police officer an urgent necessity in our town.... Her chief duty is to guard young girls and boys in all public places."[151]

One year earlier Louise de Koven Bowen wrote an article noting the increase in young people, without protection, being tempted and lured to a growing number of commercial amusement facilities. She noted that many observers of the municipal scene felt all big cities should have a morals police, with a certain percentage of them being female. It would be their job to protect young girls from pitfalls and prostitution, "that grave menace to health and morals." Bowen believed policewomen were needed in cinemas to watch for females who attended and accepted the invitations of young men who had disreputable intentions. Policewomen were needed in dance halls, "the happy hunting ground of the white slave trader," and to see girls didn't get drunk. Bowen also argued for policewomen to be stationed at beaches, to be on the alert "for conditions which demoralize children." Their presence was also needed in amusement parks "to save young girls from accepting invitations from men who hope to be repaid later in the evening.... In fact, we need women police to 'mother' the girls in all public places where the danger to young people is great." Almost as an afterthought Bowen mentioned young boys also needed protection, but it clearly was not a priority with Bowen, or other early reformers.[152]

Despite the limited policing role female officers had and despite their very limited number, they still faced resistance and discrimination, often disguised as humor. A 1913 issue of *American City* noted the many newspaper and magazine caricatures of policewomen, usually as an Amazon in uniform and always carrying a club: "It is not so very long ago that the mere mention of the term 'police-woman' could be depended upon to provoke a smile. There are those who still regard the idea as inherently humorous."[153]

Another tactic was to hold up policewomen to ridicule by declaring them inept. Raymond Fosdick, a well-known authority on police systems and methods, told of visiting an unnamed big city around 1914 where he found that the police chief "in great bewilderment, was trying to teach his six new policewomen to shoot pistols—without great success—and to learn the intricacies of handling an eighteen-inch club." This was presented by a reporter as the height of silliness from which he concluded—to explain the cases where policewomen had been failures—"Much of the lack of success which has been encountered in some cities is due largely to a complete misunderstanding of the policewoman's logical duties."[154]

Pioneer policewoman Eleonore Hutzel noted of this reform, "Police officials have questioned the wisdom of such a change in their organizations and there is still no general agreement among them in favor of the idea." Another observer wrote, "Initially, there was strong opposition among policemen in most departments to the hiring of female officers." Of this same period Elmer

Graper, who authored a text on police administration, observed; "There has been strenuous opposition to the employment of women as police officers." He also stated, "It was realized that for this particular kind of protective work women are by nature better fitted than men."[155]

Early policewomen took pains to point out and ensure that men understood that these women officers had a limited scope and had no desire or intention of performing male police duties. Darwin wrote, "The institution of policewomen is not intended to displace that of policemen in any way. Their work is merely supplementary. The policewoman has the same authority as the policeman; she can arrest people, but it is not her business to drag drunkards to the police station, to trap a burglar, or to direct Traffic. That is man's work."[156]

Policewomen held their first convention in Portland, Oregon, in September 1912, but it was limited to Pacific Coast women. Female officers then were at work in Portland and the Washington cities of Tacoma, North Yakima, and Seattle, the latter having two female officers. Discussed at the meeting were the lures that beset young women in the cities such as roadhouses, dance halls, and joyrides.[157]

Those at the conference felt that a new movement for women as protective officers in a community should be started under the auspices of a woman's society. This way the new role for women could become well established before it was brought into a close relationship with the police force. Portland's police chief told the women that only female officers could solve the problem of city vice. He stated that if he assigned 50 policemen to cases involving sexual immorality the chances were that "in thirty days half of them would have fallen for the paint and powder and beguiling ways of the women who prey on man's weaknesses." At the conference it was declared that every city "should have at least one protective officer for every twenty-five policemen."[158]

At the start of 1913 there were 38 policewomen in the United States; in 1915 this number had risen to 70 policewomen in 26 cities, and in 1917 the hiring of women officers had spread to 30 cities. Fueling this expansion were the social and economic freedom of women, their changing political status, and their more active participation in public affairs. In addition, there was some recognition of the value of a social work or preventive approach to aspects of policing and a belief in the value of women in those areas.[159]

In 1917 the U.S. Civil Service Commission established a minimum standard for policewomen, consisting of a high school education and at least two years' practical experience in social case work, or its equivalent in technical training and business experience. These standards were endorsed by the International Association of Chiefs of Police and by the International Association of Policewomen (IAP) and were then being implemented gradually in most areas. Male police had to meet a much lower standard, with high school graduation not being required in many areas until the 1960s.[160]

The IAP was founded by Wells in 1915, and she was elected president, an office she held until 1919. She initiated and founded the group only after she sought and obtained the support and approval of the International Association of Chiefs of Police. At the 1914 National Conference of Charities and Corrections, Wells secured a place on the program to propose the formation of such an organization. Then at the May 1915 National Conference of Charities and Corrections convention in Baltimore, there were enough policewomen present to form the IAP. Its functions were to act as a clearinghouse, to set standards, and "to advance, as loyal members of the police force, its general service to the community, placing special emphasis upon crime prevention and protective measures for women and children without in any wise interfering with the work as established in any police department. The policewoman is to cooperate with the police officer in every way — not in any way to usurp his place.[161]

At the 1916 Charities and Corrections convention, a report noted that early policewomen were largely drawn from the personnel of private social agencies in the community. In many instances these women, especially those of the Travelers' Aid Society and the Associated Charities were given police powers, with their salaries often paid in part by the police department, while they still retained their position on the staff of the private agency. The 1916 IAP meeting drew policewomen from 14 states, and membership rolls included females from 22 states and Canada. One year later membership was extended to the British female officer, Margaret Damer-Dawson.[162]

Wells was succeeded as head of the IAP in 1919 by Lieutenant Mina C. Van Winkle, director of the Woman's Bureau, Metropolitan Police Department, Washington, D.C. This organization folded in 1932 upon the death of Van Winkle who, besides being president, was the IAP's chief financial contributor. Under the leadership of Lois Higgins, the organization resurfaced in 1956 as the International Association of Women Police. It remains in existence today, but with an extremely low profile.[163]

4

Foreign, to 1916

The role of policewomen developed in other countries around the globe for basically the same reasons and under the same conditions as in the United States. These new officers faced the same resistance and hostility. In the state of Victoria, Australia, the National Council of Women had pressed for the appointment of policewomen from around 1902. Supporting them in their efforts were the Trades Hall Council and the Women's Political Association, groups who were in agreement with the idea that female police were an "absolute necessity for the protection of women and children." Police officials were hostile to the idea, with Chief Commissioner Alfred George-Sainsbury deriding the lobbying women as "self-advertising and self-seeking females." The police were even unwilling to concede there was a place on the force for women to perform such duties as the care and interviewing of female rape victims. Lobbying continued, and two women were appointed to the police in Victoria in July 1917. Initially, they were known simply as police agents, with their duties officially described as "restricted to dealing with females and children in a welfare capacity; it was not intended that their duties would be interchangeable with those of policemen in general police duties."[1]

These two women, one of whom was Madge Connors, were not given the drill and self-defense training given to male recruits, did not have the power of arrest, were not sworn in, wore no uniforms, and were not incorporated into the police seniority list — which meant promotions were not possible. On the job they worked with prostitutes and investigated the likes of quack doctors such as herbalists who dispensed sugar pills for money. A local newspaper commented that there was scope for women in policing but, "in its more dangerous and strenuous forms of maintaining law and order it must always be entrusted to men, for it is out of the question that women should be expected to suppress disturbances or apprehend armed criminals." The first female officer appointed in Australia seems to have been F. B. Cocks, appointed to the South Australia force in 1915.[2]

In Canada a Mrs. Whiddon became Toronto's first police matron in 1887.

Her duties were limited to searching arrested women and attending to them as they waited for their court appearances. On Canada's west coast in Vancouver, British Columbia, Lurancy Harris and Minnie Miller (perhaps Millar) were sworn in as police officers on June 18, 1912. They did not wear uniforms, which were not issued to policewomen in Vancouver until 1947. Guns were not issued to female officers there until 1973. Their main weapon was reported to be a large handbag they could swing at an assailant, if necessary. A letter in 1912 from the Central Mission Rescue and Protective Society to the city's police chief asked for women to be hired by the force to look after the "wayward girls and women" of the city. Wayward, of course, was code for prostitute. Those policewomen pounded a beat the same as men but they were assigned to places that women would frequent such as dance clubs and movie theaters. They went about their business in long dark dresses that made them relatively inconspicuous. There was a woman (Lorena Mathews) from Oklahoma charged with murder. She fled the US to Canada and was caught in British Columbia. Harris was responsible for bringing the woman back to Oklahoma, something that became, reportedly, a huge media event. Miller was the first policewoman to arrest someone — she arrested a man on one of the beaches for indecent conduct directed toward the women on the beach. In Edmonton, Alberta, Miss Annie Jackson started work as a special constable with the city's police department on October 1, 1912. She wore an ankle-length skirt and a large, prim hat on the job and was tasked with protecting "the morals of Edmonton's young girls" by warding off pimps who were hanging out at city train stations prowling for young women. Jackson, 33 when she was appointed, had to leave the force in 1918 because she got married. When that job was initially advertised 47 women applied for it. Edmonton had just two policewomen in the 1940s, and 16 by 1968. By 2012 the 353 female officers in the Edmonton Police Service represented just over 22 percent of the total. The neighboring city of Calgary, Alberta, had 316 female officers out of a total of 1,900 (17 percent) in 2012 in the Calgary Police Service. Two policewomen were appointed in Toronto in 1913. While they were sworn in as constables with full powers of arrest, they were paid two-thirds of the salary that male recruits received. They were appointed after the local council of women pressured the police commission and convinced them that there were branches of work, prostitution in particular, that could be more adequately dealt with by women. Until that time the Toronto police had hardly touched the problem of prostitution.[3]

Everywhere on the world scene fear of white slavery intensified, especially from the 1880s to 1914. In 1904 an international agreement on the suppression of the white slave traffic was signed in Berlin. At a July 1914 meeting of the Congress of the International Bureau for the Suppression of the White Slave Traffic, attendees passed a resolution unanimously stating the necessity for the employment of female police. Around that time policewomen were report-edly employed in some of the large cities in Germany, Holland, Denmark, Norway, Sweden, Austria, and Russia. With the outbreak of World War I, the problem of white slavery quickly faded away, but prostitution still remained an issue.[4]

Germany acquired its first policewoman in 1903 when the City of Stuttgart appointed social worker Henriette Arendt to deal with the problem of human distress, especially among women and children. Soon she became known as an "angel of the poor." A decade later females were on the police force in 35 German towns, including Berlin, Cologne, Frankfurt, Hamburg, Munich, Leipzig, and Dresden. These women were known as "women police assistants" who had no training, arrest powers, or career mobility, and were in no way considered as part of the regular police force. Lobbying by women's group led to their appointments where their main duties consisted in working with prostitutes. In many German cities prostitutes had to register and were forced to undergo regular mandated medical inspections. Most of the women's groups opposed prostitution, preferring to get females away from that life altogether. They felt it was important to not allow these females to be inter-viewed or registered by male police. It was hoped the influence of police-women would somehow decrease the number of prostitutes. Some of these policewomen had their salaries paid in full or in part by the various women's groups that had nominated them in the first place. Under those conditions the women's groups, and not the policewomen, were responsible to the police chief. One account of this apparently successful German police reform stated "that in towns where they were appointed as rather fearful experiments, with no fixed title or salary or tenure of office, they are now being regularly installed with full official status." German male police were reported as agreeing that the women did work that could not be done by men, and in areas without policewomen, it was work that was left undone. "This is the more striking testimony as several of the men officials admitted that at first the women had been regarded as interlopers in the force," observed one journalist.[5]

Around 1907 Stockholm began to appoint female police. Their duties involved working for the protection of women and children. These Swedish females were not sworn in as constables; they wore the uniform of hospital nurses and were generally addressed as "Sister." In addition, they took an oath similar to the one to which hospital nurses subscribed.[6]

The role of policewomen was slower to develop in England than in many other countries. It took the upheaval of World War I with its attendant man-power shortage and increased sexual fears and tensions to bring that reform. Of course, there was lobbying for female police prior to that time; it was just less successful. When Maud Darwin observed the world situation in the spring of 1914, she wondered if the establishment of policewomen in England could be facilitated by the use of a different name in order to avoid "current prejudice." Her suggestion was to call them "watchwomen."[7]

From 1883 London's Metropolitan Police had employed two women to supervise females detained in police stations. Later, this role was extended so that other women were sometimes employed on a part-time basis in that capacity, called in on an as needed basis. By around 1905 or 1907 the Metropolitan Police Force was employing Eilide MacDougall, an experienced social worker, to inquire into cases where women and children were involved, particularly cases of "outrage." She never saw herself as a police officer, but rather as an official of the Home Office. In 1910 the chief constable of Liverpool, Leonard Dunning, appointed a Miss Hughes to do similar work in that city. By 1914 the Metropolitan Police employed two full-time matrons at each of eight busy stations, with part-time, on-call matrons (usually wives of policemen) at other stations. MacDougall was then investigating white slave trafficking.[8]

One early group to preach the need for policewomen was the Criminal Law Amendment Committee, a group which became interested in the problem around 1905. A major figure in that group was Margaret Damer-Dawson, already internationally known for her work in the area of animal protection. Various women's group pressured authorities for such appointments, primarily middle- and upper-class women. One argument they advanced was that female police were needed to prevent the soliciting of respectable women by men. Generally, these efforts "met with scant sympathy from the authorities concerned." Some of these groups interested in promoting public morality employed agents to observe and report to the police conditions that they felt needed attention. Prior to the First World War there was much discussion in various publications concerning public morals and decency, including the idea that children, especially little girls, were all too frequently the victims of "degenerate men." The conclusion was that to cope with this social menace women police were needed. A delegation composed of members from the National Council of Women and other similar groups called on the home secretary in June 1914, urging the appointment of policewomen. That same year in Parliament, before war broke out, the Criminal Justice Bill was under consideration. Lord Henry Bentwick proposed an amendment providing for the appointment of two or more duly sworn policewomen in every county borough, every metropolitan borough of the county of London, and in other local authorities. Failing to gain support, Bentwick proposed to make his amendment permissive instead of obligatory. Even that failed to gather support, and ultimately Bentwick dropped his amendment altogether so as not to impede passage of the bill, which was regarded as an urgent matter.[9]

The effect of encountering the police for the first time in a confrontational way had a profound effect on middle- and upper-class females, whether in America or elsewhere. Typical was the account of Pleasance Pendred, one of four English suffragettes detained by the police for breaking shop windows while demonstrating. Pendred stated that the home secretary had lied when he said women held at police stations were in the charge of female warders. At the London police lockup where she was detained, Pendred complained she "was visited five times during the night by a man warder."[10]

From the account it is unclear whether a sexual assault was contemplated by the keeper or whether perhaps he was simply doing his job — making the rounds periodically. Either way, dealing with the police and jailers was a new and unpleasant experience for the middle- and upper-class females. They didn't like it and added their voices to those lobbying for policewomen.

The Times (of London) added its voice to the controversy with its own suggestion for combining the police and suffragettes. Citing the policewomen in Chicago, the article told how recently one of the female officers had escorted a female prisoner from Chicago to New York, noting that in the absence of policewomen the prisoner would have been put in the charge of a male escort for the 18-hour journey, and therefore arguing that "the severest mind cannot find that a comforting thought." At the time picketing suffragettes were widely viewed as an annoyance and a disruptive force by many areas of the establishment. Suffragettes commonly carried signs reading "The Right to Serve" (that is, they could serve their country by being allowed to vote). On the principle that "there is no gamekeeper so good as an old poacher," the article argued that no police "force [could] so effectively tackle the militant female suffragists as a force composed of their own sex." In favor of a limited role for policewomen, the article concluded, "We cannot believe that the career would not prove agreeable to the bolder spirits and stronger frames among the women who love serving their country better than they love complaining of their inability to serve her. And — who knows? — the publicity, the self-importance of the work might even tempt a few who now carry sandwich-boards or burn cathedrals." According to *The Times* these women should stop their grumbling and find ways to serve — ignoring the obvious fact that even if they so chose they were not allowed to be police officers.[11]

In the community of Bolton, in Lancashire, the Bolton Watch Committee appointed Eva Burton in June 1914 to the staff of the police force. She was to work in a preventive way with young girls "going astray" and to take statements from any female witnesses who might hesitate to talk to a male. At the time of her appointment she was an assistant probation officer, a post Burton was to retain.[12]

Appointments such as the one at Bolton did little to satisfy lobbyists whose pressure for the hiring of policewomen intensified during the first half of 1914. Among groups that organized deputations and agitated were the National Vigilance Committee and the Women's Industrial Council. The

Criminal Law Amendment Committee, with the support of other groups, passed a resolution calling for the appointment of policewomen with powers equal to that of men throughout the country. One speaker was Mrs. Luke Paget, who felt the lobbyists should point out "that women police were needed because they would be different from the men police." Another speaker, Margaret Ashton, referring to a proposed appointment of a policewoman in Manchester — an appointment that did not materialize — hoped that "the basis would be better than in Bolton." Ashton added that "decent women often felt the need to turn to someone in the street." Many a young girl had to go to a policeman to ask for decent lodging, and they knew of some policemen "who had misled girls into bad homes. The woman police officer in uniform would be a lighthouse preventing in some cases the wrecking of a life."[13]

The plan of action under this resolution called for groups to approach authorities in each locale and urge the officials to appoint one female in each area, "allowing such women to feel their way." A major concern was that if they demanded too much too quickly they would provoke a backlash from police authorities, men who didn't see the need of being obliged to appoint female officers against their will, "in which case they might very likely appoint the wrong kind, and curtail their usefulness by unwise regulations." It was hoped that proceeding slowly would cause the least possible friction and opposition. The groups behind this resolution acknowledged that women had shortcomings in physical strength, but they argued that "we do not want superior physical strength but superior moral and spiritual strength." Having the power of arrest was not a major issue for these groups, since women were regarded as not strong enough to exercise it, and there were always men within call for that purpose if needed. "However, we believe that, if the right women are appointed, on the one hand, they will not attempt what is beyond their power, and, on the other, they will be found to have more moral power than many of their male confreres, who are selected on other principles and under the physical force idea." Ultimately, they did indeed want policewomen to have the power of arrest, for they strongly felt that if females had to be arrested this should be done by a female officer.[14]

None of this agitation led to the hiring of policewomen in England. The event that precipitated the change was the outbreak of World War I in the summer of 1914. Soon there was a shortage of male police and males in general. Disruption in family life meant more and more children were out in the streets without supervision. Large numbers of young, single male conscripts and volunteers were marshaled together in camps in various parts of the country for training and to await transportation to their wartime destinations. A city with one of these camps nearby might see the area's population increase dramatically — even doubling. This was added stress for a society already experiencing sexual tensions through a preoccupation with prostitution and white slavery, along with a more liberated and more mobile female population. Large numbers of male military personnel from the Commonwealth (such as Canada and Australia) also passed through these English camps, further increasing the numbers and magnifying the scope of the problem. In addition, many young single women migrated from rural areas to the city in search of employment. Contemporary accounts wrote of and warned of young girls "exposed to the allurement of the uniform and the prevailing patriotic excitement" of young men "in the full lustihood of life" and of the "extra excitement and temptation to young girls."[15]

With the arrival of war, the National Union of Women Workers (NUWW) set up a committee composed of representatives from various groups interested in moral welfare, such as the National Vigilance Association, to agitate for the introduction of women police. Their initial idea was to obtain authorization for the appointment of females as special constables. However, this idea was dropped when it appeared that the existing system might not allow for women to be sworn in. Instead, they decided to get female volunteers to patrol the streets. The NUWW was able to win approval of this plan from both the home secretary and the police commissioner. The NUWW recruited women in various areas of the country, organized and trained them for the Women Patrols (WP), while the home secretary wrote a letter to chief constables throughout the country asking them to sign cards (a signed permit of authority and identification) for any WP organized in their area. The London Metropolitan Police chief constable had already signed such an agreement. Thus, when a patrol was organized in an area, the NUWW approached the chief constable to sign cards for the WP. Patrol work in London and other areas began in October 1914. The women were to maintain order in the streets, parks, and other public areas, particularly in the areas near military camps, and generally be vigilant concerning the welfare of women and children. No uniforms were worn, nor did these women have any police powers. Their only visible official denotation was an armband bearing the letters NUWW. From the beginning this work was seen only as a wartime measure and that "the promoters were anxious to dissociate the idea of patrols from any connection with the existing police force." Paid women organizers from the NUWW went to various centers when requested, to start the work and train the patrols. Mrs. M. G. Carden was secretary of the Women's Patrol Committee of the NUWW. She stated she was happy with the volunteer nature of the WP and stated, "Our patrols are most useful ... touching work which they [the men] could not do, viz the helping of giddy young girls." Rescuing girls from "a life of sin" was another way she described the role of the patrols. Carden also pointed out, "The voluntary patrols are neither police nor rescue workers, but true friends of the girls, in the deepest and holiest sense of the word." Even this minor movement into policing did not occur easily. One account noted, "All chief Constables did not welcome the scheme, and it needed much persistence and enthusiasm to overcome the objections.... The principle that women police were necessary or even desirable, frankly was never recognized."[16]

In addition, the British government was not interested in the idea of full-time paid policewomen at that stage. Women patrols were used due to a manpower emergency. The town clerk of Southampton wrote to the home secretary in December 1914 to ask if there would be any objection to that city appointing two policewomen, and if there was no objection would the Exchequer (the treasury) contribute half the pay and costs (as it did for male police). Claiming that it had no authority to approve or disapprove such appointments the Home Office reply went on to say, however, that it did encourage volunteer women workers. It would not pay any funds. Southampton had intended to hire the women on the same terms as male police, as well as having them uniformed and sworn in. But due to the Home Office reply it scrapped that idea. The Home Office then, like the promoters of the WP, saw the issue as a wartime measure only and therefore limited themselves to no more than promoting reasonable cooperation between the police and volunteer agencies.[17]

By 1916 the number of Women Patrols reached about 2,000. Duties included patrolling train stations and streets, tracing lost children, ensuring bars closed at the proper time, ensuring alcohol was not sold to minors, patrolling the areas around munitions plants, escorting female workers to and from work and trains, and dealing with female victims of sex crimes during the interview process. Male police carried truncheons; females did not. One account described these Women Patrols thus: "The duties of the policeman and the police-woman must always be different. In the one case we have the vision of the strong arm and truncheon, in the other that of Character with a specific mission and sanction."[18]

Of the approximately 2,000 Women Patrols at work in March 1915 in England, each worked about two two-hour shifts per week. Of this number, 70 to 80 worked in the London metropolitan area. While the bulk of this work remained voluntary, small sums of money were occasionally provided. The Home Office approved payments of a subsidy of 400 pounds Sterling a year to the group for training purposes. To ensure a constant supply of capable, trained patrols to fill new posts, training schools for them were established at Bristol, Liverpool and Glasgow. After conducting a survey of their effectiveness, Police Commissioner Edward Henry hired eight of these patrols, paid out of police funds, to investigate and report on conditions at cinemas in the metropolitan area. In addition, six were appointed as park keepers in Kensington Gardens, while the London County Council employed a few to work in the public open spaces under its jurisdiction. In a few areas local authorities contributed a little financial support. Some of these areas lobbied to get financial support from the Exchequer.

However, the Exchequer resisted all attempts to have these females recognized in any way as regular police since the Exchequer then would have to split all costs 50–50 with the local areas, while the females themselves would then become eligible for pensions. When local authorities paid these unofficial female police all funds had to come out of the local tax base — the rates (property taxes). A few more small grants and allowances were made to the NUWW to cover such items as heavy clothing for patrols in cold weather; but nonetheless, the vast majority remained unpaid volunteers. Even those few paid female patrols had no power of arrest and were not incorporated into the police force. Generally, those women who patrolled the streets from 1915 to 1917, uniformed by now, did so in the company of a male police officer. On such patrol duty these women did not take the initiative, and those women who did receive some reimbursement were called "part-time paid police assistants."[19]

Public attitude toward the patrols was reported to be mainly favorable. Even the home secretary was in favor of expanding their work "in the hope of controlling prostitution." However, that support did not extend to full recognition. When the chief constable of Sunderland wrote to the home secretary asking if he was in favor of female police being sworn in, the reply from the Home Office — by a civil servant on behalf of the secretary — was that females would be more successful if they were limited to "duties for which they are specially fitted ... as it is obvious that a woman could not undertake all the duties which the law imposes on a constable [so] he would not suggest that any women so employed could be properly sworn in as a member of the force." Even if the public approved the male police were less sanguine in their opinions of female police. The chief constable of Folkestone denied their usefulness under any circumstances, while some other chief constables agreed they were useful for limited purposes under limited circumstances. When Commissioner Henry conducted a May 1916 survey of the metropolitan area police divisions which used Women Patrols he found that "the attitude of the men on the spot, the local superintendents, were almost unanimously against the women patrols, and they had a low opinion of their usefulness."[20]

Measures such as the Women Patrols did not satisfy many women's organizations. Some, like the Women's Liberal Federation, continued to agitate and pass resolutions throughout the war years demanding that female police be appointed with the same powers as male appointees, stressing, however, that females would emphasize the preventive and protective side of policing. They strongly objected to voluntary police, wanting paid ones who would be appointed by the Home Office. *The Times* argued there was more to police work than strength. Citing as an example the inspection of rooming-houses (apparently conducted by police) wherein lived girls so poor that some owned only one set of underwear which had to be washed, dried, and put on before the owner could go out again, the paper argued, "Women alone ought to have entry to the rooms inhabited by such as these." Seemingly in favor of female patrols on the streets, *The Times* argued, "A child turns instinctively to a woman." Also emphasized was the supposed difference between the genders, where "there is much also in which moral force and tactful supervision are of more value than muscle." When females patrolled the streets, "The method employed is the exertion of an unobtrusive vigilance, a steady pressure of observation. 'Here I am!' says the blue armlet.... When it appears groups disperse, loiterers discover urgent business elsewhere.... The consciousness that decent well-bred women are out in all weathers taking thought for his welfare may well check a young man's reckless impulse."[21]

Another group of female police started at around the same time as the WP, just after the war's outbreak. This group was headed by Margaret Damer-Dawson who, in late August or early September 1914, was involved with a group in transporting Belgian refugees arriving in London to places where they could receive care and lodging. Spending as much time as she did at train stations, Damer-Dawson was alarmed by what she saw. While waiting for trains she saw many loitering women in various disguises. On one day she observed a woman who changed the color of her hair and dress three times, eventually being stopped in the act of taking away two refugee girls who were supposed to be transported by Damer-Dawson herself. This specter of white slavery caused Margaret to discuss the situation with her group and argue the need for trained, uniformed female police. A friend told her that Nina Boyle, a militant suffragette, held the same idea. Together these two assembled a group of some 40 like-minded women to organize a body of policewomen. Damer-Dawson was named chief of the Women Police Volunteers (WPV). From the beginning the WPV determined its objective was to train and supply a body of professional women who would give their full time to policing and who would go to any part of the United Kingdom. The members did not assume that their organization would end with the war; they felt their efforts were "undertaken in order to demonstrate, in the first place, that a force of trained policewomen was badly needed ... that women are an indispensable adjunct to any well-ordered police force." From the beginning they were against voluntary service; the WPV wanted their workers to be paid a salary. Approaching Metropolitan Police commissioner Henry, the group won his approval for a corps of women who would do police duties without being sworn in as constables, but who would wear uniforms. The uniform were designed by Damer-Dawson in conjunction with Henry. Many of the original and early members of this group had been prominent workers for women's suffrage in the militant days prior to the war. From those experiences many had been drawn to other issues, such as policing. The suffragette movement "had brought some of them into close, sometimes painful touch with the police, teaching them how very unpleasant it is for an alleged woman culprit to be handled by men."[22]

Henry suggested the names of several textbooks that should be studied, and which the women bought. Besides studying these, the women familiarized themselves with the police code. They also attended various police and children's courts to better understand the workings of the law. In addition, recruits were trained by a police drill sergeant, who also gave them instruction in police duties. Whenever a society or group in the county of London agreed to raise money to pay for two women police for any metropolitan borough, Damer-Dawson notified Henry. The chief constable then gave a letter to the superintendent of the area, who was then visited by Damer-Dawson, and the two of them then drew up a working schedule. The first uniformed policewomen to appear in the streets of London did so in the fall of 1914. This event stirred up controversy in the press, with the result that "the usual sternly repressive, satirical or darkly pessimistic letters poured in." It was a furor that passed over in a few months. With the blessing of Henry for the WPV to work in the metropolitan London region, acceptance of them in other parts of the country became easier. Many chief constables were won over, but others "remained obstinately opposed till the very end of the war to the employment of women on police duties in any capacity."[23]

Outside of London the first place to make use of the WPV was the Midlands community of Grantham. With a population of 20,000, it found itself having to cope with a military camp which housed 18,000 on its doorstep. After obtaining agreement from both civic and military authorities that policewomen would be utilized, the Women's Central Committee of Grantham undertook to raise the money to pay for two WPV. Mary Allen and E. F. Harburn arrived for duty in December 1914. Allen reported they were treated as a curiosity: "We were watched and followed by a curious crowd which was sure to collect the moment we stationed ourselves at any post." During the day the pair, in plainclothes, visited the homes of women and girls who might be persuaded to avoid the camps. Patrolling in uniform at night, they visited public houses and kept watch over "disorderly women." They raided brothels and inspected cinemas to "hinder frivolous young girls from getting into mischief" and to deter "persons of well-known bad character." Upon their arrival the WPV faced a situation where the military authorities had already imposed an order on Grantham which prohibited all women—but not men—from being on the street from 8 P.M. to 7 A.M., to prevent sexual activity. More militant women's groups strongly criticized the WPV for working in a town where such restrictions on women existed. Townswomen got around the curfew by entertaining men in their homes.

Many of the so-called brothels Allen spoke of raiding probably were not bordellos at all. Using an old military order the WPV, with their military escort, entered houses at will — with no warrant of any kind — and turned out hundreds of girls and military personnel. This activity was said to be so successful the curfew was repealed in a month. Then the WPV turned its attention to clearing courting couples out of lanes and open spaces. Private funding for the two WPV ran out in December 1915 but the experiment was considered so successful that the Grantham Town Council continued to employ the two women, who were paid from regular police appropriations. They were sworn in with the full powers of male police officers, marking the first time in Great Britain that women were officially accepted as part of the trained, uniformed police force. They worked directly under the orders of the chief constable.[24]

Now the question was raised as to whether or not the swearing in could be considered valid. The Home Office, while not legally challenging or rejecting the move, ruled that it couldn't be considered legal as under an 1890 statute women were not "persons" for the purposes of the police. That potential problem was eliminated when the Sex Disqualification (Removal) Act of 1919 established the legality of females as members of the police forces.[25]

Personality clashes between Damer-Dawson and second-in-command Boyle reached a head in February 1915. Boyle felt the WPV leader had sold out female interests by permitting women police in Grantham to enforce the restrictive order affecting only women. While Damer-Dawson leaned toward working in harmony with the male police establishment, Boyle wanted more of a separatist, feminist organization. This led to a demand for Damer-Dawson's resignation by Boyle. Calling the entire corps of about 50 together, Damer-Dawson introduced the matter to them. A resultant vote on the issue gave almost unanimous support to the WPV leader. Nevertheless, she did resign from the WPV, leaving the name to Boyle but taking virtually all of its members with her. She immediately formed a new group called the Women Police Service (WPS). Little more was heard from Boyle and her followers except "they were regarded with disfavor by the police authorities." They disappeared from the scene entirely in very short order.[26]

Relations between the Women Patrols and Damer-Dawson's group were said to be good, but not good between the patrols and Boyle's outfit for the time of its brief existence. Chief Constable Gentle of Brighton had authorized a number of the Women Patrols for duty in his area, women he described as helpful. However, he had warned the local suffragettes, who were calling themselves police volunteers, to stop parading the streets and representing themselves as police officers. Police Commissioner Henry preferred to use the NUWW patrols over the Damer-Dawson or Boyle groups because the NUWW was an organization "whose governing body is wise enough to realize the limitations."[27]

While the government was opposed to female police, its stance softened due to an increasing manpower shortage as the war continued. When Damer-Dawson wrote to the Home Office in July 1915 asking for policewomen to be sworn in, the reply stated, "It is impossible for women to take the place of men. They would not be sufficient to replace any police constables." On her first approach to Henry in the summer of 1914 to allow her female police to work in the streets, Damer-Dawson reported that the commissioner replied by shaking his head and stating, "You will get yourselves knocked on the head, and you surely don't expect me to look after a lot of women."[28]

Yet the need became greater and greater. Men enlisted in the armed forces in ever-increasing numbers, and the concentration of recruits in camps grew. Females with little or no money poured into London and other major cities from the countryside seeking employment in the relatively high-paying munitions work. Children's lives were disrupted by the absence of parents, and lonely wives turned to public houses and alcohol for comfort. As pioneer WPS members Mary Allen noted, "The protection of women by women was the root principle underlying the whole programme we laid down." The service remained very much class-based, for among the volunteers "were many women of leisure." For the WPS a major stumbling block was "the reluctance of the authorities to grant women police officers sufficient powers to make their duties worth undertaking at all." Another was lack of funds, even with Damer-Dawson making countless speeches before various groups and organizations to raise money. Not until 1916 would the government make a grant to the WPS, but even then it was not nearly enough; the group still had to raise most of its own funds. A major bar to the appointment of women, according to local officials, was that the Home Office might express objections. When Damer-Dawson explained this to Home Secretary John Simon in 1915, he responded by issuing a statement that no objections would be raised by his office to the employment of female police "on police duties of a kind they are naturally qualified for," whenever a local authority deemed such an appointment desirable. However, in some areas resistance surfaced after women were appointed.

Apparently, they were appointed in some places as a response to lack of manpower and pressure from area women's groups rather than from any real desire on the part of the chief constable. Some of these chiefs, wrote Allen, "evinced a stubborn reluctance to make use at all of the new women recruits, and put every obstacle in their path." Male citizens in some localities reportedly feared female police would be repressive in nature and "intolerant of the rougher form of natural human enjoyment." Another worry was that lack of physical strength by women would necessitate the regular assistance of male police. Allen claimed it a fact that the rougher elements of mankind were more easily controlled by women than by men and "an even more curious fact ... is the involuntary and ready submission of women to other women in authority."[29]

When the city of Kingston-upon-Hull (usually known as Hull) requested two of Damer-Dawson's police, the pair were given charge of the 40 Women Patrols already on duty in that city. Those two WPS members at Hull were not sworn in but were permitted to arrest drunk and disorderly females. Before the war ended WPS-trained policewomen had been posted for duties in numerous cities, such as Edinburgh, Birmingham, Glasgow, Belfast, Portsmouth, Plymouth, Brighton, Nottingham, Southampton, Folkestone, Oxford, Cambridge, and Reading, as well as various metro London boroughs and communities. The status of these women varied from place to place. In some areas they served under the chief constable and in others under the local committee set up for that purpose. In most provincial towns the experiences of Grantham and Hull were repeated, whereby the women were frequently told during the first week or two that they were not wanted but then were accepted. Reportedly, male constables were generally helpful and friendly with a few exceptions, although sometimes they appeared overly chivalrous. One pair of female police assigned to keeping watch one night on a suspicious house found themselves in turn watched all night by a pair of male police. While a few of these women had some power of arrest, the vast majority did not. This was a disadvantage the women tried to keep the public from learning because "where this was not possible it frequently happened that the policewoman was tainted with her inability to apply force, or was openly defied."[30]

Some of these women were paid from the local rates, and some were paid by the committees set up in the localities from voluntary contributions. In July 1916 a clause to the Police (Miscellaneous) Provisions Act was enacted, which made policewomen eligible to receive payment in the same way as male police, half from the local rates, half from the Exchequer.

From 1916 onward the WPS trained and supplied policewomen for police work in factories and munitions areas. This enabled the authorities to remove male civilian police and military police from these plants for other duties. Duties at munitions plants included checking passes, searching female workers, patrolling the areas, maintaining security, and supervising during air raids. Between 1916 and 1918 the WPS supplied 985 policewomen to munitions factories. At these plants "on various occasions on their appearance, threats were made to mob the policewomen." However, this excitement invariably calmed down when the women held their ground, proving they were able to maintain order. Stressing their moral worth, Allen noted that the language at such plants was often appallingly coarse, even among women of 19 and 20, but that the policewomen by "continued remonstrances, grave but kindly, were in the end effectual and in consequence the whole tone of the factory was raised."[31]

Part of the training for those in the London area included attending various police courts. Even here resistance was strong, for "there were magistrates who did not hesitate openly to ridicule the idea of trained and uniformed women constables.... When policewomen were first called upon to give evidence before such prejudiced magistrates, they were subject to a very unpleasant ordeal, or made the butt of the most trying form of cheap wit."[32]

In London the WPS women patrolled streets, parks, recreation grounds, canteens, cinemas, public houses, and penny arcades. In addition, they supervised dance halls, music halls, and protected children. For Allen the uniform was crucial and necessary, since "it is a notable fact that the policewoman in uniform was treated with respect by the most frivolous and incorrigible girls' while the woman constable in plain clothes, unless very insistent, was likely to be impertinently disregarded. The uniform also earned the instinctive respect of the young soldier, even when drunk and inclined to be violent." For Allen, "The policewoman instinctively finds her best field of usefulness among women and children."[33]

Whether or not they wore uniforms or had the power of arrest, policewomen supposedly brought to bear a certain moral suasion. An account of the era remarked, concerning their dealing with prostitution, that the chief use of policewomen was "to arouse by their presence a sense of shame in the men and youths bent on pleasure of the wrong sort."[34]

5

U.S., 1917–1929

Policewomen appeared in an increasing number of cities during the period 1917 to 1929; however, in absolute terms their number remained small. A questionnaire sent out in 1919 and 1920 revealed, from the 146 cities that replied, 56 cities in 26 states employed 175 women in their police departments. Results understated the true picture, since one of the cities that did not reply was New York, which had perhaps 30 policewomen and 50 matrons by that time. Of the 175 total, the proportion that were police officers and that were matrons was not known. There were 30 cities that required applicants to take civil service examinations for appointment, while 26 did not. In 21 cities some form of social service training was deemed essential to be an effective policewoman, while the other 35 required no special training of their applicants.[1]

A 1924 survey by the Bureau of Social Hygiene of New York City received replies from 268 cities. Of those cities, 210 employed women in their police departments; 71 employed both matrons and officers, 65 had matrons only, 52 had officers only, 22 employed one person as both matron and officer, and 58 had no women in their departments. Of the 100 largest cities in the United States, 92 employed females; 56 had both matrons and officers, 24 had matrons only, 10 had officers only, and two employed one person as matron and officer. Thus in those 210 cities there were at least 355 matrons, 395 policewomen and 22 who performed both functions. Being labeled a policewoman did not necessarily mean the woman performed the duties—narrowly defined as they were—of a police officer; many were used to a small or large degree as matrons.[2]

A third questionnaire was sent out by Detroit police commissioner William P. Rutledge in 1929. He received replies from 202 cities. Of those cities 164 employed women; 77 had officers only, 48 had matrons and officers, 39 had matrons only, 38 employed no women. Together these employed 465 policewomen and 294 matrons.[3]

Around 1925 out of 148 cities listed only six of them were said to employ policewomen in large enough numbers to reach double digits: Chicago 30, Washington, D.C., 21, St. Louis 18, Indianapolis 19, Detroit 31, and New York City 61 (some of these were matrons). Los Angeles then had eight police-women; all the other 141 cities employed a number of women ranging from five down to zero.[4]

A major issue to policewomen in those early post–World War I years was how the policewomen in a department should be organized. In cities with only one or two female officers the question did not arise, but most officers were concentrated in a small number of large cities. One way to organize them was to assign them all to an already existing division, such as the detec-tive squad, where they were supervised by the male head. A second way was to break them up, assigning them to different precincts where they would be under the command of the male precinct head. The third method was to assign them all to a newly created Women's Bureau with a female director — reporting to the chief — in charge of that division. The first such division was briefly established in St. Louis in 1916 and then in Washington, D.C., in 1918. A few other cities would establish women's divisions, while a few such as Indianapolis and New York City would discontinue them at a later date. By the mid–1920s, of the largest 100 cities 92 employed females on their police forces, and 68 of those had officers. However, only in six did they work in a women's division. A journalist of the day commented that this "may indicate either lack of conviction, indifference or active opposition." Another writer noted that where policewomen achieved the most they "are organized into a separate unit directed by a woman of police rank reporting directly to the chief."[5]

Decades later modern women seeking true equality in policing would criticize this early arrangement of a women's division as helping to ghettoize females into their limited and narrow range of duties. Yet in the 1920s females in the police field came to understand this was the only way they would be able to perform those duties— and at that time those limited, narrow duties were all they sought. Facing a hostile male police establishment, if police-women were under the command of a male in one division or dispersed among precincts the likelihood was that they could be and indeed were reduced to matron duty or just clerical duties of filing and typing. Assigned together to a division led by a woman greatly increased their chances to per-form what they felt to be their role in policing. A hostile male department preferred to employ no females, but if they were required to do so then they wanted those females to be under male command, since all police officers recognized that policewomen had greater autonomy in a women's division. Indeed, the male officers sometimes sought to undermine a women's division, and they sometimes succeeded. In addition, males did not like the fact that a female was in command, giving orders. True, it was only to other females, but what if it was allowed to become a more general practice? This could be a dangerous precedent. So fearful of this were the male police establishment that in many departments where a women's division existed the female head was called director. This title did not exist in the male structure. Male titles of hierarchy, such as captain and head of a division, did not exist in the female units in an openly hostile department.

An early example of success and then failure of a women's division can be found in Indianapolis. Initially, the force organized a department of police-women with 11 members in June 1918. By 1921 it had a women's division made up of 23 policewomen, headed by another female, Clara Burnside. As with policewomen throughout the United States, they wore no uniforms and made a point of avoiding making arrests where and when possible. These women kept a watchful eye on all public places frequented by women and girls, working with cinema owners to stamp out "unfit" films, and spent extra time patrolling dance halls in the 1920 season because that year saw "several vulgar dances" introduced. They also patrolled stores looking for shoplifters and spent a lot of time in public parks. In 1920 there were 4,120 cases reported to the policewomen. Of those 1,857 were female minors found to be in need of protection and assistance; the other 2,263 were adults. The total number of arrests made was 543, of which 63 were males. In addition, 64 shoplifters were apprehended, with eight of those arrested. The others were allowed to go with on-the-spot tongue lashings. Burnside admitted she had difficulty in obtaining cooperation of all the law enforcement agencies and personnel in her area. Many thought of female police and her division as a passing fad which wasted taxpayers' money. Just a few short years later, by mid–1924, this women's division was gone. Mina Van Winkle, a pioneer policewoman from Washington, D.C., noted bitterly, without providing specific details, that a "deliberate effort" was made to destroy women's divisions. One such effort "succeeded in Indianapolis" where the unit "was completely scrapped."[6]

Boston got its first policewomen in 1920 when six were appointed. This came as a result of pressure that culminated with a mass meeting in 1919 organized by groups such as the Boston Society for the Care of Girls, the Boston City Federation, the Boston League of Women Voters, the Travelers' Aid Society, and the Women's Municipal League. One of the speakers was Van Winkle. A plan proposing that policewomen be organized within their own Women's Bureau was endorsed at the meeting. However, when a special law was passed making females eligible to be regular members of the police department, Police Commissioner Edwin V. Curtis decided they should function directly under the office of the chief inspector — that is, not in their own division. One was assigned to work with male plainclothes officers detailed to clean up certain cabarets. A second, with a representative of the Better Business Men's Association, visited public auction rooms to buy sale items as if they were regular buyers. Purchases were then appraised to see if license revocation was in order. The Better Business group paid all the expenses of purchases and appraisals. Two of those six Boston policewomen patrolled the Common, dance halls, and certain streets to supervise the public conduct of young girls as well as to pick up prostitutes. If they spotted a girl for the second time conducting herself in public in such a way as to indicate a lack of decency they would warn her. If they observed her doing the same thing for a third time the policewomen were to take her home and report all the facts to the girl's parents. One of the six new officers did not last too long on the force. Early in 1922 Sabina J. Delaney resigned, objecting to certain details of duty related to obtaining evidence of liquor law violations. Specifically, Delaney resigned to protest orders directing her to buy liquor in suspected cafes as evidence against the owners. Some of the resistance to policewomen could be seen in Boston's refusal to establish a separate women's unit, as well as in the fact that through the mid–1920s at least Boston's policewomen went off duty at no later than 10 P.M. each evening, just when vice activity generally began to significantly increase.[7]

Agitation in St. Louis included having Alice Wells in to speak at a meeting. On May 15, 1916, the city appointed four policewomen to the force; they constituted the staff of the country's first policewomen's bureau. Eleven more were added in 1918; however, a few months later that form of organization was abandoned, with the women placed in the Detective Bureau directed by a male detective sergeant who reported to the chief of detectives. In the 1924 St. Louis police department report the females were listed as "18 Matrons (Policewomen)." Commenting on them in that report the chief of police stated, "Their visits to the pictureshows, dance halls, and other places frequented by young girls have been numerous, and complaints of unseemly conduct at such places have been greatly minimized as a result." Some of those policewomen were detailed as follows: one to the business district to look for shoplifters and women wanted by the police; two to answer and follow up letters of inquiry, usually for missing relatives and to investigate conditions reported by anonymous letters; two to office duty in interviewing women and girls for the purpose of general advice and "social adjustment"; two to the follow-up of desertion and nonsupport cases; two or four to patrol duty in public parks, cinemas, dance halls, and so forth; and two blacks assigned to handle all black female cases.[8]

Chicago had 30 policewomen in the mid–1920s, although "matron duty has been imposed on women police by some commanding officers," according to one report. With 17 of the 30 listed for duty under the commanding officer, the implication was that the other 13 were limited to matron-only duties. Some of those 17 were deployed as follows: six patrolled beaches and the public places, one was assigned to the missing persons bureau, two were assigned to the State Attorney's Office for rape cases and crimes against minors, and two were assigned to escort female detainees to court and stay for their hearings.[9]

Agitation in Cleveland continued with the Women's Protective Association of Cleveland in the forefront of strong lobbying, culminating in the appointment of policewomen in 1922. In his annual reports of 1921 and 1922 the chief of police there recommended the appointment of policewomen. As time passed, more groups joined in the lobbying campaign, with the Women's City Club being the most important. While most policewomen favored the separate division structure to ensure their autonomy in a limited role, some favored that structure to emphasize that women were not men; they were different, with contrasting ideas and concepts of policing. The American Social Hygiene Association and the Travelers' Aid Society sent Victoria (Virginia in some accounts) Murray, general secretary of the New York Travelers' Aid, to Cleveland for an intensive two-week educational campaign in an effort to prevent the admission of females into the police department "on the same basis as are the men and working as individuals under men officers, and with no constructive social program." Sentiment in the city was said to have swung overwhelmingly in favor of a Women's Bureau in the wake of Murray's visit. Cleveland's first four policewomen were appointed in 1922. Two years later an ordinance establishing a Women's Bureau was passed, with it being formally established in January 1925. Led by a female captain — university graduate and social worker Dorothy D. Henry — who received a captain's pay and reported directly to the chief, the bureau's mandate "shall be to do preventive work with women and children, and to deal with all cases in which women and children are involved, either as offenders or as victims of offenses." Cleveland's Women's Bureau numbered 15 when established, including the first four officers who were transferred from their existing assignments.[10]

The Portland, Oregon, department employed 11 females in the early 1920s, and they were still spoken of as operatives. Those 11 consisted of one nurse, two clericals, five patrol officers, one dance hall inspector, one assistant supervisor, and one supervisor. Available for the use of these women was one touring car. However, two male officers were detailed to drive it and make any necessary arrests.[11]

In Detroit in 1919, the commissioner of police appointed Josephine Davis, a university graduate and member of the staff of the Girls' Protective League, to interview all females detained by the force. Pressure to appoint policewomen was not placated by this move, with Victoria Murray being brought in to help agitate. The result was that Murray was appointed in 1921 as director of the newly created women's division of the Detroit Police Department. Fourteen policewomen were appointed in the first six months, the number rising to 30 in the division by 1925.[12]

Officially, Murray's title was director, but unofficially she was known as the chief of policewomen. All 14 of those first appointed were trained social workers. Murray insisted that all the male police in Detroit showed the policewomen nothing but the "greatest desire to help." Asked if her women wore uniforms Murray replied, "Certainly not. Our women have badges. It is necessary, for they may at any time be obliged to use them to enforce their authority, but they wear them out of sight. Our work is preventive, not punitive. A police woman will not receive credit by the number of arrests she makes. The fewer arrests the better, and we must get away from the idea of the strong-arm woman." Regarding the question of why Detroit's policewomen did not carry guns, Murray stated, "Our women do not know what guns are. They would not know what to do with them. One of our dangers will be that, while we have selected our patrol women with the greatest care, they may in time become too aggressive, and if they do, they must go."[13]

By 1929 Detroit had 42 policewomen with 16 of them engaged in protective patrol, four on days, 12 on night duty. During 1928 those women made investigations of 1,553 suspicious places. In addition, they made 1,079 visits to dance halls. Contact was made with 472 children and 1,642 girls who presented "serious problems." A total of 417 men found with those girls were taken into custody — but not necessarily charged and arrested. No record was kept of the large number of individuals who were questioned or advised without specific action being taken. Of the 42 policewomen 10 were university graduates (three with law degrees), 18 had some university or other formal schooling beyond high school, 10 were high school graduates, and only four had less than a high school diploma. In addition, 13 had prior work experience as social workers, six had been nurses, and two had teaching experience. In terms of background Detroit looked for social work experience as the most desired background for its policewomen, followed by teaching and nursing. A background of commercial experience was considered least desirable.[14]

When Ossining, New York, hired Mrs. Daniel O'Shea as its first officer in September 1917, the former social worker was paid $75 a month. It was reported that "one of her duties will be to crusade against spooning."[15]

Atlantic City, New Jersey, chief of police Miller announced in May 1917 that his city's first policewoman had been assigned to duty on the city's famed Boardwalk. She was described as a fully qualified official with carefully defined duties, one of which was "the suppression of flirting." He declined to describe her further other than to say she was young and knew her business. Chief Miller would not reveal her name. With respect to her work against flirting Miller said, "A mere wink, may be a ticket to City Hall," meaning jail. She also was to keep an eye on the cabarets and report anything of which she disapproved to the director of public safety. During the busy summer season she was to have an assistant to "censor feminine bathing attire on the beach."[16]

Less than two weeks later the woman's name became public knowledge when a journalist reported that Mary Green, Atlantic City's first policewoman, had furnished evidence against Professor Swami Rajan, alleged Boardwalk fortuneteller. As of May 30 the seer was being held on $500 bail. Green testified he read her palm telling her, among other things, that she would shortly marry a dark man. The policewoman was already married.[17]

At the same time Chicago's policewomen remained active in their war on flirting. In that city John Boveri appeared in what a reporter called "Morals Court" in May 1917. Policewoman Alice Clement told the court she went to a State Street cinema where Boveri became "obnoxious" to her. Clement told him he was under arrest. When he resisted Clement struck Boveri on the head with her blackjack, ran after him when he fled, grabbed him again in the street and held him, with the assistance of bystanders, until the patrol wagon arrived.[18]

New York City continued to be a holdout in the move toward policewomen. However, World War I was threatening to bring about a change. In June 1917 it was reported that policewomen for New York City was the latest plan for the war service of women. The Mayor's Committee of Women on National Defense was considering the addition of a women's division to the Home Defense League, the women to do both patrol and protective work. Miss Stella Miner, assistant secretary of the New York Probation and Protective Association, was the one who first advanced the idea. She declared, "To prepare adequately for the future New York needs a group of volunteer women workers, analogous to the Home Defense League, who should be trained by the Police Department to do police work." Miner was thinking of about 25 women. She saw them being used in the dance halls and searching for missing girls. They had, she observed, a similar group of women in Great Britain and in Ireland. "Policewomen working in couples have done regular work," she stated.[19]

Two days later Alice Stebbins Wells arrived in New York City, from Pittsburgh, to announce that her organization (the International Association of Policewomen, of which she was president) was then urging upon the Council of National Defense the establishment of policewomen in every city of the United States as a war measure. At the annual convention of her group (IAP) that had just come to an end in Pittsburgh, resolutions were passed pressing this step upon the government. At the same time the Mayor's Committee of Women on National Defense was about to ask Mayor Mitchel to establish a force of policewomen in New York City. Wells told a reporter that New York needed policewomen even in peacetime. Then she repeated her story of having been harassed in front of a New York City cinema with the perpetrator, in this version, being "a dapper young man." Nixola Greeley-Smith was the reporter and she observed that Wells "bears the queerest, most incongruous resemblance to the Mona Lisa." Wells also told Greeley-Smith, "A woman of my age does not need protection from mashers, but suppose I had been a young girl." Also, the Los Angeles officer declared policewomen were needed and necessary in dance halls and theaters. "Another phase of the work is in promoting Americanization by acting as intermediary between the foreign-born mother and the strange American duckling she has hatched and does not understand," Wells argued. The IAP then had, she said, 150 members from 24 American states and from Europe. At the conference that had just ended delegates from 14 states attended and reports were read from Canada, England, South Africa, New Zealand, Sweden, and Hawaii. All of these places were said to have policewomen.[20]

A report in July 1917 said there were then 51 cities in the United States employing policewomen who were paid for out of municipal funds. They received salaries ranging from $75 to $100 month and, in rare cases, as high as $110. California had nine of those cities, including Los Angeles, Long Beach, San Francisco, San Diego, and Sacramento.[21]

The District Commissioners in Washington were planning in October 1917, it was reported by journalist Bill Price, to ask Congress for more police-women for Washington, increased pay for the entire police force, and more money for the eight police matrons. Two policewomen were then on the force and it was said that three or four more could be used effectively. The use of policewomen in the nation's capital began less than a year earlier and had been deemed successful. In fact it was reported that how they got along before without them was a mystery "although prior to their appointment under the law they had been police matrons and had been assigned to detective work at frequent intervals, making records that brought about their promotion when Congress authorized two regular policewomen," recounted Price. The regular matrons then did special assignment work whenever the policewomen were unable to handle the extra workload they had. They were sent to cinemas to protect girls against men who annoyed them. During the Christmas shopping season and when extra crowds were to be handled in Washington they did the equivalent of police and detective duty in addition to their regular duties as matrons. The three matrons who were assigned to the house of detention were paid $600 a year while the five other matrons who were assigned to var-ious stations received $720 a year. A pay increase was sought for those women who were felt to be poorly paid for their services. "They are compelled to take charge of the vilest prisoners and are often roughly treated by vicious and drunken women who object to regulations," explained Price. The two policewomen were paid $75 a month ($900 annually), the same pay given a man when he was first hired. However, those men were entitled to a raise after three years; the policewomen were not. One of those two female police was assigned to special investigations of a "private character" and her name never figured in the daily routine of police cases (nor was she named in this article by Price). The other police-woman, Mrs. Sarah V. Farling, was said to have become well known to Washingtonians. "Her work is of a public nature and she has a record of arrests equal to that of any man on the force," noted the reporter. She had participated in the arrest of suffragists but her best work was in the reclamation of young girls attending dance halls and other places "where they meet bad male characters." Farling usually worked alone but sometimes did so in conjunction with policemen. According to Price's account, if it were not for the help of matrons in the Christmas rush of shopping Washington merchants would lose thousands of dollars to shoplifters.[22]

Mrs. Sarah V. Farling, 1918.

Days later Farling gave an interview in which she asserted Washington "teems with peril for young girls—and their mothers are very largely to blame." In this news story she was profiled as Washington's "first and only policewoman," despite what Price had published two days earlier in the very same newspaper. Sarah reached her conclusion after a searching investigation of dance halls, cinemas and various resorts, lasting more than a year, with the conclusions released for the first time now. Her work had not been with the "lower classes" but, Farling said, with girls who are members of "the better class." A majority of those girls were the daughters of prosperous merchants or government employees. Farling said that a law should be enacted, after her investigation, that it be a misdemeanor for those girls to be out late at night without an escort or a chaperon. The necessity for such a law she lay directly at the door of indifferent and neglectful mothers, she added: "When I take a girl of fourteen or fifteen home at 11 o'clock at night and find the door locked and the mother sound and peacefully asleep then I say the responsibility lies on that mother and not on the little inexperienced girl who is, after all, nothing but a child, and so needs a child's protection."[23]

According to a November 1917 news story Dr. Valeria H. Parker of Hartford, Connecticut, was the first "woman policeman" ever to be given supervision over other state policemen in the United States. She was devoting her time to "interesting, thoughtless and careless girls" near the military camp at New London, Connecticut, in recreation rooms and clubs. Parker had supervision over five other policemen.

Actually those people were "female policemen."[24]

Finally, in May 1918, New York City began to take action toward putting policewomen on the force. It was announced at that time that 12 policewomen with uniforms, handcuffs, and revolvers were about to make their debut in the municipal force, according to an announcement made on May 20 by Acting Police Commissioner John A. Leach. This was hailed by friends of the Mitchel administration who remembered that there had been an appropriation for policewomen in the Mitchel budget that was criticized by Mayor-elect Hylan "as a foolish extravagance." The Mayor's (Mitchel) Committee of Women, headed by Mrs. Willard Straight, paid the salaries of two policewomen the previous fall and it was their excellent work among soldiers and sailors in the parks that attracted the attention of Raymond Fosdick, so he wrote to Mayor Mitchel advocating the appointment by the city of policewomen. Mayor Hylan then endorsed the idea to appoint women police and dated his conversion, it was said, to the annual police parade. Those coming female police were to receive $1,000 a year — which was the salary of a first-year police patrolman. They would be assigned under Deputy Commissioner Ellen O'Grady and would work chiefly with "white slave" cases and juvenile delinquency. A large part of their work would be to patrol the parks where soldiers and sailors met young girls. Commissioner Leach made a tour of the Brooklyn Navy Yard section with Mrs. Whitehurst and was impressed with her skilful method of breaking up flirtations and escorting the young women back home to their mothers. Leach was impressed by the two women mentioned above, who were Mrs. Margaret Whitehurst and Mrs. Mary Sullivan.[25]

In July 1918 it was reported that Mrs. Sarah V. Farling had recently retired after "several years" as Washington's first policewoman. This account claimed that until recently she did not want her name known or her picture published. For nine years she did "special work" for the Department of Justice and the District of Columbia. As an example, some time earlier the Department of Justice had phoned her and asked her to help them investigate the case of a female German spy in the nation's capital.[26]

As of August 1918 Albuquerque, New Mexico, had two policewomen, their first ones. Mrs. Cora M. Swett and Miss Beulah Clement were the women. According to the reporter doing the article the pair were "lovely" and "one couldn't imagine a kinder, more motherly woman than Mrs. Swett, and as for Miss Beulah Clement, why she is just a sweet, modest little woman." Continuing on in a similar fashion the reporter declared, "They are both just dear, lovable women, but they are very much in earnest about their new work just the same, and the girls of Albuquerque had better watch out." They were the sort of women who inspired one's confidence and made one want to be good by just talking with them. The journalist went on to declare, "There was a time when the question of having policewomen in a city would have created terrible consternation. Those superior beings known as men would have lifted their eyebrows in horror at such a proposition. But veritably, 'the old order changeth,' and women are taking their rightful place in civic life." Swett had seven years experience as a police matron in the juvenile court in Cincinnati, besides the settlement work she did in Denver, and the three years experience with the Bureau of Charity in Albuquerque. Clement's work in the Travelers Aid Society was said to be well known in Albuquerque.[27]

Lincoln, Nebraska, had three policewomen as of September 1918. But Mrs. Dora Doyle, for many years a police matron, would soon take an extended vacation; therefore, the work would be in the hands of Mrs. R. M. Walsh and Mrs. W. S. Jay, new appointees. Mayor Miller said the duties of the women were the same as those of a policeman. She was given the authority to make arrests "of both men and women" and she had a right to call on any person for assistance if she needed it. However, the work of the Lincoln police-women was to be among women and girls. The new recruits were expected to look after all the girls and women brought to the police station, to chaperon all public dances, enforce the curfew ordinance, and look after women "of questionable character" found in the streets. Those women wore no uniforms nor did they carry guns or clubs.[28]

El Paso, Texas, mayor Charles Davis appointed Mrs. Julia K. Farnham (Farnum?) March 24, 1919, to become the city's first policewoman. The article advised the reader not to call a "cop" as El Paso had a new "copette" on the job. Even though it was six years or so since such demeaning descriptions were used, the practice had not entirely disappeared.[29]

Washington, D. C., became the first city in the United States, reportedly, to have a woman police traffic officer. Mrs. Leola N. King was that women. She assumed her duties on the morning of November 1, 1918, at the busy crossing of Seventh and K Streets northwest at the intersection of Massachusetts Avenue, near the Carnegie Library. Police authorities decided to try an experiment of having a female traffic cop, provided a woman with what the police called "traffic sense," could be found. King had become a police officer on September 10, 1918. She had been a school teacher in Delaware, later entering a nurses' training school, and then going into probation work in Philadelphia.[30]

At the end of 1918 District of Columbia chief of police Major Pullman asked for 30 more policewomen for his city. He deemed the experiment with King as a traffic officer a success and he wanted to use more policewomen as traffic police. Pullman stated that no woman need apply who did not have a social conscience and a desire to help humanity. The D. C. force then had a Woman's Bureau to handle most of the crimes committed by or against women and to investigate conditions that placed girls in danger. To that end the bureau had made a survey of conditions in Washington, including hotels, rooming places, boarding houses, restrooms, automobile services, burlesque shows, dance halls, movies, parks, and playgrounds. Working conditions for women had also been investigated.[31]

Policewomen were used at Union Station in Washington, D.C., in the spring of 1919. Those "little sisters," as a reporter called them, of the police department were used as "shock troops" to warn and guard "willful but not wayward girls who have been using the station lobby as a recreational parlor to meet travelers, especially soldiers, sailors and the Marines who are passing through the city." Each of the city's policewomen had been having a turn "at the new experience." That new task had been taken on by the policewomen at the suggestion of the chief of the Union Station police squad who said that there arose there each day cases that needed "a woman's tact and subtle management." Mrs. Mina C. Van Winkle was then the head of Washington's Women's Bureau. Reportedly, the young girls who gathered at the station did so because they had nowhere else to go and nothing to do.[32]

Speaking of his force of female police Washington, D.C., police chief Major Raymond Pullman declared, "The Woman's Bureau of the Metropolitan Police is really a development of the old powers of the police matron." According to reporter Hannah Mitchell Mrs. Mina C. Van Winkle then had a force of 12 policewomen under her. They had police badges and sometimes carried small revolvers but wore no uniforms; they had the same rank as a first-class policeman. Salaries for the policewomen ranged from $1,020 to $1,650 a year but most received $1,200. Some members of that group were Rhoda Milliken (graduate of Barnard College), Imra Buwalda (graduate of the University of California), and Ethel McQuistan (a newspaperwoman from Philadelphia. Van Winkle came to Washington in 1918 to work for the United States Food Administration. She went into the Women's Bureau of the Metropolitan Police when it was established, in September 1918. She was a graduate of the New York School of Philanthropy. For three years she was financial secretary of the Newark, New Jersey, Bureau of Associated Charities. As well, she had been president of the Women's Political Union of New Jersey for eight years and was an investigator of child labor for the Consumers' League in New Jersey.[33]

One part of the work of the Women's Bureau in Washington, D.C., was that, wrote a journalist, of "mothering" girls who came to them as "voluntary probation cases." Mrs. Herbert H. Votaw, who was for 10 years a missionary in India, had charge of that work since the Woman's Bureau had been established. Votaw was the sister of Senator Harding (later President Warren Harding) of Ohio. More than 40 girls between the ages of 14 and 20 had been "mothered" by Votaw. She studied each girl's personality and learned all about her past and present environments. During the period of probation each girl

Mrs. Leola King directing traffic as a policewoman on November 12, 1918, in Washington D.C.

kept a diary that she submitted to Votaw. In the diary she told of the places she went, the shows she attended and what she thought of them, what she did in her home and her ambitions, "if she has any." Votaw, reportedly, had placed many of her charges in good jobs and "practically all of her girls have made good."[34]

A photo of 11 Washington, D.C., policewomen, published in September 1919, identified them as follows: Miss Dorothy James, Mrs. Lumber, Miss Pearl Bartholomew, Miss Julia Marscher, Mrs. Cecelia Clarke, Miss Rhoda Milliken, Mrs. Louisa Sank, Mrs. Mabel Battey, Mrs. Mina C. Van Winkle, Mrs. Carolyn Votaw, and Miss Marion Flanders.[35]

Partly as a result of female lobbying and partly as a result of the war emergency, the Washington, D.C., Police Department established a Women's Bureau in 1918. Mina Van Winkle became director of the original group of four which grew to 20 within a year. With no upper limit on the number that could be hired, some urged Van Winkle to go after 30 or 40. Her reply indicated the many disadvantages of the work. She said in 1919, "It has been rather difficult to secure the full quota of policewomen allowed, because of the low

These Are the Policewomen of the National Capital

Washington, D.C.'s policewomen in 1919, top row, left to right, Miss Dorothy James, Mrs. Lumber, Miss Pearl Bartholomew; center row, left to right, Miss Julia Marsher, Mrs. Cecelia Clarke, Miss Rhoda Milliken, Mrs. Louisa Sank; bottom row, left to right, Mrs. Mabel Battey, Mrs. Mina C. Van Winkle (head of women's bureau), Mrs. Carolyn Votaw, Miss Marion Flanders.

salaries, long hours and the desire of most women to have at least one day's rest in seven. The staff has never been large enough to have a special detail for nightwork. The policewomen who are on duty all day investigating and aiding in the prosecution of court cases are compelled to go on duty at night and remain out until midnight and after."[36]

Two of those first 20 policewomen were black, one a social service worker, the other a university graduate. As with all the other policewomen in America, these Washington officers wore no uniforms. However, there was an on-duty dress code which called for them to wear a plain, dark colored, cloth suit with no "trailing trimming." Shoes were to be gray, brown, or black, with low, flat heels; and stockings had to be one of those three colors.[37]

Addressing the 1920 National Conference of Social Work, Van Winkle spoke of the role of policewomen in her department by saying, "Policewomen are aiming to bring about a close relationship between social workers, the public and the police." Her department devoted its entire time "to all cases in which women and children are involved as well as to preventive and protective work." In the future she hoped to see a Woman's Bureau, directed by a female, in every large American city. Specific duties for policewomen Van Winkle mentioned included "follow-up work for women and girls, securing employment, improving and changing environments that cause delinquency, voluntary probation ... physical and psychopathic examinations, careful investigation of questionable circumstances ... locating missing girls." Other concerns were searching for runaway girls, helping policemen secure evidence against prostitutes, and providing temporary board and lodging.[38]

Speaking in 1921, Van Winkle said there were abut 300 cities in the United States employing police and that in all they were hired primarily for preventive and protective work and "because of pressure by women's organizations." Of her own department she noted the resistance and hostility to its establishment by saying the "Bureau had a continuous struggle for existence against the forces of evil in the District of Columbia." One problem facing the movement for policewomen lay in the fact that some unsuitable women were appointed through political patronage. A second problem, according to Van Winkle, lay in departments where policewomen were not in a separate division but worked under the control of a male who decided what use would be made of the females: "Usually he places her in some clerical position and nine times out of ten concludes before he sees the woman that she is unable to render any service in the police department." Women in general had become the victims of ignorant police departments in various cities because "women's organizations have agitated for policewomen, gotten them assigned to police departments, then forgotten their existence instead of seeing that their services are utilized for the common good." With regard to salaries, Van Winkle said policewomen received equal pay in some departments, but in others they received "much lower salaries than the men although the females were better educated and had some kind of special training and experience before entering the force, in the main." Salaries were an obstacle to securing women for police work; "the salaries are so permanently stabilized that there can be no expectation of a raise in pay except through promotion, which seldom happens."[39]

At other times Van Winkle was ready to blame women for any trouble they suffered as policewomen and to display her own class bias. Arguing that where well-qualified women were employed no opposition to policewomen existed, she added, "Opposition is unavoidable where women of easy familiar habits find their way into departments either through political or other influence, and who, unable to do the work required, try to cover up their ignorance by maudlin sentimentality in dealing with persons coming under their control. Vulgar, uneducated, untrained policewomen degrade the service in the eyes of both the public and the policemen. They are a bad influence with clients in the community and a menace to police service in general."[40]

Van Winkle faced continued harassment in the early 1920s. Not only was she director of the Washington force, but she was also a nationally known figure and head of the International Policewomen's Association — having succeeded Alice Wells. On February 25, 1922, the police chief issued an order, effective March 1, whereby all matters relating to runaway children and females of any age found wandering about were to be handled exclusively by the Women's Bureau and not by the Detective Bureau, as heretofore. On March 20 two girls, ages 14 and 15, ran away from their Brooklyn homes. A few days later they contacted their fathers from Washington to say they had no money. Washington police were notified and detectives picked the girls up, took down their stories, and delivered them at 1:30 A.M. to the detention home for females, putting them in the charge of the Women's Bureau. The fathers arrived and the Detective Bureau demanded the immediate release of the girls. Van Winkle knew nothing of the case until she received the 7 A.M. release demand from the Detective Bureau. Van Winkle declined to release them immediately, saying she would first have to check the girls' records, see if the fathers checked out, and give the girls clean clothes. After the fathers complained of the delay to the senator from their area, Van Winkle was charged with insubordination. An article at the time said "this is not the first attack on Mrs. Van Winkle and her work for wayward girls. Washingtonians have observed that one of the city's newspapers has consistently endeavored to make hard sledding for her administration ever since it started. Statements in its columns are said to have been the cause, a year or so ago, of a congressional investigation which resulted in a complete vindication of Mrs. Van Winkle." That newspaper had supported a defeated candidate for police chief who was then head of the Detective Bureau. In April a trial board found her not guilty of insubordination but noted that she didn't have a "proper conception of the cardinal principle of discipline."[41]

The Women's Bureau was established by the commissioners of the District of Columbia in 1918 and existed solely on their sufferance, that is, there was no law on the books to mandate such a department. Having a law in existence did not make it impossible to eliminate the position of policewoman — laws could be changed — but the process was more difficult and more open to public scrutiny than when the positions were terminated where no such law existed. To this end various local women's groups, including the National Woman's Christian Temperance Union, the Council of the General Federation of Women's Clubs, and the National Congress of Parents and Teachers, lobbied for such a measure in the mid–1920s. Since the District of Columbia was not a state, such a bill had to go through Congress. It passed eventually, but there was an excessive delay due to opponents of the bill. Stories circulated that when policewomen arrested men who were harassing young girls, those "mashers" retaliated by claiming the policewomen lured them into a flirtation. This myth was used by Congressmen Hammer (North Carolina) and Underhill (Massachusetts) to delay the bill for several weeks until they were forced to admit they could find no truth to it. A provision of the measure called for women in a similar position as a male officer to have the same rank as that male, but Congressman Zihlman (Maryland) wanted to eliminate from the bill all such references to the possibility of promotion.[42]

It was the war emergency that finally compelled New York City to let women to join the force, allowing the nation's largest city to finally overcome entrenched opposition, doing so at a much later date than most large American cities. By August 1918 the Municipal Civil Service Commission announced that many vacancies existed in the police, fire, and street-sweeping departments. Since the age for policemen applicants, 21 to 30, was roughly the same as for the draft, and since an applicant had to be fit to be a policeman there were few applicants, mainly those deferred due to dependents. Thus, the commission announced, "The employment of women in the Police Department is to be extended as far as possible." They were not, however, to supplant men in the fire department, except in clerical positions. So severe was the shortage of firefighters that a call for volunteers went out, with the result that 200 male civilians were then sleeping in fire stations and answering calls without pay. Street sweepers were in short supply due to the draft and higher paying alternate jobs. Amid much controversy, the commission decided to employ females as street sweepers, but not as drivers of the trucks. The shortage was severe enough that the commission decided that anybody who scored a pass on the written examination would automatically receive at least a score of 70 (a pass) on the oral examination, and thus go on the list to await appointment. In the past some candidates had passed the written examination but not the oral, thus putting themselves out of the running. Lack of applicants was the reason behind the decision to basically scrap the oral section, but it was rationalized that with so much subjectivity the oral examination was unfair. As to the use of females in the police force, the commission acted to reassure people that they "will only be used for the protection of women and children."[43]

More permanent changes in the regular police force began in January 1918 when Enright appointed a 10-year veteran of the Brooklyn probation office, Ellen O'Grady, to the position of fifth deputy police commissioner. Enright stated he needed a female deputy because, "In this city every year there are hundreds of girls lured from their homes and their lives wrecked. Hundreds of other girls from all over the country, who come to this city seeking opportunities, are lured from the path of virtue, and finally are found leading a life of shame." O'Grady was to work to eliminate white slave traffic and direct the policy of the New York Police Department against men who annoyed women on the streets, in the subway, and on the elevated trains. Said Enright of O'Grady's duties, "Her time will practically be devoted to the investigation and elimination of the white slave traffic, also looking after loafers on street corners, subway and elevated trains, who make it their business to insult and annoy women and girls."[44]

Another of the first moves came in May 1918 when Police Commissioner Richard Enright announced that the Police Reserves was to have a women's auxiliary of volunteers, reorganized out of the Home Defense League. That idea originated with Special Deputy Commissioner Rodman Wanamaker, the head of the Police Reserves. Rodman argued that since New York women had the vote they should have an active part in enforcing the laws. He also made it clear these females would not have to "cope personally with rough and violent lawbreakers." Under his plan their function "would be to keep a finger on the city's pulse in an effort to detect signs of unlawful developments before they grew to serious proportions, to watch out for cases of sedition, to uplift the general moral atmosphere of the city in the neighborhood of their posts." If the need arose for the use of physical force to curb crime, a policeman would be called in. Rodman added that these women would be useful in "aiding in the Americanization of the alien elements of our population and reporting cases of sedition and disloyalty, aiding the various war activities, discovering and relieving cases of distress and destitution, comforting and cheering the unfortunate, advising and directing the weak, foolish and idle, and setting an example of high ideals, real unselfishness, and patriotism."[45]

Later that month the Women's Police Reserves began to be organized; many were the wives and sisters of policemen, and others were "prominent welfare workers." By July over 4,000 were enrolled and undergoing training. Another duty was to look for and report food and fuel violations of the ration system. Plans called for having one woman on duty on almost every block in the city but not to have them do patrol duty. Even though enrollment reached around 5,000, the Women's Police Reserves was abolished at the end of the war, almost before the group started. Of course, it was never viewed as anything other than a temporary measure.[46]

In May 1918 Enright announced he would shortly add a number of women to the police force. They would investigate white slavery, juvenile delinquency, and "attend to complaints made by women." At the time of that announcement O'Grady had five matrons doing detective work under her supervision. She was pleased to hear that New York City was to get its first official policewomen, but learned of this development from reporters not from the department. O'Grady stated, "These policewomen will be possessed of tact and discernment and have sympathy for young girls. They can instill into the mind of a girl who has erred better ideals and show her the consequences of her wrongdoing." Six policewomen were appointed by Enright on August 15, 1918, with four more on the following day. One of the first six was Mary Hamilton. Two of them, including Hamilton, had welfare work experience, and both had recently worked without compensation as volunteers in the police missing persons bureau. One was the widow of a city penitentiary warden, and another was the widow of a policeman shot to death on duty.

The other two had social work experience. These women were issued clubs, revolvers, handcuffs, and summons books; they had the same powers as men and drew the same pay, $1,200 per year. Enright had avoided using the civil service commission to select the women by calling his appointments exempt since this was an "experimental" move.[47] New York City's first uniformed policewomen, six in number, went on duty in the city on Thursday, August 15, 1918. They would pay special attention to the welfare of girls.[48]

When Police Commissioner Enright appointed those six in New York he distinctly said the policewomen were not a "war measure" to be discarded when peace returned. They were here for good, he stated. He was to appoint four more within a few days and in the coming year he said he expected to appoint 20 more. Those women had the same authority as men and would wear a uniform, at least part of the time, and carry a policeman's full equipment. They were to have zones to work, and not beats. Each would strive for the cooperation of women's clubs and welfare organizations in her district. Duties were to handle cases involving women and girls and they would be on duty at beaches and dance halls. Mashers would be one of their special areas of interest. The six that were first appointed ranged in age from early 20s to early 40s. Mrs. Mary C. Murtha (widow of a former warden at Blackwell's Island prison) was the mother of six children; Mrs. Madeline A. O'Neill was the widow of a policeman who died of wounds he received while on duty. The others, who all had experience in welfare work, were Mrs. Mary C. Hamilton, Miss Ethel L. Gay, Miss Rose Goldstein, and Miss Kathryn Hyde. They were to work under the direction of Mrs. Ellen O'Grady, fifth deputy police commissioner. In the article that listed their names their full home addresses were also published.[49]

On August 29 four more policewomen were appointed to the New York Police Department. They were to be instructed in their duties by police matrons after which the commissioner would create 10 zones and appoint one policewoman to each zone. The four new women appointed (their home addresses were also published) were Mrs. Julia F. Lee, Miss Mary Bracken, Miss Sarah Cummings, and Miss Genevieve M. McLoughlin.[50]

Reporter Elene Foster did a piece on the new policewomen in New York in September 1918. She reiterated that they were not a passing fad, not an experiment, and not even a "war measure." The policewoman was "simply the logical solution of one of our greatest problems, the proper care and protection of our women and girls and she has come to stay." Foster came across eight of them sitting around a table writing reports of their work the previous day and she wrote, "Nice, motherly, middle-aged women they were for the most part, with the exemption of two who were in the early twenties and who had the appearance of successful stenographers. They were all well dressed, in clothes that were decidedly feminine, and there was nothing about them that suggested in any way they were guardians of the law." Foster said they were then 17 female police working under the direction of O'Grady and that a "goodly number" had served as police matrons. Each morning the 17 assembled in O'Grady's office for instructions. Plans were discussed and questions answered. If a girl was reported as in need of a job O'Grady found a position for her; if a marriage was indicated she arranged for that. O'Grady furnished food and clothing and arranged temporary loans when there was need for such help. During their time on the job, Foster reported, the female police had devoted much time to improving conditions in the parks and on the beaches. O'Grady remembered a time years ago when she took her three young children for a day on the beach at Coney Island "and after searching in vain for a spot where they would be safe from sights and sounds which were unfit for them to see or hear she bundled them off home." Now she was determined to make the beaches "clean and wholesome recreation grounds." Foster went out one time and accompanied a policewoman as she walked the trails at Central Park, as the reporter had done a year earlier with Mrs. Douglas (one of the two women paid privately then by the Committee of Women on National Defense). The journalist observed that the policewomen devoted their greatest attention to 14 to 16-year-old girls, a group said to be susceptible "to the glamour of khaki and blue serge [soldiers and sailors]." When the policewoman spotted a girl and guy in the park she told the girl she was a policewoman and it was her business to take care of young girls. She then asked the girl many questions and if she was young took her home and had a discussion with her parents. From that time on she was protected and looked after by the policewoman. If the girl was unemployed work was found for her and "her name is given to the Big Sisters of her creed. It is a personal campaign with a conscientious following up."[51]

On May 27, 1919, in New York City, 10 new policewomen were appointed by Commissioner Enright, at a salary of $1,200 a year. The women did not come under civil service rules. They wore shields and carried revolvers, if they wished. That brought the total of New York City policewomen to 20. Among the new group was a black woman who was to be assigned to work in the black district of Harlem. A newly appointed Italian woman would take up her duties in the Italian quarter of the city. The new women (with home addresses published) were Mrs. Lillian J. Leffler, Miss Hortense Thompson, Mrs. Mary Coony, Mrs. Lillian A. Gordon, Mrs. Elizabeth Helms, Miss Helen M. Burns, Mrs. Sarah M. Ahern, Miss Anna Woolf, Mrs. Rae Nicoletti, and Mrs. Cora I. Parchment.[52]

Later in 1919, Ellen O'Grady, fifth deputy commissioner of police in New York City said, "It is a well known fact that boys and girls are becoming wayward and unmanageable at a young age than ever before. The work of the policewomen is protective and preventive. We must place a staying hand on the youth of the county and who is more capable or better qualified to do this than a woman?" This was a pronouncement meant to show the services of policewomen would be needed even more in the future. O'Grady concluded, "Of the many good things brought forth by the war I consider the appointment of policewomen one of the most important."[53]

One of New York City's policewomen found herself forced to leave the force not long after O'Grady made the pronouncements listed above. Miss Catherine Hyde, one of the first of the city's female police, married Detective Henry F. Schneider of the NYPD on September 17, 1919. Hyde had been appointed to her post in August 1918. A month later she met Schneider when they were put together on a missing girl case. Mrs. Schneider, 23, it was reported, would retire from the force. At the time she was hired as a policewoman she told her interviewers she had no intention of marrying.[54]

By September 1918, the women police reserves in New York City were then said to number about 4,500. Every precinct in greater New York had its quota of such women "quietly at work." The organization was then a little over two months old. They were on a "war footing" trained to meet any emergency that might come along, it was reported. The group was called the Women's Police Reserve while another group (of about 200) was called the Police Women's Training Corps. They were training to take civil service examinations for positions such as matron, policewoman, probation officer, and social investigator.[55]

Another article dealt briefly with their duties. Not much earlier one of the young women in the midnight blue skirt and coat, brass buttons and fatigue cap of the Women's Police Reserve entered a car on one of the transit lines in New York City. She sat beside a woman — and suddenly came to realize it was a man dressed as a woman. She went to the back platform. At the next stop she signaled a policeman and told him of the man dressed as a woman and said to arrest him. The officer complied and the fate of the impersonator was summed up on a police blotter by this comment, "Referred to the Secret Service." This article stated the 3,000 (not 4,500) women in the organization were being used for the benefit of the nation by the NYPD and had "uncovered scores of nests of spies, revealed dangerous aliens, spotted plotters" and reported hundreds of cases to the Secret Service. The Woman's Police Reserve was an idea that had been originally suggested by Deputy Commissioner Rodman Wanamaker. Commissioner Enright said frankly that it was an experiment — "We capitalized for the good of the nation on that extraordinary, often derided, but immensely valuable faculty known as woman's intuition." He added that woman's intuition "is a man's reasoning with much of the slower processes of the male brain eliminated and is, as has been proven by psychological tests both at Columbia and Harvard, correct twenty per cent oftener than man's slower logic."[56]

Ten more were appointed the next year. Because they proved their worth, and due to continued pressure form women's group, the state legislature passed an act in 1920 incorporating them into the police department as patrolwomen, equal in rank to patrolmen, but lacking the same pension benefits as matrons. The matrons were renamed policewomen. This confusing nomenclature was compounded by the fact that while qualifications for the two jobs differed with regard to education and so on, women were often assigned to the positions interchangeably. It was a situation which would not be resolved until 1937 when the then 95 policewomen (matrons) and 48 patrolwomen were incorporated under the single title of policewoman. In 1921 patrolwomen began to be hired under the rules and regulations of the Municipal Civil Service Commission. Applicants had to be at least 5'2", weigh 120 pounds at that height, be 21 to 35 years old, and have had experience in social welfare or nursing. Duties were described as "the moral protection of women and minors; the prevention of delinquency among women and minors; and the performance of such other duties as the Police Commissioner may assign." Enright's own views on policewomen were strictly conservative. In 1924, when England was trying to get rid of its policewomen, Enright said he agreed with Sir William Norwood of Scotland Yard in believing that women should not patrol because they were "unsuited to the task and they didn't have the necessary physical endurance."[57]

Those early patrolwomen engaged in the same duties as policewomen in other cities: that of looking after the welfare of girls and young women as well as working on prostitution, abortion cases, and fortune-telling scams. O'Grady praised these female police, noting that "the women are rendering very useful service in safeguarding the morals of young girls in their chance acquaintance with members of the opposite sex."[58]

Using policewomen to deal with prostitution was common throughout the United States; it was, of course, one of the reasons women were allowed into policing. In keeping with the male ideology of the day a writer from this period noted the reasons for having females deal with prostitution by saying — and inverting reality — "(a) the protection of men officers against a too constant contact with prostitutes, (b) the fear of false accusations by prostitutes against men officers."[59]

In March 1921 a Women's Precinct was established in New York City. This was a separate area and it had a separate building of its own, staffed entirely by females, containing a clinic, workroom, school, and a temporary hospital. The latter area was used to detain girls for a day or two after taking a venereal disease test and awaiting results. Prior to this precinct opening, females in those circumstances went through a court procedure and were held at one of the detention homes. Mary Hamilton, director of the Women's Precinct, felt such an experience for one of these girls could "embitter her whole mind and spoil her outlook on life." Hamilton added, "We feel that a great injustice sometimes is done to a woman under such conditions and that it is just one small part of our duty to right these wrongs. Women should handle these matters, question and examine these girls wherever possible." Runaway girls not charged with anything, at the request of their parents, could be accommodated in the building. Up to that time private homes were being used. In those private homes were also detained "immoral girls and women" pending investigation or trial. Hamilton was worried because in those homes "innocent girls are brought into contact with and contaminated morally and otherwise by immoral women."

When the short-lived Women's Precinct was established, the women took over a building abandoned by the men as a "dingy, dirty rathole." They cleaned it up and arranged it to be as unlike a police station as possible. Located at 434 West Thirty-Seventh Street in New York's notorious Hell's Kitchen area, the detention section for holding girls not charged with anything and keeping them separate from the hardened criminals and the "immoral" was euphemistically called the Guest Dormitory for Moral Girls. Upon the opening of this facility a *New York Herald* editorial praised the concept, saying, "The idea thing would be to keep women away from police stations altogether, to keep out of women's lives all that police interference represents.... The next best thing, unquestionably, is to make women's contact with the police as little demoralizing to them as possible."[60]

The undermining of the women police had already begun. When Hamilton was appointed director of the Women's Precinct, O'Grady had already resigned as fifth deputy commissioner. No reason for her resignation was reported. Isabella Goodwin was named acting deputy commissioner. Four months later Goodwin had lost that title, then being listed as officer in charge of the Women's Precinct. Hamilton was no longer director, having been transferred to headquarters, and there was no longer a female deputy commissioner.[61]

Women in New York City continued to lobby. A committee of 25 women representing various city groups, headed by Dr. Anna Hochfelder, called on Enright with a petition bearing 10,000 signatures calling for the appointment of at least 15 more patrolwomen. Speaking before a women's group on the question of female police, Enright stated, "There cannot be a field for women in the regular uniformed part of the department, not as patrolmen, of course; the conditions off the work bars them for the same reasons that only men are taken into the army and navy."[62]

Early in 1924 Enright appointed Hamilton as director of the police-women, said to number then about 100 (including matrons). However, the women were not organized within a separate bureau. By then the Women's Precinct had disappeared, having closed in September 1923. The commissioner also reorganized the "masher squad" that worked the subway trains during rush hours. This squad was composed of five policewomen and five detectives, with Enright having selected the women for their "comeliness." Arresting of mashers was left strictly to the male members of the squad, although the females had the same authority because "the plain-clothes men can do the subduing more easily and perhaps can save the policewoman from having a fight on her hands." While mashers were said to be a serious problem, an article of the period stated that cases were seldom reported in the press. Sentences of six months in prison were common for men caught and convicted of annoying women. It was hoped that female victims would get a fairer hearing with female police on the squad. Said one female victim of the time before women were on the squad, "it was unsafe at times to appeal to the train guard for protection, for abuse from him might follow. I have even known a policeman to take the accused man's part and counteraccuse the woman. Now, with the policewomen on duty and with the masher evil recognized as one to be put down, a woman has nothing to fear from making a legitimate complaint." However, this supposed crackdown on mashers angered those who preferred to blame the victim. They complained; "many an innocent man may be victimized on the foolish complaint of hysterical or notoriety-seeking women." This writer was not worried about policewomen arresting men, noting that since they often worked in pairs, "few policewomen have trouble arresting a man. Their difficulty begins when the captive is a woman."[63]

Policewomen in large cities often monitored classified ads in the newspapers to be on the lookout for sexual harassers. A man would place an ad for a nonexistent post such as receptionist, clerk, or model, and then harass applicants. In 1925 one of the New York City policewomen answered one of these ads as though she was an applicant: apparently, someone had complained about the advertisement. As she waited in the outer officer to be interviewed, several women came out of the inner office stating they had been "insulted." When it was her turn to be interviewed, the policewoman entered the inner office, whereupon the man who placed the ad "hugged" her, as the New York Times reported. Presumably, this was code for something more serious and specific. Upon conviction this man was sentenced to six months in jail.[64]

Toward the end of 1924 Enright made another confusing move when he announced the creation of a new Policewomen's Bureau, with Hamilton in charge. That is, he established a formal, separate division, as compared to the informal structure he had announced early in that year. The purpose of the bureau was to provide a central office where women and girls seeking aid, assistance, and advice relating to police service could go and discuss their situations with female officers.[65]

During that year Commandant Mary Allen of London arrived in New York City as part of a visit to study the use of policewomen in the United

States. She was described as the head of a training school for English police-women. Her uniformed presence seemed to unsettle the *New York Times*, which, after describing her uniform, sought to reassure those who might be uneasy by noting that "the feeling grows that she is truly feminine in all essentials of character and thought as if she busied herself only with pouring tea and household matters."[66]

Most of the female police were women over 35 in New York City in the mid–1920s. Hamilton hoped to attract younger women: "Girls who will go out among other girls." She also felt applicants must bring "the spiritual quality, which is indispensable." Hamilton was no radical; she wanted to see babies fingerprinted at birth. Yet she was fully committed to the need for women police remarking, "The police women are to the social problem what the nurse is to the medical problem. You've got to have us!... It makes me wild at the opposition we encounter.... The war changed a great many things. The police force was one.... Only women can help women." A 1924 article about her was entitled, "A 'Mother' of Disillusioned Girls."[67]

Hamilton used that same analogy by once remarking that "in many ways the position of a woman in a police department is not unlike that of a mother in a home." For Hamilton, policewomen became needed when citizens and groups started to realize that prevention and protection were important; that prevention logically started with children. Still she staunchly advocated separate spheres of policing for the genders. Hamilton cited Raymond Fosdick, a noted police authority of the period, as having said, "When policewomen put on uniforms, carried guns and clubs they became little men, but when they did their work as women, they rendered a great service." Added Hamilton, "And it is certainly a fact that no woman can really be a good police-woman, unless she works as a woman and carries with her into a police department a woman's ideals.... Policewomen have taken up policewoman-ship, not with the idea of replacing men in this work, but for the purpose of aiding and assisting them."[68]

When women began to enter policing in America Hamilton said that male officers "did not favor the idea of women entering the field." However, she thought that was mainly due to the misuse of such women. Citing an unnamed large Eastern city where a policewoman objected to her duties and was quoted as having said, "I had joined the force to help fallen women and wayward children. Instead I was forced to accompany men of the lowest type, professional stool pigeons, around town, to enter dives of the worst type and do work which could be done much better by men." Hamilton viewed the problem there as one in which that city tried to make use of their policewomen as detectives instead of preventive officers. Referring to an unnamed Connecticut city, Hamilton told of a women's league there which, by resolution, violently denounced attempts to appoint female cops because they believed

Women practicing with handguns under supervision of policeman, circa 1913 to 1920.

women wouldn't do police duty "with the ability, efficiency and promptness of a man." Females could be accepted by policemen, thought Hamilton, by showing through their work that they were sincere, honest, and earnest. Once they did so "any antagonism that the men may be inclined to display at first quickly vanishes." She wanted to see policewomen organized as a separate unit, under the command of a woman. One policewoman for every 100 policemen was then the standard that many European women lobbied to attain; Hamilton agreed, terming it "a fair ratio."[69]

While other accounts related the confusing changes in the Women's Precinct, in her book Hamilton unfortunately mentioned nothing about problems there or about any interference or hostility from the male police establishment, of which there must have been some; nor did she give any reason for its demise, or even mention its demise at all.[70]

When a policewoman was out on the streets the ideal officer, in Hamilton's view, performed the patrol function with "quiet, dignified, unobtrusive watchfulness." Patrolling was more difficult for women than for men because it was harder "for a woman to remain inconspicuously in any public place for any length of time, particularly at night.... There is one unfailing protection, and that is the knowledge of the fact that the policeman on post stands ready to come to your aid." Resorting to her powers of arrest was something a policewoman should do only as a "last resort." Policewomen of long experience were said to boast of not yet having made their first arrest. It was Hamilton's policy that her policewomen have arrests performed by men so that the reputation of a policewoman as a "friend and protector may be maintained." Hamilton based this on the idea that "the policewoman has been likened to the mother. Hers is the strong arm of the law as it is expressed in a woman's guiding hand." As to the future, Hamilton predicted more policewomen: "The field of service, however, will not change. Women protective officers will always confine their efforts to work with children, girls and women."[71]

Agitation for more policewomen in New York City continued. During 1925 Anna Hochfelder led a drive to add at least another 100 female police. Hamilton addressed one of the meetings organized by Hochfelder, lending her support. On the last day of 1925 the outgoing (on that day) Commissioner Enright appointed 25 females to the force, most of them as matrons.[72]

Mary Hamilton had gone out of her way to not antagonize the male police establishment, never speaking out about the resistance she and her policewomen must have faced. It did her no good. George McLaughlin took over as police commissioner on January 1, 1926. Three weeks later he announced that the rumors that Hamilton, the "original policewoman," had been relieved of her command were false. However, on January 26 Hamilton tendered her resignation to McLaughlin, effective immediately. Claiming to bear no animosity toward McLaughlin, she said she resigned because she had "done my bit." Her letter of resignation to McLaughlin read in part that the policewoman, "could not, by reason of her sex, do the same work that the policeman did; that if she donned a uniform and carried a gun, for instance, she was worthless, since for that type of service one policeman is equal to ten policewomen.... The policewoman's field was distinctly crime preventive and protective work with children, girls and women, she being for these purposes a kind of community mother."[73]

Early in 1927 there were 95 policewomen (matrons) and 30 patrolwomen on the New York force. An article in the *New York Times* valued them for their "tact, gentleness and diplomacy in dealing with cases involving women and children." Also remarked on was their "special facility" in dealing with the insane, fortune-tellers, and cases of missing persons. In these areas of policing females had a "woman's intuition," which gave them an advantage that policemen "could not be expected to possess." Her mere presence could work wonders: "She is said to be an influence for good ... because the sight of her arouses a sense of shame rather than fear," which keeps males "walking the primrose path."[74]

In 1928 there was a flap over whether or not all the female police should be forced to buy uniforms, even though only those doing duty in station houses as matrons in New York actually wore them. In an unusual public burst of candor and hostility New York City police commissioner Warren snapped, "That's all they're good for anyway."[75]

At a 1929 meeting of the Women's Press Club one speaker was Haley Fiske, president of the board of managers of the New York Reformatory for Women. She argued for more policewomen in New York, saying they could be more effective in some areas where policemen failed. "They can clean up the movie houses, cabarets and suppress petting in parked automobiles." Another speaker was Mary Sullivan who wanted to see 400 to 500 females on the force instead of the current 125, adding, "We are the victims of the Police Commissioners. They come and go. Some like us and some don't; some sympathize with us and some don't know we are there." The next victim was Sullivan herself.[76]

In April 1929 Sullivan ordered and led a raid on a birth control clinic. It was one of many established in New York and other cities by Margaret Sanger. A storm of protest followed the raid in which five women, two doctors, and three nurses were arrested. It was then illegal to dispense birth control information. Many prominent people protested the arrests, including officers of the New York County Medical Society and of the New York Academy of Medicine. Some 500 people, mostly females, including doctors and representatives of civic organizations, turned out at the preliminary hearing to rally to the defense of the accused. On May 11, 1929, Sullivan, who had started her

Inspector Cross and policewoman Miss Clark demonstrate how to apply handcuffs, circa 1913 to 1920.

career in 1911 as a station house matron, was removed as director of the Women's Bureau by Police Commissioner Whalen. Captain James Brady was placed in charge of the Women's Bureau, with Sullivan retained as assistant to Brady. Whalen gave no explanation for this shake-up; however, the raid was believed to have been the excuse. Sullivan refused to comment except to say she did not believe her demotion had anything to do with the raid. Speculating on the reasons, a reporter wrote, "It was believed also that the Police Commissioner had made up his mind not to have women in commanding positions in the department." This reporter also noted that the former administration under Enright "did not favor policewomen." Whalen received a letter from the New York City Federation of Women's Clubs protesting the appointment of a man to head the Women's Bureau. Nevertheless, the appointment stood, with the result that as of 1929 New York did not have, in fact, a true women's bureau.[77]

During September 1919 an investigation of the Washington, D.C., Metropolitan Police was underway, an investigation that had been ordered by the US Congress. In that probe the Woman's Bureau had come in for, reportedly, "its share of criticism." The Washington system of utilization of its female police had been selected by the International Association of Policewomen as the model to be used wherever municipal organizations put together a female force of their own. Van Winkle was president of the IAP and that group had recently ended its annual convention in Atlantic City, New Jersey. It had convened in conjunction with the Social Workers' Conference. The Woman's Bureau then had 15 members and hoped to have 30 policewomen when it was fully staffed. To answer criticism and to justify itself, the Woman's Bureau drafted a full and comprehensive list of its duties and services that it presented to Congress.[78]

Those duties and services were broken down into three categories: preventive, corrective, and general police work. Preventive had two subsections: (1) supervision and general survey of movies, dance halls, skating rinks, railway stations, parks, large public gatherings, and (2) welfare work by special workers: voluntary probation; finding positions for girls; advising as to associates, amusements, etc.; and working with family on behalf of delinquents. Under the heading corrective were six subsections: (1) voluntary probation and voluntary commitments to public institutions in other states, of first offenders over seventeen years, because there were neither laws nor institutions to cover their needs in the District of Columbia; (2) psychopathic and physical examinations with the view to securing proper disposition of the case, and treatment; (3) thorough investigation to find all negative and positive facts in a case in order to arrive at the inner mental life of the girl, so that intelligent help could be extended; (4) earnest attempt to remove or mitigate cause of delinquency; (5) locating missing girls and working with their families to prevent repeating; (6) return of fugitive children to parents, guardians or institutions. Under the heading general police work were five subsections: (1) detection of crime and apprehension of criminals: sex offenders, shoplifting, etc.; (2) helping the courts by furnishing the judges and prosecutors with the results of our investigations; (3) care of socially diseased through voluntary and court commitments to hospitals; (4) cooperation with men of the Police Department in securing information; being present with female offenders in identification bureau interviewing and searching female prisoners; (5) escorting women and girls to homes and institutions in other states.[79]

Early in October 1919 Mina Van Winkle, head of the Washington police-women announced that her people would not form a union of their own, as the policemen of the Washington force had done. At the time the policemen were organizing their union the women made an effort to cooperate, but were denied the privilege of membership in the new association. It was thought later that the women might organize their own union and become affiliated with the American Federation of Labor, but Van Winkle was said to be of the opinion that the women felt that to organize a labor union branch would be in violation of their oath of office. A bill had been introduced in the US Congress by Representative Gould, of New York, which would make it illegal for Washington policemen to be members of the American Federation of Labor, the umbrella group with which most trade unions affiliated. "I believe we will get the same privileges as the men do with their union," said Van Winkle. "We took an oath to serve the government when we became members of this force, and we cannot serve two masters.... We thought at first we would like to join with the men, but after we were not permitted to do so we were glad we had not organized."[80]

According to Ellen O'Grady's annual report on the New York City police-women, released in October 1919, 280 girls between the ages of 12 and 18 had been rescued from "perilous company" at Coney Island during the summer just ended. Thirty-five of them were runaways who were sent back to their homes and through the cooperation of other district policewomen, parents, and welfare societies, "most of them were cured of their truancy." Two police-women, Miss Madeline O'Neill and Miss Hortense Thompson, were assigned to night duty at the Coney Island resort (two of the 20 female police). They roamed the area from 7 P.M. until 4 A.M. "and through experience acquired the ability to distinguish girls who didn't belong from those who did or were properly chaperoned." Girls seen talking to "objectionable men" were led aside for quiet conversations and warnings. If necessary, the name and address of the girls were taken, "the parents notified and sometimes home conditions investigated. In a few extreme instances rebellious girls were arrested, there being no other way to detain them until inquiry could be made." During daytime hours four policewomen patrolled the Coney Island beaches and were instrumental "in sending to their homes 250 girls who, it seemed, "would be better off with their families." Others in the female police had been on similar duties in the parks of New York City. O'Grady felt strongly, reinforced by the work of her policewomen, that a curfew law was needed in the city.[81]

The Woman's Bureau of the Washington, D.C., police force appointed its first black member in August 1920. or, as a reporter described her, "a colored copette." Adelaide Child was 25 years old, a college graduate and a social worker. Policemen on the Washington force numbered 839, of which 50 were black.[82]

The problem of sexual harassment (flirting and mashing in this account) arrived back on the Washington, D.C., media scene in October 1920. In answer to the charge that "the whole male population of Washington is flirting" Mina Van Winkle declared, "It's the girl's fault." Thus did the head of Washington's female police turn an unsympathetic ear to the cry for an anti-mashing campaign from the girls of Washington, as expressed by Mrs. Sarah V. Farling, who had been the city's first policewoman. "A girl can't walk down F Street these days without being insulted," declared Farling. "Why the whole male population of Washington is flirting, the ice man, the carpenter, the chauffeur, every kind of man, and, yes, even the nice man." Responded Van Winkle, walk down F Street with me and what do you see: "A girl, a fur hung loosely around her neck, a pocketbook suspended seductively from her arm and a hobble walk. Of course the men flirt. And can you blame them? It's a shame to abuse the men of Washington this way. Why the men of Washington are the finest in the world." Van Winkle went on to declare that she did not believe in an anti-mashing campaign for Washington. "Rid the streets and movies of the unescorted girl and the problem will solve itself," she argued. Farling, on the other hand, wanted a "good old-fashioned mashing campaign." Explained the former policewoman, "It's 'Hello Cutie' and 'Where did you get that hat,' and 'I wonder who she is waiting for,' and like remarks that greet a girl when she passes a crowd of boys hanging out on a street corner. I really believe the only solution of the problem is an anti-mashing campaign." Farling said it was bad enough when she was a police officer and used to patrol dance halls and other public places but it was worse now, more serious and more widespread.[83]

Despite her unsympathetic attitude toward the flirting problem, on the night of October 18, 1920, Van Winkle was on the street with two policewomen, investigating that very situation. Four men in a touring car, reportedly, tried to pick them up. "Come on, let us take you for a ride," yelled one of the men. Yes, replied Van Winkle as the three police officers stepped into the car. She then directed them to drive to police headquarters. As soon as the car reached the First Precinct the four men (and one woman) in the car were arrested by Officer Emily Steele. A charge of disorderly conduct was laid against all five, and they were released on $25 bail each. Those arrested were Carl F. Gunnell (chauffeur), John Thomas Williams (Salt Lake City), John Wilson (Salt Lake City), William Harrison (St. Louis), and May Toomey (alias Margaret Scott — Washington, D.C.). The incident took place at 1:30 A.M. while the three policewomen were on the lookout for mashers. Steele was one of the three. Those arrests were the first in connection with the anti-mashing campaign advocated by Farling.[84]

During the spring of 1921 Mina Van Winkle announced she wanted 45 more policewomen for her Washington Woman's Bureau. That caused the

Policeman and policewoman practice self-defense.

Civil Service Commission to set examinations for the position of policewoman to be held on June 8. Qualifications for the position included: must have "personality," be a graduate of a four-year course at a standard high school, or have at least 14 college entrance units of study, and two years in "systematic social service," or educational work. Applicants had to be at least 21 years of age and under 35. Salaries were as follows: class 1, $1,400; class 2,

$1,560; class 3, $1,660; sergeant, $1,800. With respect to qualifications Van Winkle said, "I do not wish to emphasize the pulchritudinous qualification of the applicant but it is recognized that beauty in a welfare worker, such as policewomen, add to the influence she has in effecting the reform of the little wayward girl. I do not mean I want girls with doll-baby faces, but girls with sweet, wholesome faces—on the order of classic beauty." She added, "Then there is the psychological effect. One will do more for a beautiful woman than for a homely one."[85]

All 22 of the women who took the Washington civil service exam for policewoman on June 8 had to then pass a personality test before becoming eligible to be appointed to the Woman's Bureau. In that personality test the applicants were judged on personal appearance, tact, diplomacy, judgment, common sense, and general deportment. Van Winkle administered those personality tests and also engaged the applicant in conversation to draw out her personal qualifications and see if she had the ability to be a policewoman. Her Woman's Bureau was the only government bureau that required a personality test on the part of applicants. That personality test was Van Winkle's own idea.[86]

A couple of months later the Washington Woman's Bureau began to search over a greater geographic range in order to try to obtain more policewomen. It was announced that competitive exams for those position were to be held in 29 cities in the US to fill vacancies in Van Winkle's department. Successful applicants could come from any city in America.[87]

In New York City in December 1921 some 2,500 policewomen, members of the police reserve force (a wartime measure that apparently had not yet been disbanded) were ordered out to direct traffic in school streets in New York City during the milk strike. They remained unpaid volunteers. However, on the first rainy day after being ordered to show up many did not bother, as they found the weather to be cold, rainy, and in general too inclement.[88]

Duties of policewomen were essentially uniform in American cities. When a 1927 questionnaire was sent to 40 cities, 35 replied that female police supervised their dance halls, and 34 responded that policewomen regularly visited their motion picture theaters. Shoplifting was considered a crime engaged in almost solely by women, hence it often became the purview of policewomen. In Washington two officers were assigned to the stores patrol for several years, with the reported result that the professional shoplifter was "almost entirely eliminated." Policewomen sometimes were called in to assist in more major crimes, usually to deal with the female associates of criminals in the belief these women would talk to women whereas "nothing the policeman can do will induce them to open their lips." It was also believed that female criminals could get away with things when only policemen were involved by the "artful use of their feminine charms.... Not so when the policewoman is on the trail." Nevertheless, protective and preventive work with women and children, as one journalist noted, "must remain the greatest objective of the policewoman."[89]

The image of the mother remained strong. When a 1929 article in *Sunset* profiled Berkeley, California, policewoman Elizabeth Lossing, the author remarked that if someone had mentioned the word policewoman to him the day before meeting Lossing "I would instantly have visualized a hard-boiled, business-like sort of Carrie Nation, with a club in place of a hatchet — a kind of super-female-jail-warden hardened by her contact with the tough, alcoholic or dope riddled women I have seen in police-courts." Lossing, a trained psychiatric social worker, was reported as seldom making an arrest, having no beat, interviewing women and children in her office, and solving the situation herself by referring the person to some outside social service agency. The writer summed up Lossing by describing her as a "fine motherly type ... a kind of Municipal Mother Superior to all of Berkeley's lonely urchins." Like so many other American cities, Berkeley would only hire trained social workers as policewomen.[90]

At the end of the 1920s the idea that women had a role in policing — but a very limited role — was mostly unquestioned. Detroit policewoman Eleonore Hutzel commented, "It is agreed that while most of the problems coming to the attention of the police can be handled best by the men officers, there are some cases where this is not true." Helen Pigeon, executive secretary of the International Association of Policewomen, remarked that female police "are keeping house in the police department, building quietly, but very solidly for the future, avoiding the furor of a spring cleaning, and guarding what is always a woman's greatest concern, the safety and happiness of youth."[91]

When the Bureau of Public Personnel Administration studied the area it concluded there was considerable disagreement as to the duties to be performed by policewomen. However, it defined the controversy as to whether females should be confined to a role of matron only or that of having a limited policing function. "There is now almost universal agreement that Policewomen should not attempt to do general patrol work," said the bureau. The physical demands were simply too great. Also precluded were duties such as traffic regulation by officers stationed at street corners, again due to physical demands. Favoring a limited policing function, the bureau argued that runaway girls and rape victims would talk more freely and openly to a woman than to a man, and "men can't check women's toilets." Custody and care of the young should be given into female responsibility as men, in this area, were "good-hearted bunglers at best." Within policing there was a considerable field in which women could do better police work than men. However, the bureau concluded that there was another field — a larger one — in which men could do better police work than women.[92]

The International Association of Policewomen (IAP) favored the establishment of a Women's Bureau (headed by a female) in all cities in the United States. Yet this group subscribed to the limited role concept and took pains in its attempts not to antagonize the male police. Their position was that "the woman officer does not and should not do the kind of work our police officers are actually doing." She was generally not engaged in detecting crime but as a social worker doing public welfare work. The fact that female police did not wear uniforms showed, according to the IAP, "how far their activities are from those of the regular members of the police force." Women on the force were public guardians not in the technical sense but literally.[93]

Journalist Frances McMullen felt that until fairly recently the word "police" was viewed as being incompatible with "lady," and some people still believed that "decent" women would not take the job. For McMullen the fact that female police wore no uniforms was a plus, since they thus displayed "no self-assertive manner of authority," in keeping with the concept of prevention, not apprehension. McMullen pointed out that there were some cities where policewomen had been abolished and others where policewomen had resigned voluntarily because of the type of work required. Rather than consider this result to be the outcome of a hostile and harassing male police establishment, McMullen argued it was a result of an inappropriate concept of the policewoman's place or that inappropriate females were appointed, such as through political pull, with no regard to suitability. McMullen concluded by stating, "The organized policewoman movement is not a feminist one, concerned with demonstrating that women can fill policemen's shoes. Rather it is sociological, aiming to show that women are valuable as police with specialized functions ... women who are social workers with police power, and not lady-cops."[94]

Hutzel, reporting on the 1929 Detroit survey of policewomen, reported that in no city were the requirements for appointment as a policewoman lower than the requirements for appointment of a policeman. In many cities the requirements were "very much higher." By Hutzel's estimate about half the American cities employing policewomen paid them the same salaries as they did males, while in most other cities they received less. Appointment of policewomen in many cities was provided for by some legislative measure; of 85 cities surveyed 36 had a city ordinance in place, four had a state law, two had it incorporated into the city charter, while 43 cities had no legislative provision. Such a provision established policewomen formally, defined their functions, the qualifications necessary, the number of policewomen to be appointed, the provision for a minimum number, and whether or not there was to be a separate women's bureau. Hutzel considered such a legislative provision as necessary "because there are records of cities where a well-organized service of policewomen has been entirely wiped out, or at least rendered impotent, by a changing city administration." Problems for women breaking into police work, said Hutzel, centered on the fact that women were breaking into a man's world and they were bringing to policing a new type of service — preventive and protective work. She felt that whether a women's bureau succeeded or failed depended on the chief of police. If he was sympathetic, then others in the department followed suit. However, "In cities where the chief is not favorably disposed to preventive protective work and is antagonistic toward women officers the opposite is the case and the efforts which many capable women have made have not succeeded in changing this attitude."[95]

Despite the hostility and resistance of policemen to policewomen it was only briefly mentioned by writers of the era. In her history, Chloe Owings noted that "a goodly number of the directing heads of police forces and many policemen had opposed such appointments." However, she went on to state that advocates of female police pointed out that where women had proved themselves unfit it was because the wrong type of woman had been chosen or that they had to perform police functions for which their gender made them unsuitable. Owings also suggested that no concerted opposition to policewomen had arisen in police departments— where the attitude was that they had yet to prove themselves good police officers—compared to an organized movement in Great Britain where the police federations of England, Wales, and Scotland had put themselves on record as opposed to female police.[96]

In one respect that was true as the International Association of Chiefs of Police (IACP) at its 1922 convention — August Vollmer was then its president as well as being chief of the Berkeley, California, force — adopted a statement that "the primary function of policewomen is to deal with all cases in which women and children are involved either as offenders or as victims of offense." It was a statement which accepted policewomen, but only on limited terms and in limited areas. Vollmer was forward-looking in that at the convention a number of other resolutions were passed that recognized crime prevention as a major police function. In addition, minimum standards were set out for the selection of female police, standards later accepted by the IAP — standards far exceeding those set for male police.[97]

August Vollmer was chief at Berkeley from 1905 to 1932, where he was considered an innovative leader. From the start he supported Wells and her IAP. As head of the IACP he was instrumental in getting the statement supporting policewomen passed. Nevertheless, his view of female police was to see them with a very limited role, similar to that of community social workers, forging a link between the police and a community's social work resources. Vollmer once said that the "right kind of woman does not need a uniform or gun any more than other social workers do."[98]

Sometimes the male police establishment got rid of women for their own "good." In 1921 in Kalamazoo, Michigan, Chief Taffe requested the resignation of two female police as their "feminine jealousies" had disrupted the police department. "Something had to be done. The women are supposed to work together irrespective of personalities, but there has been more or less friction for weeks and co-operation has become impossible. Dismissal was the only solution," explained Taffe.[99]

One observer of the general scene wrote, "It must be acknowledged that in some cities ... there was a lack of departmental backing and cooperation which made effective work impossible" for policewomen. Also noted was that "in some instances, also, the social workers in the community have not recognized the real importance of the police function in this field and have withheld necessary cooperation."[100]

The caricature treatment of policewomen as Amazon-like creatures in the media was so pronounced that it prompted Miss E. Miner, executive secretary of the New York Probation and Protective Association, to emphatically declare that female cops did not police a beat and make arrests the way men did. However, she added, "Even more damaging than the abuse by the press was the resistance policewomen encountered from male police officers and police administrators." Antagonism stemmed from the idea that a woman's place was in the home and also from prejudice against social workers. The authoritarian, powerful world of policemen was diametrically opposite to that of the caring, casework method of social workers. While all females pursuing professional careers were the targets of a certain amount of contempt, "the disdain for women who chose to enter a traditionally male profession such as policework was even greater." Energies of policewomen "were often diverted from working full-time in areas such as protective services to defend and explain their true purpose and function." Political obstacles at the local level often interfered with or completely halted the work of policewomen. For example, the election of a new mayor often meant the appointment of a new police commissioner. Such a turnover sometimes led to a different attitude toward female police in that city: direct or indirect pressure might be applied to cause the director of the women's bureau to resign, and internal changes might take place whereby policemen stopped referring appropriate cases to the policewomen, instead handling the cases themselves.[101]

6

Foreign, 1917–1929

Agitation for female police continued throughout the world during the post–World War I period. At a 1926 Paris meeting of the International Women's Suffrage Alliance the delegates unanimously passed a resolution that policewomen should be appointed in all countries with the full power and status of policemen and to be employed particularly in cases relating to women and children. In a mocking article it was reported that these women also decided by vote that religion and domestic science were "unsuitable subjects for discussion by feminists." One of the speakers at the meeting was England's Mary Allen, "chief of the British 'Bobbyettes,' in full regalia with mannish haircut, military boots and monocle."[1]

In 1923 at Geneva, Switzerland, the League of Nations Assembly adopted a resolution in favor of the employment of females in police work throughout the world. Favoring the resolution was British representative Dame Edith Lyttleton, who declared that women "were not pressing for the employment of members of their sex as police to do the same thing as men but because they knew women in such positions could exercise a great preventive influence." She added that if you asked anyone who had anything to do with patrolling open spaces they would tell you that "the mere presence of women often produces an extraordinarily good effect. The most degraded of both our sexes have at the bottom of their souls some kind of reverence for women as women, probably due to the influence of their mothers." Lyttleton concluded by urging delegates to go home and work to get females appointed to the police; "You'll find a new influence abroad if you do."[2]

The league passed a similar resolution in 1924 and 1925 sponsored by its Advisory Commission for the Protection and Welfare of Children and Young People, Traffic in Women and Children Committee. Women police, it was hoped, would better address the problems of delinquency and prostitution and their prevention. That advisory group conducted a survey of countries to determine the extent of the use of policewomen. There were 34 replies received to this 1927 survey — 33 countries and one separate reply for the

British colonies. In nations where they were employed, most policewomen had as their chief duty the supervision of public morals and dealing with cases of sexual offenses. Responses were evenly split, with 17 countries replying that they employed policewomen and 17 saying they did not. Countries that did were Argentina, Australia, Czechoslovakia, Denmark, Egypt, Estonia, Finland, Great Britain, the Irish Free State, the Netherlands, New Zealand, Norway, Romania, Sweden, Switzerland, the United States, and the Free City of Danzig. Countries that did not employ female police were South Africa, China, Dominican Republic, France, Greece, India, Japan, Latvia, Liberia, Lithuania, Monaco, Siam, Venezuela, the British colonies, Belgium, Iceland, and Poland.[3]

Greece replied that the conditions there precluded the employment of women for the supervising of public morals. France declared that it was exceedingly doubtful whether women's employment in the supervision of prostitution would be received favorably by public opinion. South Africa stated it had employed female police in the past but the experiment was not an unqualified success, with the result that it had been discontinued. India replied that it had in the past referred the question to local governments for consideration, and these concluded that employing policewomen was not a "practical proposition." This conclusion was affirmed by the Indian central government, which added; "There was no suitable material in India for the formation of such a force and that such a force, if formed, would be of little value." When the advisory group wrote to Belgium the minister of the interior responded that it was up to the local mayors. Letters from the group to all 29 mayors produced no reply from 25, while the other four considered the proposal of employing policewomen as "useless or ill-timed." Siam stated, "It would not be wise to employ women." In addition, the group heard from the German state of Bavaria, which declared that women were not well adapted, due to lack of physical strength, for the work, as those engaged would have to pit themselves against the most cunning and unscrupulous male criminals: "Policewomen would require to be protected by male police officers. Furthermore, women lack the necessary qualities of mind — above all, resoluteness and clearheadedness in situations called for immediate action."[4]

Another questionnaire on the issue was sent in 1924 to 30 mayors of the largest French cities, drawing replies from 21 of them. Among the reasons they gave for not employing female police was that French customs would not fall into line with the appointment of women as guardians of the peace. "Women were meant to be mothers and homemakers," was one of the comments elicited, as was, "The French mind would naturally refuse to accept this possibility."[5]

While half of the responding countries indicated they did employ policewomen, their use was often very marginal. Argentina employed a few in its intelligence section to supervise the fingerprinting of women and children who needed identity documents. Australia had 26 working in all its states except Queensland; four of these were employed in New South Wales where they had all the powers of a male constable but were appointed as special constables. Denmark employed six; Finland, which had appointed its first two in 1907, then had five. Egypt employed "two European ladies" in the Bureau of the Supervision of Public Morals. Their job was to determine the locations of sites used for prostitution. Estonia stated it had a few in "Morals Police" who were responsible for registering prostitutes and supervising their medical exams. All four Irish policewomen were employed in Dublin where they had no power of arrest. Their working hours were 9:45 A.M. to 5:30 P.M. The Netherlands had a few in social work functions who were called "Children's Police." Also used in social work functions were the six in Sweden, all employed in Stockholm. Those Swedish policewomen were called "police sisters." Switzerland employed four as police assistants. New Zealand had four women called matrons who performed the typical social work policewomen functions.[6]

While Germany had hired females for its police department as early as 1903 in various cities for typical female duties, these women were considered to have even less formal attachment to the regular police forces than early policewomen in other countries such as the United States. American policewomen were regarded as second-class and second-rate, but definitely members of the force. In Germany they were second-class and second-rate but also civilians who happened to work in association with the police. Those early German policewomen positions were all abolished by the time of World War I, at the latest.

A few years after that war a new push for women police was on. This one was sparked by British authorities who were appalled at the rising rate of venereal disease among their troops stationed in occupied Germany. Their concern led to the creation of the first uniformed policewomen contingent in that country, established in Cologne in 1923, at the request of and with the help of British authorities. It was called the Women's Welfare Police. Chosen for this unit were four social workers with the most experienced one, Josefine Erkens, named to head the unit. Brought in to help set up and train them were a number of British WPS policewomen, led by Mary Allen who was then leader of that group. German women's group gave full support to the idea. As its mission this unit was to control the reportedly then rampant unregulated prostitution that caused a serious increase in venereal disease in British troops and, presumably, in German citizens as well. Uniformed German policewomen patrolled streets at night, talked to prostitutes, and took them for counseling and medical examinations. When she gave speeches Erkens emphasized the importance of organizational separation of male and female police units and of a separate career track for women that would not involve conventional police work or training. Over the next few years she would slowly retreat from that position. Briefly Erkens was the toast of Germany as she received a great deal of media attention.[7]

Cologne's policewomen's unit lasted only two years until it was suddenly disbanded. Cologne claimed it no longer had the money to fund the unit; and that made the unit's continuation impossible. Others claimed the real reason was that the unit was opposed by factions in both the regular police force and in social work agencies, both of whom felt threatened by the policewomen's unit. Amidst the controversy, and before the unit was disbanded, Erkens resigned, feeling it was impossible to carry out her work under those circumstances.[8]

A few months later in February 1926 Erkens went to Frankfurt to head up a new women's detective division being formed in that city. Prussian officials felt there would be a great advantage in having females in the same units as male detectives, in the role of "helpers of the officers." Walter Abegg, a Prussian interior ministry official, believed that using women police would bring a philosophy of caring and reform to the work, thus tempering the "authoritarian nature" of German police: "This will create the situation in which the police officer will be regarded, not as oppressor, but rather as friend, helper, and protector of his fellow citizens." Unhappy with the Frankfurt proposal was the League of German Women's Organizations, who wanted female police but only to be used in a social welfare orientation; therefore, their use in any kind of conventional law enforcement work was totally unacceptable. A compromise was struck, with the female police to become non-uniformed detectives and having to take the same examination for detective as men. These women would do standard detective work as it related to women, children, and young people, but they would not perform social work as such. However, they would be required to be trained as social workers and would have a separate organizational entity. Erkens was ambivalent about the detective work role, finally agreeing to take on that function for the policewomen she would head, saying, "It was only after getting assurances that women in the unit would only be utilized in accordance with their base nature that I consented to go to Frankfurt on a trial basis." The League of German Women's Organizations reiterated its position that "policewomen were to be used only for social welfare work and should be trained as social workers." Nevertheless, the group also insisted policewomen were not to interfere with the work of other private or public social welfare agencies. At the time Frankfurt was setting up its unit of policewomen the German states of Baden and Saxony were beginning to use females on street patrol. A few cities such as Berlin, Essen, and Hanover were also starting up units of policewomen, although mostly for station house work.[9]

Hamburg, Germany, decided in 1928 that its venereal disease problem was getting out of hand. As a solution the authorities decided to establish a female detective unit in the police department. Lured away from Frankfurt to head this unit was Erkens. Following Erkens to Hamburg were two policewomen from Frankfurt — Dopfer and Fischer. Germany's leading police journal, *Die Polizei*, ran an article at the time of Erken's appointment which read, in part, "One can postulate that women can be used in all aspects of detective work that fall naturally within their nature as women. Naturally all uses of women that go against their nature must be excluded." It argued that females were good at working with women, children, and juveniles — work that men could not do well — "therefore the duties of male police officers will not be diminished but only enhanced in a very fortunate way."

By then Erkens wanted more for policewomen. She wanted them to continue to handle the problems of women and children, but she also wanted to have the policewomen in her unit involved in each stage of the criminal process, including those dealing with men. She wanted the strict segregation of policewomen from male clients to stop. She also wanted male officers in her unit, men with training in psychology and social work who could apply her philosophy of policing. Two men were added to her unit, probably marking the first time anywhere that a policewoman was placed in direct command over policemen. Within her separate division Erkens headed a detective unit, a uniformed street patrol to deal with "endangered persons," and she was also in charge of a treatment facility for people in need. Erkens blurred the line between male and female, between police and social work, and because of this she stepped on a lot of male toes. A worried headline in a 1929 newspaper puzzled, "Women Police are Marching: It Is Now Permitted to Have Women Supervisors Over Men."[10]

Some sort of conflict had developed between Erkens and Dopfer, with the relationship becoming increasingly strained as two factions developed in the unit. Erkens recommended an official reprimand be given to Dopfer. A physical fight between the pair may or may not have taken place at the police station. On July 10, 1931, the bodies of Dopfer and Fischer were found on the island of Pellwurm in the North Sea off the German coast. A few days previous to this discovery Fischer had delivered a note to the police chief, stating she and Dopfer planned to commit suicide on Pellwurm. It was a case that was sensationalized in the press. The bodies were found tied together with each woman having been shot once in the head from close range. At the subsequent investigation the official verdict was the improbable one of suicide. The official explanation was that the women had walked into the water, bound themselves together, shot each other in the head with their service revolvers, and then fell into the North Sea. No official blame was attached to Erkens, but she was removed as head of the female unit and placed in a regular detective unit.

Soon after that, in October 1931, the women's unit was disbanded entirely, with the 12 remaining members placed into a regular division. Complaining about her treatment, even to the point of going on a brief hunger strike, Erkens appealed. She contended the disciplinary action against her was political, designed to not only get rid of her "but also the women's police division in the forum in which it had developed in Hamburg." In November 1931 the Senate of Hamburg upheld police authorities by stating she was not fit to hold a supervisory position in the police department. Erkens was allowed to retire from police service to protect her eligibility for a pension.[11]

Right after the suicides a meeting of the Presidium of German Criminal Investigators was held to inquire of all state police ministries about the usefulness of women police in light of the events in Hamburg. It was a question that went unanswered and quickly became academic. With the rise of Adolf Hitler and the Nazi takeover of Germany in 1933, all women police units were soon abolished.[12]

Prostitution was a major problem in Poland after World War I, with poverty forcing many women into that occupation. Women in that field had to register with the authorities for compulsory medical examinations and treatment. As a response to this in 1923, the Polish Committee for the Suppression of Traffic in Women and Children was set up. Working with the Polish Central Authority for the Prevention of Traffic, the committee was to coordinate and centralize the activities of all social organizations concerned with the care of women and children. The committee lobbied the Polish government to form a women's police force to be charged with combating prostitution — "traffic in women and children, and every form of depravity" — since they were convinced that females could deal with the problem much better than men. It was an idea that had many opponents, including "the majority of the police force, who feared that women would not be equal to the rigours of police work, and would therefore be more of a nuisance than a help, and a burden on the whole organization." Despite this the Polish government agreed with the lobbyists, resulting in the ministry of the interior being given the task of setting up a force of policewomen.[13]

In 1925 there were 30 women recruited, given three months training, and then 23 were assigned to the Criminal Investigation Department in Warsaw and seven to the same department in Lodz. Most of those women had a secondary school education, comparable to American junior high school, and two were university graduates. Selected to head this unit as chief commandant was Stanislawa Paleolog, then an army officer with the rank of lieutenant. Pay and benefits for the policewomen were the same as for male officers; however, the women did not wear uniforms. "In Warsaw they were made to feel the dislike of their male colleagues. In spite of this and other difficulties, unremembered or better forgotten today," the policewomen came through with flying colors, recalled Paleolog. Their chief duties were to fight prostitution and all crimes arising from it, offenses committed against, and by, women and children, and any other duties such as searching houses and people, "everywhere where the presence of a policewoman was desirable." One duty involved tracking down venereal disease infected prostitutes—they kept moving—who ignored the doctor's order to receive treatment. Waiting rooms at train stations were a major focus for patrolling, as prostitutes often congregated there, as well as to oversee the arrival of rural immigrants who might be spirited away to the clutches of white slavery. The policewomen worked closely with social work organizations in projects such as setting up rehabilitation homes for wayward girls.[14]

A special uniformed branch of the policewomen was formed in 1935 to deal specifically with minors. The first 30 members of that section hit the streets of Warsaw in August 1935. Duties included dealing with abandoned babies, abandoned children, lost children, patrol and observation of children in parks, gardens, beaches, train stations, and other public areas, and the care of children after school in crowded places, such as helping them across the street and overseeing them in cinemas. By 1939 the total number of policewomen in Poland had risen from an initial 30 to 300, distributed throughout the country in 15 cities, but still under the command of Paleolog. That number represented 1.1 percent of the Polish police, which numbered 27,000 in 1935, including all support personnel such as clerks, typists, porters, and stable hands. Even if fully half the total were support personnel, the policewomen would have amounted to no more than 2.2 percent of the force. The end of Polish policewomen came in 1939 when Germany overran and occupied the country.[15]

In Great Britain the volunteer Women Patrols quickly passed from the scene after the war, which was the original plan for this group. That left only Damer-Dawson's WPS active in the field of policewomen. From their inception until 1921, the WPS had trained and placed 935 female police at war plants for the ministry of munitions, as well as 246 policewomen in various cities. Of those latter women some 150 were employed by police forces with the others employed by manufacturing plants, other government departments, and various war social service and law enforcement groups. In 1921 perhaps 100 WPS policewomen were then serving on police forces, representing around 0.2 percent of police strength. All of these women were paid, sometimes by private groups, sometimes by police forces or other governmental groups. Soon the WPS would wither away completely as the authorities successfully tried to exclude them entirely from policing and tried unsuccessfully to exclude all women from policing. Of the WPS women at work in 1920 only on two forces were they sworn in as constables and in receipt of the same pay as men. Hull had 13 Women Patrols on duty and four WPS members in 1920;

the latter were all paid from police appropriations. The patrols were gone at the latest by the following year, while the Watch Committee of Hull decided in 1924 not to employ policewomen any longer. In addition, they declined to receive a deputation from the National Council of Women, who wished to discuss the matter.[16]

Governmental attitude to policewomen continued to be ambivalent and subject to rapid changes. When women complained about most policewomen not being sworn in, local authorities often replied that they were waiting for a lead from the Home Office as to the legality of the step. As a few had been sworn in without problems, this was simply a delaying tactic. In February 1919 the Home Office issued a circular to all chief constables in England and Wales advocating the appointment of policewomen and that they were to be paid through police channels, but it also recommended they should not be sworn in. Later that year an attempt was made to have policewomen give evidence on their pay and working conditions to an already sitting Committee of Inquiry. However, the home secretary refused the request on the ground that it was outside the scope of this committee. Another request to the home secretary for a special inquiry into the status and work of policewomen was "deferred to a later date."[17]

Faced with continued pressure, an inquiry was finally held with the Committee on the Employment of Women on Police Duties presenting its report to Parliament in September 1920. This report concluded that up till then women police had received pay on which it was impossible to live and had responsibility without authority. Acknowledged was the fact that females could be legally hired and sworn in as constables with no legal bar, particularly since the 1919 passage of the anti-discriminatory Sex Disqualification (Removal) Act. The report recommended that all policewomen should, in the future, be sworn in. Addressing the question of specific duties for policewomen, the report mentioned items such as escort duty, investigation in cases of assault on women and children, attendance at court with female and juvenile offenders, supervision of parks and open spaces, inspection of common lodging-houses, visiting of licensed premises, cinema supervision, dealing with prostitutes, and "generally speaking, any work in connection with offences committed by and against women and children." However, the report allowed that local circumstances and wishes of chief constables should take precedence in assigning duties to female police. Also recommended was that where the numbers were large enough, policewomen should be organized into a single unit, under a female head reporting directly to the chief constable. Equal pay was not among the report's recommendations, with female constables to start at 60 shillings a week. Male constables started then at 70 shillings. Even that increase, if implemented, would have been a big improvement, for policewomen were then earning around 48 shillings a week.[18]

In the Metropolitan London Police, Nevil Macready became commissioner of police in 1918. Under the control of the home secretary, not municipal officials, the Metropolitan Police force numbered about 23,000 with the City of Westminster (the city of London) force having a strength of 1,200. Macready announced in September 1918 his intention of appointing 100 policewomen to his force as an experiment. A journal account of this announcement spoke of much opposition and prejudice still to be overcome to the appointment of women police. Also mentioned was the WPS still working as an independent organization to have women police appointed to undertake "work which cannot, or should not, be carried out by male police." The WPS felt "that to institute a class of police patrols for the mere purpose of work behind the ordinary constable, without initiative, without originality, and without individual responsibility, is but a dangerous instrument to place in the hands of the male police." This journalist believed that male and female police should do different work and concluded — about Macready's new force — "The women police must not come in primarily with a desire to reform and disturb, but with a desire to learn and to co-operate."[19]

On November 21, 1918, a division of Women Police Patrols came into effect. Full strength of 100 was reached the following September; however, only about 40 were actually employed that winter as heavy overcoats were not available for the remainder. Some of the women who had been volunteer members of the old Women Patrols were incorporated into this new group. The WPS was not asked to participate in the formation of this body; all recruits were given training by the Metropolitan Police. Under this structure the commissioner had direct control over recruiting, training and all other aspects of the employment of policewomen by his force, as opposed to the commissioner employing an outside group, like the WPS, to supply women police.[20]

Most of the WPS women who had been employed had been demobilized at the end of the war — since so many policed munitions plants — but of the total of 1,200 of so WPS women trained since the group's inception, about 500 remained active members of the WPS. Most of them had no work. Damer-Dawson and Mary Allen both met with Macready as a result of his announcement to hire policewomen, but he told them he preferred to recruit and train his own women. Particularly upsetting to him was the relatively high educational level possessed by WPS members. With regard to educated women on his force, he told the two women "that they would pin-prick the men" and he did not want any friction. A few years later Macready revealed his attitude toward the WPS in 1918, a group he regarded as high-handed and pushy, by saying, "The main point was to eliminate any women of extreme views — the vinegary spinster or blighted middle-aged fanatic.... Above all things, amateur and unofficial organizations should be suppressed in the same way as bogus policemen are dealt with by law. These organizations in the past not only hampered the recognized women police, but at times brought the force into disrepute through their misplaced activities being mistaken for those of the official force."[21]

Another time Macready said of the WPS, "Another more militant organization had also grown up during the war, adopting the title of 'Women Police' and dressing in uniforms of rather a masculine type. I had several conversations with the lady at the head of this body of women, which were rather in the direction of converting everything she came across to her own point of view, which was inclined to be extreme." Macready began a specific campaign against the WPS in September 1919, when he solicited legal opinions from the Home Office as to whether or not the new uniforms of his policewomen could be regarded as a uniform of the Metropolitan Police under the section of the Police Act intended to protect that uniform from unauthorized wearers. Given the green light on this point, Macready issued summonses against five members of the WPS in 1920 on the ground that their uniforms were too close a match to those of the Metropolitan Women Police Patrols—an offense. Warned of the consequences should they continue to "masquerade" as police, the WPS yielded by changing its uniform and by once again changing its name, this time to Women's Auxiliary Service. It was the same uniform approved by Macready's predecessor just six years earlier. As a result the influence of the WPS declined rapidly, and within a few years it had dropped out of existence. Macready admitted more of his reasons for ill will toward the WPS by saying that since some of their "moving spirits had been suffragettes, he wanted to avoid stirring up the prejudices of policemen whose colleagues had been assaulted by militant ladies." He also felt that the WPS acted as if "they were there to show how police work should be done and how to purify the male force!"[22]

At the 1920 Home Office inquiry into policewomen, out of 241 chief constables heard from, 147 expressed the view that policewomen were not necessary in their city. However, of the 57 chiefs who had personal experience with policewomen only six were against their employment. Those who argued that women should not be given the power of arrest opposed it because they claimed females lacked the necessary strength. No one at the hearing could cite even a single case of such an event, while many examples were cited whereby policewomen had quelled fights and brawls among drunken men. Nevertheless, no power of arrest was recommended for females, while "the Committee agreed that women should not be regarded as substitutes for men."[23]

One prominent witness at that inquiry was Damer-Dawson. By then she had seen some of her WPS members removed from their work as policewomen on forces in various areas, including London suburbs. She regarded the reasons given for their removal as "frivolous, cynical, or both. Many of the outworn pleas—chiefly based on lack of physical strength—were repeated." Under Commissioner Henry the WPS had two policewomen employed in each of the London suburbs of Paddington and Richmond. They were paid not by the police but by local groups such as the Women's Local Government Association. When such groups raised the funds to employ two policewomen for say, Richmond, Damer-Dawson was informed. Then she wrote to Henry who wrote a letter to the superintendent of the division saying policewomen were coming to work there. Macready put a stop to all that. Since the end of the war Damer-Dawson had tried to keep the best members of the WPS together, hoping to get chief constables to take them on. However, she admitted, "The demand does not yet equal the supply." At the time of the inquiry the WPS was a London-based voluntary organization dependent on private funds. One unnamed female was said to supply most of the funding and was prepared to keep it going. Said Damer-Dawson, "We have enough funds to equip a small standing army of policewomen. We are placing them as best we can in different parts of the country." The group was not then training any new policewomen.[24]

At the inquiry Damer-Dawson struck a conservative position by blaming the victim for any policewomen failures and by stressing that women would never be able to do most police work. When she was asked if any of the chief constables who had tried her policewomen had concluded they were not a success she replied, "Yes, but I am bound to say it has been largely because the women have not been well chosen." Asked about detective work for females Damer-Dawson responded, "As a rule women are not fitted for it, and they do not like it." Avoiding making demands for equal pay she argued before the inquiry for women to be set up entirely as a separate police force from men. Emphasizing her point she cited a talk she had with a superintendent of Bristol, who told her that while he respected women police he did not look upon them as part of the regular police. Creating a new, separate and female arm of the law would eliminate friction, thought Damer-Dawson and, "It would do away with all those invidious distinctions between the men and the women if the two forces were absolutely separate.... The women are paid differently, taught differently and organized differently, and I think they do different work." Later in 1920 Damer-Dawson died, with Mary Allen succeeding her as the WPS leader.[25]

In its obituary *The Times* called her "The most feminine of women ... she yet went further than other uniformed women in adopting the outward symbols of male authority. She cut her hair close to her head, a fashion in which many of her inspectors followed her, and it was the rule of her force that superior officers were addressed as 'sir.' With the outward symbols, however, this apparent masculinity entirely disappeared."[26]

Allen toured the United States on a speaking tour in 1924 where she found one burning issue was whether or not policewomen should wear uniforms. Arguing forcefully for the affirmative, she explained "its undoubted force as a deterrent to misdemeanour and immorality." Looking ahead 20 years, Allen foresaw policewomen accepted as essential but "not in any way usurping the work or lessening the prestige of their male comrades, but supplementing them."[27]

Despite governmental hostility to the WPS, the organization was used a few times by the state in the early 1920s, although out of Britain itself where it would not be able to build any local base of support. Colonel Winter of Dublin Castle visited Scotland Yard in June 1920 for the purpose of engaging 50 "trained and tested" policewomen to work with the Royal Irish Constabulary. Unable to comply, Scotland Yard sent him to the WPS office, which soon thereafter dispatched the required number of women. These policewomen served in Northern Ireland and in the Irish Free State (Eire) until after the departure of the British Army. Two years later Allen conferred with the Ulster government, resulting in 20 WPS women being sent to serve in the North at several cities such as Belfast, Londonderry, and Newry. Ireland was in a state bordering on civil war at the time. British authorities requested British policewomen to "match wits" because they felt "Irish women chosen by Sinn Fein for political work were proving themselves cleverer than the men." A large body of the British Army of occupation was stationed in Cologne, Germany, in 1923, where it found itself bedeviled by rising rates of venereal disease. Mrs. Corbett Ashby, president of the International Women's Suffrage Alliance, was appalled by this and the sheer number of prostitutes when she visited Cologne. As a result she agitated to have policewomen in Cologne. Allen was commissioned by the government to survey conditions and prepare a report. This resulted in six WPS policewomen being sent to Cologne in July 1923 where they organized and trained a number of German policewomen before departing. In a letter praising the British policewomen a German resident wrote, "Many cases have occurred where the contact between a policewoman and a girl who had begun an immoral life has resulted in the unfortunate being helped along the right path. Often their mere presence prevents a soldier from indulging in dissipation; the sight of them arouses a sense of shame rather than fear, and he refrains from taking a step which he would regret later."[28]

The first group of 25 of Macready's new Metropolitan Police Women Patrols were trained and assumed their duties in February 1919. These women were not sworn in, had limited duties, and a meager status in comparison with many of the provincial policewomen — WPS — already in the filed. Mrs. Stanley, patrol organizer and appointed superintendent of the Women Patrols in 1920, said of their function, "At the present moment their duties only contemplate assisting police officers; they do not contemplate their being able to take the actual cases themselves." Macready added, "I don't think it is quite the thing for a full-blown constable to go and stir up ladies and gentlemen lying about in the parks. It had far better be done by the women police." He considered this an experiment he could try and scrap after one year if necessary.[29]

By September of that year this force had reached its full strength of 100 plus 10 sergeants. No power of arrest was given to them, although Macready had briefly thought of giving them the restricted power to arrest females and children up to 16 years of age. In describing the attitude of male police to these policewomen the commissioner remarked, "Now the ordinary policeman is a very conservative person, and the starting of these women police was not received with acclamation by the force ... at the beginning they looked askance at it."[30]

Lilian Wyles was one of the women in that first group of 25. She became attracted to police work when she saw the volunteer Women Patrols on the London area streets and on hand at transportation terminals. Wyles became one of those volunteers in June 1918 and then was selected in November of that year to be among Macready's new force of women. Thus Wyles had some idea of the resistance shown to female police but was unprepared for what she received, saying, "Of the downright malice and vindictive sprit to be shown by some of the men towards us we were, as yet, blissfully ignorant." Male police were certain this experiment would fail and expressed to Wyles and the others their distaste of the idea loudly and forcibly. Training for the women lasted six weeks, including first aid and drill. Upon graduation Wyles was one of five of the 25 appointed sergeant. Their uniforms were described by her as being "unspeakable apparel." The low esteem in which these policewomen were held was shown to two of the group who were then living in hotels: "They had already been given the hint by the proprietors or managers that women police officers would not be welcome in their hotels. Objections might be taken by other guests." Lacking the power to make arrests vexed Wyles, who saw it as just one more obstacle: "And limited we were; and considering all the obstructions put in our way; that we were able to justify our existence and prove our usefulness reflects the resourcefulness, tact, and courage shown by the first hundred women police." Wyles was number 23 on the female force — numbers were given out consecutively and never repeated. When she retired over 30 years later in 1949 the number was still well under 600.[31]

After training the women were assigned to various divisions in the metropolitan system, each headed by a superintendent. Tradition had it that the superintendent of a division was to introduce himself to each new arrival; this was not done for any of these first 100 females. Worried superintendents did not know what to do with the women. They worried for their safety, fearing they could be attacked by hostile crowds for these heads claimed the public would certainly resent the law being enforced by women — women who might easily discredit the force by committing some rash act for which the superintendents would be blamed. "To a man they deprecated this utterly foolish experiment — women police," Wyles said. On the job the women patrolled the streets in pairs, three hours on, one hour off, then three more hours on in the afternoon and evening hours. Following the policewomen at a distance of six to 10 yards were two male officers, as chaperons. "They had," said Wyles, "strict orders to keep the women always in sight and to rush instantly to their assistance should it become necessary to do so." Appearing on the street in uniform, they became objects of curiosity for a time. Public comments aimed their way included, "How queer," "How unwomanly," and "Not quite nice, do you think?" All makeup had been strictly forbidden for these women on duty. A major part of their time was spent looking for prostitutes. However, "Prostitutes speedily realized they had nothing to fear from us, handicapped as we were without power of arrest," remarked Wyles. If something came up in court the chaperoning male police always refused to allow either policewoman to take the witness stand to supply corroborative evidence; they always preferred instead to put each other on the stand rather than call the women.[32]

Soon the work became very monotonous, so Wyles pushed for more duties for herself and the then 12 women under her. All agreed with her plan for them to be given the task of escorting women in custody — many were deported from the United Kingdom as undesirables in this period — and to do some of the stakeout duties in night clubs where illicit drinking and gambling were suspected. The custom was when a female was needed a policeman's wife or girlfriend was used, resulting in extra pocket money or an occasional trip to the sea for a deportation for these civilian females. Lobbying for these duties made policewomen even less popular with the male police, but they felt they had to do something, fearing they could become redundant. Slowly they did get these extra duties and others, such as working with lost children and juveniles and watching for drug dealing in women's toilets. Chaperons were eventually shed. Sometimes male police were happy to drop certain duties that they never liked, such as dealing with lost children or returning stray dogs to their owners.[33]

An oft-repeated remark by male police to the women was to tell them to go back to their washtubs. At one division where Wyles worked, the superintendent never spoke to her once the whole time she was there. "Subordinates are always ready to follow the lead of their superiors. Whereas the superiors may be passively contemptuous, the subordinates become actively rude. This was the case on C division for several months. We were treated to hostility and insults from the men on street-duty," reported Wyles. She felt she and the others were looked upon as a collection "of freakish females full of fanciful and abnormal ideas." When one policewoman married a policeman it made policewomen appear more normal, yet some sniffed that this was the only reason women joined the force in the first place.[34]

Working with young, often homeless and penniless women drawn to London, the policewomen soon established a welfare department which involved, among other things, arranging hostel accommodations. Complaints about expenses such as these from headquarters soon began to arrive, causing Wyles to feel that this may have contributed to cutbacks that were soon to hit the women. Her idea of policing and welfare work was somewhat different from other pioneer women in the field. "Gradually it was borne in upon me that this was not the work of police," she said. Police are not welfare officers and welfare officers are not police." However, she did favor a close liaison between them but held that a line had to be drawn to differentiate the two areas.[35]

When she discussed the WPS in her book, Wyles noted Damer-Dawson and many others in that group were "women of means" who continued to function as "self-styled police officers," even though their authority was withdrawn after the war. The WPS continued, she said, to patrol the streets in uniform, pulling up couples and girls who they felt needed corrective advice: "Not always as prudent as they should have been when handling a delicate situation, their rashness caused a great many complaints from people to whom they had given corrective advice." Because of the WPS uniforms and their use of the word police, these people complained to the nearest station. It was these complaints that finally roused the authorities to issue summonses against the WPS, said Wyles. She thought that as the WPS women were wealthy they were indulging their inclinations—in this case for police work: "When persons of this type adopt any cause unhampered by reasonable control, and lacking in discipline, it is apt to go to the head." However, Wyles then admitted that the first complaints against the WPS were actually made by Mrs. Stanley, the superintendent of her own group, before complaints from the public were made.[36]

The Metropolitan Police Criminal Investigation Department (CID) made the statement that "here, at least, women could never penetrate, for in CID work they would be utterly and completely useless," when policewomen were first taken on the force. At the time an outside female civilian welfare worker, Miss MacDougall, was called in as necessary to take statements from females in sex crime cases, for the whole of the Metropolitan Police District, an area that was home to some seven million people. Transferred to the CID in 1922 and where she stayed until her 1949 retirement, Wyles was for a long time the lone female among 3,000 to 4,000 males in the CID. "I was not wanted in the CID. I was a sop thrown to those who had demanded that women should be appointed to deal with the child, the girl, and the woman in all cases of sexual offences," she said. She was to be sent for when any sex crime was reported to any station north of the Thames River, and she was to take statements from all complainants in such cases up to the age of 21. MacDougall was used in similar circumstances for everything south of the Thames. MacDougall did not like Wyles, the policewoman, and withheld help and information from her until she retired. The pair met only once, in 1931, one year before MacDougall retired. It was a meeting arranged by the commissioner. So strained was that meeting that at Wyles's request it was not repeated. At the CID Wyles was ignored, she was given no office and no formal instructions. She said the men at CID were "if not hostile, at least indifferent." Wyles made herself available 24 hours a day, seven days a week for she never wanted to provoke the remark, "Never at hand when wanted; just like a woman."[37]

Early in 1922 the British government released the Geddes Report resulting from a campaign for economy in public services. Among many areas under scrutiny were the police. This was a time for any hostility to surface. In the House of Commons the home secretary referred to "the disloyalty of the women's division of police," without citing any evidence. Scotland Yard's Sir William Norwood argued that females should not patrol the streets since they were unsuited to the task and did not have sufficient physical endurance. He wanted them abolished in London, calling them "not a necessity and too costly to maintain as a luxury." The Geddes Report recommended the complete disbanding of the Metropolitan Police Women, stating, "We have considered the question of the employment of the Women Patrols.... Their powers are very limited, and their utility, from a police point of view, is, on the evidence submitted to us, negligible."[38]

This prompted a good deal of opposition from women. From within the Women Patrols Mrs. Stanley lobbied to save not all the policewomen, but at least some as a nucleus, fearing that if all were terminated it might be years, if ever, before females were rehired. More prominent women also campaigned against the proposal, including one female M.P., Lady Astor. Speaking at a meeting of the National Union of Societies for Equal Citizenship she appealed to them to make the issue of policewomen a test question at the next election, stating, "It was a moral issue and the people who did not want the women police did not want to stand for the highest morals." Also campaigning was another female M.P., Mrs. Wintringham, who argued before legislators that the work performed by the women was "really police work, and not merely welfare work," and that they had accomplished much in connection with white slavery. Mr. R. McNeill argued women police were needed to interview victims of sex assault; that prostitutes arrested by a female would tell a woman they had venereal disease and ask where to seek treatment while they would not be as open with a male officer. McNeill also felt policewomen were necessary to suppress cocaine trafficking, some of which was carried on by females in women's public toilets. Another lobbyist was Mina Van Winkle, who journeyed to England to lend her support after women's groups, led by Astor, appealed to Van Winkle and her organization, the International Association of Policewomen, for help.[39]

All the agitation had an effect, for in December 1922 the home secretary announced his reform of policewomen would not be carried out with its "contemplated thoroughness." Twenty policewomen were retained. One who disappeared was Stanley, who didn't expect to hold the rank of superintendent over so small a group as 20. It would be 1930 before there was another female superintendent. While all of this applied only to the Metropolitan London Police, the Geddes recommendation and subsequent deep cutbacks tended to discourage further appointments in provincial forces, and in some cases to even cause a termination of those employed.[40]

In the face of these cutbacks women continued to apply pressure. One resultant gain came in February 1923 when the home secretary announced that the 20 policewomen, and future hires, would be sworn-in constables having exactly the same standing and powers as male officers. Henceforth, the term woman constable would be used instead of woman patrol. Said the secretary, "It will be understood, however, that they are not expected to undertake any duty which they may be physically unfitted to carry out." One year later none had actually used this power of arrest, as was noted in the police annual report, since their duties were "more in the nature of rescue work among young women and girls." An editorial in *The Times* in July 1923 added its weight to the voices calling for more women police by calling the cutback to 20 "totally unjustified." It was, said the editor, policewomen who stood "between the children and the fiends, whether mentally defective and degenerate or not.... They can protect them far more efficiently than any man.... Over and over again they have saved these children from a fate far more terrible than death." The National Council of Women of Great Britain and Ireland formed a deputation and appealed to the home secretary to preserve and restore the women's force. Finally, between 1924 and 1925 the women's force was increased in size from 20 to 50.[41]

Outside the London area, Deptford was one community that had employed women police during and after the war and then, in the wake of Geddes, refused to rehire them. One article that examined the provincial situation claimed that town and city councils were "showing themselves to be on the side of more women police; whilst most of the Chief Constables and Watch Committees and, we regret to say, the Home Office itself, standing for irresponsible and unrepresentative officials, are opposing them with every force at their command." Women's group lobbied in the provinces as well as in London. Another community that terminated its women police was Hull.

Alderman Crook of the Hull Watch Committee said of policewomen, "I never saw any work they did satisfactorily." Responding to a women's group, he said, "If we don't stand firm these women will take positions away from men. That is what it really means. Everything these women can do they will do, and it is only by the tolerance of men who cannot see their designing manner that they will succeed." In another community, unnamed, Alderman Askew of that Watch Committee claimed women were not suited for police work either temperamentally or physically. The chief constable of Cardiff regarded policewomen as a "complete failure."[42]

The National Council of Women sent out a questionnaire in 1923 to chief constables in various areas. Replies from 37 forces employing policewomen indicated that 13 towns and two county forces had discontinued their women police while five towns and one county had reduced the number employed. A committee formed by the home secretary in 1924 once again examined the question of policewomen. Essentially, this report agreed with the earlier 1920 report that stated there was a need, albeit a limited, narrow one, for women on police forces. This conclusion was reached, despite vigorous opposition during hearings. This committee noted some forces had reduced or discontinued women police, concluding that there were the following employed in all of England and Wales: on the Metro force 20, and in six counties and in 27 city and borough forces a total of 110 policewomen. Their report noted that "pronounced organized opposition to women on police forces has come mostly from the police organizations themselves."[43]

Following examples by the Police Federation of England and Wales in 1921 and by the joint Central Council of the Scotland Police Federation in 1920, the Police Committee of the Association of Municipal Corporations in 1924 moved that "there was no general public demand for the appointment of women police and that such appointments by police authorities should be optional and not compulsory." While that group accepted the idea of preventive police work, they did not believe it had to be done by women, or if women did it then they should not have police powers. Also in 1924 the Police Federation of England and Wales presented a statement to the home secretary that "the employment of women police is not justified." Worried women might be substituted for men, they also "objected emphatically to women working under any other than men officers, and to women ranking higher than constable." The Home Office resisted any idea that the duties of women police could be expanded beyond the current narrow range, arguing that sufficient experience was then lacking to decide "whether this sphere of their general employment can be usefully extended."[44]

In 1929 the number of policewomen on the Metropolitan Police force remained at 50. That same year a delegation representing 18 different groups—including the National Union of Societies for Equal Citizenship and the National Council of Women —called on the home secretary to request more female police, having clearly defined and standardized duties. The secretary told them that policewomen were a comparatively modern innovation failing to make rapid progress due to "the desire to gain a solid basis of experience as to the use of police women in practice before embarking on any stereotyped organization." Also in 1929 policewoman Margery Down arrested a drunk in Paddington. When Magistrate Hay Halkett questioned her, Down replied she had arrested the man herself because she was called and a policeman could not be found. Halkett said to her, "It is a risky thing for a policewoman to take a drunken man into custody.... You were asking for it.... It is better to leave it to a man to do this sort of job."[45]

Yet another government inquiry into the question of policewomen was held in 1928 and 1929. Journalist Alker Tripp observed the proceedings and felt compelled to point out what he called "the disability of women." Police in England depended for coercion on the muscle of "stalwart men" and perhaps also the truncheon. Failure to provide the muscular arm would immediately lower the value of law, for "law subsists by power." Tripp argued that in policing it was necessary that force be at hand and in a situation to act: "The police constable thus represents the physical power of the law, and women do not represent the physical power of the species. The radical disability on the part of ordinary women to act as constables is therefore obvious; a disability which no argument, so far, has in any way discounted." The duty of a policewoman faced with a male or female bully bent on mischief "would be to retire undamaged."

To the idea that females could overcome this physical handicap through something such as jujitsu, Tripp said no, that this must be thwarted because "violence begets violence"— which, of course, contradicted his entire line of reasoning that policing demanded violence or its potential in the first place. Much of the problem, he reasoned, resulted from a "blind push for equality," which dictated females be a part of everything. The fact that a female aviator (unnamed but presumably Amelia Earhart) flew alone over continents was a "dazzling triumph of male genius." Not that Tripp wanted policewomen abolished, only that they be "taken on as women, and not, so to speak, as imitation men." Perhaps, he thought, they should not even be called constables. Tripp argued that aside from welfare work he could not see clearly how they were to be employed other than in an ancillary role "as matrons, assistants, and so forth." Women police were recruited by different standards and for different problems than males, thus they should exist on a "separate footing of their own, and not falsely on an imitation footing for which they are not qualified."[46]

7

U.S., 1930–1969

In 1930 there were reportedly 600 policewomen employed in 289 communities in the United States. The census of 1930 stated the total number of policemen, marshals, and sheriffs was 169,240 with 1,870 females (1.1 percent), including those in private policing.[1]

That same year "progressive" police official August Vollmer introduced readers to the policewoman in an article titled, "Meet the Lady Cop." After noting that early caricatures pictured them as raw-boned, tight-lipped masculine creatures in ugly uniforms, their hair protruding in stringy locks from under frightful hats, their big-fisted hands clutching revolvers," Vollmer said that in England and on the European continent wearing uniforms was the rule for female police, while in the United States uniforms were rare. Considered a friend and supporter of policewomen in his day, Vollmer dismissed the idea of a woman having a gun or club by pointing out that if she had trouble making an arrest "she can always call a man officer to her assistance; after all, you have to leave a little leeway for the male impulse to protect the weaker sex, even in a police department."[2]

Eleonore Hutzel, then deputy commissioner of the Detroit Police Department, published her policewomen's manual in 1933. It was mainly a how-to book of field work and complaint investigation. She wrote of a "growing realization in recent years that police work is, in a certain measure, social work, and that in it there exist problems which can be handled better by women than men." She felt it was this fact that led to the employment of women in policing. Hutzel remained convinced that "the policewomen's work is highly specialized."[3]

On the pressing and important issue of whether females should be organized as a separate unit under female command or integrated into the existing force and commanded by males, Hutzel pretty much chose to pass over the politics of that potential minefield. Originally, she intended to include a chapter in her book on the organization of policewomen's bureaus but dropped it because of difficulties in formulating patterns of organizations for cities of different sizes and differing internal arrangements in police departments. When she did offer an opinion she tended to vacillate. Granting it was better to organize female officers in a separate unit, she worried about the dangers of isolation and lack of cooperation from male divisions stating, "For the future well-being of the work, women should find a place in the long established divisional police commands." Just one page later Hutzel confused the issue by claiming that the policewomen's organization could not be decentralized until female police were accepted by policemen and not regarded as an unwarranted invasion of the policeman's world. "In the meantime, it is well to go on with the present practice of organizing separate policewomen's bureaus at police headquarters. But executives should avoid creation of what appear to be little independent police departments composed entirely of women who are kept at arms' length from the main organization and, perhaps, a little despised by the remainder of the force."[4]

Hutzel supported minimum standards for policewomen of high school graduation plus at least two years of recent social work experience or two years experience as a nurse, although at that time her own Detroit force required women to be university graduates in addition to at least one year of social work experience. She felt that Detroit policewomen had started their careers in a type of social service agency which happened to be housed in a police department; but that by the early 1930s it had "become unmistakably a police unit with a social welfare point of view."

Hutzel subscribed to the conventional ideas of what the limited duties of policewomen should be. Specifically, they were best suited to dealing with complaints concerning girls of juvenile court age, boys up to the age of 10 or 12, young girls over the juvenile court age, and older women where no court action was necessary. While conventional wisdom of the era right up into the 1960s saw female cops dealing with women and children, in practice the scope was further narrowed. Rarely, if ever, did policewomen deal with young males older than 15 or 16 or women much beyond the mid–20s (except those who were victims of rape or deserters of children). Hutzel summed up this narrowing for her force — but it applied to American female police in general — by stating, "Women tramps, drug addicts, and beggars are usually handled by men officers.... These women are usually older women who do not respond to constructive efforts toward rehabilitation and are not primarily a problem for the policewoman." The same was often true for prostitutes who, by reason of their age or amount of time in the field, were regarded as hardened and therefore out of the orbit of policewomen and, of course, into the orbit of policemen.[5]

If Hutzel moved softly and confusingly around the issue of unit organization, the Citizens' Police Committee of Chicago did not. Their 1931 publication delivered a scathing attack on the treatment of women, as well as pointing out the need for a separate policewomen's bureau. Civil service requirements in Chicago were the same for matrons and policewomen, with the report noting that "this lack of discrimination between matrons and policewomen is carried through into administration and is responsible, in part, for the unsatisfactory status of policewomen." Worst of all, the distinction between the two groups was often "totally disregarded and the policewomen are allotted duties within the normal scope of a matron's limited qualifications." Approximately 25 percent of the Chicago female police were then doing nothing but matron duty, with the result that the effect on "the morale of many policewomen is far from beneficial." Chicago got around the civil service rules by hiring women as temporary, renewable appointments for six months. Twice a year these were renewed. Thus in Chicago in 1931 there had been no civil service exam for policewomen since February 1920. Integrated into the male force, Chicago policewomen were under the command of males. In some districts they did the normal policewomen duties yet, noted the report, "In others, they do practically nothing, owing to the fact that no complaints investigated by the district are referred to them for action." This Citizens' Police Committee strongly recommended that all women police be placed under the supervision of a female officer: "Until there is an almost complete reversal in the attitude of many of the district commanders toward policewomen, it will be unwise to detail them to districts where control over assignment of cases within the district must, in the nature of things, rest with the officer in command."[6]

Writing in *Independent Woman* in the mid–1930s, Josephine Nelson stated: "It is easier for a policewoman than a policeman to apprehend shoplifters (a large percentage of whom are women); to patrol dance halls and see that decent standards of conduct are maintained." She also felt women were admitted to the male domain of policing precisely because they were women, along with the growing acceptance of the idea that police work had to develop more into preventive and protective work with less focus solely on the punitive. "By and large, however," she wrote, "the American policewoman is a social worker with police powers." This policewoman could handle a gun well, "but she seldom carries the thing." Of the 150 females on the New York City force Nelson said that perhaps three regularly carried revolvers in their handbags. Nelson estimated there were 850 female police in 290 American communities in 1935. In England a policewoman lost her job if she married, while all but seven women on the New York force were married. The economic depression of the 1930s took its toll on policewomen. Baltimore, where the law permitted no more than five female police, had not filled a vacancy for several years, while New York City had made no new appointments in four years.[7]

On Hutzel's Detroit force, where she remained deputy commissioner and director of its Women's Division, 39 women were employed there, three of them sergeants. As to the future of policewomen she remarked, "The work which women can do will always be minor as compared with what men can do." Up to July 1, 1936, Detroit women were paid $200 less than similarly classified men, but after that date the situation was changed so that the pay rate was the same, $2,100 per year. New York also paid the sexes equally. George T. Ragsdale, superintendent of police training in Louisville, said he saw a place in policing for females: "I think most of the clerical work could be better performed by women."[8]

In Los Angeles there were then 34 female officers under the command of the captain of detectives. According to Captain Slaughter the majority of these women are "married, of mature age and experience, and thus temperamentally and professionally fitted to carry out the peculiar duties necessary in rehabilitating juvenile girls."[9]

Joseph Kluchesky, chief of police in Milwaukee, Wisconsin, outlined the duties of his female police in 1937 by saying that they "investigate and handle the cases involving women and children. They patrol public places and streets, inspecting all places of commercial recreation, including dance halls, skating rinks, and all other places frequented by women and children, with a view to locating any conditions which may contribute to vice or delinquency." They also dealt with missing persons and child abandonment.[10]

Women on the New York City force had been exempt from weapon handling training until 1934 when the 155 female members were issued with orders that they must learn to shoot and carry a revolver in their handbags while on duty. They had been permitted to carry weapons in the past but reportedly, few ever did. The few that did carried a small automatic. Under the new orders females had to carry a revolver of at least 0.32 caliber (standard police issue was 0.38 caliber). At the same time policemen were ordered to upgrade their shooting skills. The following year the women were ordered to buy uniforms although they were only to be worn in very limited cases, such as when policewomen patrolled beaches. That order caused an unnamed veteran policeman to snarl, "They were no bargain in civvies, and they'll be worth less rigged out in blue." Of those 155 women only about 50 were policewomen, and the others were matrons. Also in 1935 two female officers assigned to New York's pickpocket detail, patrolling in a department store, arrested a man they observed stealing wallets from the purses of shoppers. According to the newspaper report, they arrested him and took him to the station even though they were "small of stature, didn't use guns." That arrest, which of course would never have made the newspaper had it been carried out by males, was said to be the first of its kind by policewomen.[11]

By 1939 there were around 180 policewomen on the New York City force, which then totaled some 18,000. When the city's Civil Service Commission

announced an examination for the post of policewoman, with only 29 anticipated vacancies, 5,254 women responded with 3,177 actually taking the exam.
A newly appointed policewoman had to buy a uniform which she rarely or
never wore and a gun, which it was then reported they rarely carried. Either
the earlier gun order had been eased or one report was erroneous. Men had
to purchase those same items, but they used them. Only the police shield was
provided free.

A newly appointed policewoman in New York City in 1939 might be
assigned to the Bureau of Policewomen (then with a strength of 76 under
Mary A. Sullivan) or sent to join the 56 females in the Juvenile Aid Bureau.
A new recruit might have investigated illegal practices of medicine by unli-
censed midwives and suspended doctors, such as abortion providers, voodoo
promoters and other healing practices; delved into indecent exposure accusation, "degenerates and exhibitionists" in film theaters, fortune-telling rack-
ets, larceny and switch games run by gypsies and pickpockets, looked into
shoplifting charges; and dealt with fraudulent advertising whereby males
placed ads for workers and sexually harassed women who responded. New
York's policewomen were also in charge of all female detainees while they
were in police custody and were also charged with searching all the dead-on-
arrival female corpses.[12]

According to the 1940 US Census, the total number of police, marshals
and sheriffs stood at 176,988, with 2,226 of them being women (1.3 percent).
That total included both public and private employment. The number
employed as policewomen by government agencies stood at 881 females (of
127,858 in total — 0.7 percent). It was these that we think of as police. The
number of female police was up less than 300 from 1930. The remaining
females of those 2,226 were employed by private concerns or worked as
bailiffs. Less than 3 percent of the nation's 6,000 law enforcement units
included qualified policewomen in 1940, and most of those were employed
in large cities. When the International Association of Chiefs of Police sent
out a questionnaire they found that in 1945 and 1946 there were 759 female
police employed in 141 cities with populations over 25,000. Of these, 50 cities
had special Women's Bureaus; but in 51 cities they did not have equal pay for
the genders. There were 121 cities that did not respond; 155 cities reported
employing no female officers, and 24 of them stated they employed females
as matrons only. Four years later the number stood at 894 policewomen in
129 of the 143 replying cities. In cities with female police just 35 percent of
them had separate Women's Bureaus. In 1949 there were 70 black policewomen, employed in 23 cities, up from 23 black women in 1940.[13]

Close to half of the total number of policewomen were to be found in
just five cities, with 174 in New York City, 79 in Chicago, 60 in Detroit, 56
in Indianapolis, and 35 in Washington, D.C. In 95 cities that employed female

police these women were assigned to night duty as well as to the day shift. In 40 cities the women carried firearms, in 36 cities they had the option of carrying weapons if they wished, and in 45 cities they were unarmed.[14]

Little had changed for policewomen, neither their number nor their duties. *Good Housekeeping* profiled Washington, D.C., officer Mary Miller in a 1941 issue. A former teacher, Miller had a B.A. degree as well as a law degree — all D.C. policewomen had to have university degrees. The police training course lasted three months and included pistol shooting. Duties listed for Miller and her colleagues included taking women arrested for felonies to be fingerprinted, attending female accident victims, finding deserting husbands, investigating complaints about disorderly dance halls, dealing with alcoholic wives and daughters, crying babies, crooked fortune-tellers, cruelty to children, neighbors' noise, dog noise, accompanying arrested women from detention to court, convincing arrested females to pose for mug shots, patrolling amusement arcades, helping unmarried mothers, attending juvenile court, arresting female pickpockets, dealing with consumer fraud, and stopping men from annoying women.[15]

Also typical was the duty performed by Detroit policewoman Kidder, who picked up a 17-year-old girl just as the teen was about to be taken to a hotel by a strange man. The girl turned out to be a runaway from abusive parents in Akron, Ohio; in Detroit she had become penniless and homeless. Kidder promised her she would not be returned to abusive parents, that social workers would help her to get a job, a place to live and friends, and that she would be examined for venereal disease, if she wasn't still a virgin.[16]

A couple of years later Vollmer, still cited as an outstanding figure in the field of police science, said of policing as a career for women, "I can imagine no finer career for young women than in the police field where they have the opportunity of helping to save some of the 10 million children now in school who otherwise are destined to crime."[17]

While Vollmer's anti-female police attitudes were of the condescending, paternalistic type, other writers in the popular press of the 1940s were more blatantly hostile and antagonistic. When Detroit's female police were profiled in *American Mercury* in 1942, writer Karl Detzer began with the story of a young, unarmed female cop who arrested a burly male panderer by herself, without problems. In court the judge was so surprised at this that he asked her whether she had coerced the man with a gun. Another story related was how a cruiser with two males saw a pair of female officers also cruising. "The males went over to the women and said, "Evenin,' gals. We see you headin' this way and think maybe we can give you a hand." Detzer pointed out that when one woman phoned into the station she had to stand on the cruiser's running board to reach the mouthpiece of the phone. Numerous times the women were referred to in the article as "girls" and as "policegirls."[18]

Half of the Detroit women had university degrees, with 80 percent having at least some college experience. There were six registered nurses, and two were members of the bar. The strength of the Detroit force stood at 3,600 men — and 54 women, who worked in a separate women's division. They usually worked unarmed, with their main duty being to protect boys under 10 and girls under 21 from "exploiters, sex-criminals, perverts, white slavers, from immoral influences and depraved surroundings, and from their own youthful folly." They were not, said Detzer, a vice squad concerning themselves only with immorality as it might harm youth. These women told Detzer that the most intelligent male officer could not do their job as well as they did because "men are gullible. A pretty girl need only get a soulful expression in her eyes and tell a sad story to make most men believe. No man can judge a girl's age." Despite working in such rough surroundings dealing with crime, Detzer felt it "has not deprived these policegirls of the soft, motherly, feminine touch." Regarding the attitude of male police to the females, he wrote the men "are ready to help. Their attitude is respectful, almost fraternal."[19]

Anna Mae Davis joined the Chicago Police Department in December 1946. She was a founder of the Chicago Policewomen's Association, served as its president from 1970 to 1974, and once sued her force demanding equal pay for women. Policewomen made $1,000 less than the male officers in the Youth Division and she was not about to put up with it. Then she complained about women not being allowed in patrol cars and there being no female sergeants and no female lieutenants. She was born on the South Side of Chicago and held various jobs including being a fare collector in the city's transit system. Davis started studies at what was Wright Junior College before joining the force. Anna Mae Davis retired from the Chicago Police Force in 1978 and died in May 2003, aged 75.[20]

Equally derisive of policewomen was a 1949 *Saturday Evening Post* profile of the New York City women by Stanley Frank, titled "Some Cops Have Lovely Legs." There were then 190 policewomen on the New York force, 104 in a separate unit, 86 attached to the Juvenile Bureau, which Frank called "the world's largest and comeliest." Illustrating the article was a photo of a female officer in uniform, applying makeup. Frank offered the thought that "women make good cops because they're naturally suspicious." Single women numbered 77 of the 190 and were teased by the married ones with the barb, "Some cop. Can't even catch a man." A potential recruit needed to be a high school graduate and have at least two years work experience in some social welfare area such as teaching, nursing, or psychology. Of the total female group 53 had college degrees, with more than 10 postgraduate degrees, including five in law. The work week was eight hours a day, six days a week. New York City offered policewomen greater variety and diversity in assignments than any other American city as women were often used to assist in virtually every area of crime. Nevertheless, the bulk of their time was spent on conventional female police duties.[21]

Frank referred to them repeatedly as girls. To illustrate his view of police-women he related the account of two female rookies who investigated a complaint of sexual harassment against a tailor who was advertising for a cashier. One female went inside to apply for the job, the tailor harassed her, and then she identified herself as a police officer. That caused the tailor to run outside the shop in an effort to flee. The officer outside yelled "Stop or I'll shoot" but to her horror found she had the muzzle of the gun pointed at her own stomach. Finally, they arrested him and took him to the station, where the women "triumphantly waved" their guns at the desk sergeant who cried, "Don't point that thing at me! Look, you kids go out for a cup of coffee until you and I are ourselves again." Very likely that story was totally false — for one thing, rookies, male or female, were, and still are, never sent out alone or just with another rookie. The importance of the story lay not in its accuracy but in that it created the desired image of female police — woeful, emotional, and inept.[22]

The director of the New York policewomen was Irene Peters who said, according to Frank, "You can give a woman a badge, a gun and all the professional training in the world but she remains a woman at heart. To tell the truth, that's the way we want them to be." Peters went on to add, "Of course we have to smooth over petty jealousies, soft-soap prima donnas and change teams when partners have spats, but that's healthy cattiness among women." Frank then said, "It is significant that the most ardent boosters of lady cops are the men in the Police Department. They have no sarcastic or kidding nicknames for their female counterparts, and every bureau chief interviewed remarked on the willingness of his men to work with policewomen." When lethal danger loomed, wrote Frank, "the men unhesitantly risk their lives to protect a sister officer." Further undermining Frank's credibility was his assertion that females were first added to the New York police as matrons in 1888 by Police Commissioner Theodore Roosevelt. Firstly, the date was incorrect, and secondly, while the future president did serve on the New York Police Commission, his service did not commence until 1895.[23]

Promotion was virtually impossible for female officers and would remain so into the modern era. If a female were employed in a unit with separate Women's Bureau, then she had the opportunity of advancing into one of its few command positions. All other policewomen had no chance at all. They were not allowed to sit for the competitive examinations leading to advancement to which men were given access. When the U.S. Army actively recruited females during World War II, it provided opportunities for ranking female officers similar to males. This caused the New York City Policewomen's Endowment Association to agitate for promotional opportunities. However, policemen opposed the idea so vehemently it was quickly dropped. Wrote one observer of the period, "Opposition to the women's use of the titles, Sergeant and Lieutenant, and to women superiors elsewhere than the Bureau of Policewomen, was expressed by leaders of the 'line' organizations ... the matter of promotion was deferred."[24]

The National Advisory Police Committee on Social Protection of the Federal Security Agency was a national organization composed of representatives of 30 national voluntary organizations representing 23 million women members. In its 1945 federal report the group urged the employment of more policewomen. Included in the report was the group's concept of a policewoman's function. On patrol the female officer would "look for any young girl conspicuous because of the place or the hour, who is untidy in her dress, or of unkempt appearance, with excessive makeup; or any girl carrying baggage, running, hiding, obviously loitering, or disturbed in manner, or who is with an adult of obviously unsuitable appearance." Also advised was for the officer to question couples who were "excessively affectionate." In addition, she should interest herself in groups that are boisterous or rowdy or unusually quiet. As to the demeanor of the policewoman, the group noted she "should not be over-feminine nor, on the other hand, aggressively mannish. She should not play on the fact that she is a woman, but neither should she ever forget her responsibility as a woman and the dignity she owes to her sex.... She must avoid taking a position of leadership in highly controversial civic or social issues." On relationships between the sexes on the force this group believed that "police officers will accept a policewoman as a 'good officer' if her work is good.... It is only when this approval is won that fellow officers will fully cooperate with each other, no matter what orders have been given." Despite this pandering to the male establishment, this group favored the unit organization of a separate women's division instead of the dispersal and integration of females throughout the male force. The greatest fear for this group was that dispersal destroyed the value of females as "preventive-corrective" agents. In a stab at male police the group stated, "These fears seem to have had considerable foundation, as there have been a number of examples of such dispersal which resulted in definite curtailment of the usefulness of the policewoman."[25]

As the 1950s began, the unit form of organization remained a major issue. Lois Higgins, a Chicago policewoman since 1937, noted that "matron duty has been imposed on some women police from time to time by their superior officers." She agreed with the majority of females who favored the separate unit headed by a female, since "it prevents their being parceled out among the various districts or precincts, where they are sometimes used as clerks, switchboard operators, or matrons. It insures their use in a comprehensive, constructive program directed toward the prevention of crime and toward the protection of women and children." At the time there were around nine cities with separate female divisions, according to one report: Detroit, Baltimore, Philadelphia, Washington, Seattle, Portland (Oregon), Berkeley (California), Madison (Wisconsin), and New York City.[26]

Evabel Tenny, a former policewoman, noted that "at first, the appointment of a woman to the police force may be viewed with suspicion. Every move she makes will be watched." The female officer had to strike a balance being neither overly feminine nor too aggressive. Like many others, including female police, Tenny believed the onus was on the woman to fit in and somehow bring about her unconditional acceptance. For Tenny the duties of a woman officer remained unchanged, and "no arrests are made on patrol duty, except in extreme cases."[27]

Thomas Edwards, a representative for the American Social Hygiene Association, hoped to reduce or even eliminate commercialized prostitution through the use of more policewomen. His ideal policewoman would have better than average education, good health, social work experience, psychiatric training, and be "attractive, well-adjusted, emotionally mature and level-headed." Her primary responsibility was to spot young people in dangerous situations through the constant inspection of places of amusement, dance halls, railway and bus stations, and any other places where girls were apt to appear. "Above all," he added, "she should prove her value to her brother officers and win their cooperation and help."[28]

The attitude of the male police establishment can perhaps be best seen in the book written by O. W. Wilson. First published in 1950, a second edition came out in 1963. The second edition's treatment of the topic of policewomen was unchanged from the 1950 edition. *Police Administration* became the pre-eminent work at the time in its area. Outside of their normal function in the juvenile area, he acknowledged a need for female police in the Detective Division on occasion, such as to interview females or on raids in some arrest situations where it was feared a female suspect might try to hide in the women's toilets. However, if the Detective Division did not have a female officer assigned to it, Wilson suggested a "secretary, a woman records clerk, or a matron may fill this intermittent need." Where a policewoman was assigned full time to the Detective Division she should "be given either investigative or clerical assignments to occupy her time during slack periods." In the area of juvenile work Wilson was firm in the need for that division to be headed by a man and not a woman. The reasons he cited were as follows: "(1) men have a better understanding of the attitudes of other divisions and especially of the detective division toward crime-prevention work, (2) men are better able to win cooperative support from other members of the department, (3) men are physically and emotionally able to withstand the pressure of the work and are, therefore, less likely to become irritable and overcritical under emotional stress, and (4) men are usually better supervisors of women than are other women." This book functioned as a textbook and how-to manual for many police departments into at least the late 1960s.[29]

Wilson was Vollmer's protégé, having served under him at Berkeley before going on to become chief at Wichita, Kansas, from 1928 to 1939, dean of the School of Criminology at UC Berkeley, and chief of the Chicago police from 1960 to 1967.[30]

One area in the 1950s where a few female officers worked with male counterparts was in drug details. Philadelphia police bought drugs on the street undercover then arrested the seller. Recruits straight out of the academy were normally used as buyers, since dealers were unlikely to recognize them. One year one of these male recruits posed as a woman and a deaf mute so his voice would not betray him. He was so successful that real female rookies began to be used. Each girl (again the term was used often) was teamed with a pair of patrolmen who followed her in a car. When she made a buy the officer took it to the car where the material was analyzed in a small chemical lab. Patrolmen operated under orders to protect the girls from violence. One policewoman remarked, "No man will do as a woman asks. Tell a man how you want him to cover you, and he'll do it his way. Then everything goes wrong. I finally dropped my 'protection' altogether." Officer Geraldine Galcik said she sometimes felt "overprotected"; and then the writer of the article showed his inclinations by listing Galcik's measurements.[31]

Kitty Barney worked on the New York City narcotics squad, one of the 98 men and 12 women on the unit. After 11 years on the squad and 15 on the force, Barney was considered one of its best, with her commander calling her "the best narcotics detective in the country." During 1953 the squad made about 1,500 arrests, an average of 14 per officer; Kitty made 54. Yet her rank was only detective first grade, one step up from beginning rank because it was "tops for women police officers, who may not take the police department's competitive exams for higher rank and salary." Advancement to detective first grade was at the department's discretion and involved no formal procedure or application. On the question of gun use Barney subscribed at least a little to the out-of-control female image by stating, "All a woman has to do is pull out a gun and everybody freezes. They figure a woman is going to be a lot more nervous and unpredictable with a gun than a man."[32]

Openly condescending to female police was a *New York Times* article in which Officer Marjorie McCarron was quoted that one thing she did not like to talk about was her gun, which she "literally despises." Theresa Melchionne, director of the New York City Police Women's Bureau, said she was wary of giving the impression her charges were "Amazons— But usually, on hazardous assignments, male members of the force were close by."[33]

Along the same lines was a *Reader's Digest* article in 1957 which profiled the females on the New York City force. Noting they were trained side by side with males on the same things, the magazine was relieved to say that despite this "their femininity doesn't seem to suffer." Policewomen still wore no uniforms, except on special patrol duty such as on the beach (to make them readily visible to people from many countries). Regarding that fact the magazine commented that one could find "sun-tanned teams of police lovelies on the sands of Coney Island Beach in summer." All of this came under the title "Crime-busters in Skirts."[34]

For its profile *Look* magazine chose Los Angeles officer Francis Sumner whom it identified at the beginning of its article only as Mrs. Jack Sumner "a housewife par excellence who likes to knit handsome wool socks for her marine-engineer husband, and who can toss a fine green salad." Called an expert in both judo and marksmanship, *Look* stated that "nonetheless, it's when she's being most womanly that she proves most wonderful — comforting the city's lost and strayed children, listening to the problems of a confused teenager at odds with the law, coping with the problems of a woman alcoholic brought in from Skid Row." Her work in Los Angeles earned her the award as Los Angeles Policewoman of the Year in 1955. A seven-year veteran of the force, she had been a registered nurse before that. Finally the article remarked that she was not just a good shot but that she frequently instructed classes in the use of firearms. Still, said the magazine, "On the other hand, she's equally adept in instructing lady prisoners in sewing and the use of make-up."[35]

A 1950 article reported that female police were employed in at least 161 cities with populations greater than 25,000. Of 34 cities over 250,000 who responded to the inquiry 29 employed female police, but five did not. Of 429 reporting cities with populations between 10,000 and 25,000, only 51 employed policewomen. Cities employing the greatest number were Pittsburgh 166, New York City 154, Detroit 72, Los Angeles 72, Chicago 68, Cleveland 31, Washington 28, Philadelphia 19, Boston 13, Baltimore 7, San Francisco 5, Buffalo 4, and Milwaukee 4.[36]

Writing in the trade publication *Police*, James Owens reported on a 1958 survey which reported that of the 100 largest American cities 82 employed policewomen, for a total of 1,040. "The neatly dressed, well spoken policewoman, makes a very favorable impression," concluded Owens. Remarking that most of their duties were with women and children, he reassured his readers that "interested persons learn that today's policewoman is not the imagined hatchet-faced burly amazon with a brimstone tongue."[37]

The 1950 US Census reported there were 2,610 policewomen and detectives employed publicly and privately — a little more than 1 percent of the total. Ten years later in 1960 the number of such females was reported as 5,617 — 2.3 percent of the total. In 1967 municipal police agencies totaling 216 serving populations of 50,000 and above were queried. Of those 172 responded, reporting an average of three females out of their average total sworn strength of 352 (0.9 percent). When the International Association of Chiefs of Police surveyed 1,330 law enforcement agencies in 1969 only 34 percent had any sworn female officers, comprising less than 2 percent of those departments. Another report listed 784 policewomen (0.8 percent) in the United States in 1960.[38]

As the 1950s neared an end President Eisenhower sent a letter to the International Association of Police Women citing them for their "vital role" in the American way of life.[39]

Attitudes of policewomen themselves remained conservative into the start of the 1960s. Veteran officer Lois Higgins in her *Policewoman's Manual* published in 1961 wrote that police work was, has been, and always would be predominantly a man's job. Mary Anderson, a Portland, Oregon, sergeant, in her book, *Women in Law Enforcement* cautioned females that they might be the only female on the force and thus might be pinched, patted, or played with. Therefore they, the females, should not wear heavy makeup or suggestive clothing nor should they use "longshoreman's language." Finally, Anderson advised them to gain respect in their profession while keeping their good looks and their femininity.[40]

Early in that decade the number of policewomen in New York City numbered 275, which was also the quota of that era. Over one-third were in the Bureau of Policewomen, headed by a director, the only female department head. She was appointed from the ranks. There were 52 policewomen assigned to the Youth Division, 59 to the Detective Division, and the remainder were dispersed to other areas. While under the city administrative code male and female police had equal status, females were not allowed to compete in examinations for promotion. Some cities such as Los Angeles, Detroit, Washington, and London, England, did by that time allow policewomen to sit for such exams. In a few cities, such as Cleveland and Washington, legislation existed for their Women's Bureaus to have female commanding officers equal in rank to men. Thus in a few cities policewomen held ranks; Philadelphia and Chicago each had two sergeants and one lieutenant. Denver allowed women to take the sergeant's examination for a pay raise but not for a command position. Since New York allowed no women to be promoted, the female head could not be titled captain — as male department heads were. Technically, she was still ranked as policewoman. Officially, her title was director but with the same pay and responsibilities as any male captain in charge of a division. When New York policewomen agitated for promotional opportunities again in the mid–1950s they were once again stopped by male police opposition because the worry of "assignments of women superiors to commands other than the Women's Bureau caused disagreement." A few individual females, nonetheless, put in applications to take the test; however, they were rejected "because of sex."[41]

In 1961 a New York City policewoman successfully sued the city under the Fourteenth Amendment to the Constitution for the right of females to take the examination for promotion to sergeant. Four years later she became the city's first female sergeant. Until 1973 rookie policewomen in New York attended segregated training classes and received modified training compared to what the males received.[42]

That woman from the NYPD was Felicia Shpritzer. She was born on November 12, 1913, in Gloversville, New York, but soon moved with her family to New York City where she graduated from Washington Irving High School. She received a bachelor's degree in speech from the University of Michigan and a master's degree in police science from the City University of New York. She was appointed to the NYPD in 1942 and served for 17 years in the Youth Division where 57 of the 278 women in the NYPD were assigned. At the time of her lawsuit she had a spotless record and had received a number of police department awards and citations. After being rejected as a candidate to take the sergeant's qualification test she sued the city, won the court battle and then became one of two of the 127 policewomen who took the test and passed it. What led to the lawsuit was when she and five other women applied to take a test for possible promotion to the rank of sergeant in 1961. Two weeks before the test was to be given, all six women's applications were rejected. She then sued. Shpritzer also cited a section of the City Administrative Code providing that any member of the police department assigned to the Juvenile Aid Bureau would retain his or her rank and pay in the force and would be eligible for promotion as if serving in the uniformed force. In June 1963 the Court of Appeals ruled in her favor and in 1964 she and the other 126 women took the four-hour test. Their immediate assignments when the pair were promoted to sergeants (Gertrude Schimmel was the other) was to supervise the almost 160 policewomen attached to the Bureau of Policewomen. Thus no policeman was to be supervised by a woman. After 34 years with the NYPD Felicia retired as a lieutenant in 1976. Felicia Shpritzer died in December 2000, aged 87.[43]

During the period from 1952 to 1962 New York's Women's Bureau was headed by Theresa Melchionne, who found jobs in which women could excel. One of these was to organize a dozen policewomen into an abortion squad to handle all abortion investigations, previously done by all male teams. Arrests and convictions for abortion — then completely illegal — reportedly went up rapidly. Supposedly this was due to the fact that men did not know what to ask; when a suspect insisted she had done the aborting herself and told men how, the policemen had no idea if the explanation was plausible or ridiculous.[44]

Throughout her 20-year career Bessie Ibsen, Mobile, Alabama's first female officer, felt like she was held in contempt by her superiors. She joined the force in 1962. Not only was she Mobile's first policewoman she was the first policewoman in the state, according to police Major Wilbur Williams, the department's historian. When she retired in 1982 at the rank of sergeant, Ibsen said she never looked back, feeling that "it's over, it's done with, they didn't want me." According to a reporter who interviewed the 71-year-old woman at her home in Mobile in 1998, "indignation was evident" in her voice. "I never, ever felt wanted in 20 years from the people up high," she told the reporter. "The people I worked with, the patrolmen, they were fine, they didn't resent me." In 1962 the police department was under scrutiny from the US federal government to hire more minorities and women. Ibsen was 35 and working in the toy department of a local hardware store when she saw an ad in a newspaper saying the department planned to hire a woman. About 100 people applied; Ibsen was selected. "Her delight soon turned to frustration and anger when she realized she would spend her entire career doing mostly paperwork and being denied chances for promotion, simply because she was a woman," said the news account.[45]

On January 9, 1967, Mary R. Ostrander, a policewoman with the Madison, Wisconsin, Police Department for nine years wrote a polite note to the police chief, "I respectfully request permission to write the promotion exam for the position detective." On January 10 her supervisor denied her request — for the sole reason that women could not become detectives in the Madison Police Department. Nor, though they made arrests, could they carry guns or handcuffs, and they could not go through the standard training. They were paid less than the men for doing the same work. Mary Ostrander, daughter of a Green Lake County judge and a college graduate (females had to have college degrees to work in the department), was not pleased. Before she retired in 1983 she had taken on the status quo in the force on several occasions, winning back pay for female officers, the right to proper training, the right to carry weapons, equal wages and, eventually, detective status on a par with her male colleagues. Ostrander joined the force on April 1, 1958, when women were ranked Police Woman I and Police Woman II. They worked with families, and women and children, and as liaison with social agencies. Mary Ostrander died in September 1960, aged 60, from a combination of diabetes and kidney failure. As of 1994 the Madison Police Department had a female captain, a female lieutenant, four female sergeants, 11 female detectives and detective supervisors, one female special investigator and 75 female officers.[46]

When the President's Commission on Law Enforcement and Administration of Justice (popularly known as the Crime Commission) issued its report in 1967 it said, "The role of the policewoman today is essentially, what it always has been. Female officers serve in juvenile divisions, where they perform investigative and social service oriented activities for women, teenage females, preteen youngsters (both male and female) and infants." Over half of Indianapolis's 74 female officers, including most of the five sergeants, were used as secretaries. In New York City about 70 of the policewomen (of 350) performed nothing but office duties as secretaries, clerks, and switchboard operators. Giving them such limited assignments led to the view expressed by a male lieutenant, "As it is known that women cannot normally accept the full range of police responsibility, as is expected of the average policeman ... their salaries [should] be adjusted accordingly." That is, deny them the ability to do what they were trained for, give them lesser and menial work, claim that was all they could do, and use that as the rationale to decrease their salaries. In both England and Germany at that time there were strict rules in place prohibiting the use of policewomen to do typing, switchboard, or other clerical duties.[47]

Congress reorganized the Washington, D.C., women's division in 1967 (this was before that city got home rule), combining the women with the male officers into the newly created Youth Division. The rationale behind Congress in abolishing the Women's Bureau was to "free policewomen from duties which are the responsibility of other agencies." This loss of female leadership and organizational autonomy produced a strong negative reaction among the policewomen. Many resigned or retired. Of the 35 females in the Women's Bureau when it was disbanded only eight remained in 1971.[48]

However, the times were changing. The Crime Commission established in the face of riots, urban unrest, and a perception of rising crime rates, recommended police departments hire more highly educated recruits, more accurately reflect their communities' racial and gender composition, and downplay aggressiveness and strength. The commission said the height and weight standards then still in force almost everywhere frequently eliminated female applicants. Generally, recruitment became more difficult as police pay trailed private sector wages, as well as due to the popular image of police as pigs. In New York City the IQ scores of male recruits dropped from an average of 107 in 1962 to 93 in 1969, while females admitted to that city's police force in 1966 had average IQ scores of 110. Despite this, as one writer commented, the "New York department stopped hiring women when the allotted positions for policewomen were filled although many qualified women were still available." In addition, "Some departments accepted male recruits with lower IQ scores and less education rather than alter their height requirements or the limitations on the number of positions legally or informally allocated to female officers which had been in effect for many years.[49]

But total male control and domination was beginning to crack. The New York promotion lawsuit was one example. In addition, one event in Indianapolis made a big difference. Two officers on that force, Betty Blankenship and Elizabeth Coffal, had been agitating for at least a year to be put out in a patrol car to do regular patrol duty, the same as male officers. Finally, despite "departmental hostility," Indianapolis police chief Winston Churchill granted their request. In September 1968 he transferred the pair out of the Juvenile Division and assigned them to patrol car 47. He did this, giving them just 24 hours notice. They patrolled a section of downtown Indianapolis (sections overlapped with one another) but male dispatchers sent calls to them selectively, sometimes ignoring them, sometimes limiting them to domestic dispute cases, and sometimes giving them all the distasteful work. In one two-week period they had to handle 14 dead-on-arrival calls, some for corpses dead for some time. Said Coffal, "Instead of hurting us, it was beneficial because we got the worst at the beginning." Despite all obstacles and lack of preparation, the pair succeeded. It marked the start of women moving into regular policing — of being treated as individuals and not constantly ghettoized simply on the basis of gender.[50]

Coffal and Blankenship had to learn patrolling by trial and error as they had never had any in-house instruction. They were worse off than male rookies straight out of the academy who had at least some specific training. Despite the fact that on no force in the United States would two male rookies fresh from the academy be given a patrol of their own — each would first work with a veteran to make the transition from theory to practice — Coffal and Blankenship were sent out alone. Giving them only 24 hours notice ensured they could not even do minimal preparations on their own. In the end, of course, nothing went wrong. Nonetheless, they were placed at enormous and unnecessary risk. If one wished to appear to yield to female demands yet stack the deck to increase the odds that the women would fail, the Indianapolis move was one so structured.[51]

8

Foreign, 1930–1969

Progress for policewomen was as slow and ineffectual in England as in the United States. Typical of male hatred and hostility was an article by an anonymous writer in 1931 in the *Saturday Review of Politics*. Offering "nothing but praise" to matrons for their indispensable work in searching female detainees he added, "But when it comes to patrolling the streets may I ask ... what the female police are doing there?" Using the old argument that policing required brute physical force and that females were weak, he announced, "In the event of a real scrap she would be the first to demand the protection of a policeman," and if called to a riot she might faint. He concluded, "A police-woman is, in short, a contradiction in terms. I object to those amateur guardians of morality being made members of 'the force' of which we are so justly proud. I protest against the public support of this amiable but useless absurdity, the she policeman." When that article was published there were perhaps 150 policewomen in all of England and Wales. None did any regular police patrolling, only in conjunction with their work concerning women and children, as in the United States.[1]

Even though Lilian Wyles had been appointed to Scotland Yard in 1922, it was not until 1933 that three women were appointed permanent members of the detective staff at Scotland Yard. This followed experimental tests of women's aptitude for criminal investigation that proved "successful" (presumably Wyles) and apparently also lasted over a decade. The term Scotland Yard referred to the building headquarters of the Metropolitan London Police force, sometimes in a general way to police, but more usually was used as a reference to the Criminal Investigation Department (CID). It was to this unit that the three were appointed. Year after year Wyles requested more police-women at the CID. Mostly the requests were returned marked, "This is not a suitable time to increase the number of women in CID." By 1945 there were 16; and by 1948 the unit employed 48 policewomen.[2]

Agitation for more policewomen continued. In 1934 a deputation from the National Council of Women, supported by 22 of its affiliated societies, petitioned the Home Office. When that group held its convention the following year it repeated the call for more female police, stating there were a total of 161 in all of England and Wales. Claiming that in metropolitan London for every pound sterling spent on policemen, less than one-third of a penny was spent on female police, the council asked only that spending on female police in England and outside London be increased to that one-third of a penny amount. "We do not ask for anything expensive," they explained.[3]

Another source listed the total policewomen for the Metropolitan London region at 53 in 1936 (authorized to be increased to as many as 142), with English cities and boroughs outside London having 76 policewomen. When an English policewoman got married she lost her job.[4]

Lobbying for female police continued into the early 1940s with representatives from various groups by then having formed a special lobby group, a Women Police Campaign Committee. Early in 1944 the home secretary announced in Parliament, in answer to a question, that there were 348 policewomen in England and Wales, with 335 of them sworn in. However, what lobbying could not accomplish the disruptions of World War II could. As a result of a manpower shortage in April 1946 the home secretary announced a drive to recruit 200 female officers with a special appeal to young women leaving the services or war jobs.[5]

In 1947 there were 700 policewomen in England and Wales. Three years later the total stood at 1,336.[6] The small and separate force that policed the city of London continued to ban women, protesting they would be useless in the city, until 1949 when they relented, recruiting a small number of women. At that time the Metropolitan London Police force numbered 22,000; while the city of London police had a strength of 983.[7]

Expansion in the number of policewomen in England continued into the 1950s and was even more pronounced in areas outside metro London. Whereas in 1939 half of the total 200 policewomen were in the Metropolitan Police force, in 1954 — after a tenfold increase — around 75 percent were in outside forces; 548 in the metro force, and 1,453 in the 158 county and borough forces throughout Great Britain. Policewomen numbered 282 in 1940 and 418 in 1945. *The Times* remarked that the success in introducing females was dependent "first, on the keenness of the chief constable to accept the idea; next, on the willingness of inspectors and sergeants to cooperate in the plan."[8]

By the end of 1956 there were 2,200 female police employed in England and Wales, out of an authorized quota of 2,494. They had the same powers, duties, responsibilities, and training as male police, but they earned 90 percent of the men's pay. Showing more ambivalence toward them, *The Times* inaccurately stated, "That more women police are required has nothing to do with the shortage of men. Their work is complementary, not competitive, and though they share general duties with the men, the real, primary job of women police is among women and children." After commenting on the fact that policewomen were entitled to maternity leave, the newspaper used this entitlement as a springboard to show how threatened society was by working females, and not just policewomen. "But what is more than interesting, and perhaps the answer to those who feel the modern woman should be able to organize her home and family as well as an outside job, is the fact that time and time again, having returned to police work, they give it up for the claims of their family, however good arrangements may have been for the care of home and children in their absence.... They, of all people, know the 'price paid' when children lack the secure feeling of mother always being there."[9]

Female police in Great Britain began to be used in regular patrol work in 1966 when a small number were assigned the same way as men. In 1969 Liverpool used females as part of a task force patrol to combat crime. Liverpool police superintendent J. W. Carroll said of that experiment, "The policewomen have adapted themselves extremely well ... and have neither sought nor been granted any special consideration. Patrolling on foot, in vehicles or in plain clothes, their results are in excess of those of the average police officer and many have received commendations."[10]

As in the United States, there was only limited and experimental use made of policewomen in the late 1960s as officers being interchangeable with males. Also, as in the United States, the 1970s would be the period of major integration for women into the forces.

In 1969 Great Britain had 86,091 police officers, 3,490 were female (4 percent). On the Metropolitan Police force there were 19,608 officers, with a total of 548 women (less than 3 percent). Ninety percent of the policewomen wore uniforms that had skirts. Constable Joan Lock, a six-year veteran who had resigned, remarked, "Although women police are warned in training that they will be treated just like the men, it generally worked out in practice that we were treated like bone china." Speaking for the establishment side, Shirley Becke, an officer for 25 years and chief superintendent for the last two and one-half years, declared, "There is no prejudice in the force today."[11]

China got its first female police in 1933 when 18 "stalwart, unmarried Chinese girls" were given three months of training and then assigned to Peiping (Peking — now Beijing). Also in the 1930s Paris, France, appointed 18 female police assistants, after experimenting for a time with two, due to pressure applied by the Conseil National des Femmes. As of 1969 in France's national police force there were 94,000 plainclothes and uniformed personnel, of which 1,600 were female. More than 1,400 of them were employed by the Parisian police as not sworn in meter maids; thus there were less than 200 policewomen and they worked only with women and children, doing no general patrol duties.[12]

Barcelona, Spain, used 14 female officers for patrol work during its 1930 exhibition, but disbanded them after the fair. Some were appointed again during the Spanish Civil War, chiefly to search for illegal arms and ammunition that were increasingly being smuggled by women.[13]

Australia had 34 policewomen in 1936, spread among all of its states. During World War II the number in the state of Victoria went from eight to 12 to 18 between 1945 and 1949. Before the war, female officers were not permitted to drive police cars but began to do so right after the war. Victoria's policewomen were kept on a separate seniority list until 1978, when they were integrated into the male seniority list. By 1959 there were over 40 policewomen in Victoria, 54 in New South Wales, eight in Tasmania, 10 in West Australia, 36 in South Australia, and 10 in Queensland. One qualification for a Queensland female recruit — not for males— even in 1959, was "they should be competent shorthand-typists."[14]

Copenhagen, Denmark, had nine women officers in 1936 plus a few in other Danish communities. In Holland nine towns had a total of 20 female inspectors and 22 constables, but ground was said to have been lost during the depression. Switzerland had eight officers in four cities. In Hungary one of three female detectives appointed a decade earlier remained in service but was due to be pensioned off soon with no new appointments contemplated. A few were reported in the Turkish cities of Ankara and Istanbul, while the four in Dublin, Ireland, were called "in a sense experimental." During that mid–1930s period policewomen were also reportedly at work in Austria, Burma, Norway, Portugal, Sweden, Uruguay, Egypt, Mexico, and Russia. The author of this report concluded that "the duties of foreign policewomen are, in broad outline the same as in America, except that a greater proportion of their time is spent dealing with commercialized prostitution.[15]

The state of Travancore was the first in India to employ policewomen when it experimented in 1938 with the appointment of one female head and 12 women as special police constables. In 1942 all were appointed as temporary women constables in addition to the regular strength of the police force. Kanpur (Cawnpore), India, appointed a few policewomen in 1939 to be prepared for any repetition of an incident which took place in 1938. That year during a labor dispute male police were called in to remove striking female workers who lay down in front of the plant gates to prevent the entry of scabs. Their physical removal was said to have been a "very delicate situation." With those few exceptions no female police were used in India until the immediate post–Independent period, when a myriad of disruptions led to strikes, riots, and agitation that involved female participants. In addition, social disruptions led to more females out and about, seeking employment and, inevitably, more police interaction with women and children, both for social reasons and as detainees. Both Delhi and the Punjab appointed them to their regular forces

in 1948. The Punjab Police Commission observed in 1962 "there is considerable prejudice prevailing in the country against the recruitment of women in
police forces. The approach of most witnesses was pessimistic." Six years later
the Delhi Police Commission stated that policewomen's work "should start
with looking after children and women and gradually they may be utilized
for public relations work on behalf of the police."[16]

One reason for appointing them in the Punjab was the setting up of the
passport checking posts on the India-Pakistan border (the Punjab had been
partitioned into East Punjab in India and West Punjab in Pakistan at independence). Since Muslim women generally covered their entire body with a
single cloth, a need was felt to recruit women to conduct searches of these
women. However, in the Punjab "people were doubtful about their utility for
policing. They were considered a burden on the department." An advocate
in favor of their appointment even remarked that policewomen were really
an "extravagant eccentricity as they themselves were to be protected by men
police on various occasions when they were employed to perform their
duties."[17]

On March 23, 1944, the Hamilton Ontario Police Commission decided
two women should be hired on a trial basis as special officers to help the
police department's morality office. Two months later Muriel Oliver and
Leora Etherington joined the Hamilton Police Department serving summonses and executing warrants, as well as searching, guarding, and escorting
female prisoners. Hamilton did not get its first official policewomen until
January 9, 1959, when three were sworn in.[18]

Lois Beckett joined the Sault Ste. Marie, Ontario, police department in
1949 as a civilian employee. She left in 1961 to become a police constable with
the township of Tarentorus, north of the city. In 1965 Sault Ste. Marie amal-
gamated with Tarentorus and Korah townships and Beckett found herself
back on the Sault city force — which did not have any female police officers.
She was told to hand in her uniform and gun and be reassigned as a switchboard operator by the then chief, Fred Clarke. She fought her demotion before
the courts and the Ontario Human Rights Commission. An inquiry headed
by retired Canada Supreme Court justice Willard Estey agreed with her contention that she had been discriminated against and ordered Beckett reinstated. Once reinstated, Beckett worked in several departments including
traffic, safety, and intelligence. In 1968 a judge of the Ontario Supreme Court
denied equal pay to Beckett on the ground that it was "common sense" that
she should be paid less than her male counterparts. She was elected president
of the Association of Police Women in 1970 and named distinguished officer
of the year. She retired from the Sault Ste. Marie Police Department in 1991
after 42 years of service. Lois Beckett died on August 21, 1998, aged 68.[19]

Berlin, Germany, appointed women to its police force in 1948 for the first time since pre–Hitler days. This was due to the shortage of males resulting from the war. The two pictured in a *Life* magazine profile wore uniforms with skirts and were described as "stern and well-disciplined." Primarily they dealt with juvenile problems, such as keeping girls under 18 out of bars and checking out prostitutes. At training school they learned to attend to bicycle accidents, detect phony blind men, and identify forged papers. They were allowed to assist male police only in directing traffic.[20]

By the late 1960s there were about 120,000 police in West Germany, 1,600 of them were female (1.3 percent). They dealt with juveniles and women; most of them did not carry weapons and did not get assigned to patrol duty. To be recruited a woman had to have experience of a social nature such as teaching, nursing, or social work.[21]

Women in Nigeria began to agitate for females to be added to the federal Nigeria Police Force (NPF) in the 1940s when women leaders and delegates of the Women's Party met with government officials to lobby for this reform. It was their belief that women would be better able than men to deal with prostitutes and female criminals. Police Commissioner W. C. C. King rejected the suggestion, considering it too risky to entrust to women the dealings with Lagos gangsters. Nor was he convinced that female police would be able to cope with "screaming and swearing prostitutes, drunken merchant seamen of all nationalities, pimps ... touts and the rest of the unsavoury fraternity." Said King, "I find it quite impossible to visualize women police in action in Lagos." In addition, he cited the opinions of British police officers, such as the chief constable of Salford, to the effect that female cops were not generally accepted with borough and county forces of the United Kingdom and that they would be unacceptable to the people of northern Nigeria "because of the status of women there." In both 1951 and 1953 a member of the Legislative Council raised the matter, to no avail in the House, urging the NPF to employ policewomen. The following year the government announced its intention to begin the Women's Police Branch of the NPF.[22]

Late in 1955 20 Nigerian females began their seven months of training to become the first policewomen in Nigeria. They had to sign six-year contracts. The whole idea met with a great deal of contempt from all quarters, drawing remarks such as, "What a mean job for any decent girl," and "It will be a refuge for the man-hater and the ugly and the widowed." As a result few applied, causing the planned-for first group of 40 to be scaled back to half that number. They received no weapons training; their duties were the usual "welfare of women and the young." They were required to live in barracks, and if they married a male officer they could set up housekeeping in barracks. However, if one married a civilian he could not live with her, and she could not move out of the barracks to live with him. In that case if they wished to live together she would have to resign, but only after her six years were up.[23]

By the end of 1962 Nigeria had 170 policewomen. Male police still resented the intrusion, while the general opinion of such women remained low. Policewoman T. Umoffia complained of "the maliciously pious and unfounded fear that the Nigeria Police ... provide a home of vice for women and that those who join it as Women Police are low breeds and half-spoilt women who go there to be totally spoilt."[24]

Around 1953 Buenos Aires was the only city in South America with female police on its payroll. Two years later the Sao Paulo, Brazil, state government formed the Sao Paulo Police Women's Auxiliary Corps, operating on temporary regulations. To reassure the populace the state government put out a pamphlet to dispel misunderstandings about women officers. It read in part, "a group of women ... high school graduates and graduates of the Police School, of impeccable character, who do not carry weapons but are taught personal-defense techniques for use in emergencies.... Its aim is to protect and guide women and children ... and its aim is preventive rather than punitive." The pamphlet emphasized they were not "a group of masculine, physically overdeveloped, aggressive women ... who go around arresting people or trying to quell riots." Not that the pamphlet was very effective, for the head of those female officers Hilda Macedo, remarked, "We had trouble with people who thought we were trying to build up a bunch of Amazons. But of course we didn't want to do that. In fact, femininity is an important asset in our work." Recruits were not allowed to marry. Macedo said they disqualified married women initially, since "Brazilian husbands are still mighty demanding" and "motherhood and police work don't mix very well, especially in Brazil." It was Macedo's hope that as female police came to be accepted in Brazil they might start taking on married women, but never mothers.[25]

In Sweden limited use of females started in 1949. Not until 1965 were they allowed to leave their traditional female and juvenile plainclothes assignments and patrol the streets in uniform. Males in the force were incensed by this and pressured the National Police Board, the country's highest police authority. The board gave in, ordering women back inside the stations to perform their traditional assignments on the grounds that patrol duty was too strenuous for them. Two years later the Swedish government reversed that ruling, sending policewomen back onto the streets.[26]

Japan appointed its first policewomen in 1946 when 63 women were sworn in. As in Germany, a shortage of males was a major reason for this appointment. By 1953 there were 1,200 policewomen, 3 percent of the total strength, at work all over Japan. They got the same training and salaries as policemen. Two decades later policewomen still comprised about 3 percent of the total force. The prevailing view held by senior Japanese police officials was that "there are certain jobs and assignments that a woman cannot handle, such as working after midnight, stopping street fights or arresting armed robbers."[27]

9

U.S., 1970–2012 (Part I)

As the 1970s started, American policewomen and those who wished to join those ranks faced strongly entrenched opposition. Patrick V. Murphy was police commissioner of the New York Police Department from about 1970 to 1973. After acknowledging that resistance to female police was fierce, Murphy said, reasonably enough, that no one had ever proved policing was a male only job or that females could handle only certain tasks. However, Murphy wished to pass over that and "move to a more intelligent level of discourse and deployment where women are used for the special capabilities they possess.... Since none of our police departments sport a 50–50 ratio of men and women, is it discriminatory and sexist to suggest that we ought to be using those few women we have in the best possible way?" According to the commissioner, Edward Davis, chief of the Los Angeles Police Department, told him that he, Davis, had a way to get around any court order requiring the hiring of females. He would maintain the LAPD height minimum of 5'8", hiring no person under that level.[1]

When asked in 1972 if he thought there was a place in policing for women outside of their long-standing traditional duties, Chief Davis replied, "Then are we going to let a 5-foot-2 115-pound petite blond girl go in there and wrestle with a couple of bank bandits? I personally don't think that's the role for women." As to the question of whether or not the biological makeup of a woman might affect her performance Davis said, "In the history of my wife and two daughters there were certain times during the month when they did not function as effectively as they did at other times of the month."[2]

A year earlier, Davis told an audience of 100 policewomen that they did not belong in patrol cars and could not be trusted with guns during "that time of the month." Female officers were then viewed as "either lesbians or nymphomaniacs," according to retired LAPD officer Bobbi Squire. When Los Angeles and other cities were soon forced to hire female patrol officer's some LAPD men joked that the department would have to add one more pouch to an officer's belt — to hold tissues for the emotional outburst of females. It was 1981 before Los Angeles finally dropped its officer minimum height requirement from 5'8" to 5'0".[3]

In C. J. Flammang's textbook-style *Police Juvenile Enforcement*, published in 1972, the author declared that females were well-established juvenile officers in police departments. However, "some concessions must be made to the female in police work. One of the major problems faced by these women is the loss of their feminine identity among their fellow officers. The police-woman must remain a feminine entity to be effective." He believed an exhaustive selection process should be used in hiring a female officer, a process "exceeding that of the male officer." A worry for Flammang was that because a policewoman was usually one of only a few in a department there was a tendency to allow her privileges not afforded to male officers. That could lead to morale problems. Policewomen, he thought, should be given cases involving females as suspects, dependent child cases, and misdemeanor offenses perpetrated by young males up to age 15. Nonetheless, he concluded, "The policewoman can be an asset to juvenile work, but a female officer is not a necessity."[4]

If men were unhappy so were the female police. A questionnaire sent in 1971 to 150 policewomen in 14 departments drew 138 replies. The women had a median of 14.2 years of education versus 12.4 years for male officers. It was still true then that many departments required a higher educational attainment for female applicants than for males. For example, the Portland, Oregon, department required a four-year college degree for women, but only a two-year degree for a male. This study found policewomen to be less authoritarian in their outlooks and attitudes than policemen. While the women were generally satisfied with police work, they submitted low scores when asked how satisfied they were with their own chances of getting ahead in policing. This was so, thought the study, because "only rarely do police departments allow policewomen to compete in the regularly scheduled promotional examinations."[5]

In 1972 Jean Ford Clayton filed charged of sex discrimination against the Cleveland, Ohio, Police Department with the Federal Employment Opportunity Commission. Until that time, women who joined the force automatically were assigned to the Women's Bureau and limited to handling cases involving missing, neglected and abused children, juvenile delinquency and rape. Because of her actions, the Women's Bureau was disbanded in 1973, and women with the Cleveland police were able to work in departments previously reserved for men. Later that year, the Women's Law Fund filed another class action federal lawsuit on behalf of Clayton and another policewoman, claiming the city had not kept its promise to hire more women to work in all departments. The suit claimed the department discriminated in transfers, promotions, benefits, and salary. Clayton, a Cleveland native whose maiden name was Ford, graduated from Central High School in 1940. She attended Wilberforce and Kent State universities. From 1943 to 1945 she served in the Women's Air Corps. She was a bus driver for the Cleveland Transit System before joining the Cleveland Police Department in 1951. After the Women's Bureau was disbanded Clayton worked in the narcotics unit and at the City Jail. She became a detective with the vice squad before retiring in 1973. Jean Ford Clayton died at her Cleveland home on July 8, 2000 aged 77.[6]

An example of a magazine being politically correct on the surface while still undercutting the concept of women being capable and entitled to equality could be seen in a *Time* profile on the women in blue in the spring of 1972. By then there were said to be about 45 females in at least seven cities doing regular police patrol work in the country. Many of these women were sent out to respond to family dispute calls on the theory they calmed the disputes better than did men. Said one Indianapolis patrolman, "Some of these families will call you back two or three times a night but I've noticed that when the women go, that's the last time we hear from that family." Lewis J. Sherman, a University of Missouri-St. Louis psychologist was quoted as saying that male officers fed the fires through their own aggressive, provocative behavior, while females stepped in with greater tact and subtlety. Also postulated was women's "built-in calming effect" causing enraged males to not respond as angrily or violently to female officers as to male officers. That effect, thought Sherman, could be the result of cultural learning in which males were socialized to believe it was cowardly to assault a female. In spite of this even-handed approach to that point, *Time* closed out with a specific example of a female officer in action. By dealing with a named individual near the end of the story all the focus moved there. All earlier material could be erased or overridden. In its example *Time* presented the stereotypical image of the inept, overly emotional woman officer. Patrolwoman Ina Sheperd collared a muscular shoplifter in Miami in December 1971. There were no other officers or even a telephone around. Unable to summon help, she burst into tears, "If I don't bring you in, I'll lose my job," she sobbed to her prisoner. Chivalrously he accompanied her until a squad car was located. The magazine gave no other examples of specific incidents of policewomen at work.[7]

Just a few months later that same year, *Newsweek* also profiled the "female fuzz." It was more openly condescending to females from the beginning; "She is pretty, blond, svelte, quintessentially female ... the pretty blonde is herself a cop." Officer Lavette Caples was further described as a "mother of three." Male officers were said to be hostile to sending any females into dangerous neighborhoods, with some of them claiming that the presence of female officers might stimulate the violence they were trying to repress; "Others worry that in a violent confrontation they would defer to their chivalric impulses, leaving the felons to flee while they protected their female colleagues." A southern California deputy sheriff said, "I don't care if a dame is Calamity Jane and can shoot a button off my vest. My biggest weapons are that I'm tall and pretty intimidating. These gals could only intimidate my little sister." Reported was the story of Miami female officers who ruined several pairs of pantyhose in making quick exits from cruisers. In Los Angeles one almost lost her skirt while climbing a wall. They also wondered where to pack their guns—choosing their handbags. These examples all tended to show how silly the concept of policewoman could be. Unstated and perhaps unclear to most readers was that those women were required by their departments to wear skirts and pantyhose. They were not authorized to wear gun holsters. Policewomen were well aware how ludicrous such clothing was for their work. They wanted to wear pants and to have holsters. What should have come to them quickly and easily when they began regular patrol duty — proper attire and equipment — was in fact delayed for an inexcusable length of time, no doubt for political reasons. The only improvement in this *Newsweek* article in its coverage of policewomen over material 20 to 30 years old was that the women were not called girls all the time.[8]

Kathaline Salzano joined the New York City Police Department in 1968 and had done the usual policewoman's jobs, described as "switchboard duty, clerical work, searches of female prisoners and DOA's, summer details at Coney Island, where she kept kids entertained until their parents showed up to claim them." Said Salzano, "The men used to kid us. They said we made the same as they did but we only did half the work. They were right." As a result of a 1972 law change she became one of the first New York females to volunteer for and get patrol duty that same year. She was teamed with Lucille Burrascano as a sort of test within a test to see how an all-female team would fare. They worked out of the Seventy-Seventh Precinct in Bedford-Stuyvesant. Salzano stated, "There are always a few men who like to give women a hard time. There probably always will be. You just have to get used to it.... For the first few months the sergeant sent a backup car every time we answered a call." While male officers may have been hostile to policewomen, residents of the area were not. "The residents like the idea, especially when there's a family dispute. A lot of women think men all stick together," explained Salzano.[9]

In New Jersey the male police establishment put up a solid wall of resistance as late as the summer of 1972. James Alloway, president of the New Jersey State Civil Service Commission, announced that women could now apply for public safety jobs formerly open to men only, such as firefighters and police officers. However, he noted that women would have to meet the minimum height standards, which were 5'7" for the police. Such height standards remained in place on many police forces in the very early 1970s and, depending on the exact height, had the effect of automatically eliminating 70 to 95 percent of all females in the general population. Newark Police Director John Redden did not like the idea of equal roles for male and females saying, "I think men and women are equal, but different. And that difference obviously determines the different roles people will undertake." He felt women performed very well on special assignments as policewomen but "would not be able to handle general police work." Paterson police chief James Hannan said he would follow the directions of the Civil Service Commission but saw some problems ahead. "First of all, we'll have to change our physical plant, including the locker rooms, showers and toilets. And I can foresee some domestic problems when the spouses of the men and women police officers start to complain."[10]

The Indianapolis experiment was successful enough that two more policewomen were assigned to a patrol car early in 1970. Two years later four more were assigned. In Peoria, Illinois, six female officers were patrolling the city's streets in one-person squad cars in 1971. In Florida nine of Miami's 28 female officers performed patrol work. While there were a few exceptions like these, in the vast majority of cases the outlook for policewomen achieving equality was bleak, and business continued as usual. New York City listed 65 of its policewomen (18 percent of them) as detectives, yet some did mainly clerical work. When the Police Foundation — a nonprofit funding agency established in 1970 by the Ford Foundation to help American police agencies by developing and funding programs of innovation and improvement — queried the 60 largest police departments in the United States in the fall of 1971, not one was accepting women applicants even though many departments were below authorized strength and were actively recruiting male applicants. Most of the police departments had established female quotas of less than 1 percent of the total sworn force. San Francisco, for example, had 1,795 sworn positions, nine of which were designated for women. St. Louis had not hired a woman officer since 1956 and had just 13 female officers among its 2,232-member force. The largest quota for females in the country was at Indianapolis with 74 positions (6.5 percent of its force) set aside for women. However, only 14 of those 74 women did any outside work away from the police station. The need for quotas was explained by a high-ranking official from the Washington, D.C., force who said they were necessary because "without them, departments would be flooded with female recruits."[11]

In 1971 policewomen totaled 1.3 percent of the total police strength in the 32 largest American cities. By 1974 it was 2.4 percent in those cities, 2.6 percent two years later. Sixteen of those cities had less than 1 percent in sworn female officers in 1971, but by 1976 only six did so. Of the nation's 166,000 state and local police in 1974 only 2,859 were female, less than 2 percent.[12]

A survey by the Police Foundation of 286 municipal law enforcement agencies serving populations over 50,000 showed that 3.38 percent of sworn personnel were female, at a time when women made up 38 percent of the national labor force. Of that total, 2.67 percent were white females, 0.71 were black. At the police officer rank 4.26 percent of the sworn personnel were female; at all higher ranks the figure was 1.69 percent. Leading the way among cities, and labeled progressives as they had sworn female components above the average, were Denver with 67 females, 4.9 percent; Houston with 181 females, 6.1 percent; Miami with 49 women, 6.2 percent; Washington, D.C., with 307 women, 7.3 percent; and at the head of the list Detroit with 644 women, 11.7 percent. One reason for the meager percentage of females at ranks above officer, according to the Police Foundation study, was "the tendency toward assigning women to nine-to-five desk jobs after a few years in the department and psychologically discouraging them from applying for promotions to supervisory positions requiring that they supervise men."[13]

The Federal Bureau of Investigation (FBI) appointed its first two female agents in July 1972 after the death of long-time director J. Edgar Hoover, who said of women in the FBI, "The Bureau's responsibilities were too taxing, too physically demanding, too complicated and serious for women, except insofar as they would help out in menial or subservient roles." When the FBI had needed a female for various assignments they had to use an untrained female civilian clerk or borrow a policewoman from a local force. In early 1972 the Secret Service appointed its first female agent. Also in July 1972 the Pennsylvania State Police became the first state police agency to employ female officers for identical duties to those performed by male officers. However, as one observer noted, "Women have not had an easy time of it, though, at the state police level and their 'intrusion' into state police agencies has been strongly resisted by such agencies as the South Carolina Highway Patrol, the New Jersey State Police, the Alabama Highway Patrol and others." By the end of the 1970s women comprised only one or two percent of the state police agencies in most places. A 1975 study of these agencies found that of 42,000 state police officers only 135 were female, 0.033 percent. In 1971 the FBI's *Uniform Crime Reports* said that females were 1.4 percent of the country's municipal police officers. The 1977 edition of that publication put the number at 2.7 percent. According to the 1984 edition there were 28,027 policewomen in America, 6 percent of all sworn officers.[14]

By 1993 the Secret Service had 2,000 agents with about 190 being women. They were assigned to all areas, including guarding the president of the United States. Nonetheless, female agents admitted that they "still brace themselves for discrimination and believe that they continually have to fight the agency's male heritage."[15]

Requiring a college degree for women and a high school diploma for men was common practice on many forces. One rationale for this was that since openings for policewomen were few, departments could afford to hire only the best. Separate eligibility lists for men and women were kept so that women were not hired even when their scores were higher than the men's scores. In many departments male and female recruits were given separate training. One academy instructor said, "Why should we waste our time on them when they won't need to use it, sitting behind a typewriter?" Some police departments, like San Francisco's, did not allow women to take promotional examinations at all. Others allowed it only when there was an opening traditionally filled by a woman, such as head of a Women's Bureau. One woman waited 14 years before being allowed to take the sergeant's exam. In St. Paul a woman who sought to take the sergeant's examination hired a lawyer to present her claim to the Civil Service Board. She succeeded without suing. A policewoman in Seattle who had been a sergeant for 15.5 years applied to take the examination for lieutenant; it was four years before the Seattle Civil Service Commission would even consider her application. Joanne Rossi was refused an application for the Fairmount Park Police in Philadelphia because at 5'6" and 112 pounds she was under the 5'7" and 140 pounds minimum. The courts decided in 1973 that these requirements had no relation to job duties. Also in that year Veragene Hardy brought a class action suit in a California state court to order the City of Oakland to create a civil service classification for police officers with the Oakland police department that would be open to males and females with a single standard, related to the duties that would be performed. Hardy was not eligible for the position of policeman because of her sex, and she lacked the education required for the position of policewoman. Hardy had graduated from a two-year junior college but the Oakland police required female applicants to have a college degree or four years of police experience, while male applicants needed only a high school diploma. In 1967 Philadelphia policewoman Ruth Wells challenged the practice of requiring both an oral and written examination for women seeking promotion to sergeant but requiring only a written exam for men. The court held in favor of this practice as long as males and females did not compete against each other and job duties were different for the sexes. Part of the court's decision read, "Many of the tasks performed by the police force are of such a nature, physiologically speaking, that they cannot and should not be assigned to women; using firearms, patrolling the highways, maintaining roadblocks, conducting raids, ferreting out dangerous criminals, quelling gang warfare and riots are just a few examples."[16]

Something as seemingly simple as uniforms proved difficult for policewomen. It was another way of delaying putting females on the street and making things hard for them. In Miami the initial uniform for women was a miniskirt. This was still true in 1971 or 1972 when pants were expected "sometime in the future." Dallas had no uniforms of any kind available for women until 1971. Referring to the general situation, the Police Foundation noted in

1972 that "short-sighted superiors initially assigned the patrolwomen skirts, handbags and heeled pumps" — wholly impractical. Chief Jerry Wilson of the Washington, D.C., force recalled the first uniform design for the policewomen on his force, saying they "looked like air hostess uniforms, done up in yellow, blue and pink. I just asked them where they thought the girls were going to carry their guns." As late as the summer of 1974 *U.S. News and World Report* observed that "many departments are adding the option of pants to women's uniforms." After much bother and delay, by the later 1970s female uniforms became the utilitarian outfit of trousers, flat-heeled oxfords, and Sam Browne belt equipped with handcuffs, extra ammunition, nightstick, gun, mace can, and whistle — the same as the male police uniform.[17]

When Deputy Kathy Stanley moved from the Los Angeles County Sheriff's Department to a job as an officer on the University of California at Los Angeles police force in 1975 female university police officers in that nine-campus system still wore miniskirts as uniforms.[18]

The great push to achieve gender equality in policing began in the late 1960s, fueled by the Crime Commission and the movement in society as a whole by different groups to redress various grievances. It came out of the civil rights era and was one aspect of the feminist movement. The second important event in promoting a move to equality was Title 7 of the 1964 Civil Rights Act, which banned sex discrimination. When that law was enacted in 1964 it applied only to the private sector. In 1972 the act was extended to public as well as private employees — including for the first time police departments among others — as the Equal Opportunity Act of 1972. The following year Congress passed the Crime Control Act that, among its provisions, banned sex discrimination by recipients of federal aid to law enforcement agencies. The Law Enforcement Assistance Administration (LEAA) that managed the aid required recipients with 50 or more employees and $25,000 or more in grants to set up women's equal opportunity plans.[19]

The legal activity in the early 1970s meant an end of things such as separate educational requirements for male and female applicants, separate promotional lists, irrelevant height and weight requirements, and the abolition of separate women's division within departments. In a few areas some discriminatory practices had already been abandoned. Miami dropped its higher education requirement for females in 1965; Washington, D.C., followed suit in 1969. The latter city had abandoned its Women's Bureau in 1967, with officials terming it wasteful and inefficient.[20]

Even with these laws, discrimination remained well entrenched. When the Civil Rights Act was extended to the public sector, it outlawed discrimination in employment on the basis of race, creed, color, sex, or national origin. In 1972 for the first time it became illegal to deny women the opportunity to compete with men for police jobs solely on the basis of sex. The Equal

Opportunity Commission (EEOC) created in 1968 was the executor of the Title 7 provision. However, "because it failed to provide sufficient legal sanctions, even the passage of Title 7 did not appreciably alter the male-dominated ranks of police departments— unless pressed by a lawsuit," noted one writer to explain why the theory of equality in practice fell so short of the mark.[21]

Another source noted that discriminatory practices such as keeping women off patrol duty and subsequently off promotion eligibility lists continued, despite the extension of the Civil Rights Act. When females asked for patrol duty they often received the usual spurious arguments about women being too emotional and too physically weak to carry out the duties. Patrol experience was important for promotional consideration. In the examinations for the promotion lists bonus points were sometimes given for military experience, which applied to less than 2 percent of the females, even though no evidence existed that officers with military backgrounds were better than those with no such background. Oral examinations were sometimes given, making it easier to downgrade female applicants.[22]

While a few departments altered standards such as height minimums prior to 1973, it took a lawsuit settled that year to cause the height minimums to fall to more reasonable levels, or be abolished altogether. In September 1973 the court held in the case of *Smith v. The City of East Cleveland* that its 5'8" and 150 pounds standard was discriminatory under the Civil Rights Act of 1964 and that larger size did not improve police performance. The city was enjoined from imposing that standard in the future. In the wake of that case police departments around the United States lowered their minimums, down to 5'0" as in Washington or abolished a minimum completely as did New York City in 1973.[23]

Despite its mandate of only funding agencies with equal opportunity programs the LEAA was found to be a weak enforcer. In 1974 the United States Commission on Civil Rights found that the LEAA was not enforcing equal employment opportunity for women because "it believes sex may be a valid criterion for selecting persons for police work." LEAA did withhold funds from the Chicago Police Department in 1974, yet 26 of the 50 largest police departments receiving funds from LEAA were defendants in lawsuits alleging discriminatory practices. In 1974 one researcher discovered that 65 percent of all law enforcement agencies surveyed gave preference to veterans and 57 percent of all municipal agencies granted absolute preferences. Less than 2 percent of veterans were females.

This resistance to women police, displayed in weak or unenforced laws, was strongly reflected by the male officer on the street. One said, "Policing is men's work. The only woman I'd feel comfortable with is built like an Amazon. I prefer the muscle of a man.... A woman's nice to have in a family argument call but she's not physically able to do the job." Said another, "Women can't hold up their end in fights. I'm no babysitter. Equal pay means an equal amount of work. No woman performs the same way or amount as a male." A third stated, "I kind of look down on any type of female who wants to do this job. I don't think it's a woman's place. I've been taught that women should be treated as queens and I try to treat any woman who rides with me as a queen." Commented a fourth male cop, "Sure there's some stuff women can do like type, but they shouldn't jump into fights.... I don't know how their husbands put up with it. It takes his masculinity away when a woman is trying to do a man's job."[24]

The first policewoman killed in the line of duty was 24-year-old Gail Cobb of the Washington, D.C., force, who was fatally shot in September 1974 while chasing a shotgun-toting fugitive. It was even suggested in some quarters that this incident would help ease the way for female entry into policing, that it would be a sort of baptism under fire and show that females were made of the right stuff. Needless to say, it had no such effect; discrimination and harassment continued apace.[25]

This beginning of a movement toward equality was unsettling to some policewomen already on the forces: women who were apparently content with the limited role assigned to women officers. Said Inspector Dorothy Cay of the Detroit force, "Women feel very specialized and are concerned about their backgrounds. They would rise up if they were put into regular patrol and would view it as downgrading. They're very snobbish." Another account mentioned that some felt uneasy about unisex training and deployment, saying they didn't join the force to do "men's work." A third report noted that some women hired for specific positions did not like the change to street duty and "resigned after a brief period of time."[26]

According to one source in the mid–1970s, with the exception of male police "the most outspoken foes of sexual integration are a small but scrappy band of police wives." In New Orleans a group of irate women descended on the force headquarters when their husbands were assigned to train six female rookies by riding with them in patrol cars. In Dallas Chief Frank Dyson was treated to a similar protest when he launched a training program for female officers. During the summer of 1974, 35 members of the New York City Policemen's Wives Association staged a two-hour march from the police headquarters building to City Hall in protest over the assignment of female officers to patrol duty with their husbands. A second source from the same period claimed that "one headache which failed to materialize to a significant extent was jealousy of police wives."[27]

Since those incidents above seem to be the only examples of enraged wives ever reported in the media, one can create a quite different impression by labeling them as major or insignificant. Ostensibly behind the wives' protest was concern that the women would not provide adequate backup for their husbands. A more cogent explanation was that of sexual jealousy. In the end sexual activity did take place, but it was the sexual harassment of policewomen by policemen.

A third major event which propelled women into greater participation in policing was an experiment conducted by the Washington, D.C., force in the early 1970s. Until then the major arguments for not allowing females to perform all policing functions were that they lacked the necessary physical strength and were too emotionally volatile. These arguments were accepted as given facts; no one provided any data to show just how often police work was physically violent or how physically small male police performed compared to physically large male officers; nor was there any evidence to show that females were more or less emotionally volatile than males.

In 1969 newly appointed Washington police chief Jerry Wilson indicated his determination to utilize policewomen throughout his department, including on patrol. To that end he recruited around 100 women over the next couple of years. It was late in 1972 when these women were sent out as a group of rookies and studied on patrol, along with a control group of male rookies, each group numbering 86 officers. On the time it took to launch the program Wilson remarked, "Exemplifying the tendency of minutiae to become substance, more time was spent on the selection of a proper uniform for policewomen than any other aspect of the program." When these females were introduced, Inspector Claude W. Dove of the Washington force commented, "Our biggest problem was to overcome the chauvinistic tendencies of the male officer." Male officers and officials on the force in general had negative attitudes toward women in policing. They believed men were more likely to be "calm and cool," "decisive," and "emotionally stable."[28]

This experiment marked the first time such a large number of females had done unisex policing in an American city. When first assigned to patrol these women were outfitted in skirts, medium heels, and pocketbooks for their guns. Obviously impractical, these uniforms evolved over the decade until by the mid–1970s policewomen in Washington wore the same uniforms as the males. For these new women the chief issued clear guidelines for the equal treatment of the sexes. Implementation of this policy was left in the hands of district supervisors, "some of whom were strongly opposed to the use of women on patrol and who permitted their subordinates to undermine the guidelines," noted one observer. While Peter Bloch, the man who conducted the experiment, concluded these guidelines were "reasonably well observed" several of the experimental women "noted that in reality the women often did not receive the same initial on-the-job instruction as male officers, that their assignments were changed during a tour of duty," and that they faced a great deal of informal opposition and harassment. These discriminatory practices and harassments were often not brought to the attention of higher-ranking officials because many of the females feared complaining to immediate supervisors, who themselves were often guilty of discrimination.[29]

Bloch's study was done by the Police Foundation and studied the two groups of officers for one full year. Both groups had to meet the minimum height standard of 5'7". An initial evaluation was published in February 1973 based on four months of study. As to the question of whether it was appropriate to hire females for patrol assignments on the same basis as men, "this report indicates that it is. The men and women officers were observed to obtain similar results in handling angry or violent citizens. There were no reported incidents which cast serious doubt on the ability of women to perform patrol work satisfactorily." One major difference between the genders was that females made fewer arrests. They also gave out fewer traffic citations. The above conclusions all held when Bloch issued his final report in 1974, based on the full year-long study. Bloch stated that the equal treatment order given by Wilson was reasonably well observed "despite the first six to eight months of the program. Even during that time the rookie policewomen got station duty 10.7 percent of the time, twice as often as the rookie comparison men."[30]

Even before the preliminary report was issued by Bloch, Chief Wilson publicly declared in December 1972 that the policewomen patrol experiment was a success. He also declared that males and females would be hired from the same civil service list, and in April 1973 he dropped the minimum height requirements for police officer from 5'7" to 5'0". By the end of 1972, with the experimental study still ongoing, the special equal treatment order was no longer in effect — ostensibly at least not needed any longer. Differences in assignments for the two experimental groups occurred so the program coordinator was reassigned. A study of assignments in August 1973 revealed that only 45 percent of the new policewomen remained on regular patrol, compared to 71 percent of the comparison men; and 31 percent of the females, but only 12 percent of comparison men, were given inside assignments. "It was not possible to determine whether the high frequency of station assignments was due primarily to the desires of the women or the attitudes of their supervisors." This difference in assigned duties could explain a lower arrest rate for females, since they had less opportunity despite so-called equal treatment. More importantly, no one had questioned the idea that more and more arrests were a good thing, that it reflected proper policing methods. One could argue the hostile, aggressive, and belligerent attitude displayed by some male officers led to encounters escalating and in turn led to higher arrest rates. These measures of police efficiency were all drawn up by the male police establishment, which did not give much thought to the idea that violent male police may be a major hazard on the streets and a principal reason for high arrest numbers.[31]

Citizens of Washington, D.C., regardless of race or sex, were more likely to support the concept of policewomen on patrol than to oppose it. Male officers experienced much less favorable public response than the females, with males perceiving the public as much less cooperative, and they reported receiving 50 percent more insults and close to three times as many threats or attempts at injury, with less than half the compliments as the women reported. All of these male and female rookies were given the normal performance rating and reviews. Sensibly enough, "For comparison men, a few men with lower ratings tended to be reassigned to station duty." However, "those new women with higher performance ratings tended to be reassigned to an inside assignment."[32]

Police officials and male police entered the experiment with negative and hostile attitudes toward policewomen. One Washington police official said, "Most women panic easily and have neither the courage nor physical strength to make an arrest unless they are backed up by a man.... Ninety-nine percent of women police are just social workers picking up 26 checks a year and alleviating the welfare rolls." Said one male officer, "I would improve the policewomen's program by taking the women out of regular uniformed patrol and letting them do jobs they are better suited for." Said a second, "Only 5 percent have the ability to do street work. On the other hand, policewomen have the ability more than a policeman to do office work or station work and to enable the department to bring the policemen out on the streets where they belong." Said a third, "Women should be used in places their bodies and minds are suitable for — youth aid, station personnel, captain's clerks, administrative and morals." Said a fourth, "They are not stable, strong or emotionally ready to take the hours and abuse from the public. They belong in an office where they can do administrative work. They can also be assigned to the juvenile squad and the sex squad." Said a fifth, "If I had to work with one in a scout car my life would be in danger, almost all the time. Improve the policewomen's program by taking women off the street." Despite this marked prejudice by policemen against the women, despite the fact that the women had to work with these men, and despite the fact the equally prejudiced male command structure rated these women, the Bloch study still concluded that "it is appropriate to hire women for patrol assignments on an equal basis with men." The only disadvantage Bloch could find to hiring females equally was that "police management must accept the additional obligation of monitoring ... to insure that women are given the opportunity to perform the work and ... must find ways of carrying out effective police service in the face of extreme prejudice against women on patrol by most patrolmen and male supervisors." Notwithstanding this successful experiment Bloch noted, "There was little change in the attitudes of patrolmen toward policewomen between the start and the conclusion of the experiment."[33]

While males in this study made more arrests than females, there was no evidence that females failed to make arrests that should have been made. Male officers were involved with more serious misconduct, with offenses ranging from traffic accidents to improper use of a gun. By the time the study ended in the fall of 1973, 17 percent of these new male officers and 1 percent of the females had been involved in such problems. In addition, four men and two women had been fired "in the best interest of the department."[34]

Officer Jude Walsh discussed the Bloch study in the trade journal *Police Chief*, where he wrote, "Obviously, I have quoted only portions of the report, and those which I quoted were mostly negative in their treatment of policewomen. I am not supporting nor discouraging that policewomen be used on patrol." With no real negative results to rely on Walsh could only feebly call for "more research."[35]

Other, smaller studies took place around the same time. New York City compared 14 females with 14 males, coming up with "essentially similar findings" to Bloch's. Lewis Sherman evaluated the performance of women in St. Louis County, in suburban, one-person squad cards. St. Louis County Police Department had then 555 sworn officers. It had used policewomen on patrol since August 1972 and had 26 women on active patrol duty at the time of the evaluation. Despite this small number, St. Louis County ranked fourth in the United States in the number of women assigned to general patrol, trailing New York City, Washington, D.C., and Dallas. Results obtained by Sherman paralleled those of Washington and New York. "Women were able to perform the duties of one-person motor patrol in a suburban police department equally as well as men ... women can do the job." He also concluded that policing style differed by gender: "Policewomen perform in a less aggressive fashion than male officers; they made fewer arrests." Citizens of the area felt females could handle their service calls and domestic quarrels better than men. They perceived females as more sensitive to the human element involved in those interactions and considered them more responsive to personal needs expressed by complainants. Independent observers riding with the officers rated the genders the same. Citizens felt no less safe when their calls for help were responded to by women instead of by men. Paradoxically, a frequent objection to policewomen on general patrol duty, voiced by policemen, was that "the public would refuse to accept them." Yet when sampled, citizen attitudes have often refuted that idea. Attitude surveys of policemen were conducted before women were introduced to general patrol work and again six months later in this St. Louis test. Despite its success, Sherman commented, of the male police, "The overall male evaluation of policewomen on patrol still was negative; however, the trend was toward less negativism after six months of contact." Those in favor of more women in policing hoped they would bring with them greater degrees of sympathy, understanding and compassion tempering and perhaps altering all-masculine, aggressive departments. Others feared that "rather than women changing the police system, the police system may be changing the women."[36]

Just before he retired in late 1974 Jerry Wilson said, "Women have demonstrated they can do the job. Some women are going to be better than others. You cannot classify people on the basis of sex. I think it's possible to have a police force of all women, and I would be willing to run it."[37]

By the mid–1980s many more research studies on female police had been completed. In all of these studies women proved as capable as men in all aspects of police work. They required no more assistance from supporting units than men and they worked as well with their partners. Policewomen did not require sick leave more often than men, nor did they sustain any more injuries on the job.[38]

Other major evaluations of policewomen besides those noted above included Pennsylvania State Police, 1973; California Highway Patrol, 1976; Denver, 1977; Newton, Massachusetts, 1977; New York City, 1978; and Philadelphia, Phase 1 and Phase 2, 1978. In all of these studies it was men who were the raters; it was men who set the study standards, and yet females still came out to be as capable police officers as men.

The one exception was the Philadelphia twin studies. Phase 1 reached the same conclusion that all other studies had reached, namely that the genders were equally capable. This conclusion did not sit well with the Philadelphia police establishment, which ignored the conclusion and launched Phase 2. In Phase 1 officers were positively evaluated for avoiding unnecessary arrests and for making prudent calls for backup assistance. In Phase 2 these activities were negatively evaluated. In addition, a high number of arrests in violent confrontations were positively valued. Not surprisingly, Phase 2 concluded that policewomen were not as capable as males.[39]

Philadelphia used this Phase 2 report in court in an attempt to avoid having to hire more females for its force. Filed in court in July 1978, the report stated, "It should be understood by the police department that use of female officers in sector patrol work is being done so at great risk, potential hazard and at increased cost." Outside consultants Bartell Associates of State College, Pennsylvania, who had prepared the report, acknowledged inconsistencies in its findings.[40]

Philadelphia's problems began in 1974 when a sex discrimination suit was filed against the police force by the Justice Department and policewoman Penelope Brace — she became Philadelphia's first female detective in 1978 after she was reluctantly promoted as the result of a federal court order. The idea was to force the city to hire more female officers. To stall for time the department won court approval to conduct its study, ostensibly to objectively determine if women were capable; in reality to prove women were not capable. In

1976, before this study, Philadelphia entered into a consent decree that 20 percent of new police officers hired would be female. Thus in Phase 2, Bartell Associates concluded that females did not perform as "safely and efficiently" as men. It was a statistically unreliable study which unaccountably credited male officers with more arrests, fewer assaults, and fewer calls for assistance than policewomen. Inexplicably, men were also rated higher in building searches. Generally this study was branded for what it was, "absurd."[41]

In September 1979 Federal District Judge Charles R. Weiner ignored the obviously flawed Phase 2, ruling that 25 percent of all police officers hired by the Philadelphia force should be women. This ruling by Weiner blocked the hiring of 225 men who had been selected by the department. Despite past court rulings and the consent decree that females be hired, this group of 225 contained no females. Weiner stated that the city had failed to comply with his earlier ruling in 1979 that found the police department's policy discriminated against women. He ordered the city to stop discriminating. The judge noted that females then made up 1.6 percent of the 7,936-member force. He also noted that the city had adopted a new physical performance test without his approval. This new test was passed by 97.2 percent of men but only by 30.9 percent of women. Weiner said this test had an adverse effect on females. In the summer of 1980 the federal Justice Department obtained another consent decree. This one required Philadelphia to hire women for 30 percent of the next 2,670 police officer vacancies. All remaining outstanding aspects of the sex discrimination suit were also settled, with the city ordered to pay $700,000 to 96 women victims of the force's past discrimination. Justice Department officials felt this settlement was finally reached due to a city administration changeover. Frank Rizzo, a former police commissioner, was mayor at the time the original suit was initiated. Since then he had been succeeded as mayor by William Green, who was described as being more cooperative.[42]

The California Highway Patrol (CHP) undertook its two-year study in 1974 to determine the feasibility of hiring women as state traffic officers (TOs). This study was motivated by a class-action suit launched by Jennie Schultheis in 1973, arguing that the male-only requirement for state traffic officer was discriminatory under Title 7 of the Civil Rights Act. Proceedings in that suit were postponed, pending the results of the study. Ultimately, the finding was for the plaintiff and the CHP agreed to open its application and hiring process to qualified women applicants. The study consisted of hiring 41 females and 42 males, giving them the standard 16-week training, placing them in the field, and evaluating their performance for one year. Of the group, 27 women and 30 men completed training and were placed in the field. One year later 22 women and 28 men remained on the force. Application standards had to be changed before the study. The minimum height of 5' 8" was dropped, since there was no evidence it had any validity or that it was job related. It was also impractical, as the State of California stated, "because surveys report that less than 5 percent of women in the United States between the ages of 18 and 34 are that tall." Attempts by the CHP to fund the study from outside sources failed, with five public and four private sources all declining the project. Ultimately, the department had to fund its own study. One agency that turned down a funding request was the Ford Foundation, because its representatives "were generally of the opinion that the Washington, D.C., Police Department study had settled the issue of women in law enforcement." In the application process the 41 women had an average score of 91 points; the 42 men averaged 86 points. That was without veterans' preference. Vets received an additional ten points added to their scores—in this group 23 males and one female had military experience. When this was included, the average male score moved to 91.25 with females averaging 91.24. The men averaged 49.6 college semester units, the women 67.1 units. As in all other studies the females and males both performed acceptably in the field. The only negative factor cited was a higher cost in employing women due to their higher attrition rate in the field. Left unsaid was that perhaps a higher turnover rate was due to harassment in the academy and in the field. Women cadets did claim life was made harder for them in the academy, while over half the male officers thought females "had it easier" than male cadets in the academy. As to the question of female physical strength, the number of arrests of combative individuals was too small for any conclusion to be drawn.[43]

As part of this study attitude surveys of officers and citizens were also taken, before women were assigned to the field and then one year later. The results showed in all cases that public and departmental personnel felt women had a lower overall ability to perform as officers than males. Members of the public who had contact with female officers had a much higher opinion of their ability to perform than those who did not. The female public thought women were nearly as capable as men; the male public thought a little less of female ability, while male CHP officers thought less still. On the second survey the public gave male and female officers higher evaluations than did uniformed personnel, with the public ranking the genders close to equal in ability. Uniformed personnel gave female officers much lower ratings than they gave male officers. Comparing before and after surveys, the study concluded there was "no major shift in attitudes." Male officers who had personal, professional contact with the female officers had a less favorable opinion of them than other uniformed personnel. Sexist attitudes were strong, for the study noted that "some male TOs believe that the CHP should not hire female officers in the future; other male TOs tend to be overly protective of their female partners and in some instances tend to 'dominate' when highway stops are made. Male

Traffic Officers have also expressed concern that women may not be strong enough to back them up in a volatile situation."[44]

The physical strength issue had always been a red herring, as had the concept that suspects would resist policewomen more than policemen. In Miami, Florida, it was found that the number of people resisting arrest by female police was the same on a proportional basis as for male officers.[45]

Yet another needless and repetitive study was undertaken by the Los Angeles Police Department in 1980 when they studied the performance of 68 policewomen, the first large female group to be hired to go out on patrol. As in other studies a male-female team was as productive and efficient as a male-male team. When male training officers rated the women against a group of men hired at the same time in (1) tactics, (2) initiative and self-confidence, (3) writing and communications, and (4) public contact, male officers rated lower than females in all four areas. Unsatisfactory probation reports were given to males two to four times as often as to women. Each gender drew about the same number of public complaints; however, policewomen received significantly more commendations from the public.[46]

The evidence was overwhelming. Lee Brown, commissioner of public safety in Atlanta, said, "We are satisfied with the performance of our female officers. The women are better equipped than men to handle things like calming down a situation and establishing rapport." The project director of the Police Foundation, Roi Townsey, noted that much of the effectiveness of female police officers stemmed from their willingness to talk to an offender: "The women officers seem to have a general awareness that aggression is not the only answer. They seem to be more open than the men in resolving the situation without the use of aggression." One Los Angeles policewoman said, "A lot of these guys feel they have to assert their virility. More often than not, they end up turning a situation that could be defused into a full-scale brawl." Added a female detective, "Women are not much for walking tall — they have to use their heads." Regarding the unanimous evidence from studies showing females were effective officers, Townsey commented, "Many people refuse to look at the data that indicates the effectiveness of women officers because they simply don't want to hire women."[47]

The Denver study found no difference between men and women in being effective officers. What it did find was that policemen reported resistance from suspects at almost double the rate of policewomen. In addition, male officers averaged a rate of citizens' complaints about 50 percent to 66 percent higher than females. It was not just American studies that showed that policewomen were as effective as policemen. Other countries, such as Great Britain, Canada, Guyana, Sweden, and New Zealand, had all reached the same conclusions.[48]

Many American cities hired more female officers only because they were under some type of court order or consent decree to do so. Early in 1974 Maryland, under Justice Department pressure, agreed to substantially increase its hiring of blacks and women. That same year, and under the same pressure, Jackson, Mississippi, agreed to hire females for one-third of all vacancies. Also in 1974 a federal judge ordered the Detroit Police Department to eliminate sex discrimination in hiring and promotion. The order declared that affirmative action hiring should be extended to women, with the result that for every white male hired or promoted a female would have to be hired or promoted. Additionally, the order included court-mandated computations of retroactive seniority dates for policewomen who had been delayed in joining the department by discriminatory eligibility requirements. This retroactive seniority saved some of the women from being laid off in coming recessionary times. In May 1975 in San Francisco the police department was ordered to hire 15 females for every class of 40 until 60 females were hired and their performance could be studied. The cities of Denver and Miami also hired more females in the 1970s under court orders.[49]

In 1975 New Jersey signed a consent decree with the Justice Department agreeing to hire more women, black, and Hispanic applicants for the state police. Over the next 5 years New Jersey was able to graduate only two females from the State Police Academy. By the end of 1979 New Jersey's 1,943-member force had 51 black men, 27 Hispanic men, four males of Asian background, one black female and one white female. In the previous two classes in the academy 20 females were accepted, along with 350 men for training. Of the men who entered 60 percent graduated, while all 20 females dropped out — one of them ousted by the force. State Police commandant Clinton Pagnano said he hoped to try having an all-female class at the academy. He said that lack of peer support had been suggested as a reason for the high dropout rate of women from the academy. Around the same time the New York State Police were ordered to hire more females until they made up 10 percent of the force. The then 3,400-member force contained 31 black males, 25 Hispanic males, one Asian American male, seven American Indian males, one black female, and 14 white females.[50]

In June 1977 the U.S. Justice Department obtained a consent order in federal court that required most of the large cities in Louisiana, with the exception of New Orleans, to hire more females and blacks for police and fire departments. The order applied to all municipalities over 7,000 in population. The decree abolished minimum height and weight requirements and required departments to fill 25 percent of all police vacancies with females.[51]

Lawsuits were initiated against the City of Los Angeles, with regard to its discriminatory police employment practices, by five women in 1973 and then, separately, by the Justice Department in 1977. Both were resolved when Los Angeles signed two consent decrees in 1980. The city agreed to pay

$750,000 to a group of 175 to 200 women who were hired as police officers before July 1, 1973. In addition, another $750,000 was to be paid out to as many as 8,000 females and minority group members who had been rejected for police officer jobs since August 1970. Regarding the Justice Department suit, the force agreed to establish annual hiring goals until women comprised at least 20 percent of the LAPD. To meet that goal the department agreed to a 25 percent quota of women for hiring in officer positions the first year, 22.5 percent the second year and 25 percent each succeeding year until the goal was met. This would necessitate a vast change since in 1980 the LAPD employed 7,300 officers, only 2.4 percent of whom were female.[52]

When the Police Foundation conducted a 1986 survey, 15 percent (45) of the 297 responding municipal agencies had court-ordered affirmative action policies, 42.5 percent (126) had voluntary affirmative action plans in place, and 42.5 percent (126) had no such plan. In those agencies under court order to increase the ratio of women and minorities, females male up 10.1 percent of the sworn personnel. Of the agencies with voluntary affirmative action plans females comprised 8.3 percent, and in those with no affirmative action plans women were just 6.1 percent of the force. Birmingham, Alabama, signed a consent decree in 1981 after seven years of litigation. Still in effect in 1986, it required the personnel board of Jefferson County when certifying for police officers to have one black applicant for one white applicant and one female for every three males, and those hired had to be of the same ratios. In 1986 the Birmingham force had 15 percent female officers and 10 percent female supervisors. Progress made in the hiring of females and minorities in Detroit was lost to a large extent by layoffs that hit the force from 1979 to 1984. New hiring only started again in 1985 after the recall of all laid-off officers. In 1986, of Detroit's officers, 18 percent were female, as were 12 percent of the supervisors. Detroit then operated under both court ordered and voluntary affirmative action programs. Washington, D.C., with a voluntary affirmative plan, then had 13 percent female officers and 7 percent female supervisors; while for Phoenix, Arizona, also with a voluntary plan, the figures were 7 percent and 2 percent, respectively. In Chicago policewomen did not receive the same pay as male officers in the Youth Division (to which all females were then assigned) until 1976, after protracted litigation. That same year Chicago entered into a consent decree whereby each class of police rookies would be 33 percent white male, 34 percent minority male, and 33 percent female. Yet by late 1986, still under that order, Chicago policewomen comprised 10 percent of sworn personnel and 2 percent of the supervisors.[53]

These suits and many others were instrumental in allowing many women to get hired as police officers. However, a reversal came with the change to the Reagan administration in 1981 as affirmative action programs were deemphasized. In 1985 the Justice Department called on 56 cities, counties, and states to modify affirmative action plans in order to end the use of numerical quotas designed to increase employment of women, blacks, and Hispanics. Reagan's administration considered such preferences based on race, sex, or national origin unacceptable under Title 7 of the Civil Rights Act of 1964. The Justice Department sent letters to all 56 public employers asking them to join the Justice Department in urging federal courts to amend the decrees. Among those 56 were the police departments of New York State, New Jersey, Buffalo, Syracuse, Los Angeles, Philadelphia, San Francisco, and Cincinnati. While many orders and decrees remained in effect, the likelihood of vigorous prosecution by the federal authorities for failure to comply was decreased under the Reagan and Bush regimes.[54]

One of the biggest problems for policewomen was the attitude taken toward them by male officers. Occasionally, policewomen themselves echoed some of the negative statements made about them by the males. In 1973 a questionnaire was sent to 27 policewomen and 22 policemen in a large metropolitan area in the South. One question was do women make as good police officers as men? In reply, 4.5 percent of males strongly agreed, 13.6 percent agreed, 18.2 percent were undecided, 31.8 percent disagreed, and 31.8 percent strongly disagreed. As for the policewomen, 37 percent strongly agreed, 25.9 percent agreed, 14.8 percent were undecided, 14.8 percent disagreed, and 7.4 percent strongly disagreed. This survey taker concluded that "for the male officers, the presence of women on the force lowered the status of their job by defining it as a 'woman's job.'"[55]

A questionnaire sent to Ventura County California sheriff's deputies in 1974 to try and measure how well females were being accepted was returned by 16 of 20 female officers and by 159 of 200 male officers. An example of questions asked was, "Do you think that the average citizen prefers to have a male as a police officer? In reply, 98.1 percent of the men and 62.5 percent of women said yes. Another question was, "Considering patrol functions, do you feel that female officers as a whole possess the physical strength necessary for the job?" The reply was that 91.2 percent of the men said no, as did also 56.3 percent of the females. In addition, 57.5 percent of men and 93.8 percent of women indicated that females could cope as well as males with handling family disturbance calls. A further question was, "Do you feel that your safety would be jeopardized if your partner were of the opposite sex?" To this, 100 percent of women said no, while 67.7 percent of the men said yes. When asked if they felt that male officers were psychologically better suited to police functions, 68 percent of men said yes, while 87 percent of females said no. Asked if their spouses would object to their working a full shift with a partner of the opposite sex, 32.7 percent of males said yes, with 6.2 percent of females agreeing. When asked if they would object to working under the direction of a female watch commander, 100 percent of the females said no, while 52.9

percent of the men said yes. Queried as to whether female officers performing in limited assignments should receive equal pay with male officers of equal rank who are performing in all assignments, 87.5 percent of females said yes, 54.8 percent of males said yes. Asked how department morale would be affected by the full employment of female police, 50 percent of females thought it would have a positive effect, 31.2 percent perceived a negative effect, while 18.8 percent thought it would have no effect. Of the male officers 58.5 percent thought it would have a negative effect, 20.2 percent said no effect, and 16.9 percent saw a positive effect, while 4.4 percent did not answer. The author of this study concluded, "An overall review of the survey indicates that there is a low acceptance factor for females to be used in all police functions, especially those areas which could be termed hazardous in nature." In the space for comments the study author said that a number suggested the creation of a report writing unit in which patrol divisions could utilize the services of female deputies.[56]

During a stint as a police reserve officer in one district of the Metropolitan Police Department of Washington, D.C., in 1975 and 1976, author Susan Martin interviewed a number of policewomen. Several spoke disdainfully of the role of being a junior partner and expressed annoyance at the "overprotection" by the male officers. One said, "If you're a man and a police officer, it's accepted that you can do the job. Nobody's watching to see if you can.... But if you're a woman, everybody's watching to see how brave you are, how commanding you can be, and how well you can take charge of a situation. You have to prove to the citizens that you're a police officer ... and you have to do twice as much to prove to your partner and officials that you can handle the job." Martin found some women displayed their loyalty to the department by resolutely defending it and its policies, "concurring in the men's negative evaluations of policewomen." One reported that she refused to help a group of policewomen fight an instance of discrimination because she feared being tagged a "women's libber." Some minimized or denied the existence of sex discrimination in the force, blaming the female officers for the problems they encountered. One said, after running down female officers for being flighty, interested only in dating, and not being aggressive enough, "I can see why the men dislike the women on the street." Some women felt females should not be on patrol; it should be an option. "There are other parts of the department where women are much better." Another one remarked, "No, I don't think women should be on patrol.... For women to be on patrol they must prove they're as good as a man.... In some situations we are, but when it comes to tooth and nail, we're not physically equipped."[57]

A decade later, in the mid–1980s, little change had taken place. A survey was taken of 62 female and 89 male officers in Michigan regarding their attitudes toward police handling of family fights and spouse abuse. One conclusion was, "Policemen tended to view policewomen as lacking assertiveness, while policewomen viewed themselves as more patient and understanding, and as less likely to escalate a conflict." Female officers saw themselves as not taking sides, not having trouble calming the male combatant down, and not altering their partner's behavior. On the other hand, policemen saw female officers in a negative light, as taking sides with the woman combatant, as having difficulty in calming down the male combatant and as offsetting the policemen's own behavior. In response to the open-ended question, "If you agree that females handle fights differently, in what way?" 35 male and 33 female officers replied. Of those 35 male comments only two were clearly complimentary toward women, two were ambiguous, with the remaining 31 comments being clearly negative. There were 10 who complained of "feminine" traits such as being too emotional or too talkative and siding with the women, and 21 comments had to do with women lacking assertiveness. Said one male officer, "They are slower to respond, in hope of a male officer arriving first. They are very passive, allowing males to take the lead." Another commented, "They don't know what the hell they're doing." In contrast, all 33 comments from women were favorable to policewomen viewing them as being more patient, helpful, understanding, and as less likely to escalate a conflict. Said one, "Women from early years must learn to survive physically without fighting or using force — talk is their own best defense, consequently they automatically try to talk or reason rather than use force. Some males do this too."[58]

Lesli Lord surveyed 24 policewomen and 32 policemen, all members of a large southern California metro police force, to ascertain their perceptions of female police. Male officers "generally perceived women as being too soft, too weak, too emotional, and too irrational for contemporary street policing." Lord stated that "male officers still harbored grave reservations about women's suitability to be competent police officers." Her research supported "the notion that women were still not totally accepted in the police function." For Lord it was all part of the cultural stereotypes whereby women do not carry guns, women do not fight, and women do not arrest people. Lord also concluded: "There remains a tremendous resistance and opposition to their presence — mainly by their male peers.[59]

Also surveyed in the mid–1980s were 191 males and 42 female officers of the Illinois State Police. At that time 63 members (4 percent) of the 1,557-member force were women. This survey concentrated on showing male attitudes toward what they saw as preferential treatment of women by the police establishment. Over 90 percent of the males thought females were more likely to get promoted because of their sex, 71 percent of males thought police work currently provided greater career opportunities to women than men, and 83 percent of the men believed female officers were given more lenient treatment for official misbehavior. Among the men 95 percent agreed that "if it weren't for legal and government pressure, few police departments would hire many female officers." These attitudes had, of course, no basis in reality and represented a rationalization of male hostility to women. The men did not hate the women because they were female but because they were a group receiving preferential treatment. The author of this study noted that the greatest resistance to female officers usually came from their male colleagues and mentioned the real but unspoken belief of male officers that "if a woman can do it then the job isn't worth much." While the study concluded that older males were more resistant to the hiring of female officers "even young officers showed a reluctance to fully accept females as legitimate police officers."[60]

When Ruth Masters rode along with the Fresno, California, County Sheriff's Department in the early 1980s, one male officer told her, "Females are good for two things: having kids and taking care of a house." Another one commented, "I don't think females are useful in patrol. I just don't think they have any business in patrol." Masters found that for most men in law enforcement, officer safety was the primary issue with regard to having female partners. Most of these men agreed that women had a place in law enforcement; however, they did not think it was as patrol officers."[61]

While the attitudes of male police toward policewomen were usually harsh and negative, attitudes of citizens showed a greater range with less negativity, although many of the attitudes reflected traditional notions of a woman's place in law enforcement.

In conjunction with his 1972 study in Washington, D.C., Bloch sampled the opinions of Washington citizens by interviewing 420 of them over the telephone. Generally they approved of having policewomen patrol the streets and respond to police calls. Respondents did not have a preference as to whether an all-male or male-female team answered their call (there were no all-female teams). Those respondents who had experience with female officers were more likely than those who did not have such experience to prefer a male-female team instead of an all-male team.[62]

A few years later a questionnaire was administered to 203 residents of Champaign-Urbana, Illinois. Asked if they preferred a male or female officer to be on patrol, 44 percent had no preference, 52 percent preferred a male, and 3 percent a female. Women were preferred over males in such traditional areas as dealing with rape victims and children under the age of 13. The more education a respondent had the more likely he was to have no preference with respect to which gender should patrol. For those with less than a high school education, high school diploma, or college degree the percentages expressing no preference were, respectively, 19, 33, and 49 percent. This study concluded that "citizens are more favorable toward women in traditional female police roles than in expected nonviolent or in potentially violent police roles, and

(b) citizens are more favorable toward women in expected nonviolent police roles than in potentially violent police roles." Expected nonviolent incidents would involve traffic violations or shoplifting, while potentially violent roles would be family disputes and fistfights.[63]

Around 1980 a questionnaire was distributed to 569 respondents, 233 male and 336 female, in two major cities in New York State. To the question whether it was not good for female officers to supervise male officers, 55 percent of the male respondents agreed, 45 percent disagreed; 26 percent of females agreed, 74 percent disagreed. Faced with the statement, "Policewomen are as competent as policemen," 66 percent of males agreed, 34 percent disagreed; 87 percent of female respondents agreed, while 13 percent disagreed. When asked to respond to the statement, "For a policeman, a policewoman is as good a partner as a policeman," 51 percent of males agreed, 49 percent disagreed; 76 percent of females agreed, 24 percent disagreed. Asked to compare the effectiveness of policewomen to policemen, 50 percent of males said they were less effective, 24 percent said as effective, and 26 percent replied more effective; 16 percent of females said less effective, 27 percent replied as effective, and 57 percent replied more effective. For the author of this study the overt attitudes toward policewomen correlated positively with general societal attitudes toward working women. She concluded that sex discrimination was very much a reality and that it was especially prominent in male evaluations of females, and that, "As a major source of negative attitudes toward policewomen derive from anti-feminism without our society, the policewoman may well be viewed as an obvious and blatant index of the inroads achieved by women into the fortified domain of the 49 percent majority.'"[64]

When a 1982 survey presented 144 Detroit area people with the statement, "Females are capable of being full-fledged police officers," a nearly even split was recorded with 49 percent agreeing and 51 percent disagreeing. Those who commented felt police department admission standards had been lowered too much in order to recruit women and blacks into previously white- and male-dominated police work. In the decade prior to this survey the number of blacks in the Detroit Police Department increased from 6 percent to 32 percent of the force, and the number of females rose from 1 percent to 12 percent — the majority of them being black. This survey concluded that the Detroit area "community is not giving women police an unqualified welcome, and probably the increase in women police in regular, traditionally male police roles is a factor detracting from the police image."[65]

Two other studies, one in St. Louis County and one in New York City, found that female officers were preferred by respondents in handling aggravated situations. A questionnaire returned by 259 residents in the city of Irvine, California, asked respondents what type of officer they would prefer in different situation. In the case of robbery 184 chose a male, three a female, 29 no preference, and 43 did not answer. For a burglary situation 61 percent opted for a male, and for a vehicular accident 78 percent also preferred a male officer. In rape cases a female officer was preferred by a two to one margin. More women than men preferred female officers or had no preference. The mean age for people choosing a male officer was above 40, while the mean age of those opting for a female or the no preference category was under 40.[66]

A survey that dealt specifically with police response to family violence was conducted in Detroit when 90 women from three Detroit-area shelter homes who had had contact with police officers as the result of a family disturbance were interviewed. Of these, 40 percent preferred to have two male officers respond to a future call, eight percent preferred two women, and 52 percent preferred a male-female team; thus 60 percent preferred at least one female. Of the 31 who had past experience with both genders, 71 percent said there was no difference in helpfulness, 16 percent said females were more helpful, while 13 percent said males were. Of the 59 respondents who had no prior contact with policewomen in a family dispute, 54 percent preferred at least one female officer in the future; and of the 31 who had prior contact with a policewoman, 71 percent preferred at least one female officer in the future. This study concluded, "In general, contact with policewomen resulted in a more favorable evaluation of them. However, while policewomen were more able to calm a situation than the subjects had anticipated, they did not automatically take the woman's side in an argument between cohabitants."[67]

The image of female officers in the general media was often limited to the depiction of them either as sex kittens or inept or both. Most female officers were quick to criticize television police shows at the start of the 1980s, such as *Police Woman*, *Get Christie Love*, and *Charlie's Angeles* (the women here were officers turned private detectives), for portraying women as bouncy, effervescent sex kittens. Male police, they felt, were presented as tough, take-charge, decisive types, as portrayed on shows such as *Baretta* and *Kojak*. Said Officer Gloria Davis of New York about *Police Woman*, "I mean, Angie Dickinson runs around with a purse in one hand and high heels on. I've never seen a police woman running down the street chasing a suspect in her high heels. She couldn't get very far. But that's the image people have of us."[68]

However, playing that role for real also got women into trouble. Cibella Borges was sworn in as a New York City officer in 1981. Then it came to light that she had posed nude in a men's magazine under the name Nina in 1980. She was summarily kicked off the force. In 1985 she won her lawsuit, resulting in her reinstatement on the force and being awarded $70,000 in back pay. The New York City Police Department stated it would not appeal the decision.[69]

People magazine latched onto the story of Anita McKeown, "a 5' 9" blonde with a movie star's face and Hulk Hogan's muscle power." She joined the Santa Monica, California, police force in 1984, finishing in the top 17 percent of her class and second among the 16 females. During her first 10 months on the job she suffered more serious mishaps "than anyone can remember in the department's history." Her colleagues took to calling her Calamity Jane and jokingly dove for cover whenever she strolled into the station house. Injuries incurred included two broken ankles, one broken finger, a wrenched back, and stab wounds that altogether caused her to spent 29 of her first 50 weeks sidelined with injuries. Due to this time lost she was told she would have to repeat her year as rookie. These events were enough to get her invited onto national television talk shows and for the rights to her life story to be purchased by Hollywood producer Andrew Fenady. When she started at the police academy she lost her boyfriend because "he just couldn't handle the fact that I was a cop." Her then current boyfriend was fellow Santa Monica officer Mike Hurt. Not overjoyed with her being on the force, Hurt commented, "Look, I just figure if you've got a bad guy out there and he's built like Arnold Schwarzenegger, you need somebody just as strong to take him out." Here was a female officer who could be portrayed as a sex object and defined as inept on the job—clearly a concept meant to be generalized to all female police. Despite being intelligent enough to finish high in her academy class, it wasn't enough to allow her to overcome the disadvantages incurred from being a "girl." National television and Hollywood were also interested for the same reasons, with the moral being that if you move outside of your sphere then bad things occur; not to mention that you may lose a boyfriend or two.[70]

Elizabeth "Betsy" Watson became chief of the Houston police force in January 1990. She was the first woman to head a major urban police department. The 40-year-old, 17-year veteran originally applied to the force because working in its Juvenile Division seemed a more appropriate use of her psychology degree than taking stenographic dictation at the city tax department. In the early 1980s she was informed that she could not be a supervisor in an investigation division because it was "too tough a job for a woman." Her husband, Robert "Chase" Watson, was a sergeant on the Houston force. When *Time* magazine profiled her, the idea that she was a feminist was downplayed. To further reassure its readers *Time* noted, of Watson's home life, that the power balance "shifts the moment they walk through the front door." According to Elizabeth's brother John, "At home Chase is the center of the family. Betsy makes sure that Chase's needs are satisfied." On February 17, 1992, Watson was removed from her post as chief as a result of what appeared to be personality clashes and infighting among Houston politicians.[71]

Time followed up its 1972 article with another general one on female police in 1980, one which painted a negative picture of them. It cited sociologist Patricia Weiser Remmington, who rode several shifts a week on police patrol in Atlanta. She concluded that male cops dealt with their female counterparts by "dealing with them as natural subordinates — and the females accept the situation." A second pronouncement was that "because women cops were not trained in the martial arts or encouraged to handle tough assignments, they often showed a lack of confidence, and sometimes deliberately drove slowly to a potentially violent call." In fact, female cops by that time all received the same martial arts training at police academies as men. Indeed, every objective study that had been done showed females equally capable as males in all situations. *Time* cited the Bloch report, emphasizing that women made fewer arrests than men, without commenting on the possible lack of validity of this measure. Worst of all *Time* noted that "a Philadelphia study concluded men could handle violent situations better than women can." This was the Phase 2 study that was by then wholly discredited. The magazine failed to mention that Philadelphia conducted Phase 2 only because they did not like the results from Phase 1, which found female police as capable as males in all situations.[72]

Some of the hostility directed to policewomen in the early stages was masked as chivalry. One article noted that some men jumped out of the car to open doors for female colleagues, adopting a "you sit tight while I look after this" attitude. Velma Holmes, of the Washington, D.C., force said of one of her first partners, he "kept holding the door open for me when I started. It made me so self-conscious. I told him to stop." Another male partner suggested she wait for him in the car on a burglary call but she pretended not to hear him. "I wasn't going to stay there and then have to explain why he was hurt and I wasn't," Holmes explained. Officer Marian Sleeth was patrolling in Peoria when she heard a dispatcher announce a trouble call in her area. She radioed she was just a couple of blocks away but the dispatcher hesitated to assign the call to her until the chief broke in on the transmission, ordering the man to "Send her! She's the same as any policeman." However, most of the hostility that had surfaced previously, and still does, appeared in a more vicious and uglier fashion.[73]

A reporter in the Pacific Northwest observed in that nearly 25 years after the Civil Rights Act amendment put women out on patrols they generally were outnumbered nine to one by men and were effectively shut out of some specialty units. Some female officers said they had to constantly prove themselves to their male colleagues. "I'm not naïve enough to believe that everyone's excited about me being her," said Commander Vera Pool of the Multnomah County, Oregon, sheriff's office. "I know there are people who are counting the days until I fall. That goes back to why I work twice as hard — so I don't meet those expectations." A 1994 U.S. Justice Department study found that nearly 10 percent of officers around the nation were women; Oregon had about 8 percent. It took a power base of 20 percent to 25 percent women to overcome the good-old-boy network and make police agencies friendly to women, said Penny Harrington, the director of the National Center for Women and Policing, in Los Angeles. Many Oregon policewomen told the reporter that sexual harassment was the exception in their state, not the rule. A U.S. District Court jury awarded a former Multnomah County sheriff's deputy $225,000 just a week earlier for her harassment claims. Lana Mockler said a male deputy referred to her in sexually derogatory terms in front of a sergeant and other deputies during roll call in 1992. After filing an internal complaint she said she was denied a transfer and a supervisor told her boyfriend she might not get backup in dangerous situations. The Justice Department study found that promotional interviews or supervisors' recommendations — usually done by men — were another barrier facing female officers.[74]

The decision in favor of Mockler was appealed by the defendants and heard before the United States Court of Appeals for the Ninth Circuit in 1998. Without contradiction Mockler testified that she filed a complaint with Chief Deputy Amudsen, spoke to the sheriff about Officer Dennis Fitz's offensive conduct, and filed additional complaints when Fitz and other deputies took retaliatory action against her. Mockler's evidence also showed that Fitz received a one-day suspension, that the Sheriff's Department of Multnomah County deviated from its usual procedure for investigating complaints by not interviewing witnesses, that Fitz did not receive a letter of discipline until months after the incident reported by Mockler, and that he was allowed to work overtime the day after his suspension to recoup his lost wages. Fitz admitted that he had monitored Mockler's activities, filed complaints against her and encouraged her supervisors to discipline her after his suspension. The sheriff stated that it was clear that Fitz was not going to relent even after being told to stop interfering with Mockler's activities. The evidence also established that neither Fitz nor any other officer was disciplined for retaliating against Mockler. Mockler spent three months on stress leave and eventually transferred to the Portland Police Bureau in June 1994.[75]

Writing in a newspaper in 1996 reporter Christina Nifong said that as an outgrowth of what experts said was the growing influence of women in uniform the situation was becoming one of us and them instead of us against them. She said, "Indeed, as more women enter the ranks, there is an emerging recognition that they bring a distinct style to policing, one that depends more on negotiation than machismo." Chief Elizabeth Watson of the Austin, Texas, police, and former chief of the Houston, Texas, police force remarked, "Women as a rule tend to be more collaborative. We come together and talk about issues. We want the same things, we just have different ways of going about them." But, noted the journalist, women still represented less than 9 percent of all sworn officers nationwide, according to 1993 figures from the U.S. Justice Department. Their numbers were higher in the cities, at almost 14 percent. But of all the women in blue only about 3 percent were high-ranking officers, including chiefs in Atlanta and Austin, Texas. "Potentially volatile situations that reach the hair-trigger stage are calmed by the presence of a woman," said Hubert Williams, president of the Police Foundation in Washington and former police chief in Trenton, New Jersey. Research over the past five years and recent anecdotes, said Nifong, revealed a woman's way of walking the beat. In general, studies found, women depended less on physical strength and more on verbal skills than men did; women were less likely to be confrontational when first answering a call and more likely to use physical force only if the situation required it. The most striking example, however, of women officers' tendency to avoid violence came from the Christopher Commission, which studied the Los Angeles Police Department after the infamous beating of motorist Rodney King in 1991. That report revealed that women were rarely cited for using excessive force. It found that women officers were involved in fewer expensive lawsuits against the department. Since the report the Los Angeles City Council had ordered the LAPD, then 16 percent female, to strive for a force that was 44 percent female. Other recent studies, continued Nifong, by criminologists had shown that women cops generated fewer citizen complaints than did men cops, were less inclined to use deadly force in general, and were involved in fewer shooting incidents. Especially cited were domestic violence crimes—roughly half of all police calls. It was no coincidence that the police forces at the forefront of community policing also had a higher percentage of women officers. For example, the department in Madison, Wisconsin, which used a community-policing model, had 28 percent women officers.[76]

Kristen Leger conducted a study in 1997 that involved the perceptions that residents of two Kentucky counties had of female patrol officers. When policemen were asked if they accepted women officers on patrol it was revealed that only 27.9 percent of officers surveyed in the states of Washington, Oregon, Idaho, and Montana actually accepted women on patrol, while 38.6 percent were neutral and 24.7 were either non-accepting or strongly non-accepting (1994 data). Leger's study consisted of 200 residents within the Louisville, Kentucky, metropolitan area. At the time of the survey the Kentucky State Police had a sworn force of 898, 2.6 percent of whom were women. The Louisville Division of Police had a total sworn force of 679, 13.5 percent of whom were female. Overall findings from the study indicated a positive citizen attitude toward female police officers on patrol and a decrease in citizen skepticism about the ability of female officers to handle violent encounters. When asked if police work was an appropriate occupation for women the study found 34 percent of the respondents agreed with the idea,

44 percent were neutral, 15 percent disagreed, and 6 percent of the respondents strongly disagreed. In response to the statement that female officers could effectively contain violent encounters 22.5 percent of the respondents agreed, 54.5 percent were neutral, 13 percent disagreed, and 9 percent strongly disagreed. Some 39.5 percent of respondents thought more female officers should be on patrol, 38.5 percent were neutral, 5.0 percent wanted less, and 17.0 percent of the responses were invalid. In general, the study found that respondents with a lower level of educational attainment showed more disapproval of women in patrol work.[77]

Complaints that had been filed with the internal affairs office of a large police force in the Southeast United States were examined over a three year period in 1998. It was a study to explore the possible difference between the male and female officers named in the allegations of misconduct in the following areas: overall number of complaints, characteristics of the officers named (age, race, and tenure), characteristics of the complaint, and characteristics of the citizens lodging the complaints. While male officers were overrepresented in the allegations of misconduct, there were no significant differences found in other areas of the study. Many researchers in that area believed that because of the differing socialization of men and women in society, one should see marked differences in how police men and women interact with citizens and perform their duties. Female cops have been assumed to have a greater commitment to public service, have a calming and beneficial impact of police-citizen interactions, be more effective at diffusing potential volatile situations, and be more likely to provide comfort and sympathy to crime victims than their male peers. That inclusion of women in modern police forces was harmonious with the current emphasis on community policing. According to researcher Kim Lersch no consistency had been reported by researchers to date to support the idea of differences. One area of consistency that had been reported with respect to differences between male and female officers was with respect to citizen complaints in allegations involving the improper use of force. For example, the Christopher Commission in Los Angeles (an investigation launched in the wake of the Rodney King beating in that city) found that of the 120 officers with the most allegations against them concerning the use of force, all were male. In this particular study over a three-year period from 1992 to 1994 a total of 527 citizen complaints were filed. Those 527 complaints translated into a total of 682 allegations of wrongdoing (a single complaint could name more than one officer). Complaints involving force numbered 149; non-violent complaints of non-threatening behavior, harassment and lack of courtesy totaled 339; dereliction in performance of duty complaints came to 159; and miscellaneous complaints totaled 35 (such as conducting personal business while on duty, and inappropriate driving). The unnamed city where the study was conducted had a population of just under 240,000 with 77.8 percent being Caucasian, 19.6 percent African-American, and 2.6 percent other. The police department in that city employed just over 500 sworn law enforcement personnel with an average age of 36.05 and a mean length of service of 11.97 years. Within the force 81.8 percent were Caucasian, 15.2 percent African American, and 3.0 percent were other. Male officers made up 87.6 percent of the force; females were 12.4 percent. With respect to educational levels 61.6 percent of the officers had only a high school education, 15.1 percent had a two-year degree, and 23.3 percent had a four-year degree or higher level of education. Of the officers named in the complaints 643 (94.3 percent) were males and 39 (5.7 percent) were females. Minority males were significantly overrepresented in the complaints. Neither citizen gender nor race was found to be a significant predictor of officer gender. No significant differences were found for female officers with respect to race. "The findings of the present study suggest that while women were less likely to be accused of misconduct, no significant difference was found in the type of complaint filed against male and female officers," concluded the researcher. "Once an officer was accused of misconduct, both male and female officers were equally likely to be accused of misuse of force. Male and female officers named in citizen complaints did not differ significantly with respect to age, length of service, or citizen characteristics."[78]

A study by the National Center for Women and Policing (released in 1999) found that nation's law enforcement agencies were recruiting women at "an alarmingly slow rate." The center said, in a report entitled "Equality Denied," that women will never have equal status in police departments, especially in the highest ranks. The report showed that women represented about 14 percent of law enforcement positions nationwide, up half a percent from 1997. Since 1990, their numbers had increased by 3.2 percent. Other findings in the report included that more than one-third of the 176 police departments surveyed had no women in top command ranks and nearly three-quarters had no high ranking women of color. Also, of the 10 big-city police departments with the largest number of female officers, eight were forced to hire more women by federal court orders. Beverly Harvard, the first black female chief of police, in Atlanta, and the only female chief executive of a large American police department, said that movement "within the ranks is going far too slowly" for women. She added, "It means something when prospective female officers see other women in uniform with stripes on their arms."[79]

Researchers looking at discrimination suits, in 1999, stated that the history of such suits had shown that though cities might be willing to remedy discriminatory practices against women, police unions were often not as agreeable to such concessions. Another fact suggesting the presence of co-worker discrimination was the difference in female employment rates for protective services in the military versus the civilian sector. In the United

States military the percentage of female police officers (as a percentage of total military police) was triple the percent of female civilian police officers. From that researchers drew three conclusions. One was that anti-discrimination legislation clearly promoted the hiring of new female police in the early to mid–1980s. In contrast, female representation on city councils or in mayoral offices did not significantly affect the proportion of female recruits. Results suggested litigation was more likely to influence gender hiring policies of cities than gender identity of elected representatives. A second conclusion was that police hiring policies were influenced by the gender composition of current officers. Increases in the proportion of male officers were associated with a reduction in the proportion of new female recruits. Male-dominated departments were more likely to employ fitness tests solely for new recruits, which impeded entry by women. As a third conclusion the researchers declared the effect of labor unions on female police employment was somewhat ambiguous. In contrast to the apparent opposition to female employment observed in past legal battles, union status was positively associated with the proportion of female new recruits in the mid–1980s and early 1990s. However, the incidence of fitness exams for new recruits, a possible vehicle for discouraging female entry, was either positively associated with union status or uncorrelated.[80]

Diana Grant conducted a study of perceptions of policewomen in 2000. Her analysis of the research already done supported, in her view, that gender stereotypes, both favorable and unfavorable, shaped public expectations of female police officers. Public opinion research supported that members of the public generally supported the idea of policewomen but often believed female officers were less able than male officers to effectively handle violent confrontations. In more recent research, policewomen described citizens refusing to speak with them and instead requesting a male officer, expressing disrespect or ignoring them when a male officer was present and similar experiences of gender bias. Grant's research involved 379 college student participants, all aged 18 to 22. Participants were asked to estimate a probability that the officer was guilty of the charge by the plaintiff of alleged misconduct. A hypothetical situation was described in which a cop called to one of three incidents: a rape, a shoplifting, or a noisy party. In the rape situation the female officer was found guilty more often than the male officer (74.6 percent to 66.2 percent). In the shoplifting case the female officer was found guilty less often than the male (63.15 percent versus 76.7 percent). Gender was not a factor in the noisy party condition.[81]

Another piece of research published in 2000 assessed the attitudes of 835 undergraduate students at a mid-size, state-supported university in the northeast of the US towards women in the field of policing. Several earlier studies done in the late 1970s and early 1980s found that male college students tended to harbor, to vary degrees, negative attitudes toward female officers very similar to those of male patrol officers. That is, both those groups felt the women lack physical strength and ability and also lacked emotional stability. Female students in those earlier studies showed that females were much more supportive of female police officers than were male students. In fact, on most survey questions pertaining to women in law enforcement, male students' support was, on average, 20 to 25 percentage points below that of their female counterparts. In this 2000 study the respondents were given a series of questions with a five-point agree-disagree scale. It was found that males, when compared with females of the same major field of study, were anywhere from 10 to approximately 40 percent points less supportive of female police officers than were female students on any given item. The difference was most pronounced on the item "Females have the physical skills and strengths to do police work," as male criminal justice majors were twice as likely to disagree with the statement than their female counterparts (43 percent versus 86 percent).[82]

A study by the Feminist Majority Foundation's Center for Women and Policing, published in 2001, found that women police officers were involved in significantly fewer lawsuits for excessive force, sexual assault, and domestic violence, than male officers. The study, which reviewed the Los Angeles Police Department, found that male officer payments in lawsuits for brutality and misconduct exceeded female officer payouts by a ratio of 23 to one. Male officers payouts that involved killings exceeded female payouts by 43 to one. For assault and battery the ratio for male officer payouts to female payouts was 32 to one. That study confirmed earlier research both nationally and internationally that women police officers relied less on physical force and more on verbal skills in handling altercations. In addition, the study revealed the LAPD had to pay out $10.4 million for lawsuits involving male officers for sexual assault, sexual molestation and domestic violence.[83]

From 1990 to 2000 the number of full-time, sworn local policewomen increased 2.5 percent, according to preliminary numbers released early in 2002 by the Bureau of Justice Statistics in Washington, D.C. In 2000 10.6 percent of local police, or 46,000 officers, were women as compared to 8.1 percent in 1990. Some municipalities reported a number as high as 15.9 percent.[84]

In the summer of 2002 a jury found that two women police officers from Santa Barbara, California, were harassed and discriminated against because of their gender by the City of Santa Barbara and the Santa Barbara Police Department. The women were awarded $3.2 million in compensatory and punitive damages. One of the major issues of the case was that the department had never promoted a woman in its 102-year history until the suit was filed. According to the Feminist Majority Foundation's National Center for Women and Policing annual survey, women accounted for only 12.7 percent of sworn officers nationwide in 2001, down from 14.0 percent in 1999. At 7.3 percent women were also virtually absent in top command decision-making positions. The National Center declared that it "promotes increasing the number of women at all ranks of law enforcement as a strategy to improve police response to violence against women, reduce police brutality, and strengthen community policing reforms."[85]

A retired New York City police commander was suing the NYPD in the spring of 2002 charging she was passed over for promotions because of her pregnancies. In a lawsuit filed in United States District Court in Manhattan, Catherine M. Volpe-Wasserman, who retired at the rank of deputy inspector in June 2001 after 20 years with the force, described a pattern of harassment and discrimination that she said caused her to retire 10 years earlier than she had planned. Her lawsuit also changed that other women in supervisory positions throughout the department had suffered similar discrimination because they were mothers.

As of February 2002 there were 6,088 women on the NYPD — about 16 percent of the more than 38,000 officers on the job. But while 684 men (2.1 percent) held a rank of captain or above, just 40 women (0.6 percent) held such a position. In her suit Volpe-Wasserman, who rose quickly to the rank of captain and joined the Internal Affairs Bureau in 1992, painted a portrait of a department rife with discrimination at the top. Just weeks earlier the City of New York had agreed to pay $500,000 to settle a 1997 federal civil rights lawsuit that embarrassed the department and raised questions about how aggressively it investigated sexual harassment reports. In an interview with a reporter Volpe-Wasserman, 43, said she suffered many negative comments about her maternity over the years. Coming to work became such a hostile experience, she said, that she retired. "I was put on the back shelf, twice," she said.

In November 2001 the department's Office of Equal Employment Opportunity investigated her allegations without her cooperation. The allegations were found to be unsubstantiated. Chief Wilbur Chapman, a former police official named in her suit, called Volpe-Wasserman's claims "ridiculous and bizarre." He added, "This sounds like someone is twisting the truth for her own agenda." Chapman had been chief of patrol in New York and was then the police chief in Bridgeport, Connecticut. But the federal Equal Employment Opportunity Commission ruled in December 2001 that Volpe-Wasserman could sue the department. In 1992 after less than 12 years on the job she was promoted to captain. By the fall of 1996, superior officers were promising to promote her to deputy inspector, the lawsuit said. But when she announced that December that she was pregnant, her career abruptly "hit a glass ceiling," said Jonathan C. Moore, her lawyer. When she returned from maternity leave, Chief Chapman told her, "They couldn't promote you because, how would it look for a pregnant woman to walk 'across the stage,'" said her lawsuit. She went on maternity leave again in 1998 and became a deputy inspector at the end of that year. Soon after she was made executive officer of the Quality Assurance Division, which evaluated commands. While there, she wrote a report that was critical of the way the Office of Equal Employment investigated discrimination cases. In 2001 she was passed over for the position of commanding officer of the Quality Assurance Division; the job was given to a deputy inspector with less time on the force and in command. When Volpe-Wasserman asked about it a supervisor said she had less patrol experience than the successful applicant. But the same man later admitted, according to the suit, that "patrol experience" was just an excuse; "Hey, it's the old boy's network."[86]

A study published in 2005 examined the use of force in a large, suburban police department during a seven-year period, 1993 to 1999. Force was used in only a small percentage (5.9 percent) of the arrests made. Use-of-force incidents totaled 1,863 out of a total of 31,778 arrests. The study found no statistically significant difference between female and male officers in the overall use of force or in the rate of unarmed physical force. Female officers had a lower rate of weapon use when all types of weapons were considered together but not when the different types of weapons were considered individually. Female officers also had a lower rate of any suspect injury, but there was no statistically significant difference in the rate of suspect injury resulting in treatment at a hospital for the suspect. Injuries to suspects occurred in 1.6 percent of arrests and injuries to suspects resulting in treatment at a hospital (usually emergency room treatment) occurred in 0.7 percent of arrests. This study was done in the Montgomery County Police Department, on the outskirts of Washington, D.C.[87]

In May 2006 the federal Equal Employment Opportunity Commission ruled it had found cause for a former Eagle Lake, Florida, police officer's complaint that she was not hired permanently after she filed an internal discrimination complaint. Leslie Barr was the city's only female officer when the complaints were filed in 2005. Title 7 of the Civil Rights Act of 1964 was violated, ruled the commission. Having found violations had taken place the commission attempted to settle the issue through informal methods of conciliation. Barr was hired by the police force on October 6, 2003, as a gang resistance education and training officer. Barr's position was funded through a law enforcement grant. Because she was in that position Barr was paid $9 an hour, a salary below that of other officers on the Eagle Lake force. She was to work at the city's two elementary schools, but because of training conflicts she did not start right away. Instead she performed regular police work. During the first couple of months of her employment Barr learned she was pregnant. She continued answering calls until two days before her delivery in May

2004. When she returned to duty, Barr said, she spoke to Police Chief J. R. Sullivan on numerous occasions about a pay raise. In October she received a $1-an-hour raise. She was still paid below the starting officer pay in Eagle Lake of $11.50 an hour. Because she was performing the same duties as other officers Barr thought she deserved the same pay. On March 4, 2005, Sullivan recommended Barr be fired stating she had violated hiring general orders and the city's personnel policy. Sullivan claimed Barr did not follow proper procedures for filing a grievance when she wrote a letter to police commissioners. When Barr found out she was to be fired she hired lawyer Alex Pujol. After Pujol became involved, Barr's firing was changed to a five-day suspension without pay.[88]

For years the Suffolk County Police Department on Long Island, New York, allowed officers to take desk jobs or light-duty assignments when they notified superiors they were pregnant. That's what veteran patrol officer Christine Blauvelt did in 1999 when she was expecting her first child. She worked a desk job, responding to walk-in complaints and inquiries until just days before her delivery. By late 2001 Blauvelt was expecting her second child and asked for a similar assignment. That time her request was denied. The year before that police department had implemented a new policy that denied limited-duty assignments to any officer, pregnant or otherwise, who was not injured on the job or facing some disciplinary action that would result in a desk assignment. Pregnant women thus had no choice under the new policy — go home and use sick leave and unpaid days during the later stages of pregnancy and after delivery, or stay on patrol, even though bulletproof vests did not cover their growing bellies and in some cases made it difficult for them to reach their side arms. (Because of the vest issue, the policy was altered and pregnant women were given 90 days of light duty if the vests no longer fit them.) However, six female officers did not let the issue drop. Enlisting the support of the New York Civil Liberties Union and the American Civil Liberties Union's Women's Rights Project, Blauvelt and five other female cops challenged the new policy in federal court in New York. In June 2006 a four-man, four-woman jury found the policy discriminatory and that the department discriminated intentionally against two of the plaintiffs. All six were awarded damages of at least $5,000, and up to $23,000.[89]

The National Center for Women and Policing mailed out a survey questionnaire in 2007 to 2,000 randomly selected policewomen with 531 of them responding with a completed survey. Of those respondents 39 percent indicated they were made to feel less welcome than males in their police departments and almost 32 percent indicated they were treated worse than male officers when they first began their careers in law enforcement. A total of 377 of those respondents (72.8 percent) reported that they had never been sexually harassed.[90]

Attitudes toward women in policing among undergraduate college students was examined in 2009. Findings revealed that feminist orientation was the most consistent predictor of support for women in policing, with academic major also having a significant influence. Gender, race or ethnicity and support for the police were generally not significant predictors. Separate analyses completed for men and women indicated that there was some difference in the factors that predicted support for women in policing.[91]

The female proportion of all state and local sworn police in the United States nearly tripled from 1971 to 1980, then more than doubled again by 2000 but had since slowed considerably, said the authors of a 2011 report. Proportions of women were given as follows: 1971 (1.4 percent), 1980 (5.0 percent), 1990 (8.6 percent), 2000 (11.0 percent), and 2009 (11.7 percent). Those number came from the Uniform Crime Report statistics put out by the FBI. The Law Enforcement Management and Administrative Statistics (LEMAS) provided similar numbers with the female proportion of sworn local police having increased by more than 40 percent from 1987 to 1997, but it had increased by less than 10 percent since then. Their numbers were as follows: 1987 (7.6 percent), 1990 (8.1 percent), 1993 (8.8 percent), 1997 (11.0 percent), 2000 (11.0 percent), 2003 (11.3 percent), and 2007 (11.9 percent). As of 2011 the female proportion of the workforce aged 20 years and over was 47 percent. The authors of this study observed that there were then plenty of individual police agencies that had 20 to 30 percent female officers on their forces: "Thus, a plausible explanation of the plateau effect is that external pressure, in the form of fair employment litigation [1964 Civil Rights Act and the 1972 Equal Employment Opportunity Act] was greater in the 1960s and through the 1990s but has since waned." The report concluded that the current level of female presence on forces seemed to have stagnated but was not a "natural plateau level" in the United States because there were individual police agencies with 20 percent and more female officers on staff, including Chicago, Detroit, Philadelphia, and Washington, D.C. At the national level, it was pointed out, Canada had a reported 19 percent sworn female officer component, as of 2009, while Australia had 23 percent female, as of 2006; "These figures tend to suggest that the current U.S. national 'plateau' of 11 percent to 12 percent is substantially lower than it could be."[92]

Researchers Cara Rabe-Hemp and Dawn Beichner analyzed the print advertisements of police officers that appeared in the US professional police magazine *Police Chief.* There were looking for gender stereotypes and analyzed all the ads that appeared in that publication over the years 1996 through 2006. It had a professional audience of over 21,000 law enforcement professionals. Their study was published in 2011 and results suggested that women "are numerically underrepresented and socially excluded from the imagery of crime-fighting, rather, they are portrayed as being in lower ranks, stereotypically as caretakers and nurturers." Women in society were, on average six inches shorter than men (62" versus 68") or 90 percent as tall. Yet the researchers found the women in the study ads, if real, would have averaged out to about two feet shorter than men, or 63 percent as tall — that was because more often they were depicted in the background of these ads.[93]

10

U.S., 1970–2012 (Part II)

While the formal legal barriers that worked against females being hired and promoted as policewomen had largely fallen by around 1973, or soon would, hostility and resistance from the male police establishment remained rampant. New York City police headquarters spokesperson Lucy A. Acerra said of policewomen on patrol in that city in 1974 that they were meeting "resistance from the men at every level and at every rank. There is a great deal of resentment and a constant attempt to keep them out of radio cars and out of certain precincts. Women are constantly being told, 'I don't think you can make it.' It will take a long time to change this."[1]

Newton, Massachusetts, was offered a federal demonstration grant in 1974 to add 12 women to its police force of about 200 members—two of whom were females. Police Chief William Quinn and Mayor Theodore Mann were agreeable; however, Newton's policemen launched an all-out assault on the project. They charged reverse discrimination as women who passed the state civil service examination would receive priority over males already on the waiting list. In addition, they argued that the safety of citizens and policemen would be endangered when policewomen faced violent situations. Wives of the Newton men joined in to agree that women could not deal with violent criminals. Some city aldermen sympathized with the protestors and worried about what would happen when men and women started sharing night duty in cruisers. In the end Newton's aldermen voted to hire the additional women — provisionally and as a supplement to the regular force.[2]

When Bloch did his Washington study he found in 1974 that policewomen were assigned to station duty about twice as often as men and less frequently assigned to two-person or one-person squad cars than the men. Author Susan Martin found a similar pattern of assignments in that city in 1975 and 1976. A July 1978 report prepared for the Washington police department found that although females comprised 8 percent of the force assigned to patrol districts, they received 25 percent of the station house assignments. Said one of the sergeants who gave out the assignments, "I wish I could say

I don't treat them differently. I try not to but I suppose I do unconsciously. I tend not to put them together by themselves for everybody's good, so they won't get hurt." Another sergeant said, "I try to be as impartial as possible.... She should be holding her end up but most can't." Bloch noted that by August 1973 only 45 percent of the new policewomen and 71 percent of the new males remained on regular uniformed patrol while 31 percent of the new women but only 12 percent of the comparison new men were given inside assignments such as clerical, youth, or community relations. When women were first assigned to patrol in Washington they were outfitted inappropriately. When they complained about the cold they were temporarily removed from street duty as no other uniforms were available. Another sergeant commented, "I give the girls in this district credit. Those girls earn their pay ... although they're not doing the job a man would do. Ask the men, deep down they're looking out for the girls."[3]

As recently as 1966 the International Association of Chiefs of Police, at a workshop, defined a policewoman as someone appointed "for the increased moral protection of women and minors and for the prevention of delinquency among such women and minors, and for such other police duties as can best be performed by a woman."[4]

Another problem for female police was that most chiefs and senior administrators felt women should not be supervisors. Others believed that women should only supervise other women. It was an attitude often shared by policewomen. One female officer commented, "Women supervising men I don't think would be very logical. I just don't think it's in the scheme of things for a woman to supervise a man. I don't go for that myself. I couldn't comfortably supervise men. Personally, we [women] look to the man for leadership and everything, and I couldn't tell him what to do. I would if I had to and they said do it, but I wouldn't be comfortable." Said a female sergeant, "The role doesn't fit. Men are not made to be subjected to a woman. And they resent it, and I don't blame them. But, you see, you get a lot of attitudes from policewomen, 'Well I can do the job — I can do it as good or better than any man.' Well, that's the kind of attitude that men resent, I think. So I really don't feel that women should be higher than sergeant."[5]

Policewomen had some problems in New York City in 1975 when a massive layoff was imposed due to the city's financial crisis. In total 3,000 officers were laid off, about 375 of them being women. Prior to those layoffs the New York City Police Department had 618 policewomen on the force. Those women who remained were mostly on matron duty, with few female officers still on patrol. Ken McFeeley, president of the Patrolman's Benevolent Association, was elected to that post on a platform of removing women from patrol duty. One of those laid off was Maureen Kempton, a member of the force for 26 months. After her application to join the force was accepted she had to wait five years to be appointed. Following her appointment about 4,000 new officers were hired, so she still should have kept her job as only 3,000 were let go, and she would have, except for veterans preference. Ex-service personnel, whether draftees or those who enlisted, automatically received 30 months extra seniority and five bonus points on the police examination score. Even when examinations for police officer were theoretically evened out for the genders and only one list of appointments was compiled, some sort of preference, such as New York's, remained in most jurisdictions for ex-service personnel. Since the vast majority of them were male, they had an obvious albeit sometimes slight advantage in being hired and promoted.[6]

One of the most sexist arguments against equality for policewomen came from Anthony Vastola, a sergeant on the New York City Police Department, who aired his views in the trade magazine *Police Chief* in 1977. Vastola, who claimed to be working on his Ph.D., tried to disguise his views under the cloak of academia, but they were a throwback to an earlier and more overtly discriminatory time. The sergeant argued that women should not aim for complete assimilation into policing, as he felt the women's movement wanted them to, because it would be difficult if not impossible as resistance to females in policing would increase as their percentage in the occupation enlarged. Vastola felt females should aim for a social, pluralistic approach to integration: "They should, instead, seek to maximize employment of women in policing along pluralistic lines; i.e., equally prestigious roles but in some respects different from men. The movement, ideologically, should recognize that perhaps there currently are some areas in police work where women should not attempt to invade, at least not on a complete assimilation role basis with men. The most prominent area, in this regard, is general patrol work." In working toward voluntary acceptance by the police establishment, women should not take the position that they be allowed to work in all areas of general patrol because they are equally as capable as their male colleagues. He thought females could be used in certain areas of patrol work, such as family quarrels and business disputes, and perhaps could start their careers by being titled "crisis intervention specialists." Another role he considered suitable for women was the area of traffic enforcement. It was all in keeping with his approach that sought "entrance for women into special areas of patrol work by virtue of the positive cultural attributes ascribed for women in current literature and social thinking in this country." If women wanted to achieve large-scale entrance into policing they must "not significantly threaten the long-standing social system of the men." Vastola envisioned a "male policehood" and a "woman policehood," with roles "different but nevertheless equal." This would put an end to worries about physical fitness for females as his roles for women would not require it. For him it was a major concern that females in a dangerous situation, such as trying to mediate a bar brawl, would act inappropriately by drawing a revolver needlessly or crying. With regard to policies assigning females to all areas of patrol equally with males the sergeant said, "It is clear that the majority of men do not support these policies. Instead, they take a popular view — one not necessarily limited to men — that women have a special, rather than a general role to play in law enforcement.... There is, too, evidence that a substantial group of female officers themselves support the view that women should be used primarily in specialized functions." As an odd bonus this approach could also "channel prejudice against women along functional lines." He wrote, "By discriminating against women, in terms of prescribing the police roles they are to occupy, men may in effect be creating greater opportunities to hire larger numbers of women to fill these roles." However, even if that happened, "prejudice and discrimination against women may not disappear completely. But it would likely be less intense and more functional in nature, in terms of integration of women in policing."[7]

Much of the discriminatory harassment directed at the women who broke into policing in the early years, before 1975, remained vivid in women's memories years later. Frequently it was malicious, blatant, organized, widespread, involved supervisors, and, on occasion, life-threatening. When Susan Martin interviewed some of these policewomen over a decade after incidents had taken place, several of them broke down in tears, some choked them back, some remained evasive, and some obviously were filled with anger. One called her boss a "sexist, racist bastard." Another, recalling an incident with her male supervisor said: "The bastard deserves to die." The discrimination took various forms: male colleagues organized to avoid working with a woman and, if assigned a female partner, would give her the silent treatment so that "eight hours could seem like an eternity." Often men would refuse to share job knowledge or refuse to teach women skills they routinely passed on to new men. Occasionally, policewomen had their lives put at unnecessary risk by male partners and other male squad members who failed to assist in a physical confrontation or were slow to provide backup. Said one policewoman, "The males didn't want to work with females.... I was at the precinct ten days before I knew I had a partner ... because the first ten partners called in sick." When that eleventh male was on a day off another male was assigned who did not know his partner was a female. At roll call he said, "'I won't work with a dumb female and get my ass kicked.' Everybody at roll call laughed." Some supervisors abused their position by directly harassing women — some did it indirectly by ignoring harassment and discrimination by male officers, encouraging mistreatment by peers. Other discriminatory behavior directed at these policewomen included denial of lockers in the station, denial of regular scout car duty, denial of training opportunities, overzealous enforcement of rules, lowered performance evaluation ratings, sexual harassment, and overprotection and favoritism that singled them out — causing male officer resentment. One policewoman said of her supervisor, "He created rules that only applied to me. I was the only one who had to wear a hat inside the building.... It was outright harassment; he didn't even try to cover up. It was always verbal, not physical harassment, but it was constant." Most of these women suffered in silence, not wanting to make waves as they were trying to fit in. "Before EEO and sexual harassment laws," said one policewoman, "I didn't think of [what we faced] as discrimination. It was just the cost of doing the job."[8]

When a panel of six black female officers met in 1974 to discuss their experiences, one, who patrolled in Washington, D.C., said, "I don't like to use the term ugly, I'll use the term irregular-looking. If you are an irregular-looking police officer and you happen to be female, you're going to get a bad detail! If you are good looking, you don't have much of a problem." Five of the six panelists had worked or then worked on patrol and each of them had faced hostility and harassment from their fellow officers in one fashion or another. One year later a second panel convened. A male inspector on the panel did not look favorably on women on patrol, voicing his opinion that women failed to perform adequately on patrol. He wanted to see them play a more traditional, and limited, role in policing. Peggy Triplett, special assistant to the director of the National Institute of Law Enforcement and Criminal Justice, was the author of the article on the two panels. Triplett mentioned the Washington, D.C., Police Foundation study, pointing out that it showed the sexes to be equally capable officers. However, she then went on to say that the most controversial issue about women in policing was whether or not they could do the job. Her conclusion was, at the moment, "We don't know."[9]

By the mid–1970s Lucille Abreu had served on the Honolulu Police Department for 22 years without a promotion. When she graduated from the police academy she was the only female in a class of 36. All her former classmates had been promoted, with the lowest-ranked male being a sergeant. Eight times during her long career Abreu took the examination for promotion to sergeant. Each time she passed with high marks, and each time she was not promoted. Finally, she filed a sex discrimination complaint with the Equal Employment Opportunity Commission. After the suit was filed and only after formal conciliation talks between the EEOC and the Honolulu Police Department, as well as intervention by the federal Law Enforcement Assistance Administration, was she finally promoted. In 1975 Abreu was moved up to the rank of detective (equivalent to sergeant) and posted to the Juvenile Crime Prevention Division to become the first female in the Criminal Division. At that time the Honolulu force had over 1,000 male officers and 13 other females; of those, five were in the Juvenile Division and three in training. Also as a result of the suit the Honolulu force dropped restrictive height requirements

which barred females from patrol work and promotion. Lucille was 5'1¾".
Summing up her long fight and the reaction of her male colleagues on the
force Abreu remarked, "They felt I was to blame — my persistence. They didn't
see that they were breaking the law.... I found so many inequalities that I've
definitely never regretted it. I would do it all over again."[10]

Two black Detroit policewomen, Katherine Perkins and Glenda
Rudolph, got a taste of the male police establishment workings in August
1979. Years earlier, in 1971 or 1972, Perkins, 5'2", applied to join the force.
The white male officer who took her application tore it up in her face saying,
"You might be able to get two years of college, Katherine, but you will never
grow. Come back when you grow!" Soon thereafter, under legal pressure,
height restrictions were reduced, allowing Perkins to join. When Rudolph
joined the force she found a lot of racial and sexual harassment at the station
house. Guys would tell her, "In order to get ahead on this job, you have to
jump on the jolly pole."[11]

On August 26, near midnight, the two officers were patrolling when they
saw a naked man, Calvin Rowell, in the street burning dollar bills while shout-
ing about the evils of white people. The officers called in the situation,
requested backup, then approached the man and began to talk to him. Backup
came in the form of white sergeant Paul Janness, who jumped from his car,
moved in on Rowell, and was then attacked by Rowell. Rudolph said she and
Perkins jumped on top of the two brawling men and got Rowell handcuffed.
Both women said Janness yelled something like, "Don't cuff him, I'm going
to beat his motherfucking ass." Janness denied this. Another cruiser arrived
on the scene containing officers Vicki Hubbard and Lawrence Estelle, who
said they saw the women do nothing to aid Janness. Perkins and Rudolph
claimed the pair arrived too late to witness any help — the whole incident
took two minutes. Within an hour of the event rumors began to spread that
the two policewomen were to be "jammed" for some kind of malfeasance.
Next day at roll call a sergeant exclaimed that "if a woman wants to become
a patrol officer, she had better know how to handle herself on the street."
Then the two officers' superior told them they would be charged with cowardice. Perkins felt the officer delivered a message to all blacks and females
on the force: "If you get out of line, the same thing will happen to you that's
happened to Katherine Perkins." It should be remembered that the situation
with Rowell was under control until Janness arrived on the scene. A few
months later the two women were officially charged with three offenses: cowardice, making a false statement in saying they had helped Janness, and making a false statement when they accused Janness of threatening Rowell. By
mid–March of 1980 the pair were officially fired after being found guilty on
the first two counts; count three was dropped. Perkins appealed to the board
of police commissioners that, in June, acquitted her of cowardice on the ground

that the legal definition required that a person "acted or failed to act out of fear." The policewomen were not afraid of Rowell and were in fact laughing at him during the encounter. Her conviction on charge two was upheld but she was returned to work, drawing a ten-day pay penalty for her offense. Rudolph took a different appeal route waiting for an arbitrator. In July 1980 before arbitration a deal was cut whereby the force would take her back if she accepted the ruling given in Perkins's case: innocent of cowardice, but guilty of making a false statement. She accepted the deal because she needed the money. Soon after the incident with Rowell the story circulated that Janness had been beaten up while the women just stood by. In fact, the sergeant was not hurt seriously and did not even go to see a doctor. He refused to talk to news people about the story but several of his friends claimed he did not want to make the cowardice accusation. Said Rudolph, "The story fell right into a lot of guy's fears. The men were always saying that you could never count on women to back you up in a pinch." When Rudolph returned to work a couple of male officers stood around and said, "Here comes the cluck, cluck." Five weeks after her return to work Rudolph, Perkins, and 690 other Detroit police officers were laid off. Of that number 271 were female.[12]

When *Time* was showing its hostility to policewomen in its 1980 article, it also mentioned this incident. The magazine said Rowell went berserk and attacked Janness; in fact, he did not. It claimed Janness was "badly beaten," but he was not. Concluding comments held that "some women on the force are bitter because their two colleagues were not given the chance to resign quietly. Even if Perkins and Rudolph are cleared they say the case will leave the lingering impression that female cops are not up the job."[13]

Black females had more difficulty breaking into policing than white women. A study of the situation in 1979 reported that "black women are at most negligibly present even among the sworn supervisory and command personnel of five of the more progressive municipal agencies." Black women advanced beyond the rank of officer less frequently than did white women. At that time the Detroit police department had 644 policewomen, 11.7 percent of the force; of these 7.5 percent were black women, while 4.2 percent were white women. However, in the ranks of sworn supervisory personnel women made up 3.7 percent, 2.7 percent white and 1.0 percent black. "The advancement of black women in American policing has been minimal, and less than the general advancement of women and black males ... institutional racism, coupled with sexism likely operates in monumental measure to the disadvantage of black women."[14]

Constance Barron was an agent-in-training in the Oklahoma City office of the federal Bureau of Alcohol, Tobacco, and Firearms (ATF) in 1991. White colleagues routinely used the term "nigger" in her presence. A white agent once called her a "black bitch." On an office wall where she worked a card read, "State of Oklahoma Nigger Hunting License." The ATF was an agency of the Treasury Department that collected federal excise taxes on alcohol, tobacco, and firearms and enforced federal laws on firearms, among other duties. When Barron first was called "nigger" she said her feelings toward the agency changed dramatically: "This is a federal agency. We're supposed to be upholding the law. To me, they were breaking the law." Barron filed an internal equal opportunity complaint. Without admitting any violation of her civil rights, the agency quietly settled her case in 1991 by paying her attorney's fees, purging job evaluations from her files which she said were unduly harsh in retaliation for her complaints, and transferred her to the Dallas office. Her complaint was echoed by many black agents (mostly male) who brought a class action suit against the ATF, resulting in a 1993 agreement allowing a federal judge to supervise its employment practices for a five-year period. At that time the ATF had about 2,000 law enforcement agents in 22 districts, 11 percent female, 10 percent black, and 7 percent Latino. Among supervisory agents each of these three groups accounted for about 5 percent. Around that time rookie ATF agent Sandra Hernandez told her supervisors in Chicago that she had endured two years of sexual harassment from a higher-ranking male agent who repeatedly pawed her, forcibly kissed her, and propositioned her for sex. Only after Hernandez and two other women with sexual harassment allegations went public on the CBS television program *60 Minutes* did ATF director Stephen E. Higgins call on the Treasury Department's inspector general to investigate the charges. When an internal investigation verified Hernandez's allegations, the ATF recommend the firing of the harasser. Charges that the agency was sexist and racist continued to beset the ATF.[15]

Hostility to policewomen often began in the training academies themselves. At the Southeast Florida Institute of Criminal Justice in Miami in 1983 it was found that women entering training were generally idealistic and self-confident about their roles and interactions with male colleagues. However, after just eight weeks in training their feelings about peer relations worsened by 80 percent, and those percentages did not improve significantly after that time. The more traditionally "feminine" a woman was, the worse she felt about herself. One commented, "I'm proud of what I'm doing, but when the guys put female officers down, I find myself laughing with them. Then I feel like a traitor to myself and my sex."[16]

At abut the same time an article in *Police Chief* stated that there was a higher turnover rate among females than males. Many believed this was due to the "discrimination of male officers, unfairness in male and female promotional opportunities, and the stress in proving 'a woman is as good as a man on the job.'" Policewomen felt themselves to be frequent recipients of anti-women comments and rumors. Policemen frequently remarked that the "police department didn't really want women." The idea of "one rotten female apple" was pervasive, whereby if one woman screwed up then all females were branded as inept.[17]

Judie Wexler studied stress among female patrol officers in 1981, interviewing 25 policewomen, all from a large metropolitan police department in California. Females had first entered the academy to train for patrol duty in 1975. The women experienced all four types of stress as reported by males: external stressors (such as negative public attitudes), organizational stressors (such as training), task-related stressors (such as danger), and personal stressors (such as health problems). In addition, women suffered from female-related stressors, mentioned by 23 of the 25 respondents. These included negative attitudes of male officers, group blame, responses of other men, and lack of role models. Of the 25 officers 13 reported male coworkers were very concerned with the women's sexual orientation and sex life and spent considerable time talking about this, nine said males refused to talk to them, eight mentioned males made blatant anti-female comments, three reported threats of no backup, and three reported a refusal to let them drive. Some of the males made persistent passes, both verbal and physical. One female officer reported that a male officer ended the roll call one night with, "Let us pray that _____ [woman's name] gets shot tonight." Other females reported spending eight hours in a squad car with males who refused to talk to them, and two women were assigned to units wherein none of the men would speak to them if they could be seen doing so by other male officers.[18]

Over the six years women had been assigned to patrol in that police department the anti-female attitudes had not been eliminated. One positive change was a reduction in official harassment. Females were first placed on patrol only because of the requirements of a court order, which the department and police union fought against in a joint legal action. Some of the first females to arrive in that department's stations found that the lieutenant had ordered that they be locked out or that they had been assigned a locker in the middle of the men's locker room. That type of official harassment had stopped. Of the 12 females in the first two training classes to incorporate women, seven reported difficulties. One training officer said, "This is my personal opinion; I don't think you should be in this job. You should go home and have babies." Said a policewoman, "They didn't know how to train us. The department tried to fire us every week. The federal courts kept saying, 'Go back and teach them over again.' So they would hire us again." Even six years later three of nine women reported anti-female training officers who tried to harass them into resigning. Rumors were often spread about the women. One was said to be a lesbian. Fully half of the 25 female officers interviewed felt they were affected not only by their own actions but by the actions of all the women in the department as well — the idea of group blame. This study concluded that after six years of experience with females on general patrol, "the men in the department still did not seem to accept them as officers. They were ignored, harassed, watched, gossiped about, and viewed as sexual objects. The hostility of their male co-workers has been so substantial that other stressors recede in comparison." Commented one policewoman, "The worst part of the job is the attitudes of the people I have to work with. It is harder to be around them than the bad guys." While police work has been singled out as a high-stress occupation for men, the actions of policemen increased the stress level for women. Of the stressors under which policewomen worked, "the most common ones seemed to center around their being women."[19]

Odd, discriminatory practices harking back to an even more anti-female world remained in place in some areas. In July 1984 policewoman Gail Kello of Pasadena, Texas, handed in her badge after marrying fellow officer Larry Kello. The marriage put the couple in violation of a Pasadena civil service rule barring married couples from working in the police department. Mayor Johnny Isbell and Police Chief David Mullican came up with a job offer for Gail, one day after she resigned — that of Isbell's secretary. It meant a salary cut of $1,000 a month but Gail was able to keep her sick pay and retirement benefits.[20]

When author Susan Martin assessed the status of policewomen in 1986 she found that women had a larger number of non-patrol assignments than their male counterparts, leading her to suggest there had been both "integration and 'reghettoization' of the women in policing." A combination of old-boy ties, sex role stereotypes, and paternalism continued to informally influence assignment decisions. Rookie policewomen were "protected" into station house assignments. This protection led to incompetent street performance, which, in a self-sustaining cycle, justified the need for further protection and non-patrol assignments. Martin thought it was still true that females were presumed to be incapable patrol officers until they proved otherwise. "They face overt hostility from some men, double standards of performance, sexual harassment, and exclusion from informal social networks that are keys to gaining self-confidence and acceptance." While agreeing that sex discrimination continued to exist, Martin felt it was "less frequent, blatant, and organized than in the past." Of the women interviewed by Martin 66 percent identified at least one instance of sex discrimination or were able to illustrate an instance of clearly discriminatory treatment. Another 8 percent claimed to have suffered racial discrimination. Of the policewomen who entered the service before 1975 there were 83 percent who perceived themselves as victims of sex discrimination. For those joining between 1975 and 1980 the figure was 73 percent, but for women sworn in during 1985 and 1986 just 27 percent felt they were the victims of sex discrimination.[21]

Bias against women surfaced in other ways. In the late 1980s the forms used for the performance evaluation of police officers in cities such as Birmingham, Chicago, and Detroit used the masculine pronoun throughout. Birmingham rated officers on the "physical ability to perform the job." In Chicago one rating area was the quantity of work, with suggested criteria including arrest activity and traffic enforcement, while activities such as crime prevention and public service received no consideration. Criteria for judging personal relations included the ability of the employee to cooperate in team efforts, with the rater being instructed to consider whether the employee is "someone with whom most other members are able to work comfortably." When men were not comfortable working with a female it was she who was the one receiving a negative evaluation due to her "inadequate" personal relations. Even if a policewoman lived up to male standards it was not necessarily acceptable. One female lieutenant told of a rookie policewoman who made many arrests. Male officers, she said, "several times have tried to cut her out on the radio when she stopped a car and gave the location." Thirty-five percent of policewomen, but only 8 percent of policemen, cited officer or superior harassment as their greatest initial problem. While Martin believed sex discrimination had diminished somewhat from the past, she noted that "some men continue to oppose the presence of women in patrol assignments (and probably in policing)."[22]

Some lawsuits charging discrimination dragged on for years. In New York City tests for police officer were segregated into the early 1970s. Between 1960 and the end of 1970 the force held 54 tests open to men only, while over that same period only three tests were open to women. In March 1964 both men and women were tested; however, males who passed were appointed to the force in 1964 and 1965, while successful females who passed the test on the same day were appointed between 1966 and 1969. This had an effect on seniority and promotion. During New York City's fiscal crisis 2,864 were laid off in 1975, including 399 of the approximately 700 females—55.3 percent. Remaining policewomen were reduced to doing more matron-type duties of searching and guarding female prisoners. In response to this layoff a class-action suit against the force was brought through the New York Human Rights Commission in 1976. This was not settled until 1991, when the commission found the NYPD had discriminated against 124 female officers. By then four of the women were dead and about 50 percent no longer with the department. The settlement meant that these women, or their estates, were entitled to monetary damages to be determined at a still later date.[23]

The lead plaintiff in that suit was Beraldine Kalra. She, like most of the others, was rehired once the fiscal crisis passed. However, she filed a new suit, alleging she was harassed because of her role in that first suit. She was, she said, verbally abused and denied the promotions and assignments she sought. In a separate 1991 ruling the Human Rights Commission ruled that Kalra was in fact discriminated against because of her involvement in the first action.

Kalra was awarded over $200,000 in damages and more than $100,000 in pension payments. By then she had left the force.[24]

Susan Bouman joined the Los Angeles Sheriff's Department in 1971 as part of the first class in which women were enrolled with men at the training academy. After graduation she was assigned to the county women's jail. While there she applied for transfers to other positions but was told that she needed patrol experience to qualify. But women were not allowed patrol experience. Eventually, she was transferred to the Lakewood Station in 1975 where she was part of a pilot project which put female deputies into the field. What she had defined before as resistance to her presence became out-and-out hostility. It ranged from a training officer who peppered her with profanity, to a captain who did not believe women belonged on patrol, to a lieutenant who refused to allow her to work at night because she was a woman, and to a dispatcher who refused to speak to women, necessitating that she get work assignments through somebody else. Later she was transferred to the Pico Rivera Station where she received pornographic pictures placed in her mailbox. It was then 1977 with Bouman having taken the examination for promotion to sergeant. Despite her high ratings she found herself, suspiciously, ranked at only 128 out of 250 successful candidates. Bouman started to hear rumors she would not be promoted, and that the police establishment considered her a troublemaker. People on the list were being promoted. Finally, the first 127 were moved to the rank of sergeant. Bouman was then at the top of the list, next to go. Suddenly the department cut off the list, calling it expired. When Bouman complained she was told that no vacancies existed. She checked on her own and found there were vacancies. Attempting to complain through department channels, Bouman was informed that a complaint could not be initiated about an active list as it was possible she would still be promoted. On the other hand, a complaint could not be initiated about a dead list since she was not on an active list. She was then transferred back to the women's jail as her "previous position had been eliminated." Bouman launched a class-action suit at the end of the 1970s, charging that the Los Angeles Sheriff's Department had unfair promotion practices. In 1988 a federal judge in Los Angeles held in favor of the women, awarding over $150,000 in compensatory and punitive damages to Bouman. Three years later the U.S. Ninth Circuit Court of Appeals upheld the earlier ruling, agreeing that the force engaged in intentional sex discrimination by failing to promote women to sergeant, even though vacancies existed. One lawyer for the women estimated that hundreds of passed-over female officers were eligible for damages that could exceed, in total, $2 million. None of the money had yet been collected. Bouman spent five more years stationed at the women's jail where she was basically a matron. During this time, and after the suit was filed, she was promoted to sergeant in 1981. Bouman was given a stress disability retirement by the sheriff's department in January 1990. Privately, many policewomen supported her but none would testify on her behalf for fear of losing their jobs. In mid–1991 of the department's 6,322 deputies 862 were female (13.6 percent) while 86 of the force's 942 sergeants were women (9.1 percent).[25]

When the Christopher Commission released its report in the summer of 1991, most of the attention to this well-publicized report focused on its discussion of the use of excessive force by the police in Los Angeles. The commission was convened in the wake of the beating of black motorist Rodney King by LAPD officers in March 1991, an incident captured on videotape by a bystander and aired around the globe. Nevertheless, the report did contain some information on policewomen.

At that time 13 percent of the LAPD were females, yet none of the department's 132 officers who were the worst offenders in shootings, the use of force, or as recipients of citizen complaints were females. This report concluded the women were better at averting potential violence and that they did a good job at policing by any measure. Still, the report termed them unwelcome on the LAPD, "perhaps more than minority male officers, ridiculed in computer messages and doubted by Chief Daryl F. Gates." Assistant Chief David Dotson testified to a conversation he had with Gates in which they discussed research showing females did the job as well as men. At the end, said Dotson, Gates shook his head and said, "But I really don't think they belong out there." Messages on computer screens in patrol cars used terms like "sweet cakes ... babes ... Barbie dolls ... Sgt. Tits ... cunt." The LAPD was then still well under the court-ordered 20 percent female force. Christopher Commission interviews with 90 training officers showed many of them did not believe women were "as capable, effective or trustworthy" as men. Other computer messages between officers in 1989 and 1990 included: "Pound her into submission ... and then have her make you breakfast"; "We got rid of our two lovely young ladies.... They both need a few rounds with the old baton ... wouldn't you say"; "Hey slut, when do you want to take a code 7 (a break)"; "Most policemen treat women like shit ... and I have heard of some guys even getting away with rape because they're officers"; and "Don't give me any lip, woman, just obey." When a Soviet policeman visited the LAPD around that time he told a roll call session that Soviet policewomen were limited to desk jobs or juvenile duties. Upon hearing this, male officers in the back of the room cheered. The Christopher Report concluded that accepting women was more difficult when police continued to define the job as one requiring "a major emphasis on physical strength" over other skills, disdaining a more patient, less aggressive approach."[26]

In June 1992 a group of about a dozen Fairfax County, Virginia, policewomen took sex discrimination grievances to the Equal Employment Opportunity Commission in a move that reflected growing resentment. Said one,

"For years and years we've put up with it because it would make it worse for other women. It's gotten to the point where we're not going to take it anymore." Of the 946 sworn Fairfax police officers 86 were female and 86 were black. Both those groups also complained about lack of promotions. Detailed complaints included a high-ranking police official who referred during a meeting to a female officer as a cunt, and a female civilian employee was discouraged by a male supervisor from pursuing a sexual assault charge against a male officer. The complaint was pursued, with the male officer subsequently pleading guilty to a misdemeanor. A policewoman was told not to apply for a position because she had children, but this vacancy was filled by a male officer who also had children. Male officers were given individual coaching by their superiors to help them prepare for promotion examinations, but females were denied such assistance. Their complaint also alleged there was a pervasive "locker room attitude" in the department that subjected policewomen to sexist statements as well as causing them to be overlooked in promotions and assignments. Also alleged was that some women were denied promotions in favor of less qualified males.[27]

Sexual harassment of policewomen was pervasive. In earlier years the attitude adopted was that it was just something to be put up with, something the female herself was largely responsible for. It was an attitude that applied to working women everywhere, not just in policing. Mary Anderson, a Portland, Oregon, police sergeant captured that idea in her book *Women in Law Enforcement*, when she warned that a woman may be the only female on a force and "thus may be pinched, patted, or played with. They, therefore, should not wear heavy make-up or suggestive clothing and should not use longshoreman's language."[28]

Some writers almost ignored the problem. In his 1980 book Peter Horne devoted less than half a page to the issue, noting it was "a very small problem percentage-wise," which also confronted private industry. He cited one policewoman who said it was almost an unwritten rule with certain male supervisors that "you've got to make love to get a day off or a good beat, and you've definitely got to put out to get a superior performance evaluation." Stating that such things could not be tolerated, Horne went on to devote over a full page to how policewomen could and did use sexuality to manipulate male supervisors.[29]

As the number of policewomen increased so did the sexual harassment. When Susan Martin rode around as a Metropolitan Police Reserve Corps volunteer officer in Washington in the mid–1970s she was told innumerable stories. One policewoman assigned with others to protect a visiting foreign dignitary's hotel had her sergeant say to her, in front of other males, "Come on, I have a room. I want a header." At the conclusion of one shift signing out several policemen looked at one female officer's chest and asked, "How long do you think she can float?" That policewoman told Martin, "I know this is sexism and I try to put them in their place but if I get snippy they'll get me for insubordination." Another policewoman was greeted as a newcomer to the area by the remark, "Officer, I don't mean any harm but I just want you to know that you have the biggest breasts I've ever seen on a policewoman." She upbraided him verbally, humiliating him in front of his peers. This caused her to acquire a reputation for being "stuck up, snotty and evil; even being a lesbian." But, she remarked, "I preferred it that way. Then they'd leave me alone." Another new policewoman said, "They all tried to hit on us when we arrived, to see who could be the first to get one of us. When we had the _____ detail [and had to remain at a fixed post], they'd line up their cars trying to get our phone numbers." She remarked that some of the women did date the men, but they then got a bad reputation. In order to reject the men some females had to resort to unladylike bluntness or threats of public exposure, tape recordings, or telephone calls to their wives to make their unavailability very clear. Some sergeants singled out females for harassment. One policeman found his sergeant "on his back" when he worked with one particular policewoman partner — the sergeant was sexually interested in the woman and thought the man was dating her. Because of this the man requested not to work with the woman as he "could feel a dereliction coming." Martin reported a strong feeling among both male and female officers that women who were sexually harassed "asked for it." According to many policewomen, "It all depends on how a woman carries herself." One said, "If a person cannot deal with their own sexuality, they have no business having a gun, arresting people or making serious decisions about other people." However, she did not apply that standard to men.[30]

Other researchers found similar problems on the Washington force in that time period. Officer Peggy Jackson complained in 1975 that intercourse was expected of her in order to get good assignments. Penny Bolden reported that her male partner pulled their cruiser into a Washington park, requested that she have sex with him, and warned her to say nothing about it. Most of the women victimized by sexual harassers would not formally complain since they feared retaliation from their superiors. Almost half of the district's then 333 policewomen were assigned to patrol duty. In interviews half of those admitted to having been sexually harassed. One of the more regularly heard stories from these women was one that "consisted of male officers — many of whom outrank the women — punishing policewomen who would not submit to sexual advances and rewarding those who did with better treatment and assignments." Washington police chief Maurice Cullinane called these allegations "unsubstantiated innuendo and back-alley gossip." He dismissed the charges on the ground that up until then he had received no official complaints.[31]

Ten years or so later Martin found the situation little changed when she surveyed the policewoman situation in 1986. With regard to police turnover rates she concluded, "Sexual harassment also appears to contribute to turnover for women." While she found that policewomen hired in recent years were less likely to report themselves as victims of sex discrimination, such was not the case for sexual harassment. For policewomen hired before 1975 approximately 77 percent said they had been victims of sexual harassment; for policewomen hired between 1975 and 1980 the figure was 76 percent. Of the policewomen hired in 1985 and 1986 there were 67 percent who reported themselves as the victims of harassment. Of the overall 75 percent who indicated being subjected to some form of sexual harassment, 49 percent of them reported being pressured for sexual favors by a supervisor or fellow officers. In addition to sexual propositions, policemen sexualized the workplace through frequent pranks, jokes, and comments based on sexual stereotypes of females, or calling attention to women's sexuality. One commented, "There were constant comments and always a *Hustler* lying around." When she went into the locker for supplies "there'd be an enlarged centerfold. I never said anything, but every time I had to open the locker, I had to see it. The shift commander had a sexually explicit photo on the front of his desk when I was working inside.... It made me uncomfortable and he put it there for that reason." In the 1980s one policewoman said, "I was going to the parking lot and saw two officers in plainclothes. I trusted this one guy, who said the other guy wants to talk to you. I walked over to the car and he had his groin out." Another had refused to go out with her supervisor, saying she did not date her boss. She said, "Suddenly my work was no longer acceptable; he will not speak to me at all now. Up 'til last May, I had rave evaluations; all of a sudden, it changed." Eventually she transferred to another squad. In comparing her two surveys Martin found "the persistence of sexual harassment and practices that allowed [the men] to preserve their ideology of male supremacy while accepting or tolerating the presence of women."[32]

Policewoman Cheryl Preston filed suit against the Detroit Police Department in 1984, alleging sexual harassment. She maintained that on-the-job harassment, sexual and otherwise, caused her to suffer a nervous breakdown and prevented her from working for two years. She said she was harassed by coworkers who thought her job should have been given to a male officer who was laid off and who felt she did not need the job because she was married to a doctor. Preston won the first round in 1987, when the court held she was sexually harassed, awarding her $900,000 plus interest.[33]

Late in 1990 in San Francisco a federal district court jury awarded $2.7 million to three female sheriff's deputies in the Santa Clara County Sheriff's Department who alleged a male officer demanded sex in exchange for favorable work reviews. In making the award the court ruled also that the department and several officials did not do enough to discourage the harassment. The deputies launched their suit in 1985 charging department officials with failure to investigate their complaint against Deputy Sheriff Craig Nelson. Nelson was dropped as a defendant earlier in 1990 after his insurance company agreed to pay $150,000.[34]

In some cases the woman lost, as in Michigan where a policewoman alleged sexual harassment by her colleagues. One specific act mention was that of a male officer putting a flashlight between her legs from behind. The court ruled in that case that it was not sexual harassment; rather that it was merely "horseplay" and as such was more indicative of the female's acceptance as a coworker than harassment.

In some cases the evidence was so overwhelming as to leave no doubt as to the court outcome. In *Arnold v. the City of Seminole, Oklahoma*, a policewoman outlined in court a series of incidents of sexual harassment directed at her, which included: a lieutenant who told her he did not believe in female police; superior officers who sometimes refused to speak to her; obscene pictures posted in public places in the station with her name written on them; epithets and derogatory comments written next to her name on posted work and leave schedules; false misconduct claims filed against her; work schedules manipulated to prevent her from being senior officer on duty, thus denying her command status; she was singled out for public reprimands without receiving the required notice; officers interfered with her office mail and squad car; attempts to implicate her in an illegal drug transaction were contemplated; she was denied equal access to station house locker facilities; and members of her family were arrested, threatened, and harassed. In this case the court ruled she had been sexually harassed. The contention that it was all simply office camaraderie was dismissed.[35]

Karen Sorlucco's nightmare began in 1983 when she was a probationary policewoman with the New York City Police Department. Sorlucco reported being raped by a man at gunpoint in her Nassau County apartment. One week later she identified NYPD officer John Mielko as her assailant. Due to the consistent effort by both Nassau County police officers and investigators from the Internal Affairs Division of the NYPD to refuse any investigation into Sorlucco's charges against Mielko, Sorlucco was found guilty by a Nassau County District Court jury of making a false police report. An appeals court later ruled this conviction was a direct result of the police refusal to conduct an appropriate investigation. The federal appeals court ruling in Manhattan in 1992 was critical of the NYPD for sexual discrimination against Sorlucco. The three-judge panel unanimously reinstated a jury verdict award of $264,242 to Sorlucco. That reversed a federal district verdict which had overturned the jury verdict and ordered a new trial at the request of the NYPD. Said the court, "In our view, given the undisputed fact of Sorlucco's brutal sexual assault, the New York Police Department tragically failed to show the sensitivity to the physical trauma and the resulting psychological manifestations commonly experienced by rape victims." It reiterated that the department had not investigated Mielko and had treated Sorlucco "harshly," all of which led them to find "an unconstitutional departmental practice of sexual discrimination." Mielko was never charged with any crime. Later he retired with a full pension. When news people tried to contact him following the 1992 ruling, an NYPD spokesperson said the department did not know how to contact him.[36]

That same department came under fire in 1992 when two policewomen complained they had been sexually harassed by policemen and that their One Hundred Tenth Precinct commander in Queens, Deputy Inspector Hugh Selzer, failed to take any action, despite their complaints. Allegedly, an obscene statement was written on a station house wall, pornographic pictures were placed on the women's lockers, and lewd phone calls were made to their homes. In October that year Selzer was transferred to the Fifteenth Division in Brooklyn as an executive officer. The head of the NYPD's Inspectional Services Bureau said "part of" the reason for the transfer was the harassment complaint. Selzer's new division post involved less direct supervision of rank-and-file officers than did a precinct commander's job. However, Inspector Lawrence Loesch said the transfer was a promotion: "It's the next level of supervision."[37]

In September 1991, after a one-month trial, a jury awarded Lindsey Allison and Melissa Clerkin $3.1 million for sexual harassment during the pair's tenure as officers in the Long Beach, California, Police Department. Both left that department in 1988. They and other officers testified that sexually harassing behavior was "endemic" on that force. Witnesses told of male officers often using obscene language to degrade women and then retaliating if a female complained about it. Allison was one of the first women assigned to the Long Beach canine unit. She said that some policemen told her graphic sex stories, urinated outdoors in her presence, and allowed their dogs to attack her. Detective Estelle Martinez stated that while a cadet in the Long Beach Police Academy in 1985 she and other recruits were instructed in the presence of supervisors to run and sing in cadence a suggestive rhyme that began, "I wish all women were holes in the road." Clerkin testified that her sergeant and one-time lover had harassed her; then male officers retaliated by refusing to provide her with backup assistance, by calling her vulgar names, and by sending her offensive messages over police car computers. Officer Cheryl Perkins related that she heard officers say they would not back up Clerkin on calls. Officer Melissa Williams (then with Pismo Beach PD) testified that she was called an obscene name by her partner on her first night on the job and that policemen sometimes blocked transmissions between dispatchers and policewomen they did not like. After the verdict Allison said, "For so long we were told 'we' were the problem. 'We' couldn't get along. How good it feels to prove it wasn't us."[38]

After the court decision a reporter for the *Los Angeles Times* contacted several Long Beach policewomen for comment to see if the situation had changed. None would comment on the matter, fearing retaliation. As of spring 1993 neither woman had received any money as the case was still under appeal. CBS television aired a television move *With Hostile Intent* in May 1993 based on the case. Officials for both the city and police department of Long Beach complained that no one connected with the movie had contacted them for their side of the story. Filmmakers, who relied on official transcripts, countered that they had contacted city and police officials but none would comment, saying the case was being appealed. Screenwriter Alison Cross worried the movie would not do justice to the women's experience because of television's limitations. "The language was so horribly degrading, but you can't use that on television," she explained. Cross's opinion of the real-life case was that "the guys in the field could get away with these things because of the silence above at the top. The women complained constantly, and right away. But no one paid attention.... The silence acted as license." When the film aired Allison was worried about retaliation and feared for the safety of herself and young son. "It started with exclusion," she recalled. "Right from the beginning there was a negative tension that I wasn't welcome. So much happened and it was so extreme. The movie is a very condensed version. It barely touches the surface of what really happened."[39]

Five male deputies were fired by the Los Angeles Sheriff's Department in 1991 for harassing a female deputy. The incidents took place at a county jail where the deputies encouraged male detainees to expose themselves to the female officer and to throw tomatoes, eggs, and water balloons at her. In addition, the detainees screamed obscenities at her and threatened her safety. The deputies were terminated following a five-month internal investigation.[40]

Despite the firings in this case, reporters for the *Los Angeles Times* said the Los Angeles Sheriff's Department had been "plagued for years by allegations of lewd and unfair conduct toward women in the ranks." One other case was that of Deputy Laura Beard, whose 1990 suit alleged "almost daily abusive and demeaning remarks and sexually offensive posters and pictures." In December 1992 the Los Angeles Sheriff's Department signed a consent decree ending both Beard's suit and the previously mentioned Bouman suit — then still under appeal after 12 or so years. Under the decree the department agreed to spend $4.5 million over the coming four years to improve the working atmosphere for females by establishing an ombudsperson and by holding gender sensitivity training. One change was to a defensive driving training film in which a topless female motorist was shown distracting a male deputy who was driving a patrol car.[41]

June 1993 saw a few details of a harassment suit launched the previous February against the Irvine, California, police force made public. Four female officers, two of them on medical leave then, were suing on the basis of alleged harassment and discrimination against women on the force. According to the women, male officers boasted of their on-duty sexual exploits and had formed a Code Four club in which membership and pins were awarded to an officer when he had sex with a policewoman in his patrol car. Code four meant, in police lingo, that an officer was all right.[42]

Near the end of 1992 former Los Angeles Police Department officer Teri Lyons began a lawsuit against the department, alleging she had been raped by a superior then fired for reporting the attack to the LAPD's Internal Affairs Division (IAD). Alleged was that Lyons had been raped the previous spring by Commander Maurice Moore. When she reported this to Moore's superior she was told "these things happen." A second superior told her not to discuss the rape. Thereafter her employment was terminated.[43]

Lyons was one of about six policewomen who alleged they were raped by LAPD male officers during the period of 1989 to 1993. Another was Suzanne Campbell, who said she was raped on the police academy grounds by Officer Ernest Hill in 1990. In October 1992 she filed a lawsuit stating the LAPD and the city's unofficial policy was to ignore and discourage females— sometimes with threats of disciplinary action —from filing complaints of sexual harassment. After she made a formal departmental complaint the LAPD took 15 months to process Campbell's charge before sustaining the rape complaint, culminating in the firing of Hill. During those months Campbell alleged she was harassed further for pursuing the complaint. The first step in the departmental process was an IAD investigation.

After three months they sent a report to Chief Daryl Gates with a recommendation to send Hill to a board of rights. Calling the accusation not sustained, Chief Gates reversed that decision. According to Campbell, Maurice Moore recommended to Gates that all charges against Hill be dismissed. Unsatisfied with this Campbell, asked LAPD for an explanation, but none was given. Detective Kena Brutsch, women's coordinator on the force, told her that if she continued to press her complaint she would be charged with "lewd conduct in a public place." Also alleged by Campbell was that IAD captain Jan Carlson told her it was LAPD policy to take no disciplinary action in "one-on-one" incidents of sexual harassment. This woman also reportedly told Campbell that if she persisted in her complaint she would be charged with having sex on company grounds. Ignoring standard procedure, Campbell appealed Gates' reversal directly to the police commissioners, who ordered a board of inquiry to review the handling of the case. Eventually, Hill was terminated and the IAD found negligent, specifically for failing to interview key witnesses.[44]

Katherine Spillar, co-chair of the Women's Advisory Council (WAC) to the police commission, said that some Los Angeles field-training officers made it clear to recruits that sex could be traded for favors. Spillar found the number of females reporting sexual assaults to the WAC to be "disturbing." Speaking anonymously, a male officer told of a field-training officer who put the lives of sexually noncompliant women recruits in danger by provoking suspects into an altercation with them. When his behavior was finally documented he was transferred quietly to a different division. Another LAPD officer suing on an alleged rape charge was Teresa Wallin. She did not report the rape for four weeks, fearing retaliation and that filing a complaint might ruin her career. In the cases of both Wallin and Campbell, IAD investigators questioned their associates about the social and sexual history of the women.

Commander Daniel Watson of the force's personnel division said that sexual harassment on the LAPD "is really bad, but it's not as big a problem as women think it is." IAD made the decision to alter its procedure by characterizing charges of sexual harassment as "conduct unbecoming an officer" instead of harassment, offering the rationale that this was easier to prove than charges of harassment. Women countered that this change perpetuated the idea that harassment was not worthy of consideration on its own merits. They also argued that if harassment charges were entered into a personnel file only as "conduct unbecoming" it would be much more difficult to find a pattern of sexual misconduct. When Willie Williams took over as chief in the wake of the Rodney King beating, he reviewed the WAC's recommendations and ordered anti-sexual harassment training for the entire LAPD command staff — including himself — which began in 1993. During William's tenure the LAPD's board of rights decided that a case in which a male officer pulled a policewoman's face into his crotch was not sexual harassment because the man received no gratification. That officer was finally suspended after being found guilty of inappropriate conduct involving the same policewoman. Spillar was not optimistic that the sexist ways of the LAPD would change with the departure of Gates. "Willie Williams has a problem," she explained. "He's sitting on top of a department that is philosophically opposed to change."[45]

One problem faced by females trying to pursue complaints was the unwritten code of silence. Another was that the IAD was a division of choice for many officers. Problems potentially arose when IAD detectives had to investigate higher-ranked officers, men who had power and control over the detectives. If a female complainant tried to evade the system by going straight to the district attorney's office with a rape complaint, the DA would almost always send the case back to the IAD. Los Angeles Police Commissioner president Jesse Brewer said of sexual harassment on the force, "It's a problem everywhere, but especially in a predominantly male police department, where there's a lot of resistance to women being there."[46]

Southern California's Newport Beach Police Department was hit by sexual harassment charges that started to unfold publicly on September 24, 1992. Four current and former department employees filed a sex discrimination lawsuit in Orange County Superior Court that day against Newport Beach as defendant and accusing Captain Anthony Villa and Police Chief Arbra "Arb" Campbell of misconduct. The civil suit was brought by Officer Cheryl Vlacilek, records supervisor Mary Jane Ruetz, communications supervisor Margaret McInnis, and fired officer Rochell Maier. The women charged Villa with harassment and Campbell with condoning that behavior. Allegedly, Villa made sexual advances which included touching the women's breasts, and made sexually suggestive remarks, including an explicit description of a pornographic movies. With the exception of McInnis, all complainants contended they had been disciplined then fired on spurious charges after rejecting Villa's advances. Vlacilek and Ruetz were reinstated by the Newport Beach Civil Service Commission while Maier's reinstatement appeal was then under consideration. At the time of filing Ruetz was on disability leave, claiming to be suffering from stress due to the sexual harassment. According to their lawsuit, the women were told to socialize with male officers off duty, especially commanding officers, and to wear short skirts to show off their legs and wear other clothes deemed desirable by the men. Some female officers involved with high-ranking male officers were said to receive favorable treatment at the expense of female employees who would not "go along to get along." According to the suit, a number of women had left the department because of sexual harassment and discrimination. After filing the action the women told a reporter they were "petrified" of retaliation but determined to proceed as they felt the department was an intolerably sexist workplace, describing the force as a "hotbed of sexually offensive conduct at the top levels of the command structure." Vlacilek said, "It's been extremely stressful and very retaliatory.... At times, it's very unbearable to work there, and with the powers that be, I worry about what could happen." Ruetz commented, "It's been almost unbearable as far as fear and pressure and retaliatory treatment." Newport Beach PD had at the time 250 employees. Of those, 76 were female, including seven officers. At about the time the suit was filed the department announced that Villa was being transferred from patrol captain to captain of administration. A police spokesman said it was just part of a routine rotation.[47]

Both men declined to comment publicly on the charges. Their attorney issued a denial on their behalf, describing the complainants as disgruntled employees who were properly disciplined and fired. On October 14 Campbell announced his retirement, to take effect May 15, 1993. He gave no specific reason.[48]

Just one day after that announcement a fifth woman, dispatcher Peri Ropke, joined the lawsuit of the other four. She alleged that 11 years earlier in 1981 when she was 22 she was raped and subjected to other sex acts by both Campbell and Villa. Following the rape, which took place at a landfill site in a vehicle after a departmental party, Campbell ordered her out of the vehicle and, claimed Ropke, told her to never discuss the incident with anyone, threatening retaliation if she did. For the following decade the two men allegedly told Ropke to be "a good girl" and "keep her mouth shut." Villa warned her that Campbell was a force to be reckoned with who fancied the job of chief (which he got in 1986) and that Villa would rise along with him. Due to the six-year statute of limitations for rape, no criminal charges could then be brought. Said Ropke, "Working for Arb and Tony for the last 11 years, it was very difficult. I was constantly living in fear.... I hope that by my coming forward, other women will have the courage to do the same." Later that same day Newport Beach city manager Kevin J. Murphy responded to the latest charges by placing Campbell and Villa on paid administrative leave and appointing an acting chief. Bruce Praet, the attorney hired by the city for the two men, issued another denial for his clients concerning the latest charge. Praet said, "We're going to respond on our own and set these people for independent psychiatric evaluation which, we think, especially in Ropke's case, will be very enlightening." Near the end of October the Police Employees' Association announced an overwhelming vote of no confidence in the chief.[49]

In November Campbell and Villa filed a federal civil rights lawsuit against Newport Beach, charging their removal from duty was improper. By then Campbell had withdrawn his resignation.[50]

Early in December four more female police department employees joined the lawsuit, bringing the number to nine. They also alleged they had been touched against their will by Villa, told to socialize with male officers off duty, denied promotions because they were women, and harassed in other ways. These women were officers Shontel Sherwood and Katherine Heinzel, dispatcher Molly Thomson, and animal control officer Michelle LeFay. The latter two had taken medical leaves from the department. Two of the women corroborated Ropke's story to the extent they stated she told them about the assault years before her public accusation. Sherwood remarked, "I believe that by my actions in joining the lawsuit, other employees will not have to endure the wrong that made me a victim." Praet continued to deny everything on behalf of his clients. He now contended Ropke confused the party at which she alleged rape with another sexual encounter involving two different men while she was employed by another police department. Regarding the latest four women to join the suit, Praet stated their case had no merit and added,

"The more people who jump on the bandwagon, the less credibility it gives the original plaintiffs, if there was any credibility in the first place.... You can cry wolf too many times."[51]

Shortly after the first suit was filed, the City of Newport Beach hired outside attorney Harold Bridges of Los Angeles to investigate the charges. He reported on his "substantially complete" investigation to the city council in mid–December following the questioning of 169 members of the police department. Bridges concluded, "The interviews revealed information from which a trier of fact might find that conduct of a sexually harassing nature occurred." However, he added that the women who filed the suit may have themselves "engaged in sexually harassing conduct." Continuing, he stated that apart from sex "a substantial number of those interviewed believed there to be a hostile work environment." Bridges gave no names or specifics for any of this conclusions.[52]

Response by the city council to this report was only that they were "saddened." This listless response angered an editor at the *Los Angeles Times* who demanded, "Where is the council's outrage about the trouble in the department? Where are the promises to clean it up?" Acknowledging there were serious problems in the department, the newspaper termed the council's reluctance to confront the problem as "disturbing." It urged a stronger response.[53]

This stronger response came on December 22, 1992, when Murphy fired Campbell. No specific reason was given other than that the grounds were "many" and "varied." Four days prior to that steps had been initiated to fire Villa as well. As Campbell was an at-will employee it was procedurally easier to terminate him than it was Villa. Other insinuations about Campbell surfaced. Reportedly, Campbell diverted to his person use a 1985 Mercedes-Benz sedan seized in a drug raid and turned over to his department for law enforcement purposes. In addition, Campbell allegedly granted special favors and police services to a wealthy friend who had sold Campbell some property. The firing had the full support of the Newport Beach City Council. This move met with approval at the *Los Angeles Times*, which described it as showing admirable decisiveness.[54]

Campbell made his first public statement on the situation a day after his firing. Denying all charges of harassment, he claimed he was the victim of a conspiracy and a "witch hunt" and that "the inmates are now running the asylum." In the face of the overwhelming no confidence vote in him by the department he insisted he could effectively run the department if he was reinstated. Campbell accused some of his immediate subordinates in the department, members of the city council, and the city manager of orchestrating his removal by utilizing sexual harassment complaints to fulfill the city manager's political agenda.[55]

In January 1993 city officials announced they would no longer pay the legal bills of Campbell and Villa in the court action. The next month four female employees (not party to the suit) of the police department who said they had been sexually harassed on the job accepted cash settlements ranging from $2,000 to $7,500, in exchange for a promise not to take legal action. Mayor Clarence Turner explained, "We investigated, and made a determination that we think they were harassed, and acted accordingly." The 10 women suing (one other had joined the first nine) reportedly rejected a proposed settlement around that time that would have given them between $300,000 and $500,000 in total. While that suit remained outstanding, a settlement was reached between the city and Campbell and Villa in June 1993. In return for a promise to drop their lawsuit, to waive their right to civil service hearings, and for a promise not to seek reinstatement to active duty on the Newport Beach police force the two men were reinstated on June 10 but immediately retired that same day. The settlement agreement with Campbell stated that the city had "no corroborated evidence that Campbell sexually harassed any female employee of the department" or that he condoned any misconduct on the part of any others in the department. No such statement was included in the settlement with Villa. Newport Beach agreed to pay all their legal bills. Under the agreements the city would not oppose disability retirements for Campbell, 54, and Villa, 48, who claimed injuries dating back as long as 15 years. Retirement packages would total around $50,000 a year tax free for Campbell and around $40,000 tax free annually for Villa. In addition, the city agreed to pay each man a lump sum of about $30,000 to settle workers' compensation claims. Beno Hernandez, a lawyer representing the 10 women, bitterly exclaimed, "They're rewarding the people who have allegedly raped and pillaged their employees. If you're going to be a victim of sexual harassment in Newport Beach, forget it.... They're going to protect their own and they don't care how they protect it."[56]

By 1983 women comprised 5.7 percent of total police strength in America; by 1989 they were 8.2 percent, 41,146 policewomen. Another source claimed the percentage of policewomen rose from 5 percent in 1978 to 10 percent in 1986. According to this source, over that same period the percentage of female sergeants went from 1.0 to 3.7 percent, lieutenants went from 0.7 percent to 2.5 percent, and for those in higher ranking command staff the figures moved from 0.5 percent to 1.4 percent.[57]

In 1988 in New Jersey females accounted for just 230 of the 18,315 municipal police officers. Of the close to 500 municipal police departments, 119 included policewomen, 81 of which had only one female each. One decade prior to that New Jersey employed 17,262 municipal police officers, of which 55 were women. Newark was the state's largest city, yet in 1988 it had 1,064 policemen but just 12 policewomen. New Jersey State Police numbered 1,779 male and two female officers in 1978; 10 years later the numbers were 2,603 and 62, respectively.[58]

When the Police Foundation conducted their study in 1987 surveying municipal police departments serving populations over 50,000, the proportion of female officers had grown from 4.2 percent in 1978 to 8.8 percent at the end of 1986 (5.3 percent white, 3.5 percent minority). On state police agencies, females were, at the end of 1986, just 3.7 percent of the officers, 3.1 percent white and 0.6 percent minority female. In supervisory ranks 3.0 percent of supervisors were female in municipal departments and 1.0 percent in the state police. Females had higher annual turnover rates than men in both municipal (6.3 percent versus 4.6 percent separations for 1986) and in the state police agencies (8.9 percent versus 2.9 percent). The report noted that "sexual harassment also appears to contribute to turnover for women." It also concluded, "Without changes in recruitment or application rates, the representation of women will not grow to exceed 20 percent." Writing much earlier, one author predicted in 1979 that "at the start of the twenty-first century women will only comprise 10 to 15 percent (at the utmost) of our national sworn police officer population.[59]

That Police Foundation study received replies to its questionnaire from 319 of 446 municipal agencies and 38 of 49 state police departments (Hawaii did not have a state police agency). Minority women made up 40 percent of policewomen, while minority males made up 21 percent of all municipal policemen. In cities with over one million in population 10.4 percent of the officers were female (5.7 percent white, 4.7 percent minority); in cities from 500,000 to one million women were 9.3 percent (4.5 percent white, 4.8 percent minority); in cities of 250,000 to 500,000 female officers were 9.1 percent (6.1 percent white, 3.0 percent minority); in cities of 100,000 to 250,000 women were 6.8 percent of the officers (5.3 percent white, 1.5 percent minority); and in cities of 50,000 to 100,000 female officers comprised 4.9 percent of the police (4.0 percent white, 0.9 percent minority). Despite the low percentage of policewomen and still lower number in supervisory ranks, when a number of policewomen were asked whether or not a glass ceiling was imposed on their gender in police command staff positions 47 percent said no, 31 percent said yes, with 22 percent not sure. When policemen were asked the same question 79 percent said no, 11 percent responded yes, while 10 percent were not sure.[60]

During September 1992 the Los Angeles City Council unanimously approved a package of initiatives which they said would require the police department to hire thousands of women and increase the proportion of females on the force to 44 percent by the year 2000. The LAPD was still operating under the provisions of a more than 10-year-old civil rights lawsuit which required the force to have at least 25 percent of each new class of rookies be female, until the force was 20 percent female. The city council initiative was to have each class contain 30 percent women, until the 44 percent goal was reached. The *Los Angeles Times* presented this news without comment or even noting the mathematical difficulties involved. The idea of adding more policewomen stemmed from the recommendations of the Christopher Commission report, which found, in addition to widespread sex discrimination and harassment, that women were better equipped to peacefully resolve potentially violent situations. Los Angeles, like many other American cities, was annually paying out tens of millions of dollars in settlements and court judgments for assaulting its citizens. No one in the Los Angeles area was able to recall even one case of a policewoman being involved in an excessive force case. In 1992 the Los Angeles force had about 13 percent female officers, roughly the same as New York, Chicago, and Miami. However, at the rank of sergeant and up only 3 percent of Los Angeles' finest were women.[61]

The Police Foundation reported the percentage of policewomen in the six largest cities in the early 1990s as follows: Detroit 20.8 percent, Philadelphia 16.5 percent, Chicago 16.5 percent, New York 15.5 percent, Los Angeles 14.0 percent, and Houston 10.2 percent. Nationally, American policewomen comprised about 10 percent of the total strength.[62]

A week or so later the *Los Angeles Times* published a total of three letters to the editor commenting on the city's plan; all were openly hostile, all were from males, and one was from an LAPD detective. Every old bogey was brought out in these letters, such as, "reverse discrimination," "hiring officers who are not qualified," "latest fad," and "men need not apply."[63]

The call to raise the ratio of policewomen to 44 percent of the LAPD total went nowhere, as hiring was at a near standstill in the cash-strapped city. Nevertheless, many Los Angeles policemen opposed the idea by mentioning the old clichés about physically and emotionally weak women having no place in patrol cars. Said one, "If we have gender parity, the criminals will have one big party. As a citizen I want guys around who can take care of business."

Sometimes it was dangerous business. A 1990 study of the New York Police Department found that women fired their guns less than half as often as male officers, which prompted study author Long Island University criminal justice associate professor Sean Grennan to declare, "Men draw their guns when they shouldn't. They play with their guns." In 1993 the LAPD had a total of 7,708 sworn personnel — 6,632 men, 1,076 women (14 percent). Women were absent entirely from the elite SWAT unit. In the rank of police officer (three grades) were 4,338 men and 913 women (17.5 percent). At the rank of sergeant (two grades) and detective (three grades) were 2,012 men and 155 women (7 percent). At the rank of lieutenant (two grades) and captain (three grades) were 259 men and eight women (3.0 percent). At the top were the chief, nine deputy chiefs in two grades, and 13 commanders. These 23 positions were all held by men. When the City of Los Angeles surveyed its employees it found that 48 percent of females in protective service departments had been sexually harassed at work in the past year. Of those harassed, only 30 percent had formally complained.[64]

The City of Chula Vista, California, agreed, in 1994, to pay police officer Ruth Schaefer $45,000 to settle her claim that she was sexually harassed and molested by supervisors on the job. She filed a claim in April 1993, through the State of California Department of Fair Employment and Housing, saying she had been harassed and discriminated against for two years. Her formal complaint to Chief Richard Emerson was met with retaliation and underserved disciplinary measures, her claim asserted. Assistant City Attorney Ruth Fritsch said the city settled quickly before an actual lawsuit was filed because we felt "Schaefer's claims, to the extent we were able to investigate them, were not without merit. She was quite likely to prove at least some of her claims." Schaefer joined the police department in 1982 as a dispatcher and became an officer in 1985. She was married to policeman Tom Schaefer. In her initial claim for damages, Schaefer alleged that her supervisor, Lieutenant Richard Strickland, made inappropriate remarks about her breasts, touched her breasts and made sexual references during conversations through the fall of 1991. Strickland also allegedly ordered her to make coffee and clean the station. When she complained to Captain Keith Hawkins, the harassment continued, she alleged, until she filed a formal complaint in April 1992. After that, she said, Hawkins retaliated by giving her undesirable work shifts and duties.[65]

As a Hollywood, Florida, police officer, Melody Fortunato said, her peers and bosses grabbed her buttocks, talked about her breasts, invited her for dips in a hot tub and made her the subject of sexual jokes. On December 14, 1994, a federal jury in Fort Lauderdale attached a price tag to the treatment: $150,000. The city also had to pay Fortunato's legal fees, which could double the cost. During the trial Fortunato alleged a history of sexual harassment during her 10 years on the force but lawyers for Hollywood police tried to portray her as a loose-talking cop who boasted of her own sexual affairs. They said she didn't leave the force in 1992 because of harassment but because she got her law degree. And if Fortunato was really upset, said the department, she did not let anyone know about it. As an officer in training, she said, she was forced to do push-ups in a dress and stand before the class giving the definition of a word involving a man's sexual organ. Later, as a full-time officer, she was on the receiving end of sexual jokes and physical advances. She was afraid to complain up the line of command, she said, because some of those laughing were her superiors. The jury's verdict ruled the City of Hollywood subjected her to a "hostile environment" of sexual harassment. The settlement was awarded for "pain, suffering and emotional distress." Her attorney, Timothy McDermott, said he offered to settle before the trial for $60,000: "If I were a city of Hollywood taxpayer, I would be irate with city fathers. Now it's going to end up costing them five times more." He was referring to the fact he would be billing the city another $150,000 for his fees and costs. McDermott concluded, "The evidence was overwhelming that between 1982 and 1992 there was an attitude of a sexually hostile atmosphere that pervaded the Hollywood Police Department."[66]

Nearly 80 percent of Dallas policewomen answering a survey in 1997 on sexual harassment said it occurred on their police force, and more than half said it has happened to them. The study, solicited by Police Chief Ben Click after a group of female officers requested it, also showed most female officers said they did not think the department took sexual harassment training seriously. Meanwhile, only 30 percent of those respondents said they felt free to report harassment without fear of reprisal. Click and other Dallas police officials disputed some of the findings, noting the study did not define sexual harassment. "On the specific issue of sexual harassment, I do not believe it is widespread in the organization," said Click. "And when any type of sexual impropriety comes to our attention we deal with it aggressively." In the previous two years, the department had fired nine employees for inappropriate sexual behavior directed toward citizens and fellow workers, police officials said. That study asked an array of questions regarding abuse that female officers might have been the target of while on duty. "Sexual teasing, jokes, remarks and questions" were the most commonly cited behavior, followed by "sexual looks, staring or gestures." None of the sworn officers, who responded, reported being the target of rape or assault. Criminal justice experts at Sam Houston State University conducted the study and included more than 200 questions administered to 1,000 female employees in February 1996. It drew responses from 419 police department employees, including 180 sworn officers. Over 140 of those officers said sexual harassment was occurring in the department and more than half said they had been sexually harassed. Under the police department's General Orders, sexual harassment was defined as "unwelcome sexual advances, requests for sexual favors, and other verbal or physical conduct of a sexual nature." As well, the police department designated two types of harassment, "quid pro quo" in which a supervisor pressured an employee for sex, and "hostile work environment" in which harassment was "so severe that it creates an intimidating, offensive workplace."[67]

In 1998 the town of Simsbury, Connecticut, agreed to pay more than $200,000 to settle a federal civil rights suit filed by the town's first female police officer, who claimed officers continually harassed her while she was on the job. Former Simsbury police officer Sharon Boudreau accused the police department in 1995 of a persistent campaign of harassment against her during her tenure with the department. She first filed complaints against the department in 1989 with the Connecticut Human Rights and Opportunities Commission. With respect to the settlement the U.S. District Court in Bridgeport, Connecticut, sealed the terms of the agreement prohibiting both sides from speaking about the terms of the deal but several sources knowledgeable about the deal placed the value of the settlement at between $200,000 and $300,000 plus other benefits. Town officials said the cost of the suit should be covered by its insurance policy. However, the National Casualty Company informed the town it would drop Simsbury's coverage at the end of the fiscal year because of a poor loss record on the part of the town. Boudreau, in her suit, alleged she was pulled off serious duty in favor of male officers, denied stipends for college courses, and that supervisors refused to provide emergency medical training to her — benefits offered to male officers. She first joined the Simsbury Police Department as a dispatcher in 1981 and became a police officer in 1984. Boudreau left the force in 1994.[68]

In an article published in 1999, journalist Alexandra Marks observed that across the United States, police departments found recruiting women to be difficult. Harassment suits launched by women police officers remained common. The former top person in charge of investigating sexual harassment charges in the NYPD had herself filed a harassment lawsuit. A police sergeant in Denver had gone to court claiming sexual harassment was so rampant in her department that she was not safe. Marks said that from New Jersey to California to Hawaii the number of sexual harassment complaints filed by women who worked in criminal justice "appears to be on the rise," although she cited no figures. The number of women officers— once seen as the key to improving solution oriented community policing techniques— had remained stagnant despite a major push in the 1980s to recruit more women and the addition of 100,000 new police officers nationwide since 1994, wrote Marks. At the time she was writing, about 13.8 percent of the nation's law enforcement officers were women, up only 3.0 percent since 1990. Said Penny Harrington, director of the National Center for Women and Policing in Oregon, "There is absolute resistance to hiring more women. People are terrified that if women have an equal voice things will have to change." Harrington, a former cop, said it was unusual that so many women officers were filing suit. For years, most women officers just tolerated what were sometimes difficult working environments. Studies had found that 80 percent of women officers said they had been subjected to some sort of sexual harassment during their careers, but only 5 percent had filed complaints. "Filing suit is a last resort because you know that it will either end your career or make your life intolerable," said Jamila Bayati, a former Los Angeles sheriff's deputy who left after filing a complaint in 1995. Experts said filing a sexual harassment complaint was the equivalent of breaking the so-called blue wall of silence. And like other officers who've cooperated in internal police investigations, women who have filed complaints often become ostracized. Many claim they've received anonymous death threats, been set up on false drug charges, or been reported anonymously to social service agencies for allegedly abusing their children. "It gets to the point where people won't cover you or emergency calls so your life is in danger," said Harrington. Said attorney Joel Berger, who dealt with harassment cases, "I don't want to stereotype but many of these men are poorly educated, very sexually immature, and have a hard time dealing with women as equals and colleagues." Experts also said the recruiting and training process was set up in a way that discouraged women. The focus was on military bases for recruits, tough strength standards, and boot-camp-style academy training.[69]

Researcher May Texeira published an article in 2002 that explored one group of women's experiences in a United States sheriff's department. Interview data was gathered from 65 African American women who were active and former law enforcement officials. Black females then made up less than 3 percent of all sworn police officers nationwide. A City of Los Angeles personnel survey found that policewomen generally experienced sexual harassment at higher rates than other female city workers. That survey found that 48 percent of women in the protective services (police and firefighters) reported at least one type of harassment in the year before the survey. The occupational category with the second highest number of reported sexual harassment incidents was the skilled crafts—another area traditionally dominated by men. In addition women police officers indicated more extreme cases of harassment than women in other city departments. Nonetheless, of all city employees, women police officers filed the smallest proportion of formal complaints. That Los Angeles survey found no difference in the reported rate of harassment among women of different ethnic groups. A second study mentioned by Texeira was done specifically of women police officers. It found that 68 percent had been sexually harassed (1988) with the majority of victims being younger officers. The masculine bond, wrote Texeira, was a much more unifying factor than the "brotherhood of policing." Texeira's survey featured data from 50 active duty and 15 retired African American women. At that unidentified sheriff's department the force comprised 64.5 percent white males, 6.3 percent black males, 7.5 percent white women, and 2.5 percent black females. The white people on the force were of European ancestry so the remainder, not identified in the study, were, presumably, others such as Hispanics. Texeira's group had an age range of 22 to 70 years with a mean age of 35 and had joined the force anywhere from 1954 to 2002. Before they joined the force some 87 percent of the women had low-paying clerical jobs. When asked why they sought employment in policing most of the women

(86 percent) answered that it was because of financial reasons. Although they occupied nontraditional jobs, most of the officers considered themselves politically conservative, declaring that they were not feminists. In questioning her respondents Texeira used the legal definition of sexual harassment that described unwanted or unwelcome sexually explicit words, touch or intimidation based on a perceived power difference and on which one's employment depended. A majority of the women in this study (59 percent) could recall no occurrence of sexual harassment. The 27 women who perceived they had been sexually harassed reported 114 separate incidents—situations that were described as humiliating, demoralizing, and physically harmful. Six of the women (almost 10 percent) reported experiencing an actual or attempted rape or sexual assault. With respect to the race of the harasser, the study revealed that black men were named 41 percent of the time and European white men 59 percent of the time.[70]

Early in 2003 the City of Seattle, Washington, agreed to pay a former Seattle policewoman $225,000 to settle a federal lawsuit alleging that her supervisor and two fellow officers sexually harassed her and that department leaders tried to force her out of the ranks for reporting it. The agreement meant that neither the city nor the officers involved admitted any wrongdoing, which, of course, was standard for such agreements. Heather Hottle was the woman involved. The officers accused of harassment had been recommended for discipline but the Seattle Police Department declined to release details. The city never denied that Hottle was harassed, but it denied department leaders tried to cover the situation up. Hottle, 34, sued the department a year earlier, alleging that Sergeant Eddie Rivera, who was serving as Hottle's commander in the South Precinct, harassed her in 2000 after she spurned his advances. She alleged that officers Michael Goetz and Miguel Torres were enlisted to contribute to the harassment, which, she said, included breaking into her home. Hottle also alleged that when she reported the harassment the departments' former human resources director, Janice Corbin, and a sergeant then in charge of equal-employment opportunities, Terri MacMillan, belittled her allegations and then focused on Hottle's fitness for duty.[71]

A Seattle man, Joseph Wilson, who said he was beaten by three Seattle police officers after he jaywalked near his home in the summer of 2009, filed a lawsuit in 2010 against the Seattle Police Department and the City of Seattle. One of the three officers named by Wilson was Sergeant Eddie Rivera. After the incident and before the lawsuit was filed, all three were exonerated by an internal police department investigation.[72]

A jury awarded $3.5 million on June 2, 2003, to three female Glendale, California, police officers who said they were groped, propositioned and exposed to pornography by coworkers and supervisors who later retaliated against them. The jury of eight men and four women found that members of the department created a hostile and discriminatory work environment while failing to prevent harassment. They awarded Kathryn Frieders $850,000, Jaime Franke $1,361,250, and Renae Kerner $1,305,176 for lost wages and benefits. Lawyer Brad Gage (for the women) called on the department to take additional steps to discipline the officers named in the suit, including William Hallorsen, Darrell York, and Art Crabtree. Instead, he said, some of the officers had been promoted, given specialized assignments, or allowed to retire with full benefits. Irma Rodriguez Moisa, attorney for the City of Glendale, said the police department took the allegations seriously, even though some of the alleged misconduct occurred as far back as 13 years ago: "The department could have said that this stuff is so old it shouldn't even be looked at. It didn't even do that." Gage said that officers in the department constructed pornographic web sites, grabbed breasts, made lewd comments and implied that if the female officers did not date them they would lose their jobs, while at the same time denying them activities that would have enhanced their chances for promotion. Moisa said the Glendale Police Department disciplined York after determining that he had used his office computer to look at Internet porn for 17 minutes. "It is inappropriate for the workplace. Absolutely. The department would agree," said Moisa. In reaching its decision the jury found the City of Glendale had been negligent in preventing the harassment and discrimination that the three officers had been subjected to from the late 1980s through to the mid–1990s.[73]

Sue Collins undertook a study and analysis, published in 2004, of the disciplinary measures taken by the Florida Criminal Justice Standards and Training Commission against law enforcement officers found guilty of sexual harassment. While sexual harassment cases were widely known about through media attention to such incidents, said Collins, it was much less clear what happened to the harassers. The agency named above was the regulatory charged with licensing and disciplining law enforcement officers in the state of Florida. In Florida, of the 39,655 sworn officers employed by state and local agencies in 2000, approximately 37,508 were employed full-time and 12.4 percent were policewomen, compared to a nationwide figure of about 13 percent in 2000. A statewide Florida study of sexual harassment of policewomen was conducted in 1993 when all 3,790 active duty female officers were sent a questionnaire. About 33 percent of the sampled population (1,269) returned completed surveys. The results revealed that 61 percent of the respondents (775) indicated they had been sexually harassed in the workplace within the previous 12 months. More than 40 percent stated they had been exposed to sexually-oriented materials or the telling of sexually-oriented jokes on a daily basis, and 20 percent believed they worked in an overtly hostile environment. In her survey of disciplinary actions Collins looked at the commission's decisions taken during a five-year period that ran from January 1, 1993, until December 31, 1997. Between 1993 and 1997 the commission received a total of 89 cases involving male police officers charged by their employing agencies with sustained complaints of sexual harassment. Only 33 cases met the criteria for inclusion in the study conducted by Collins. To be included that harasser had to be a male police officer who had been administratively charged with sexual harassment; at least one of the harasser's victims had to be an active duty female police officer; the case was investigated by the employing police agency and resulted in a sustained complaint against the harasser; the case was submitted to the commission for corrective of disciplinary action; and the commission reviewed the case and entered a final administrative action closing the case between January 1, 1993, and December 31, 1997.[74]

In 1997 there were 37,508 full-time police officers in the state of Florida with 88 percent of them being male. Within the male total 70 percent were white, 8 percent black, 9 percent Hispanics, with Asians and other racial minorities making up the remainder. Of the cases studied by Collins, 70 percent (23) of the policemen involved were white, 21 percent (seven) were black, 9 percent (3) were Hispanics. Of the victims, 85 percent were white (28) while fewer than 10 percent were black (2) and Hispanic (1). The remaining two cases had insufficient data to classify with regard to race. Despite the fact that all the cases submitted to the commission had been "sustained" complaints at the level of the individual and referring police agency, the discipline entered by the commission in 39 percent (13) of the cases was that of "no cause." The difference was explained by Collins as lying in the fact that the employing police agency needed only "probable" cause to sustain a complaint while the commission imposed the higher standard of "clear and convincing" cause before taking action. The commission imposed administered corrective discipline in 24 percent (eight) of the cases and imposed punitive discipline in 36 percent (12) of the cases. Corrective discipline involved sending the guilty policeman a letter of guidance, sending him to an intervention program, or sending him a letter "of acknowledgment of significant agency action." Punitive discipline involved things such as reprimands, remedial training, probation, suspension, and revocation of an officer's certification (equivalent to firing). In the cases reviewed by Collins remedial training, probation, and suspension were the punitive methods most used. One of the things about this study that surprised Collins was the low number of cases, 89, received by the commission over the course of five full years, compared to the earlier cited study of 61 percent of those policewomen who reported harassment in response to a survey. Although Collins was, presumably, very upset by her results she was the model of diplomacy and tact when it came to her recommendations. "The Florida Criminal Justice Standards and Training Commission's current policy position on sexual harassment are out of sync with women's realities and deny the nature of sexual harassment experienced by many female officers working in law enforcement," she wrote. "Currently, the Commission limits the sexual harassment cases that it exercises jurisdiction in to those involving actual physical touching or misuse of official position," she added. "Specifically excluded from the Commission's jurisdictional net are all cases involving gender harassment, unwanted sexual attention, or sexual coercion, unless the officer misuses his official position, or commits an act involving actual physical touching." With respect to the commission's discipline, Collins recommended it should revise its policy on the nature and severity of discipline administered in sexual harassment cases: "The inadequacy and arbitrariness of the Commission's position becomes quite apparent when the penalties for sexual harassment are juxtaposed to those meted out for consensual sex on duty and solicitation of prostitution." For the latter two offenses the discipline imposed was usually much harsher and often involved revocation of certification (firing).[75]

A study published in 2007 looked at sex discrimination lawsuits in law enforcement. A case study of 13 women who sued their law enforcement agencies for sexual harassment or another form of sex discrimination revealed that when the women reported the behaviors they experienced myriad forms of retaliation. When women in law enforcement were asked how often they experienced sexual harassment or other sex discrimination their responses varied depending on the way the question was asked. For example, in one study 24 percent of female officers indicated they had experienced a "constant atmosphere" of offensive remarks. In another study, 100 percent of the women interviewed described experiencing at least one sexually harassing behavior within the workplace. However, most of the existing research, according to this account, converged on a range of approximately 53 percent to 77 percent of American women in law enforcement having been subjected to some form of sexually harassing behavior from their male co-workers. Yet very few of the targeted victims considered themselves victims of sexual harassment or reported the incident with a formal complaint. Research revealed that only 5 percent to 25 percent of women filed a formal complaint after experiencing sexual harassment. That was true even for women who were sexually assaulted by a co-worker. In one study of women who experienced an attempted or completed sexual assault in the workplace, only 21 percent of these women filed a formal report and 19 percent quit.[76]

11

Foreign, 1970–2012

Great Britain announced in late 1972 that it was abolishing the separate women's police division within the Metropolitan Police force. Policewomen would be integrated into the force, which meant that female officers would be competing with males for jobs and promotions. The force then had about 600 women. As to their duties, a force spokesman said, "Apart from certain jobs which are considered dangerous, they will do the same duties as men." Until that change women had been paid 95 percent of a male officer's salary. They had rank structure with only a certain number of posts set aside for them. Thus, while the genders took the same promotional examinations, females had to wait for openings to occur in their own limited promotional structure. All this ended in 1973.[1]

Equality was still a long way off. Less than a year before that announcement 12 policewomen had to cancel a Christmas outing to Danny La Rue's nightclub in London due to a club rule that unescorted women were not allowed entry.[2]

In 1979 policewoman Lorraine Edser of Felixstowe, Suffolk, won a national contest to find Britain's prettiest policewoman. Her name was entered by her chief inspector. Edser's prize consisted of two portraits of herself and a year's supply of tights.[3]

Only in 1977 were policewomen in the South Yorkshire police force issued with trousers. This came after agitation by the women, who were the targets of wolf whistles when they climbed over walls and out of cars in their skirts.[4]

A major change in Great Britain came with the passage of the Sex Discrimination Act, which came into effect at the end of December 1975. It integrated men and women at work, putting an end to any separate women's divisions that still existed. At the start of 1976 the Greater Manchester force had 408 policewomen, 5,497 policemen. By November 1977 there were 658 women versus 5,652 men. Over half the probationers in the force (under two years of service) were women, compared to one-third at the beginning of

1976. The proportion of foot patrol officers who were female ranged up to 21 percent in one Greater Manchester division. However, the policewomen still wore skirts in Manchester in late 1977.[5]

The overall representation of women in policing in the United Kingdom increased from 5.4 percent in 1975 to 10.5 percent in 1988. Paralleling that increase, fueled in part by the Sex Discrimination Act, was a decrease in the proportion of women holding ranks other than that of constable. In 1971 the percentage of policewomen sergeants was 11.2, a figure that decreased steadily to 5.8 percent in 1988. Newer recruits had not been on the force long enough to be promoted, but numbers indicated perhaps discrimination was at work keeping the number of higher ranks down — almost as if an unofficial numeric quota was in effect.[6]

The Sex Discrimination Act, in the case of policing, placed women on the same 24-hour-a-day operational basis as men, and therefore raised a lot of hostility among the male police establishment, which portrayed females as weak and inept, in the face of the threat of an increased female presence. In 1977 fully 25 percent of those entering police service in the United Kingdom were female. Philip Knight, chief constable of the West Midlands, in his annual report noted this increase in female police and worried, because, "Firstly, we shall see an increasing number of women in the uniformed patrol force who cannot be expected in a general way to handle public order matters without at least some support from their male colleagues. Secondly, as women are now patrolling much more, we are likely to see more assaults on them."[7]

Chief Superintendent Peter Hawkins of the Avon and Somerset Constabulary and president of the Police Superintendents' Association of England and Wales delivered a speech to that group's annual conference in 1977. Noting the increasing proportion of female police, he warned, "there was a greater need for more men because of public disorders." Hawkins continued, "It might be necessary to reconsider the application of the Sex Discrimination Act to the service. The replacement of trained officers by young women just to maintain numbers was ideological idiocy." That challenge to the government to think about exempting police service from the Sex Discrimination Act did not pass unnoticed. Speaking for the Home Office, Deputy Undersecretary Robert Andrew said any prospect of a change in the act was unlikely without clear evidence that the performance of policing was permanently prejudiced by its implementation. "I don't think that evidence yet exists," said Andrew.[8]

When Kenneth Steele, chief constable of Avon and Somerset, addressed a Bristol meeting in 1978, he said that policewomen on night patrol in rough areas had needed policemen with them for protection. He blamed the Sex Discrimination Act for this state of affairs. To solve the problem Steele proposed setting up new specialist units for policewomen that would operate 24 hours a day and "handle much of the work of the former women's police department to do mainly with women and children."[9]

Opposition to policewomen from policemen continued through 1978 as more male officers complained to the Home Office in an effort to convince the government to exempt police from the Sex Discrimination Act. According to the policemen, an increase in public disorders required more men in policing rather than women. Part of the opposition sprang from the suspicion that females were being recruited to build up the force without having to raise police pay. While older, retiring males were more highly paid than rookie females, this argument was nonsensical in the entry level ranks since rookie males and females drew equal pay. P. A. Myers, chief constable of North Wales and president of the Association of Chief Police Officers, said, "The natural chivalry of men does not allow rank and file policewomen to go out alone. They go out with men. And the net effect of the Act has been to turn the clock back. Thirty years ago the main complaint of policewomen was that they were answering the telephone and making tea, and they are having to do it again because of the Sex Discrimination Act."[10]

Detective Sergeant Frederick Conner, chairman of the Scottish Police Federation, complained at that group's conference that poor pay and conditions made it harder and harder to recruit men. However, he added that the recruitment of a higher proportion of women was not solution, "as they were incapable of handling the violence that officers on the beat had to face." Conner continued, "I am not saying there is no place for women in the police service ... but they have their limitations. God made us differently and an Act of Parliament cannot change that."[11]

The Times (London) editorialized in the wake of Conner's remarks. Mentioning the fear that women recruited en masse might depress wage levels, the editor said, "Nevertheless, it is reasonable to suppose that too high a proportion of women in a force must affect its ability to respond to the varied and challenging demands of modern peacekeeping and throw an excessive burden on the men." Examples given for this included dispatchers and supervisors reluctant to send a female on a violent call, routing more of these incidents to less and less men. Even if that were true, the blame should be attached to the dispatchers and supervisors who were not performing their duties correctly, not the policewomen. *The Times* editor then wavered a little, concerning the present ratio of females in policing: "That is not to say that the proportion is already too high." But the conclusion was that "warnings such as Sergeant Conner's should be carefully regarded."[12]

Ten years after the Sex Discrimination Act was enacted, a survey of a typical but unidentified "Midshire" constabulary confirmed that policewomen remained a small minority and were not given full opportunity. It documented the failure of that act as far as the police were concerned. While formal policies spoke of equality, informal practices precluded equality. Comparing policemen who joined the service after the Sex Discrimination Act was in place with men who joined prior to that time, the survey said, "Modern male police hold the same chauvinistic views as their 'Traditional,' and older male colleagues, and often hold these attitudes to a greater degree ... there is every prospect of current discriminatory decisions on deployment and promotion being perpetuated by this young group as it moves up and through the ranks." Recruiting literature stressed the equal opportunity aspects, but recruited females were frustrated to find it was not true. This may have been a cause of higher turnover among women, a fact twisted around by the police establishment so they could declare that due to the turnover the police force "continues to see this unacceptable wastage in terms of lack of motivation and commitment on the part of women," so "informal discriminatory practices ... become formalized on economic grounds." According to this survey, policewomen were still disproportionately deployed on desk, station, or office duties.[13]

An article on policewomen in 1989 by Robert Chesshyre stated, "It took until 1985 for women to be admitted to the police on equal terms with men, and even then all sorts of silly games were played with heights and quotas to restrict their numbers." The passage of the Equal Opportunities Act in 1985 furthered strengthened theoretical equality in the United Kingdom. It was a year after that before policewomen were issued with truncheons, hitherto always carried by males. Females received a shortened version to fit their handbags. Chesshyre found old-fashioned chivalry still prevailed, with male recruits getting upset if instructors drove the females too hard. In addition, "sergeants and inspectors tend to assign women to tasks like answering the radio or patrolling school crossings." It meant policewomen were less likely to get front-line experience, without which advancement was very difficult. West Midlands policemen still claimed that when things got tough women could be "the weak link in the chain." He added, "The prejudice faced by policewomen is not confined to male colleagues. The public instinctively feels that a policeman must be more effective than a female counterpart." Chesshyre cited no support for that final statement. Perhaps it represented a patronizing and condescending attitude toward them. He opened his article with an item about a policewoman calling for assistance in the field after she had been knocked down and slightly roughed up, describing her "whisper of pain" and that her "cry was desperate."[14]

Occasionally women lashed out at the unfairness of the system. Superintendent Rachael James retired in 1986 after 30 years of police service. She was the only female superintendent in Devon and Cornwall. During a 13-year period she was rejected for the rank of chief inspector by an all-male promotion board 12 times. When she retired she attacked the attitudes of the male-dominated police hierarchy by saying, "Women have to be 20 times as good at their job as men to get on. So much expertise is going to waste simply because women are not being allowed to develop their potential in jobs.... We are women in a man's world and we are discriminated against to the detriment of the police force in general."[15]

Near the end of the 1980s policewomen (WPCs) made up close to 11 percent of the police service yet only about 1 to 2 percent of the senior officers were women. Discrimination and sexual harassment were major problems. A Midlands policewoman related that for years the police establishment said, "We won't issue women with truncheons because there's a danger that they could be taken off them and used against them. Now somebody's decided: We'll give them a little one—so it will only hurt them a little bit if it's used against them." Said another Midlands female officer, "They're very discriminative against women" with remarks like, "She wouldn't know, she's only a woman." Yet another officer remarked that if a baby is brought to the station with a drunken woman the policemen "all start wailing for a WPC to come and look after it." This policewoman protested she knew nothing about kids, but the policemen said, "Women's instinct. You know all about this." When she tried to get them to take the baby (they had children but she did not) they replied, "No, you're the WPC, you have the baby." A male superintendent on the Metropolitan London force commented, "A woman's probation, although it is only supposed to be two years, is about three or four. It takes them three or four years to gain the competence of a man after two years' service. They are used to having things done for them. It takes them ages to become assertive in the way a man is." A policewoman from Central London related how her senior officer was replaced by a man she described as a "frightful little creep" who made a pass at her. She laughed at him, but then "he made life extremely difficult. He blocked any applications I made to do anything more interesting." From a large northern force a female sergeant told of experiencing severe problems because on more than a couple of occasions "I wouldn't sleep with senior officers. If you say no, they take it as a personal insult; and no matter what they say, they really do take it out on you." As a young constable she was "totally ostracized by my superior. Everything I did was wrong. He put me through it so badly I was about to pack it in. Another one gave me a bad report on my Sergeant's course because I failed to give him the goods." Another London female officer said, "I'm amused when I hear of some outraged West Indian Beryl Somebody-or-other alleging sexual harassment in her job because Mr. So-and-so pinched her bottom and brushed against her breasts in the canteen. Jesus, if she tried being at any police station. It's just a way of life and you have to take it in good part." A female constable from the Home Counties received sexual propositions from constables up to the chief inspector. She thought harassment had worsened since when she first joined one might be sexually harassed by a constable but never by a chief inspector. She had a chief inspector (married, with children) turn up at her door one night, in uniform, with a bottle of wine. She made an excuse. The same thing happened two nights later. That time she told him to go and not return, in no uncertain terms. "And he then made my life hell, for two months. Just being bloody awkward, being rude to me, not letting me do things I should have been allowed to do." After two months she verbally confronted him, which put an end to the harassment. Sexual harassers were known as canteen cowboys. Being "one of the boys" meant sleeping around. A policewoman who said no to propositions was a "lesbo" while one who said yes was a "relief bicycle." According to one woman inspector on the Metropolitan force, if rumors spread it might affect promotions. A senior officer might say, "She's a bit free and easy. We don't want her."[16]

Chief Inspector Jennifer Hilton noted the many difficulties women faced in trying to advance in policing when she spoke of the old boys' network, wherein members of the male police establishment socialized together and drank together in the same bars, forming a club that was hard to crack. Drive and ambition were neither expected nor accepted from females. "Male camaraderie will always be a subtle bar to the advancement of women when men, as in policing, are the selectors and promoters," said Hilton.[17]

In Britain male officers were designated PC (Police Constable), while female officers were WPC. After a recommendation from equal opportunity experts the Metropolitan London Police force dropped the "W" from WPC in July 1990. A large number of persistent complaints from policewomen led the force to quickly reverse its decision. Supporters of WPC said the letter's absence caused confusion among the public and on the force.[18]

WPC Joy Court won financial compensation for sex discrimination from the Derbyshire police in 1992, and an apology from her chief constable, after proving her attempts to become a detective were blocked by a quota system operated within the force's criminal investigation department. Court had tried for five years to win a transfer to the CID and although she became a detective in 1991, she continued her action. An unofficial quota system operated within the CID to restrict the number of women detectives to no more than two at any subdivision. In 1991 the Derbyshire force was composed of about 1,770 officers, of whom 177 were female. There were 212 male detectives versus 33 females. Of the 28,000 officers on the Metropolitan London force, 3,734 were female, while in the London CID there were 3,817 male and 277 female officers.[19]

Discrimination remained pervasive in 1992. Baden Skitt, chief constable of Hertfordshire and chairman of a national police committee on equal opportunities, told of a policewoman who wanted to join a motorcycle course but was told she would first have to lift a heavily loaded 1,000cc machine left lying on its side, a test no man had to perform. Skitt said it was not an isolated example. He asked a female officer to question her colleagues about discrimination; all 14 queried said they had been discriminated against and 13 also reported being victims of sexual harassment. A policewoman who wanted to be a detective was questioned by her sergeant about her religion. When she said she was Roman Catholic he told her he would recommend her only if she could prove she was taking the pill. In 1991 there were 15,061 policewomen in the United Kingdom, a little over 11 percent of the total police strength.[20]

Alison Halford became assistant chief constable in Merseyside in 1983, the first female in Great Britain to hold such a position. She was then the country's highest ranking female officer. Over the coming years she made nine unsuccessful attempts to win promotion to rank of chief constable. The three male candidates she defeated for the Merseyside post had all since achieved promotion beyond assistant chief constable. While Chief Constable Kenneth Oxford was kind and supportive for the first few months, Halford said he quickly became "abrasive, aggressive, dogmatic, demanding and, I suppose, outright rude to all my colleagues." In 1990 Halford initiated a sex discrimination suit against Merseyside and the home secretary. Later that year, after the suit was filed, Halford was suspended on full pay, pending disciplinary hearings. The charges had to do with Halford being accused of being inebriated and swimming in her underwear with another police officer in a private pool at the home of a businessman. Her case was heard before an industrial tribunal where she was supported by the Equal Opportunities Commission. Beverly Lane, a witness for that body, testified that files relating to Halford's work as assistant chief constable were "significantly altered and unavailable." Allan McGwire, a Merseyside constable, testified that senior officers forced him to lie about alleged drunken frolics to blacken Halford's name. In July 1992 a settlement was announced before the hearing was complete; in fact, only Halford's side had been heard. Under its terms all disciplinary charges were dropped and Halford, then aged 52, was to retire at the end of August of that year on health grounds. Her pension was to be 35,000 pounds Sterling per year, enhanced by an undisclosed amount because of her ill health — stress and an arthritic knee — plus she was to receive a lump-sum payment of 142,000 pounds Sterling. By then she had been suspended on full pay for 19 months. She was to remain in that status until her retirement officially started. Cost of the 39-day hearing had reached one million pounds Sterling. In a statement read by her lawyer, Halford said, "The way has now been eased to allow other women of courage and commitment to follow me up the greasy pole of promotion. Although I have not achieved my goal in becoming chief constable, a rank I know I could have worthily held, I believe that no woman will ever suffer as much as I have through discrimination in the police." James Sharples, chief constable of Merseyside, said her claims of victory were "farcical."[21]

Policewomen in Norway worked in uniforms only from the mid–1960s onward. With a total national police force of 5,500 at the end of the 1970s, there were slightly over 100 females who were mainly employed in Oslo where they did traditional female police duties. They were not utilized for police tasks where "their sex sets natural limitations when it is necessary to use force." Also utilizing a single, centralized national police force was the country of Israel, where out of a total force of 15,500 at the end of the 1970s women numbered 2,200 (14 percent). Females had been a part of that force from the beginning. However, 90 percent of the traffic police were women. Senior public officials believed females could not be used on night shifts or for large male public demonstrations, that they had less physical strength and stamina than men, and that family problems, pregnancy, and child care interfered more with policing by women than men. So Israeli policewomen played a limited and secondary role.[22]

Canada's national police force, the Royal Canadian Mounted Police (RCMP), did not hire its first policewoman until 1974, when 32 women were hired and sent to the Regina, Saskatchewan, Academy for training. They were assigned to duty in April 1975. Several years later there were 300 females (2.3 percent) out of a total strength of 13,200. The major provincial police forces, the Ontario Provincial Police and the Quebec Provincial Police, began employing policewomen in 1974 and 1975, respectively. Canadian city forces had employed females for a much longer period of time, but they still comprised only a token percentage of the forces. The Metropolitan Toronto Police had started employing policewomen in 1913. While they were used for more than just matron duties they were not armed, not issued uniforms, received less pay than men, and were not considered full-fledged police officers. In 1945 they were issued uniforms and granted equal pay but were used exclusively in traditional female policing duties. That changed in 1974 when policewomen were armed and assigned to regular police duties. By 1979 policewomen numbered 100 (2 percent) of the force's 5,400 members. At the same time policewomen comprised 2.5 percent and 3.0 percent, respectively, on the Winnipeg and Calgary city forces. Winnipeg's first policewoman was hired in January 1917. Calgary hired its first policewoman in 1943.[23]

The National Police Force of New Zealand was a single, centralized agency which started to employ females in 1941, mainly in clerical roles, but they also sometimes assisted males in dealing with women and children. These women began to wear uniforms and carry firearms in 1952. A separate Women's Division where policewomen worked mainly with women and children was disbanded in 1966. When they were granted equal pay with policemen around that time, the commissioner of police directed they should perform the same duties. However, a study conducted in 1973 concluded the policewomen did not have equal job assignments or equality of status with policemen, resulting in de facto segregation of the force. As a result, greater efforts were made to see that females were given exactly the same work as men in all areas of police work, except they would not be assigned to field duties on their own between the hours of 11 P.M. and 7 A.M. By the end of the 1970s about 2.5 percent of the 3,300-member force was female.[24]

A survey of citizen attitudes toward police officers was done in Wellington, New Zealand, in 1984. Male and female respondents did not differ in their overall view of law enforcement officers. Policemen were rated as strong and suspicious while policewomen were described as fair, kind, protective, and patient. This study concluded that "female police officers were viewed as more competent than male police officers in areas such as youth aid, domestic problems, rape-victim counseling and other social services police work."[25]

Since the 1920s Denmark has had laws providing equal opportunities for both genders in the public service. However, as policing was considered to be so physically strenuous, the police force was exempted from the rules, in the modern era. Until 1977 the Danish Police Service consisted exclusively of male officers. Pressure to admit women arose in the late 1960s and early 1970s as debate on women's rights heated up. In 1973 the Danish national commissioner of police set up a group to examine the issue. When this group advised hiring policewomen, 18 female recruits were appointed as a test in 1977. On the basis of that successful test the final decision was made to open up policing to women. Major fears expressed in Denmark when policewomen were first admitted were that they would jeopardize the safety of their male colleagues and that females would be assaulted more frequently in the performance of their duties. Neither outcome occurred. Major incidents of disorder and confrontation between the public and the police were frequent in the metropolitan Copenhagen area. Policewomen participated in violent incidents on an equal basis with policemen, and this led to a study conclusion that females were not the "weak link in the chain." The Danish national commissioner of police conducted a study of officers who had committed criminal offenses or offenses of misconduct: "The findings show that women are proportionately under represented in this respect. Generally, our study showed that the majority of our 'problem children' are men." By 1990 the Danish police contained about 600 women (5.8 percent) out of the total 10,300-member force. Most of those women served in the Copenhagen area. Until then no policewoman had been admitted into the Danish SWAT teams. Physical requirements for entrance were identical for the genders, with the few women interested being reportedly unable to meet those physical requirements.[26]

Around the mid–1970s India had about 1,711 policewomen. Almost all Indian states employed female police, with the state of Maharashtra topping the list with 409 females. Nonetheless, these women played only a peripheral role, limited to working only with women and children. The police establishment in all states agreed that "policewomen cannot effectively play the police role which is still considered a 'man's job,' and in case women have to be recruited, their duties should be limited to dealing with only those cases where women and juveniles are involved." Conditions of service and pay were equal for both genders.

Despite the low number of females recruited in India, applicants remained hard to find, with the result that standards of recruitment had to be lowered. This resistance by females to joining the police service was attributed to the masculine attributes of the job, exposure of police to antisocial elements, and interference with familial role objections; citizens looked down upon women employed as police, and a police role exposed females "to relatively greater contact with men at odd hours." Most policewomen were recruited from the lower classes. In the state of Punjab in 1977 there were 148, one to every 175 policemen; in Haryana that year there were 28 female officers, one to every 400 male officers.[27]

At the training academy females were allowed, through a statutory provision, to be excused from doing physical exercises for three days each month — menstruation. Male instructors were often partial to certain of the trainees. Amarjit Mahajan, the male author of a study done on the Indian police system, encountered only two of 110 policewomen who made a formal harassment accusation. However, a female research associate of the author, in informal talks with the women, found that many more agreed with the allegations. When the associate reminded the policewomen that this was not what they had said in their formal interviews, their usual answer was, "How can we tell these things to him?" In his study Mahajan said of female officers, "It seems as if they have been recruited to ward off public criticism of male police when they have to deal with women population. They are mainly put on duty to provide protection to women criminals against male police while checking cases of sex violation." Generally, policewomen were posted at a district headquarters and sent out when needed, usually after a woman was picked up. When they were sent for, no less than two were dispatched and they were also accompanied by male police officers. In practice the female suspects had already been searched by male police by the time the policewomen arrived. When the female police did interrogate women detainees they did so under the guidance of and in the presence of male officers. Males rationalized this by saying they doubted the ability of policewomen and felt female detainees were not afraid of policewomen who, reportedly, accepted this arrangement without objections. Escorting of female detainees from cells to courts was a duty of policewomen, a minimum of two; however, two male officers were also assigned. During public demonstrations a few policewomen were always on hand, but all the duties were performed by males. A poll of male Punjab officers found they contended that policewomen could not perform their job as efficiently as males could. Almost half the men believed policewomen were of "easy morals." Policewomen were aware of this reputation, but argued that "generally when policewomen are recruited they are not bad, but are made bad.... They sometimes fall prey to the sexual lust of the male officers. To be young and beautiful is a curse of girls and women in the police organization." Mahajan concluded, "The male officers' negative attitudes towards policewomen's moral character, their inability to perform police jobs, and their refusal to treat policewomen at part with their male counterparts have been the most significant factors that have hindered the emergence of clearcut role definition of the policewomen and the advancement of the policewomen force." He added, "The women's new role in police remains unattractive to the women population. It has yet to gain recognition and acceptance from the policemen and society at large. It can, however, be made more attractive if the nature of work is made to resemble that of a social worker."[28]

In 1991 author Shamin Aleem concluded, about Indian policewomen, that they are "generally not taken very seriously by those at the helm of affairs. For this the police department, which has not been able to capitalize on the potential of women police, is to blame." A need for policewomen was perceived, since many female citizens believed there was a danger to their personal safety when they approached a police station, as there were many cases reported in the media where the "modesty of women was violated by policemen." There were then about three women police stations in the entire country staffed exclusively by women and dealing exclusively with cases pertaining to women. In 1987 India had a total of 875,000 police officers, of whom 7,706 (less than one 1 percent) were women. Aleem said, "There is no doubt that the police service, due to the stigma attached to it, is generally not the first preference of women. In other words, it is difficult to obtain suitable personnel for the police service."[29]

Typical was the state of Andhra Pradesh, which had 500 policewomen, less than 1 percent of that force's total strength. Most of those were concentrated in the city of Hyderabad, where their duties included searching females, guarding and escorting detainees, regulating crowds of females, traffic duties, and the interrogation of female detainees. The Ramachandra Reddy Commission in that state noted, "Women police are very useful in performing functions like interrogation of women criminals, examination of women victims and witnesses, rescuing and rehabilitating exploited women from brothels. Though women police are not in a position to handle all these problems independently, they are very useful in performing these functions with some support from men police." Aleem concluded, "In the case of women suspects/criminals, women police are used mainly to protect the honour of women and to save them from molestation."[30]

When the republic of Singapore police faced a manpower shortage around 1986, the idea of solving this problem by hiring more women police was discussed. It was felt that they would come in handy in cases involving women. In addition, with the emphasis on crime prevention and community-oriented policing, there were more opportunities for females to serve since "it is generally true that women police officers in Singapore do not like to perform investigative work."[31]

Amid charges of massive police corruption the Mexico City department organized a new squad in 1993, The Eco Cops, composed of about 100 policewomen. Male officers allegedly pulled motorists over for real or imagined offenses, and then solicited bribes instead of issuing tickets. The new squad was to be charged with pulling motorists over for pollution violations. Women were assigned exclusively to this detail as it was believed they were more honest than men. Critics of the plan argued that what was needed to combat corruption was better pay and working conditions for police officers. Mexico City policemen than averaged less than $400 per month. Countering this, an official said, "A low salary doesn't justify corruption. It's an excuse. The policewomen are paid less than the men but look at their record."[32]

A study done in the Netherlands in 1982 and 1983 compared the position of females entering the traditional male-dominated field of policing (5 percent of patrol officers in the Netherlands were female) to that of males entering the traditionally female-dominated field of nursing (males were about 19 percent of the nursing staff in general hospitals). Policemen resented the intrusion of the women, doubting their ability to do the job and handle all the calls. Overall, the female officers spent more time than males on tasks like making coffee, tidying up, and buying presents for colleagues. Ninety percent of the female officers reported sexual harassment by way of crude remarks, such as "a rotten fish smells better than the cunt of [a female colleague]." And 69 percent of these women knew of cases where policemen showed sex films, mostly during the night shift. Males entering nursing faced no such hostility. The study noted that "male nurses enjoy advantages from being one of the few among female colleagues. Also, while the male majority in police teams do indeed resist women ... the female majority in the nursing teams do not show a similar resistance to men." The opposition in policing was said to be due to a status loss associated with changes in the workplace. The entry of women (inferior status) into policing lowered the status of the job by emphasizing the feminine side of patrolling, such as patience and empathy at the expense of force, violence, and authority. On the other hand, the entry of males (superior status) into nursing elevated the status of that occupation by emphasizing the technical aspects of the job at the expense of nurturing.[33]

Male motorists treated Amman, Jordan's first female traffic cops as a joke when they hit the street in 1986; "men harassed them or flirted outrageously," noted one observer. The women were quickly removed and assigned to other duties. By early in 1993 the situation of Jordan's policewomen was reported to be improving. The force was even said to be considering putting them back on traffic duty — gradually. Said Jordan's top policewoman, Lieutenant-Colonel Hind Fouad Hammouka, "In the beginning my male colleagues used to wince when they had to salute me." She said the country's 700 female police officers were, in 1993, carrying out most of the duties of their male colleagues — previously they were confined to traditional roles such as searching women, typing, and other administrative jobs. "Compared to other Arab states, we have reached a very advanced stage and we are always striving to improve," explained Hammouka. Women entered Jordan's police force in 1972 with the encouragement of King Hussein, seeking to widen women's role in society and to modernize his kingdom along Western lines. Three years after that he gave women the right to vote and to stand for Parliament. Women formed about 11 percent of the Jordanian workforce, in 1993. Concluded Hammouka, "People's acceptance of policewomen has improved — but I cannot say acceptance is 100 percent."[34]

In her survey of the Israeli police force Dahlia Moore reported that until the early 1960s very few women were employed by the Israeli Police Department. The few women who worked in the force were employed as secretaries and as typists. In the 1960s and 1970s women were encouraged to join and allowed to hold a variety of male-type jobs. Regardless of policy charges, however, these women were only partly integrated, because only a few of them were actually given field jobs. The majority of those women were still placed in administrative jobs at police headquarters. In 1976 only 7 percent of the forces were comprised of female officers. But the growing worldwide movement for more women in policing encouraged more women to join the force. In 1995 20 percent of the entire police force was made up of women and about 24 percent of all supervisory officers were women, but only 2.7 percent of the three highest ranks. In the various riskier police units such as bomb disposal squads and detective squads only about 5 percent of the members were policewomen. In contrast female officers constituted 70 percent of the passport control units at the airports and more than 80 percent of all police administrative workers.[35]

Another researcher who looked at the Israeli Police was Erella Shadmi. She found the percentage of female officers in the Israeli Police (including Border Police and Civil Guard) to be as follows, in certain years: 1948, 5.5 percent; 1956, 4.7 percent; 1966, 7.8 percent; 1976, 15.7 percent; 1986, 18.9 percent. During those years the percentage of female commissioned officers (including Border Police and Civil Guard) was as follows: 1948, 1.1 percent;

1956, 0.9 percent; 1966, 1.4 percent; 1976, 7.0 percent; 1986, 19.3 percent. Women had served in the Israeli Police since it was established in 1948. Shadmi argued the employment of women in the force had undergone three main phases: segregation, breakthrough, and partial integration. Segregation existed in the period 1948 to 1959. In that period women were confined to specific jobs. Opportunities available to women to enter the police or be deployed in various jobs were severely restricted. Women were employed either in female occupations such as typists and secretaries or in jobs in which for legal reasons their presence was unavoidable such as body searches of female suspects and as women's jail custodians. Due to manpower shortages a very limited number of women also served in traffic and communications jobs. The official police position during this period was that only those jobs in which their presence was necessary would be opened to women. For Shadmi the breakthrough period covered the years 1960 to 1969 when, for the first time, women entered typical police jobs. However, only a limited number of such jobs were open to them and the police attitude towards employment of women remained discriminatory. For the first time women entered male jobs—at first only traffic and later—in limited number—on patrol. Police reports explained women's "natural limitations" such as motherhood, pregnancy, the inability to work night shifts, and the idea that most of them did not make the police a lifetime career, as a rationale for limited opportunities. Israeli law prohibited women from working nights but allowed nurses to do so. The Israeli Police adhered to that ban. Partial integration, for Shadmi, covered the period from 1970 up to the time she was writing, 1993. During this time women had been gradually accorded more and more equal rights and treatment and given the right to enter new jobs and positions, although they did not reach the point of full equality. A comparison of the distribution of female and male officers in 1986 in the four main task groups of the Israeli Police, namely patrol and operations, traffic, investigation and intelligence, and administration, revealed a clear division among female, male and mixed occupations. Border control, city traffic control and school safety instruction were almost exclusively staffed by females while patrol, highway traffic control, detective and intelligence were almost exclusively staffed by males. Bomb disposal was 100 percent male. All administrative jobs had a mixed staffing, yet women comprised the majority. Said Shadmi, "Full integration of women into policing is far from being achieved. Sex discrimination still exists in the IP, although it is difficult to determine its extent. Thus, like in the United States and England, a gap between formal policy and informal practice still exists."[36]

Female sworn officers were initially appointed to the Bermuda Police in 1961 but were limited to social work functions and later to general patrol. Promotions were limited up to the rank of inspector within a separate

Women's Department. After 1977 the recruitment of females increased in response to difficulties in the recruitment and retention of male officers. During the 1990s the introduction of human rights legislation in Bermuda guaranteed female officers equal career opportunities and promotion to management ranks. Bermuda Police strength by gender was as follows: 1960 (197 men, 100 percent); 1961 (total strength of 235 officers, 233 men [99.3 percent] two women [0.7 percent]; 1962 (267, 259 men [97.1 percent], eight women [2.9 percent]; 1973 (377, 366 men [97.1 percent], 11 women [2.9 percent]; 1980 (413, 383 men [92.7 percent], 30 women [7.3 percent], 1990 (467, 416 [89.1 percent], 51 women [10.9 percent], 2002 (416, 328 [78.8 percent], 88 women [21.1 percent]. Gertrude Baker joined the Bermuda Police in 1966 and retired in 2003 as the nation's first female command rank officer. With respect to those early years, she said, "At the time there were just eight female officers, and they were placed in a separate Police Women's Department under the leadership of British Inspector Isabelle Lee. We didn't work around the clock like we do now, the ladies worked until midnight." Baker added, "We weren't part of the police because we were only dealing with children's issues and anything to do with female prisoners. Except for the community side of policing that was the extent of our contribution."[37]

In August 1985 in a move motivated both by progressive politics and political opportunism the state government of Sao Paulo, Brazil, inaugurated the country's first of many all-female police stations charged with investigating and prosecuting cases of violence against women. It was a move that attracted worldwide media attention. Those stations were charged with investigating and prosecuting cases of violence against women. It came about — despite the macho culture of the country — from demands by feminists that the state did not treat violence against women as a crime. Police, almost always men, routinely ignored and rarely prosecuted cases of physical and sexual abuse of women and often blamed and harassed the victims. That first one in Sao Paulo was located in the center of the city adjacent to a regular police station with which it shared police cars and holding cells. The main one in that city in 1994 was the only all-female station open 24 hours a day, seven days a week. All the others observed regular business hours and were closed at night. As of February 1995, there were 126 of these stations in operation in Sao Paulo and over 200 throughout Brazil. The opening of all-female stations led to a dramatic increase in the number of complaints to police from women, a trend that continued over the years. As of 2004 there were 125 women's police stations in the state of Sao Paulo, and 339 throughout Brazil. Before July 1985 only 1 percent of police officers in the state of Sao Paulo were women. Just 13 months after the first station opened there were 23 of them in Brazil. On the day the first station opened it had a line of 500 women patiently waiting to file complaints. A woman transferred to that first all-female police station was Ivete Ramos (she was transferred from a regular police station). Ramos said she felt she was not a police officer anymore after she was transferred. But the huge number of women daily filing complaints changed her views. As she said, "Although we had seen some cases in regular police stations, we had no idea about the gravity of the problem. It seems that all women decided to report when the first women's police station was opened, the lines were always enormous." In 2000 for example, 310,058 complaints of violence against women were registered in the women's police stations of Sao Paulo. "Nevertheless, existing research shows that very few cases go to court. Researchers and police officials have reported that the Sao Paulo Police Department and other police departments throughout Brazil still discriminate against policewomen and women's police station," commented a researcher.[38]

In 1996 Mangai Natarajan conducted a survey of women police officers in one Indian state, Tamil Nadu. In 1938, during the colonial era, the participation of women in political movements generated the need for women police officers to deal with them. For this reason women officers were appointed in Kanpur in 1939. During the same period one of the Southern states, Travancore, first appointed women police constables. At first one woman head constable and 12 female constables were appointed as special police constables. Women were recognized and appointed in greater numbers as police officers for line duties only after independence (August 15, 1947). After 1947 women were assigned to the prime minister's security detail and to check Muslim women (who covered themselves head to toe with purdah). For these purposes Delhi and Punjab began to employ women officers in increasing numbers. The 1961 Punjab Police Commission had a mixed reaction to the issue of women officers. One person testifying before the commission said women police were an "extravagant eccentricity" as they themselves had to be protected by the male police on various occasions when performing their duties. A very large increase in the number of women offenders in the 1970s necessitated the employment of more women in the police force to deal with the situation and, said Natarajan, "in spite of deep-rooted prejudice against women in the police, almost all states took steps to employ women officers." A 1987 survey of 10 states revealed that in none was the proportion of women officers greater than 4 percent and in half was 1 percent or less. According to statistics (from the Indian National Crime Records Bureau) for 1991 the numbers remained about the same. Of the 861,119 police officers in the 25 states of India, 11,938 (1.4 percent) were women. Their role continued to be only a peripheral one, largely limited to protective and preventive tasks involved women and juveniles. Tamil Nadu was one of 25 states and seven Union Territories in India. According to the 1981 Census the population was 48.3 million (23.9 million women) with approximately 46.8 percent of that population being literate (58.3 percent of males and 35.0 percent of females). Total police strength in the state was 66,856 of which police constables comprised just over 90 percent, with inspectors being 9 percent. In 1989 there were 770 female police constables and 88 female inspectors in the state. In 1991 that number was up to 1,262. In her survey of these women police in Tamil Nadu Natarajan distributed 300 questionnaires with a total of 183 being completed and returned — a response rate of 60 percent. The survey disclosed those women to have a mean age of 30.8 years, a mean length of service of 8.3 years, 68 percent had high school education, 29.5 percent had a bachelor's degree and 2.2 percent had a master's degree. One-quarter of the respondents were in a supervisory position; the rest were constables. Half of those respondents believed women were less competent than men on a range of police duties — general purpose motor patrol duties, surveillance, foot patrol, dealing with traffic offenses and accidents, dealing with crowds of males on the street, dealing with situations where someone had a lethal weapon, and interviewing male suspects. The majority saw themselves as more competent than men on only the following tasks: clerical work, writing reports, interviewing female suspects, dealing with domestic disputes, and dealing with juvenile offenders. Fully 35.5 percent of the respondents favored the establishment of separate policewomen departments, with a separate career structure that would specialize in female offenders and victims, juveniles, children and missing persons; 38 percent favored the above but in stations staffed by both male and female police officers. Finally, 26 percent favored a fully integrated police department for all officers in which men and women performed the same duties.[39]

Early in 2002 it was reported from New Delhi, India, that initial steps had been taken to address the problem of gender discrimination and sexual harassment in the Indian police with the holding of the first National Conference for Women in Police. Two hundred policewomen from 31 states and union territories in India had come together for the first time. The idea, it was reported, was to inculcate self-esteem in women and teach them how to deal with difficult bosses and colleagues. Joint Commissioner of Police Kiran Bedi said, "We are like the British police in the 1960s. Even now, the Delhi Police needs to review its posting policy. Despite having a good number of policewomen they are not given investigations to handle." Bedi added, "They are hardly even seen in police stations. Sometimes when the police HQ assigns them to a station the [supervising] level officers give them the softer jobs."[40]

The 1,300-odd women in the state of Karnataka, in southwest India, police force were reported to be an unhappy group in the summer of 2003. Faced with discrimination with respect to promotions to handling cases, a majority of women in the service were reduced to just "counseling" harassed women, said a journalist. Even the small percentage sometimes used in law and order capacities or in traffic management ended up assisting their male counterparts. Said a woman constable with 25 years of service, "We are used only for ushering women during processions or guarding women prisoners. During a VIP visit to the city, we carry out security checks for women and ... that's all." A female head constable remarked, "This is my 36th year of service and I am yet to be promoted as inspector. Promotions are slow and sometimes given just before we retire. Who wants such promotions? Why has the government created a women's police force?" The women underwent the same nine-month training program as men but, said the reporter, "none of this training is put to use." At an all-female police station in the state a dozen constables sat in a cramped office and tried to save marriages by reasoning with quarrelsome couples. "We handle only harassment and dowry cases here. If the parties do not reach a compromise we refer the case to court," said Inspector P. Munirathnamma of Ulsoorgate station, who had put in 30 years of service. Reportedly, nearly 70 percent of the women got no exposure handling hardcore crime.[41]

In a 2003 story in the Indian press it was reported that militants had asked Muslim women to quit jobs in the police in the Indian states of Jammu and Kashmir and set January 25, 2003, as the deadline or these women would "face serious consequences." A poster to that effect also said that all Muslim girls should get married after they turned 15 years of age.[42]

Another story in the Indian press, near the end of 2006, featured an interview with a woman police officer who had been on the force for 30 years and had only one promotion in all that time. This unnamed woman told a reporter she was not alone and many other women were suffering the same fate silently. Several policewomen came forward to tell the journalist that the police stations had neither separate changing rooms nor restrooms for them. "We have to beg the inspector to lend room for us to change our clothes. We become the object of ridicule because of this," said one. Inspector-General of Police B. S. Sial said no one was denied promotion because of gender. "There are jobs that are suited for women, while some can be given only to men. This is not to say that one is less efficient than the other or anything." He explained. With respect to sexism in the police department Sial said that although the force was male-dominated, not many cases of bias had been reported.[43]

On March 3, 1998, for the first time, uniformed women police patrolled the streets of the Moroccan capital of Rabat. Their deployment in blue uniforms that were similar to those of their male colleagues coincided with a public holiday marking the 37th anniversary of King Hassan's accession to the throne.[44]

According to research done by the Criminal Justice Commission in Australia, female police officers performed the same physical activities as men despite a perception they were less effective. Researcher Linda Waugh said a traditional opinion existed that women did not belong on patrol because they lacked the physical strength and the ability to maintain an authoritarian presence. That research was a joint project between the Criminal Justice Commission and the Queensland Police Service and showed there was little difference between the physical activities male and female officers performed. Of particular importance to the researchers was the absence of any differences between males and females in activities involving the management of offenders—moving noncompliant offenders, using handcuffs or batons, applying pressure-point control tactics and breaking up fights.[45]

On June 1, 1998, Victoria, Australia, policewoman Narell McKenna was awarded a record damages payment of $125,000 (Australian) for claims of sexual harassment and sexual discrimination brought against the Victoria Police and three of its employees. The state's Anti-Discrimination Tribunal found McKenna had been subjected to sexual harassment by one of her superior officers, and discriminated against and victimized by other senior officers during her employment at two country police stations. In awarding the record payment the tribunal described the behavior of the senior police officers as "very serious" and ruled that, with the exception of the sexual harassment, the incidents "were initiated, supported or endorsed at high levels in the district hierarchy." She had been subjected to discrimination during her placement at the Bairnsdale station from August 1993, which prompted her application for a transfer from that station two years later. During that period, Acting Sergeant Brian Mansfield had sexually harassed McKenna on three occasions during night shifts, including an incident in which he violently dragged her into a holding cell while she screamed and physically fought him. While awaiting the outcome of her transfer application senior officers discriminated against her including upgrading a disciplinary notice against her without giving her the right of a hearing. As well, she was passed over for promotion. The amount awarded to McKenna was the highest damages order made by the tribunal—whose previous highest award for sex discrimination was for $55,000 in 1991, against a college.[46]

A brief 2003 news story reported, without detail, that at least four policewomen had received confidential settlements from the Victoria, Australia, Police in the previous 18 months, after taking complaints of sexual discrimination or sexual harassment to the Australian Equal Opportunities Commission.[47]

A victim of serial sexual harassment in the New South Wales, Australia, Police was told three times by police management not to complain about her treatment before she was eventually forced out of the service. She left the New South Wales Police in 2006 and at the start of the following year was receiving treatment for depression. She said she encountered sexual harassment in her first week on the job back in 2001 when an officer obtained her mobile phone number from employee records and send her lewd text messages. But when she spoke to an education officer she was warned not to lodge a complaint. The fact she had spoken to the education officer was relayed back to the offender and she was suddenly ostracized by all her peers— including the female officers. The following year, 2002, she was grabbed on the ass by a sergeant. Another sergeant who witnessed the incident reported it, but the woman was again cautioned against complaining because the offender was soon to retire. She was transferred to a country station but the harassment continued. Yet again the matter was raised, and yet again she was cautioned not to proceed. Things came to a head in 2006 when a superior officer grabbed hold of her despite her asking him not to. This time she did lodge a formal complaint, but only because she had decided by this point to leave the New South Wales Police. All that occurred when she reported the assault was that the officer involved was given "advice and guidance." With respect to the complaint-handling process, this woman (never named) remarked, "It's an absolutely pointless exercise. You see it all the time, where girls are treated disrespectfully. The whole thing is wrong."[48]

For the fiscal year 2003–2004 the percentages of sworn female officers in the Australian and New Zealand Police were as follows: Australian Federal Police (24.29), New South Wales (33.0), Northern Territory (29.0), Queensland (21.81), South Australia (22.91), Tasmania (22.81), Victoria (18.94), Western Australia (16.04), Australia total (24.43), New Zealand (15.68). For the year 2007–2008 the percentages were as follows: Australian Federal Police (22.0), New South Wales (34.0), Northern Territory (28.2), Queensland (25.1), South Australia (24.20), Tasmania (26.04), Victoria (23.48), Western Australia (19.73), Australia total (26.62 — up 2.19 percent over 2003), New Zealand (17.14 — up 1.46 percent over 2003).[49]

The total police strength in Pakistan in 1999 was about 258,000 and only 1,200 of that total were women. Only nine women had achieved the rank of deputy superintendent. As well, there were a few women-only police stations. The first women officers were appointed in the state of Sindh in 1976. That initiative resulted from a view among senior police at the time that women would be more efficient than men at keeping records of reported crimes, and that women would be less corrupt than men. Two years later that initiative was abandoned and the women recruited were moved to duties such as being traffic education officers for schools. Slowly over time more were appointed and their roles diversified somewhat. Much of that change was a reflection of the highly gender segregated way of life in Pakistan. For example, it simply was not permissible for a male officer to be alone with a woman suspect, witness, or victim. As of 1999 policewomen were sometimes used for their investigative skills because a perpetrator was known or thought to be a woman and that female officers would better understand the "psychology" of a female

criminal. Nevertheless, "It is rare for a woman investigator to be used in operations simply for her general policing skills," said researcher Pauline Amos-
Wilson. The establishment of women-only police stations by Benazir Bhutto
in 1994 (when she was Prime Minister) raised the profile of women police
officers and generated much debate in the media and in the professions and
in parliament over their roles in policing.[50]

It was said to be common knowledge, in 1999, that to get out of a traffic
ticket in Mexico City one simply had to pay the police a bribe. In order to
try and change that situation Mexico City's Ministry of Public Security put
female police in charge, hoping to recoup an estimated $50 million a year in
unpaid fines that was lost. The government deployed the first all-female police
traffic patrol, christened the Swans, that year. They had the singular duty of
handing out traffic tickets. The 950-strong patrol was expected to exude,
wrote a reporter, "naturally occurring feminine traits of firmness, fairness,
and, most of all, incorruptibility." Early into the changeover the female
officers were reportedly issuing three times as many tickets as their male
counterparts. "Women are less corrupt," said new recruit to the squad Mireya
Magog Gutierrez, "because when we aren't working we are busy being housewives and taking care of our children." This situation did not sit well with
Mexico's mostly male police force. "It's just another way to discriminate
against us," grumbled traffic cop Daniel Quiroz. With a monthly salary of
$400, officers bought their own uniforms and paid for patrol-car repairs.[51]

In the fall of 2003 Iranian policewomen were back on the beat for the
first time since the 1979 Islamic revolution. Two hundred and fifteen graduates from police training wearing the all-enveloping chador garment and carrying either ceremonial swords or firearms trooped past President Mohammed
Khatami on October 4 that year. Iranian women served as police officers
under the pro-Western shah — toppled in the revolution — but since then
their role had been restricted to administrative tasks and conducting body
searches on female suspects. However, the new graduates, on duty as of October 5, had polished their judo and fencing skills and were able to serve alongside men in police stations and at border posts. A police training official said
the female officers would not be required at all times to wear the chador.
Instead, he said, they would wear a loose coat and trousers while on patrol
(wearing the chador was obligatory in some government offices).[52]

Several months later the police commander of the Greater Tehran, Iran,
Region, Brigadier Morteza Tale, I said that given half of the country's population were women, establishing a female police force was a need in that society. Reportedly, some 4,000 women had joined the Iranian police. A female
commander in a training academy affiliated to the police academy, Mohtaram
Mas'Ud-Manesh, said they had been women police officers before the Islamic
Revolution in 1979 but after the revolution "due to special conditions" women

were banned from working as officers and all of them were given administrative jobs.[53]

As of January 2003, for the first time in a decade, Afghanistan's national police academy was training female officers to serve in the capital, Kabul, according to interior ministry officials. More than 60 women began a six-month training course late in 2002 at the police academy in Kabul and were expected to graduate in two months, said Interior Minister Taj Mohammad Wardak. "We need more policewomen, and we're asking more to come," Wardak commented. "Eventually we want 50 percent of our police force staffed by women."[54]

Later in 2003 a journalist observed that the female recruits at Afghanistan's new police academy were an oddity in that country where the former Taliban regime banned women from working and society had treated them as second-class citizens for centuries. Dressed in her police uniform of green pants and shirt, and a black headscarf, 19-year-old female cadet Khadidja Ghulan Ali said, "I came here to show ... that women can work together with men ... even in the police. Some women don't think this is the right thing to do, so we want them to understand that they can do it." Reportedly, Afghan police commanders hoped to build a 20,000-strong force, including 2,000 female officers, before the country held national elections slated for June 2004. However, only 30 women had graduated from the academy since it opened in March 2002 and apart from 20 cadets then being trained, few other females had expressed an interest to join the police force. "We suffered 23 years of war and poverty, and women's minds are still indoctrinated by the al-Qaida propaganda, so it is difficult," said the chief instructor at the academy, Major General Abdulzia. "Also, the security in Kabul is not good and even men interested in this job are scarce." The academy had launched a television and radio recruiting campaign and was even sending police cadets and their trainers to high schools to try to enroll female students. Said 17-year-old female cadet Sepideh Muhadesseh, "In one school, some girls said it was anti–Islamic and unholy to work as a policewoman. They wonder how we can remain Muslims and be police officers at the same time." Female recruits at the academy were taught a range of skills including how to investigate child abuse, sexual harassment and domestic violence.[55]

Taliban gunmen shot dead the most high-profile female police officer in Afghanistan and wounded her teenage son as she left home to go to work in September 2008. Attackers waited outside the home of Malalai Kakar (late 40s in age), who was head of the city of Kandahar's department of crimes against women. After the murder the Taliban took public credit for the killing. Kakar was a mother of six. A captain in the police force and the most senior policewoman in Kandahar, she headed a team of about 10 women police officers and had reportedly received numerous death threats. During their

1996 to 2001 hold on power in Afghanistan the Taliban stopped women from working outside the home and even leaving home without a male relative and an all-covering burqa. Kandahar was the birthplace of the Taliban. Kakar was the first woman to enroll in the Kandahar police force after the 2001 ouster of the Taliban and she had been involved in investigating crimes against women and children, and conducting house searches. Earlier that same year, in June, gunmen shot dead a female police officer in the western province of Herat in what was believed to be the first assassination of a female police officer in the nation. Bibi Hoor, 26, was on her way home when two armed men on motorbikes opened fire killing her instantly. The reason for the murder was unknown and no individual or group took public credit. At the time of Kakar's murder the Afghanistan police strength was reported to have numbered about 80,000 people, including a few hundred women. Just in the six months before Kakar's murder approximately 750 policemen had been killed, mostly in the insurgency-linked violence then sweeping the nation.[56]

According to a 2012 news report, some of the women who had joined the Afghan police would not admit to their families where they worked. One female officer who lived and worked in the northern city of Mazar-i-sharif told her family that she was employed by a foreign aid organization. That was because the rumors about sexual abuse in Mazar's police force were so widespread that many of the women were ashamed to say they were police officers. In Afghanistan simply wearing the wrong clothes, sitting in the front seat of a car, or working outside the home, was enough for a woman to get labeled a prostitute, even in the most modern parts of the country. The law reflected that. With sexual assault the woman was often sent to jail along with her rapist. The assumption was that any woman who put herself in a situation to be vulnerable to rape must be immoral. That seemed to apply even to police officers. One unnamed female officer told a reporter that some women were being promoted only if they agreed to give sexual favors to their superiors. Most of the females on the force were poor and many had children and for them the $300 (US) a month salary was higher than that paid by any other work they were likely to find, such as maid or teacher. "It's a fact. Women in the police are being used for sex and as prostitutes. It has happened to me. Male cops ask for sex openly because they think I joined the police just to work as a prostitute," said another woman on the force. Still another said she was forced to have sex with her superiors: "Put it this way. If there's a young woman and she wants to remain in her post, she accepts being used this way." All the policewomen that spoke to the reporter declared the sexual abuse was widespread across the police force. Georgette Gagnon was head of the United Nations human rights office in Afghanistan. She said, "We've received many reports of abuse of Afghan women police in various parts of the country. We are very concerned."[57]

Women made up only 3.2 percent, or 9,097 members, of the 275,294 officers in the national police force of Indonesia, as of late 2006. No police-women held senior positions. Said researcher Fitriana Sidikah Rachman, "Most policewomen are also posted in stereotypical assignments, like desk jobs and administrative work." During the recruitment process, among other conditions, female cadets were required to be virgins. Once they were accepted into the force few of the females escaped desk work. For a policewoman to be recruited up the ladder, according to this account, "she must get an okay from her relatives." Remarked one male police officer, "Before appointing a policewoman, I would call her husband and ask his permission. I don't want to cause a family feud when she had to go on a business trip or some-thing."[58]

Late in 2007 the Iraqi government ordered all its policewomen to hand in their guns for redistribution to men or face having their pay withheld, thwarting a US initiative to bring more women into the nation's police force. The Ministry of the Interior, which oversaw the police, issued the order in late November. It affected all officers who had earned the title "policewoman" by graduating from the police academy, even if their jobs did not require them to be on the streets. The order did not apply to men in the same type of jobs. Critics said the move was the latest sign of the religious and cultural conser-vatism that had taken hold in Iraq since the ouster of Saddam Hussein ushered in a government dominated by Shiite Muslims. That tendency was hampering efforts to bring stability to Iraq by driving women from the police force, said US Army brigadier general David Phillips. Without women police, said Phillips, there would be no officers to search female suspects, even though women have joined the ranks of suicide bombers in Iraq. Another US advisor to the Iraqi government said that forcing out female officers would hamper investigation of crimes such as rape, which stigmatizes women in Iraq, because few victims feel comfortable reporting it to men.[59]

So controversial was the move to disarm Iraqi policewomen that Iraqi police officials announced they were dropping plans to disarm their female officers, about a year after implementing the policy. One of those affected was Hanan Jaafer, a policewoman in the Shiite holy city of Najaf, who guarded the revered shrine of Imam Ali. She said none of the roughly two dozen female officers posted at the shrine had a gun or a uniform (because of the policy), even though they searched women and children entering the complex and faced threats from the increased use of female suicide bombers. Their male counterparts at the complex were armed. In the previous year Jaafer personally stopped a woman from entering the shrine with explosives she had apparently swallowed and that caused her abdomen to swell. Her young son was holding a remote control device to detonate them. She was stopped because she had "an oddly shaped body" and she felt "very hard" to the touch. Since US forces had introduced female recruitment in Iraqi in late 2003 about 1,000 women had qualified as policewomen.[60]

At the start of 2009 the Iraqi Ministry of the Interior graduated a class of 490 women police officers—the first all-female class to graduate since the fledgling force was established. Those women would take to the streets with some working in counterterrorism while others would staff the many checkpoints on Baghdad's streets. Since militants began sending in female suicide bombers, female officers had been needed more and more to search women and staff checkpoints. Those women took a 30-day training course providing rudimentary English language skills as well as training in human rights, counterterrorism, the penal code, self-defense, and competency with weapons.[61]

During January 2004 there were 32 cases of physical injury or verbal abuse of police officers in Lima, Peru; in all but five cases the victims were female traffic cops. Two of those cases attracted headlines in the press. One involved Miguel Angel Mufarech, the president of the regional government for the area around Lima; he was alleged to have roughed up a woman officer who gave him a ticket. Another involved an unnamed American diplomat, with no details provided. Mufarech was applauded for his machismo at a meeting of his political party after the incident. Policewomen were said to be especial targets because "they refuse to accept bribes, which bothers people accustomed to paying when they break the law." Because they were seen by police officials as less corrupt than their male colleagues, 75 percent of traffic cops in Lima were female.[62]

As of 2006 South Korea had policewomen for some 60 years. However, it was reported that policemen did not recognize policewomen as their partners but considered female officers as being fit only for specific duties. A survey conducted by a university professor of 1,124 policemen and 114 policewomen in 20 police stations in Seoul and Kyonggi Province was undertaken in 2004. It was conducted by the Korean Institute of Criminal Justice Policy. Results showed fixed ideas on gender roles among the male police officers indicating that female police faced a glass ceiling and discrimination at work. When asked whether policewomen were necessary in general police work, 81 percent of the females and 42.1 percent of the males answered yes. More than 55 percent of the men said increasing the number of policewomen would weaken the image of the whole force while 20.9 percent of the women said it would not. Some 53 percent of the men said policewomen had less ability to perform duties than male officers, but only 6.3 percent of the women said so. More than 44 percent of male officers said they did not want female police to be their superior officers; 21.9 percent said they did. When asked whether the duties of policewomen should be expanded, 75 percent of females said yes while just 28.9 percent of male officers said yes. At the end of 2004 policewomen comprised about 4.1 percent of the total strength of the South

Korean police force. But the National Police Agency announced at that time that it planned to adopt a 20 to 30 percent quota for female officers in recruitment with the goal of increasing the total proportion of female police to 10 percent by 2014.[63]

Since the Islamic group Hamas took over in Gaza City, Palestine, in June 2007 it had been recruiting policewomen as well as policemen. From mid–August of that year up to the beginning of 2008 a total of 60 women had been accepted into the force. Mostly they worked on cases that involved dealing with women in areas such as drugs and prostitution. Restoring internal security to the lawless Gaza Strip was one of the main challenges for Hamas upon taking over the area following a civil war with Fatah. Most of those policewomen wore the niqab (a full veil leaving only a slit for the eyes).[64]

In 2003 the Fiji Police put measures into place to widen the pool of recruits and to remove certain compulsory selection criteria concerning height, weight, and chest size of candidates that discriminated against ethnic Indians and Chinese. That same year saw a new policy initiated that gave 35 percent of places in the police recruitment process to women and 65 percent to men.[65]

The Women's Police Directorate was set up in the Kingdom of Bahrain in 1970 as a gender-segregated police unit that handled cases involving female and child victims and offenders. As of May 2006 there were 368 policewomen in Bahrain out of a total of approximately 3,000. In that later year a new female recruit entered the Women's Police Directorate or the Community Policing Unit. Female police did not participate in police duties such as traffic patrol and investigation of cases involved men. In the Community Policing Unit female officers worked in separate teams from the male officers, and closely with policewomen from the Women's Police Directorate. In police stations female police occupied a separate wing of the building. They also staffed the juvenile detention center and the women's prison in Bahrain. Most of the policewomen queried by a researcher felt gender segregation was appropriate for female police in Bahrain. That researcher concluded "any move toward gender integration is unlikely to be demanded by the policewomen themselves, even a small minority of them."[66]

Studied in 2010 were the Gulf Cooperation Council countries of Bahrain, Kuwait, Qatar, Oman, Saudi Arabia, and the United Arab Emirates (UAE). Those nations shared a common language, and a religious and cultural heritage. With the exception of Saudi Arabia, all of those countries were constitutional monarchies. Women achieved the right to vote in Bahrain in the early 1970s, in Oman and Qatar in 2003, and in Kuwait in 2005. The UAE monarchy "hand picks voters for elections." In the national police forces in those nations policewomen were primarily in segregated units that focused on women and juveniles as victims, witnesses, and offenders. Women made up approximately 5 percent of the forces in Oman, the UAE, and Qatar, and 10 percent in Bahrain. For those six nations the statistics were as follows: Bahrain, 10 percent females on the force (1970, date of first appointment); Kuwait, unknown (2009); Qatar, 4.7 percent (1980s); Oman 4.5 percent (1974), the UAE, unknown (early 1990s); Saudi Arabia, zero (nil). At that time the highest proportion of females on police forces was to be found in Eastern European nations where in many countries there were 20 percent or a bit more on some forces. However, duties of policewomen in the Gulf countries were more limited than in Western nations.[67]

The Turkish National Police were part of the national government in that country and from 2001 to 2005 the percentage of women in the force grew 0.6 percent, up from 4.9 percent in 2001 and 2002 to 5.5 percent in 2005. Women made up approximately 25 percent of the total Turkish workforces. In urban areas during 2006 women comprised 16.7 percent of that workforce. The first systematic recruitment of women into police schools in Turkey occurred in 1979. A survey of 70 Turkish policewomen was undertaken in 2010. That number amounted to 5 percent of that total number of sworn female police officers working in Ankara, which was 1,405. Only officers with three of more years of service were surveyed. All of the respondents said they had never experienced sexual harassment from their coworkers, supervisors, or family members. Of the 70 respondents, 45 indicated they had no problems with their male colleagues (that is, discrimination other than sexual) related to their jobs as policewomen. The others complained about being seen by their male colleagues as second-class citizens, and so on.[68]

Late in 1993 Sarah Locker of the London England Metropolitan Police Force settled an action against her employer alleging sexual and racial discrimination. That settlement was for £32,500 and under its terms Locker could not discuss those allegations as she was under a gag order. However, said reporter Geraldine Bedell, much of the substance of those allegations was known. During hearings before an industrial tribunal Locker said she was repeatedly and unreasonably turned down for jobs in the Criminal Investigation Department (CID). A fellow officer handed her a spoof application he had written as if from her. It read, for example, "A few of them courses is right up the street of a Third World effnic girl like me." Locker described herself as "very ambitious." She initiated first an internal grievance procedure and then, backed by the Equal Opportunities Commission and the Campaign for Racial Equality, an industrial tribunal action. The police establishment fought her all the way. She expected her case to last six months but an out-of-court settlement was reached in December 1993 after just two days of pre-trial negotiations. Locker alleged she was repeatedly passed over for jobs in the CID while men with less service and experience were given those jobs. She had four commendations for work on various serious crime cases. Hardcore pornographic material, described by one news account as "homosexual and with animals" would be left in her tray at work. She was once sitting at her desk and realized a man was underneath it, looking up her skirt. Other men would snap her bra strap as they passed. Locker commented, "I went into the police because I felt it was a career that offered a range of different types of jobs. I knew I was qualified, although there is a tendency to give women jobs thought of as 'women's work' and then complain that they aren't qualified for promotion." In her case the women's work was translation, which she did willingly because speaking Turkish was a rare skill that she felt was valuable. Once she set in motion the grievance procedure colleagues stopped speaking to her. When she walked into an elevator it would clear. A female colleague phoned to warn her that threats had been made against her and suggested someone might tamper with her car. That was back in 1991 and Locker had not been back to work since that date. She was born in east London, the daughter of Turks, and joined the police force straight from school. Paul Condon, the Metropolitan Police commissioner, apologized to her in December 1993 for the abuse she had suffered although he denied that racial and sexual discrimination had prevented her promotion to detective work. However, as part of the settlement Locker would return to the police as a detective constable in the CID, working in financial investigation. She had been offered £250 to settle her case in 1991. She told a reporter she had no idea if the past two years would prejudice her future; "I'm willing to start afresh. I can't forget, but I'm willing to put it all behind me. I hope there isn't bitterness, but I won't know until I go back."[69]

Sarah Locker had joined the London police when she was 18. She was invalided out of the force in 1996, but was still fighting in 1999 at the age of 37. Later that year she was slated to take the police force to the High Court where she was suing for breach of contract and negligence. When Sarah first became a policewoman she said she learned very quickly that women in the force were treated as "second-class." She recalled, "It was literally, 'You make the tea,' I didn't fit in. Some women would join in with it, try to be one of the boys, but that was never me." Nevertheless she did extremely well, gaining a number of commendations. She wanted to join the CID and she was one of only two women accepted to join the drug squad, working for John Grieve. And it was there that her problems began in earnest. "Most days it was the most gross abuse. You'd go in and they'd say 'Did your husband fuck you last night? Are you wearing stockings? Come and sit on my cock.'" Then she got passed over for promotion in favor of men who had less experience than she did. And that led to her grievance procedure launch in 1991. Her husband was and remained a policeman. And he endured taunts about his wife's case. Then she achieved her 1993 reinstatement and seeming victory. But when Locker went back to work things were even worse. Her life was made intolerable and she was forced to leave the force, according to reporter Hester Lacey. "I instigated charges, I took on the old boy's network and I feel the most hated policewoman in the Met," said Locker. "The job I loved was taken away from me twice." And that, said the journalist, was why she was taking legal action against the force for a second time. "Women and ethnic minorities are both used and abused in the police," Locker declared. "There is no point in just paying lip-service to cleaning it up."[70]

In June 2006, the day before Locker's case was to be heard by the High Court, Scotland Yard agreed to pay her a compensation package worth an estimated one million pounds Sterling. When she returned to work in 1993 (she had specifically been promised fair treatment as part of the 1993 settlement) her promised job as a financial investigator in an elite squad turned out to be little more than a desk job. The hate campaign started again, including obscene phone calls. Within weeks she took sick leave and left the force after 16 years. She received £215,000 cash and a pension and police injury award of around £20,000 a year for life. After that settlement Locker said, "My colleagues shunned me. It was a kind of torture. I began to realize that the agreement [of 1993] was all show. I had no real work to do and no one to talk to. I cracked up and left with a nervous breakdown. So I brought these proceedings." She added, "My life's ambition was to be a professional police officer. I gave 16 years of my life to the police and they have torn it apart." Her solicitor, Jane Deighton, said the Met's failure to admit liability despite the large payout was arrogant. She said there were two things Locker did not achieve. One was an apology, as the police refused to admit responsibility. But, said Deighton, why pay out so much unless they knew they would lose in court. The second things, said the solicitor was that "the public and police have no guarantee that despite the commissioner throwing money at this disaster, another one is not around the corner. The police are saying they have changed. If they had changed they would have apologized.[71]

English journalist Stewart Tendler remarked in 1994 that nearly 20 years after women police won equal status with male officers in the United Kingdom "they remain isolated in a service dominated by a masculine culture." Women made up nearly 13 percent of the police strength there but in an investigation by his newspaper, the *Times* of London, it was revealed those women were held back by Home Office inertia "and often outright hostility from male colleagues." When a woman applied to join a canine unit, a senior officer on the appointment board said, "We don't have bitches with the dogs and we are not going to have them among the handlers." Tendler declared that attitude "and frequent sexual harassment and innuendo have put huge obstacles in the way of policewomen." New figures from Scotland Yard showed that 41 women in the Metropolitan Police lodged formal grievances in 1993 alleging sexual harassment. Behind those figures, he wrote, lay other complaints resolved at the local level. Such discrimination explained, continued Tendler, why there were only five women among the 173 most senior officers in England and Wales. Within the 28,000 strong Metropolitan force, which was at the forefront of equal opportunities campaigns, figures for the end of 1993 showed there were 65 women holding the rank of inspector or above out of 3,896 women officers. Women were then still fighting to breach male bastions such as the motorway patrol units and CID. One woman who applied to join a motorcycle unit was told she would have to lift a 1000 cc machine before being accepted. It was an impossible task that no male officer was required to undertake. One female officer told Tendler, "One of the worst problems is sexual banter. You go into a room and three or four men will run their hands over you to see if you are wearing the 'full tackle' suspenders. It happens frequently." The Home Office's inspectors of constabulary were urging chief constables to recruit more women. Reportedly, those chief constables had publicly attacked sexual harassment in their forces. The Police Federation, the largest staff organization, had recently issued a leaflet to its 100,000 members urging them to fight harassment. That new drive came in the wake of several harassment cases that had received wide media coverage, such as the case of Alison Halford, the Merseyside assistant chief constable. More women would get a better deal if more were prepared to fight, but policewoman Tina Martin, chair of the British Association of Women Police, said that complaints were being deliberately delayed until it was too late to go to an industrial tribunal. As parts of any settlements that were reached between the parties, policewomen were being ordered not to talk to the media.[72]

A female detective in England was given a six-figure compensation payout, in September 1996, after her promising career was blighted by sexual harassment from male colleagues. Libby Ashurst, 27, a former WPC (woman police constable) with North Yorkshire Police was the party in one of two out-of-court settlements made by the force to avoid embarrassing details becoming public at industrial tribunals. In the second case former WPC Amanda Rose, who was on secondment to the same CID at Harrogate, was understood to have received £10,000 in her settlement. The allegations made by the two women led to a two-year investigation at Harrogate. Reportedly, several officers have since been disciplined (fined, transferred, or both). Some of the abuse was directed at male officers as well, in the form of bullying and bizarre initiation rites for new officers. Most of the incidents happened a few years previously. Besides sexual harassment complaints the women also complained about always being given the worst jobs and suffering a barrage of sexist and deprecatory remarks. Ashurst's father, Terry, principal of Doncaster Further Education College, called for a public investigation. He said, "I do not believe the chief constable's statement that none of the hierarchy was involved. I believe the culture is pervasive of sexual harassment and bullying and I cannot accept that senior officers are so lacking in knowledge of what is going on at various levels within the force. If they don't know, there is even more wrong with the force than one might believe already." Libby Ashurst had signed an agreement not to talk about the case. Tony Lidgate, press officer for North Yorkshire Police said, "The Chief Constable, David Burke, has apologized to Miss Ashurst for the treatment she received. He has said this was an isolated incident which departs radically from the very high standards of North Yorkshire Police. The force will strive to ensure similar circumstances do not arise again."[73]

A woman detective in England who was nicknamed "Massive Cleavage" and subjected to a barrage of sexual abuse by male colleagues won her case on November 10, 1997, for harassment. An industrial tribunal ruled that detective constable Dee Mazurkiewicz had suffered months of harassment by Thames Valley Police. During the hearing, Dee, 41, described how she was tormented by fellow officers at Aylesbury, Buckinghamshire. At one stage they claimed she got confessions from criminals by "getting her boobs out." They also accused her of wearing no underwear and performing sex acts on prisoners in exchange for confessions. She eventually went on sick leave and complained in November 1995 about the harassment. Inspector George Pugsley investigated her allegations and she was transferred after he found no evidence for her claims. John Hollow, chair of the industrial tribunal hearing the case in Reading, England, accused him of misrepresenting the facts. Pugsley conceded he thought indecent remarks had been made but then said he could not be sure they had been made by two officers accused of discrimination. Said Hollow, "The most charitable view we can take is that it was disingenuous to say there was no evidence whatsoever. It is in our view a misrepresentation of the facts." Hollow said it was clear that within the CID office there was a culture of bawdy repartee between the officers. After the tribunal announced its decision in favor of Mazurkiewicz, Ian Blair, assistant chief constable of Thames Valley, said, "We feel sorry that Miss Mazurkiewicz has felt distress at this case. We will learn from it. She is welcome back and the decision as to whether she would like this is up to her."[74]

After negotiations over the amount of the award it was announced on May 14, 1998, that Mazurkiewicz was awarded £300,000. She retired from the force on May 16, 1998, on the ground of ill health.[75]

In June 1995 Britain's first woman chief constable — Pauline Clare — was appointed to lead the Lancashire Constabulary. However, Clare was one of only six female officers to hold any of the 240 most senior posts in the police service in England and Wales, as of late 1997. Moreover, she headed a force of 3,200 officers, of whom only 15 percent were women. Nationally, women constituted 13.7 percent of the total strength of police forces and occupied only 2.9 percent of the senior management positions. Researcher Kevin Gaston did a survey of officers of an unnamed British police force. When officers who were eligible to set for promotion examinations were asked if they had, in fact, sat the promotion examinations, 47.6 percent of the males had but only 17.9 percent of the females had done so. Success rates were not significantly different by gender with 10.8 percent of males and 7.7 percent of females being successful on those exams. According to Gaston, a central factor affecting the decision to sit for promotion exams concerned the support received from others. Of particular interest was the encouragement and support given by candidates' partners, colleagues, immediate supervisors and others in supervisory roles. "For each of these categories male officers reported higher levels of support and encouragement than did female officers," reported Gaston. Male officers got significantly more support from their immediate supervisors (most of which were male).[76]

A police inspector in Warwickshire, England, had her ambitions for promotion derailed by a "wrong and sexist" decision made by her boss, an industrial tribunal decided on May 22, 1998. Inspector Shirley Daniel, 49, found herself unable to apply for a chief inspector's job in the career development department of the Warwickshire force because the rules were changed at the last minute. Chief Superintendent Richard Allsopp, who had retired since the incident happened in June 1995, limited applications for the post to chief inspectors with two years of experience. Industrial tribunal chairman Christopher Goodchild declared in his judgment he believed Allsopp had acted "specifically to prevent a woman getting a job." The hearing was then adjourned to allow the parties to try and reach a settlement over the amount of compensation. Goodchild said the alteration in the job description had been made because Daniel was "perceived as a woman and as a woman would not be up to that particular job — it's as simple as that. It was a straightforward sexist decision." The tribunal had been told that no one applied for the post after Allsopp altered the job description, and finally a serving officer had to be "recruited" to fill the vacancy. Goodchild said the panel thought Daniel would have got the job under normal circumstances.[77]

On September 5, 1998, it was announced that the Midlands Police had agreed to pay Shirley Daniel £35,000 in compensation. Daniel would retire from the force on September 17, 1998, after it was agreed to retrospectively promote her to chief inspector — the rank she had been earlier denied because she was a woman. Her promotion increased her pension to about £14,000 a year, and included a lump sum of about £85,000.[78]

A 32-year-old Warlingham, England, mother was awarded a £150,000 sex discrimination payoff in December 2000 from the Metropolitan Police after an industrial tribunal ruled she had been discriminated against. Catherine Moore was a highly rated police constable at Wandsworth Police Station. But after she retired from the force with severe depression in March 1998, she complained she had been forced out of the job. She alleged that after her 1996 return to work from maternity leave her performance was unfairly criticized and that the force refused a request for a modest change to her working hours because of childcare commitments. She said from that point on she was bullied out of her job and had been unable to work since. A Croyden employment tribunal held earlier in 2000 ruled she had been discriminated against because of her gender and because of her request to work flexible hours. The tribunal concluded Moore had become a scapegoat for the section's ills after her return from maternity leave, that her sickness record was greatly exaggerated and that an unduly punitive attitude had been adopted towards her. The £150,000 settlement was agreed to a day before a scheduled further compensation hearing.[79]

Reporter Jane Simpson declared, in March 2006, "One of Scotland's largest police forces has been operating a secret policy to block the promotion of working mothers." Legal documents obtained by Simpson's newspaper indicated Grampian Police overlooked WPCs with children when selecting officers to promote. In those documents, part of a court case in which a WPC took legal action against the force, solicitors for Grampian Police said even though the woman had passed her sergeant's exam it was "unlikely" she would be promoted because she subsequently had children. They went on to say that because of the commitments of her new family, the department would expect her to look for other employment "in social work, counseling or general administrative work." Said Simpson, "Scotland already has the worst record in Britain for promoting female officers." The case referred to involved Julia Bain, 39, of Elgin, Moray. She had passed the sergeant examinations which normally led to promotion within a year. One in five Grampian police officers was a female but the force had only two women of chief inspector rank, one of whom was a mother.[80]

A survey of two county police forces in the United Kingdom in 2007 compared the promotion of men and women police officers controlling for tenure and then compared the organizational commitment of male and female officers. According to the researchers their aim was to establish empirically whether there was any foundation in the premise that female officers' lesser tenure or lower levels of commitment to their police forces explained their under-representation in the senior ranks. "Our findings revealed that women are less likely to achieve promotion than men and this cannot be attributed to less service experience," declared the researchers. It was also found that if commitment to the police force was seen as essential to promotions there "is no lack of it in female officers. They are as committed as their male colleagues, and like them their organizational commitment is most strongly influenced by how they are managed." Concluding remarks from the researchers declared their data clearly "refute some of the widespread beliefs about reasons for women's lack of progress in their policing career since gender differences in length of tenure and organizational commitment have been discounted as possible explanations in these two police forces."[81]

A newspaper report in August 2009 reported that after months of taking a beating in the media over allegations of heavy-handedness Britain's largest police force was trying a new approach: handing women commanders the reins—in potential riot situations. London's Metropolitan Police Service was taking a "softly, softly" approach that week as environmental campaigners undertook five days of action against targets ranging from government buildings to the offices of multinational mining firm Rio Tinto. The hope was for an outcome that was sharply different from that of London's Group of 20 conference in April 2009 during which major clashes broke out between hundreds of riot police and protesters—many of whom accused the police of unprovoked attacks upon them. The change of gender in the command structure was based on the theory that policewomen often viewed their work as a public service, while policemen approached their task from the perspective of "control through authority." The two females slated for command during the expected protests were Superintendent Julia Pendry and Inspector Jane Connors. Pendry had, in the past, reached an out-of-court settlement with her police force over allegations of sexual discrimination against her.[82]

In December 1994 Lenna Bradburn 34, was appointed chief of the 142-member police force in Guelph, Ontario, becoming the first woman to head a police force at the municipal, provincial or federal level in Canada.[83]

Alice Clark joined the Royal Canadian Mounted Police (RCMP) in Canada in 1980. Two years later she was posted to the 60-member detachment at Red Deer, Alberta, where, at first the men she worked with were welcoming and helpful. Then she was transferred to city traffic duty where, she said, "The officers on my shift made no bones about how they felt about female members. They didn't like women in the force—period." In 1987, after repeated episodes of sexual harassment and intimidation by male Mounties, Clark quit. She sued the force for damages, telling the Federal Court of Canada that she had been grabbed and propositioned, publicly humiliated by her supervisor and embarrassed one day to find life-sized plastic breasts taped to her desk. In 1994 the court awarded her $93,000. Clark, 37 in 1995, was then working for the British Columbia provincial government, in Nanaimo, BC. Journalist Rae Corelli observed that there were 4,286 women among the nations' 56,991 municipal, provincial and federal police officers and "the RCMP, the Ontario Provincial Police and most metropolitan police departments across the nation have introduced — and claim to be enforcing — tough policies against harassment and discrimination." In Clark's lawsuit 26 separate incidents over a five-year period were listed in the court documents. For example, a plainclothes officer once drove up while she guarded a body at a murder scene and suggested they have sex in the back seat of his car. A supervisor told her in front of other officers "that I was a waste of a uniform and that I should quit and let a real man have a job." When she asked a male cop about his United Nations peacekeeping ribbon he told her he got it "for making five female members quit." The male officers would occasionally play pornographic movies seized from a local video store and when she and another woman officer objected "they told us if we didn't like it to hit the road." Allegedly, male officers told her she "wasn't a real woman until I had a child ... referred to me as a 'bitch' ... and a meter maid. One officer grabber her one day in a back office and kissed her, "He told me to call him when my husband was away if I wanted a real man." The environment became so poisoned she hated going to work, Clark said, choosing to do paperwork in her police cruiser. "I found it difficult at certain times to work with particular members because I knew of their hostility toward me," Clark said in court testimony. She added, "I found I didn't belong or have a place in the office to do my work.... You could never pay me enough to go through that again ... I felt like a piece of shit." Clark finally quit because, she said, "I wasn't there to put up with that sort of garbage." She quit after filing a formal complaint of sexual harassment against the force. Then she was charged — vindictively in her view — with having assaulted three civilians in separate incidents during her time at Red Deer. She was acquitted of those allegations the following year and her husband RCMP officer Bruce, fed up with the way his wife had been treated, resigned from the force.

Meanwhile, Clark said she had stayed in touch with many of the policewomen who had phoned or written her after they read about her case; their experiences led her to believe that harassment was still commonplace. "A lot of us talk about it among ourselves, but for them to go public with it is a different ball game," Clark stated. "If you go public, you know it's going to get worse." Lorne Goddard, a Red Deer lawyer who represented Clark, said nine or 10 other former policewomen who claimed to have unresolved grievances had called him in the last year. But all had waited too long and their right to take legal action had expired under the statute of limitations.

According to Corelli, as of 1992 women accounted for less than 8 percent of the nation's cops. And only 20 women were among the 2,680 who had reached officer rank. In the intermediate ranks women did somewhat better; of the 14,631 noncommissioned officers, 233 were women. Of the three levels of policing in Canada (municipal, provincial and federal) the RCMP had recruited the highest proportion of women, 1,434 in a force of 15,662, but only 56 were noncommissioned officers and only two were in the officer ranks. In a major study of women in Canadian law enforcement, the federal solicitor general's ministry published a 1993 report titled "The Status of Women in Canadian Policing." It looked at police departments in Moncton, New

Brunswick; London, Ontario; Ontario's Halton Region; and Delta, BC, along with RCMP detachments in Burnaby and Surrey, BC. Two-thirds of the women who took part in the study said there was sexual harassment in policing but that most of it was manageable; sexist or suggestive comments were accepted as part of the job. One-fifth of those interviewed said anti-harassment policies were inadequate and the balance said harassment was a serious problem. In an attempt to discourage male cops from preying on females, most medium-sized and large police organizations had adopted stiff measures against sexual harassment. In 1993 the RCMP published a 15-page directive that declared it would "neither tolerate harassment nor any discriminatory practice." A constable with the Ontario Provincial Police spoke to Corelli only if her name and detachment were withheld. She had served for more than 15 years and was one of the force's 25 peer support officers. She got about five distress calls a month, usually from new female recruits. "They say he did this to me and that to me and guess what the sergeant's doing to me," she said. "I tell them if you don't do anything about it, then whoever comes after you is going to have to deal with it. But the women don't want to lose out; they just got a $50,000-a-year job, and they feel if they buck a 20-year officer they're going to lose it. I mean who are they going to believe — you or a 20-year officer? You very soon begin not to trust the levels of appeal." This unidentified female officer added, "There are women quitting all the time. A lot of them leave because you can't pay them enough to put up with what they have to put up with."[84]

Inspector Connie Snow, of the Royal Newfoundland Constabulary in Canada, told an audience at the annual conference of the International Association of Women Police in 2000 that she had been ostracized, insulted and harassed by her male colleagues during her 25-year career. She was a senior female police officer and she compared her experiences as a woman in male-dominated policing to being a victim in an abusive relationship. "In my police career, I've often felt like I'm in an abusive relationship…. There was tremendous pressure to conform…. I wouldn't complain or correct…. I still felt isolated," she told the audience. "You don't want your family or friends to know about it…. They might even want you to leave the force." She added, "It's easier to give up. I've had my bad days. I do it for my daughter. Personally, I feel a great responsibility to help make things easier for the next generation of women." Snow remarked that only 9 percent of Canadian police officers were women and that was far too few because it made it harder to speak out against the discrimination: "I broke through the glass ceiling. I didn't know I'd hit the brick wall," she said, describing what she called an old boy's club environment. "It is still very much there at every level. It doesn't seem to matter really, what the next level is that you're going to move on to. Your struggles change a little bit, but they're still there," stated Snow.[85]

When women were first recruited into the RCMP in Canada in 1974 they were dubbed "The Greatest Mancatchers Alive" by the media. That first class had 32 female recruits. Prior to 1974 Mountie wives often functioned as "unpaid Mounties," being pressed into duty as and when necessary as for matron duty and as escorts for female prisoners.[86]

At the start of the 1970s the Royal Commission on the Status of Women in Canada recommended that "enlistment in the RCMP be open to women." It would take the RCMP another four years and several studies to act on that recommendation. But in May 1974 the federal force announced it was recruiting women for the first time in its 101-year history. Some 292 women applied for that first intake and on September 16, 1974, the RCMP accepted 32 female recruits. One week after that those women began the standard six months of recruit training at the RCMP's academy in Regina, Saskatchewan. After six months of training 30 women successfully finished with the graduation ceremony held on March 3, 1975.[87]

Late in 2011 the RCMP exploded onto the media scene in Canada again over sexual harassment in its ranks. It all began in November of that year when a prominent BC RCMP officer went public on national television alleging she had suffered years of sexual harassment in the force and was then off work on sick leave suffering from post-traumatic stress syndrome. She was Catherine Galliford, a former spokeswoman for the RCMP. As the usual media spokesperson for the force she was regularly seen on newscasts telecast across the country. She was the main media person for the force during the Air India bombing of 1985 (which took over 300 lives and was never out of the news for long through to 2011). Galliford was also a main spokesperson for the force during the Robert Pickton serial killing investigations during the first decade of this century. Both cases were highly controversial, and lasted a long time with the result that few Canadians did not recognize Galliford from her many, many television appearances as she struggled to explain what many in Canada viewed as the errors and shortcomings of the force during those two particular cases.

When she went public she said she faced sexual advances from senior officers in the RCMP during the 16 years she was with the force. She went off-duty on sick leave in 2007, had launched an internal RCMP complaint and was then considering suing the force. She told the country's national broadcaster, the Canadian Broadcasting Corporation (CBC), that one of her bosses tried to have sex with her and she had been asked by her bosses to sit on their knees. "It just got to the point that after I had about 16 years of service, I broke. I completely broke," she said. It was the second case in just a couple of months in which a female officer alleged she was sexually harassed. In October 2011 RCMP constable Susan Gastaldo claimed her boss coerced her into having sexual relations with him. Mike Webster, a former member of the RCMP and now a psychologist who often worked with police forces, said these allegations illustrated the need for an RCMP union. Sexual harassment is as frequent in a municipal police service or fire service, he said, "the difference being, in a municipal police service or fire service, the female victim has a union. She can take her complaint forward, sit down with management, they iron it out ... and she can go back to work. In the RCMP, that doesn't exist." Without an independent union to represent them female officers who experience sexual harassment have no one to turn to. The masculine culture and command and control structure discouraged them from speaking up. There was also, said Webster, the question of who to complain to. "They are going to complain to the guy who is harassing them; their supervisors," said Webster. "Or they're going to complain to somebody who has influence over their career, and they don't want to appear like they're not one of the boys. They want to be tough."[88]

One day after Galliford went public with her allegations another officer, Krista Carle (retired), came forward to say she knew several female officers who had experienced sexual harassment in the RCMP workplace. She told a reporter the Galliford revelations brought back horrible memories and that she knew of six female officers, personally, that had left the force or were still there but had suffered similar sexual harassment. All were afraid to come forward because of reprisals. Carle said when she complained, RCMP management tried to cover it up. "When I spoke out against the harassment, it wasn't taken seriously, and I felt diminished and I felt revictimized every time I told what happened to me," Carle explained. Carle was one of four female officers who sued the RCMP alleging Sergeant Robert Glendell sexually assaulted them in the late 1990s. They said they were reprimanded and the case settled with all parties agreeing to keep the terms secret. Glendell was docked one day's pay, later promoted and was then in charge of protecting VIPs in Vancouver, BC.[89]

Krista Carle went on to explain she was constantly sexually harassed by male colleagues during the 20 years she was on the force. She said she was diagnosed with post-traumatic stress disorder in 2004 after being sexually harassed by colleagues for all those years. Carle applied for a medical discharge from the force in 2009 due to stress. She started with the RCMP in Alberta in 1991. Pornography was placed inside her desk and she endured sexual jokes and inappropriate touching from male colleagues throughout her career. "There was an internal review and nothing ever came of it [the pornography]," she said. Once she formally complained her male colleagues shunned her. Raul Champ was a lawyer who had represented RCMP officers in similar cases. He said internal grievances were not adequately addressed in the force: "This process often takes years because the RCMP often does not treat complaints as a priority. Most complaints are dismissed out of hand, or dismissed with no remedy offered to the complainant, other than, 'We talked to him about it.'" At the end of September 2011, the RCMP was comprised of 20 percent women, 8 percent visible minorities, and 8 percent aboriginals.[90]

In another story about Galliford at this time it was reported she said she spent years being treated as a potential sexual plaything by some supervisors, being called "baby" and repeatedly propositioned. On one occasion a superior showed her his genitals and asked her if a mole on his penis was "cute." During the Air India investigation she said she was dragged along on pointless trips to Eastern Canada to meet with the families of victims. She said there was no news for the RCMP to impart to those people, but her superior used the road trips as an opportunity to try to have sex with her: "I was not prepared for the harassment in the workplace, I kept on waiting for it to end and it didn't end." RCMP officers were prevented by statute from organizing a union while most municipal police forces had a union. One of the most bizarre of the RCMP provisions was that the force had unlimited full-pay sick leave. Of the 6,000 Mounties in BC the RCMP said 225 members had been off the job for more than 30 days (the definition of when long-term sick leave began, after 30 consecutive days off sick). Of those 225 members, 48 were off for some form of workplace conflict (as opposed to being injured in the line of duty, for example). Mike Webster said he had several RCMP officers in a support group he ran who had been on such paid sick leave for four years. The record for longevity on the unlimited, full-pay sick roster in Canada was 13 years. The record for E-Division (British Columbia) was 11 years. Said Webster, "Females don't have anywhere to go, so they end up turning to a lawyer and they can't go back to the workplace because that's where the abuse took place, so what do they do, they flee into this unlimited sick time. This ridiculous thing that the RCMP has enshrined in the RCMP Act, where they have unlimited sick time." When asked if she would recommend any woman opt for a career in the RCMP Galliford remarked, "Don't even think about it. No. Run like your hair is on fire ... do not join the RCMP."[91]

At the start of 2012 it was reported that 94 current and former female members of the RCMP from every province had asked to join a class-action lawsuit against the force that was then being prepared.[92]

Around the same time the RCMP named a new commissioner for the force. Bob Paulson, at the end of January, outlined steps he had taken to address the problem. Testifying before a House of Commons committee he said he had centralized oversight of all harassment complaints in Ottawa to ensure they were dealt with in a timely fashion. He had met with his deputy commissioners and commanding officers to discuss how to better manage discipline and noted that a gender-based audit of the workforce was then underway.[93]

By the summer of 2012 it was reported that nearly 150 female RCMP officers across Canada had retained legal counsel to pursue civil claims against the force for sexual harassment — certification by the courts of the class-action suit was still pending. Galliford had been on medical leave since 2007. She had been sworn in as an officer in 1991. In class-action suits, as part of settlements, plaintiffs were required to sign a document releasing the defendant from further liability, and an acknowledgment that the receipt of settlement monies did not constitute an admission of liability or wrongdoing on the part of the defendant. It was also standard practice that a release had to be signed that prohibited the plaintiffs from disclosing the details of the settlement. An alternative to class-action was lodging a complaint of sexual harassment with the Canadian Human Rights Commission. The RCMP, reportedly, pursued internal disciplinary proceedings against female RCMP officers who had reported harassment. After allegedly being coerced into sex with her supervisor, RCMP officer Susan Gastaldo complained to her supervisor's boss. Not only was her complaint ignored, but she was subjected to disciplinary proceedings for violating the RCMP's non-fraternization policy that prohibited members from having a sexual relationship with co-workers. While Gastaldo's supervisor was also cited for conduct unbecoming, Gastaldo was unsuccessful in convincing the disciplinary hearing members that she did not consent to sex. A civil suit was filed by Gastaldo against her harasser and the RCMP.[94]

By late in 2012 the federal government of Canada (on behalf of the RCMP) had begun to formally respond in court to some of the lawsuits then mounting up. In one of the several lawsuits filed by women the government filed a statement of defense denying the charges and suggesting the courts were not the appropriate venue to air such complaints. Karen Katz had launched a lawsuit in January 2012 alleging years of harassment and eventual sexual abuse by one of her colleagues when the pair worked for the RCMP in Vancouver. The statement of defense said Katz should have filed a grievance under the RCMP's formal grievance process rather than by filing a lawsuit. If the plaintiff was dissatisfied with any administrative decisions by RCMP officers (during the initial and informal step) she was obliged to grieve formally. By this time Galliford had also initiated a civil suit, as the sole plaintiff. The federal government filed a statement of defense in her case, in July 2012, denying all her allegations and casting her as an alcoholic who refused treatment and who rejected the RCMP's efforts to keep her away from one of the men she alleged harassed her.[95]

Results of the internal gender-based audit of the RCMP's workforce in November 2012 revealed, said a report, a "clear unassailable" bias against the promotion of women in the upper ranks.[96]

When researcher Jennifer Brown looked at women in policing on a more global scale, in 1997, she observed that countries varied in the dates when they admitted women into the police "but the opposition to their admission was almost universal. The role of women in policing was to be an extension of the domestic sphere and organizationally they were to be kept within separate lines of management." The first policewoman employed in the Dutch police in 1911 followed pressure from women's groups because of changes in the law concerning sexual offenses and the increasing number of prostitutes. It was the Polish Committee for the Suppression of Traffic in Women and Children's representations to the government that was instrumental in the formation of the Polish Women's Police Brigade in 1925. Opposition to women officers came from male police officers as well as from some sections of the public. Sweden, Britain, Netherlands, Germany, Norway, and France all saw women's entry into the police occur between 1904 and 1913. Denmark admitted women in 1917, Finland 1926, Hungary and Belgium 1944 and 1945, Portugal 1957, Ireland 1960, Spain 1978, Austria and Luxembourg 1983. At the time Brown did her study the percentage of female officers ranged from a high in the 12 percent to 14 percent range (in Sweden, Britain, and the Netherlands) down to 1 percent in Spain and in Austria. Sexual harassment of women officers by policemen had been established, reported Brown, to be present in some degree (at least 20 percent of the women) in the Belgian and Danish police. In studies of Dutch and English police, respectively, were found high levels of harassment reported by nine out of 10 policewomen in their national samples. One speculation was, said Brown, that as the numbers of policewomen rose beyond a token presence, but before they achieved a critical mass of about 20 percent to 25 percent, levels of harassment were predicted to increase. The European Network of Policewomen was founded in 1989 with the aim of "optimizing the position of women in the European police services." When Brown was writing there were 1,200 members in the organization.[97]

A study published in 2009 revealed that in the United States federal government workplace 44 percent of women and 19 percent of men were confronted with sexual harassment in a two-year period (around 1995). In workplaces in the European Union approximately 33 to 50 percent of women and 10 percent of men experienced sexual harassment (1999). A survey among serving policewomen from 35 countries revealed that 77 percent experienced sexual harassment from their male colleagues.[98]

Conclusion

The history of policewomen shows the importance of grassroots organizing and lobbying by groups to initiate changes in the law enforcement system. The major modifications in policing took place in the very early part of this century and again in the very late 1960s through the 1970s. During both of those periods there was a very active and vocal feminist movement. Once can also see the limitations of such agitation. Without an active involvement from a sympathetic government, any gains made are likely to be restricted and limited. Early policewomen were employed in limited roles and numbers as the U.S. government took no part then. Those women wanted no more than a limited and token role and would have been appalled at any suggestion they seek anything amounting to parity; in fact, such a movement would have been rigorously opposed by females as well as males. Early policewomen achieved their goals in spite of considerable opposition, precisely because they were modest aspirations. Even with a modest agenda the male police establishment often threw up considerable opposition. Pioneer policewomen almost always wanted more female police hired, but apart from that, they were satisfied. The other major point of contention was whether women should be organized into their own division under female command or integrated into the force under male command. Overwhelmingly, the women wanted their own bureau, since only then could they be assured they would be able to perform the functions they had determined for themselves. They sought this, knowing that in a fully integrated force they were more at the mercy of a hostile male hierarchy — which could limit them further or reduce them to matron-only duties or typing and filing. Discrimination and harassment of these women must have been rampant, although it was not mentioned much in writings of the period. Sexual harassment did not "exist" in that era; instead, women were "insulted." Books by pioneer policewomen rarely mention the discrimination they faced, while account from periodicals of the day sometimes did.

Individual women fought their own battles in these periods and in the time frame between them — a particularly lonely time. Brave women who, for example, tried over and over to get promoted, never giving up no matter how often they were rejected and discriminatorily denied. Women pioneers on general patrol in the late 1960s and early 1970s were observed and rated by often hostile and hateful males, yet they almost always distinguished themselves.

During the second period, involvement of the U.S. government was crucial to aiding women in their move toward full equality in policing. No matter how hard and long and loud women agitated for reform, there were many, many forces that would not budge an inch. LAPD is but one example, being among the last to drop the height standard. It took federal government involvement to strike down such discriminatory and nonsensical standards, and it took federal government involvement through lawsuits, orders, consent decrees, and affirmative action plans to compel forces to take a certain minimum percentage of women into each new class of recruits. Some cities did these things on their own, but only because they saw what was happening in other cities under court compulsion — to they were being practical and pragmatic. This modern period of the history of policewomen has been marked by a continuing hostile male police establishment. Policewomen are subjected to enormous harassment of all kinds and discriminatory practices— not from suspects on the streets but from their own peers and commanders. There is little to suggest policewomen are more accepted today by their departments than they were in the early 1970s. In fact, there is much to suggest they are not. While many areas remained under various court orders and consent decrees to hire certain percentages of female police, the whole affirmative action concept fell into disuse and disrepute, in large part due to the propaganda machine of right-wing U.S. administrations starting in 1981 and beyond. Because of this, the percentage of policewomen is likely to stall where it is. Unsympathetic courts make the systematic enforcement of old orders more problematic, while new ones are less likely. Even through to 2012 the incidents of discrimination and harassment against policewomen remained unabated.

Policewomen should be recruited in greater numbers simply on the basis of fairness, justice, and equality. If that is not sufficient reason then they should be recruited on the basis of economics. Policewomen are more cost effective than policemen. They do not involve their employers in costly excessive force settlements. They do not involve their employers in costly harassment settlements initiated by citizens and policewomen. We need more policewomen, not fewer.

Chapter Notes

Chapter 1

1. M. Herman, *Prisoners' Rights Sourcebook*, p. 21.

2. "A Woman's Prison," *The New Northwest* [Portland, Oregon], August 8, 1878; "Making a Prison Cheerful," *Daily Globe* [St. Paul, Minn.], March 24, 1878.

3. "The Tombs," *New York Times*, January 16, 1870, p. 3; Katharine Bemet Davis, "The Police Woman," p. 14; Lois Higgins, "*Historical Background of Policewomen's Service*," p. 822; and No Title, *Western Reserve Chronicle* [Warren, Ohio], September 7, 1870.

4. "Police Matrons" *Harper's Weekly*, p. 675; Alice Fleming, New on the Beat, p. 14; "A Needed Police Reform," *New York Times*, March 23, 1890, p. 20; "City Policewomen to Wear Uniforms," *New York Times*, January 14, 1935, p. 17; "Nellie Bly," *The Norfolk Virginian*, April 11, 1895.

5. Higgins, "*Historical Background of Policewomen's Service*," pp. 822–23; "A Needed Police Reform," and "Police Matrons," *St. Paul Daily Globe*, August 7, 1887.

6. Higgins, "*Historical Background of Policewomen's Service*," pp. 822–23; and Elmer D. Graper, *American Police Administration*, pp. 268–269.

7. "A Needed Police Reform," p. 20; "World's Fair Notes, *Los Angeles Herald*, July 1, 1890; and "Police Matron Many Years," *The Jackson Herald* [Mo.] May 5, 1904.

8. *Ibid.*, and "Adjourned Sine Die," *St. Paul Daily Globe*, July 22, 1886.

9. "A Needed Police Reform"; "Station-House Matrons," *New York Times*, March 3, 1882, p. 3; "Police Matrons Wanted," *The Sun* (NY, NY), March 3, 1882; and "Captains Opposed to Police Matrons," *New York Tribune*, February 10, 1883.

10. No title, *The Sun* (NY, NY), May 5, 1882; and No title, *Sacramento Daily Union*, May 17, 1882.

11. "For the Ladies," *The Forest Republican* [Tionesta, Pa.], June 28, 1882; "A Girl Burglar's Sentence," *The Sun* (NY, NY) July 15, 1882; and "Brooklyn Police Matrons," *The Sun* [NY, NY], July 11, 1887.

12. No title, *Sausalito News*, May 3, 1888; and "Matrons in Police Stations," *New York Tribune*, May 30, 1888.

13. No title, *New York Tribune*, May 30, 1888; No title, *Omaha Daily Bee*, June 5, 1888; and "A Population Puzzle," *Daily Alta California*, June 6, 1888.

14. No title, *New York Tribune*, October 23, 1888; and "Why women may win." Pittsburgh *Dispatch*, November 1, 1889.

15. "A result hard to reach," *New York Times*, December 10, 1889, p. 8; and "Police Matrons," *The Sun* [NY, NY], August 2, 1890.

16. "A Needed Police Reform," *New York Times*, March 23, 1890.

17. "Police Matrons," *New York Times*, August 3, 1890, p. 4; and "Police Matrons at Last," *The Evening World* [NY, NY], March 21, 1891,

18. "No Police Matrons Yet," *New York Times*, August 13, 1890, p. 8.

19. "Police Matrons," *Harper's Weekly*, p. 675.

20. "Police Matrons," *New York Times*, October 1, 1890, p. 4; and "Police Matrons Needed," *New York Times*, December 25, 1890, p. 8.

21. "Police Matrons," *The Sun* [NY, NY], December 28, 1890.

22. "The Question of Police Matrons," *The Sun* [NY, NY], December 29, 1890.

23. "Want to be Police Matrons," *New York Times*, May 21, 1891, p. 10; "Police Matrons Begin Work," *New York Times*, October 6, 1891,

p. 9; "Matrons May Not Be Matrons," *New York Times*, June 29, 1899, p, 3; "Brooklyn Police Matrons," *The Evening World* [NY, NY], March 13, 1892; and "Wish to be Police Matrons," *The Evening World* [NY, NY], May 20, 1891.

24. "City and Suburban News," *New York Times*, October 24, 1891, p. 3.

25. No title, *Albuquerque Daily Citizen*, April 7, 1899; and "Police Matrons in New Uniforms," *New York Tribune*, October 17, 1899.

26. "Ladies of Temperance," *St. Paul Daily Globe*, July 31, 1886.

27. "Additional Minneapolis News," *St. Paul Daily Globe*, March 8, 1887.

28. "The Police Matron's Work," *St. Paul Daily Globe*, June 26, 1888; and "Minneapolis Globules," *St. Paul Daily Globe*, July 24, 1888.

29. "Seeing how it is oneself," *St. Paul Daily Globe*, March 17, 1889.

30. "The Matron on Duty," *St. Paul Daily Globe*, March 23, 1890.

31. "And now the Matron," *St. Paul Daily Globe*, October 29, 1891.

32. "No police Matrons," *National Republican* [Wash., D.C.], February 5, 1888; and "Police," *Evening Star* [Wash., D.C.], November 30, 1889.

33. "Police Commission," *Los Angeles Daily Herald*, August 2, 1888; "Low-down Journalism," *Los Angeles Daily Herald*, August 31, 1888; and "Prison Notes," *Los Angeles Herald*, November 28, 1895.

34. "Ordinance No. 123," *Los Angeles Daily Herald*, June 10, 1889.

35. "Police Matrons on Duty," Pittsburgh Dispatch, June 3, 1899; "Money for Matrons," Pittsburgh Dispatch, December 10, 1889.

36. "Quite natural," *The Carbon Advocate* [Leighton, Pa.], July 13, 1889; and "In the World of Women," *Evening Capital Journal* [Salem, Oregon], April 28, 1890.

37. "Woman's World," *Los Angeles Herald*, December 31, 1893; and "15-year Police Matron," *Kansas City Journal* [Mo.], January 2, 1898.

38. "Concerned for their Sex," *Los Angeles Herald*, February 15, 1894.

39. "Cleveland Women Win," *Los Angeles Herald*, April 22, 1894.

40. "That Matron Matter," *Fort Worth Gazette*, February 12, 1895.

41. "The Army in the West," *Los Angeles Herald*, January 18, 1896.

42. "Will begin today," *Kansas City Journal* [Mo.], February 5, 1896; and "Out of a God Job," *Kansas City Daily Journal* [Mo.], July 3, 1896.

43. "Matrons at the City Jail," *Omaha Daily Bee*, September 12, 1900.

44. "History of the Police Matron," *The Evening World* [NY, NY], October 22, 1892.

45. "Mrs. Sarah B. Schaeffer," *The Minneapolis Journal*, January 16, 1901.

46. "Russell Sage Police Matron's Friend," *New York Tribune*, March 21, 1901.

47. "Police Report," *The Courier* [Lincoln, Neb.], May 11, 1901.

48. Modeste H. Jordan. "Twenty-four hours with the Police Matron in the St. Louis Four Courts," *The St. Louis Republican*, January 26, 1902, magazine section.

49. "How women prisoners fare at the Central Station," *The Saint Paul Globe*, March 30, 1902.

50. "Life of Police Matrons," *New York Tribune*, May 13, 1904.

51. "Police Matrons Divide Work," *Los Angeles Herald*, July 30, 1906.

52. "Work of a Police Matron," *Omaha Daily Bee*, September 26, 1909.

53. *Ibid.*

54. *Ibid.*

55. "Woman Policeman is favored by Commission," *Los Angeles Herald*, June 14, 1910; "Salary Increase Made," *San Francisco Call*, December 6, 1910; "Answers to Queries," *San Francisco Call*, August 2, 1910; and "New Honors for Women," *San Francisco Call*, September 17, 1911.

56. "To awaken an Interest," *Los Angeles Herald*, January 19, 1896.

57. Elmer D. Graper, *American Police Administration*, New York: Macmillan, 1921, pp. 268–269.

Chapter 2

1. No title, *The Anderson Intelligencer*, [Anderson, SC], June 23, 1881.

2. "Policewomen," *New York Times*, March 31, 1880, p. 4.

3. Alice Fleming, *New on the Beat*, New York: Coward, McCann and Geoghegan, 1975, p. 20.

4. No title, *Daily Alta California*, March 15, 1886.

5. No title, *St. Paul Daily Globe*, April 14, 1887.

6. "The Female Police Officer," *St. Paul Daily Globe*, September 18, 1887.

7. "Lily Pines for a Billy," *The Washington Times* [D.C.], November 21, 1894.

8. "A Police Woman in Prospect," *The Washington Times* [D.C.], November 21, 1894.

9. "Women back the Widow," *The Washington Times* [D.C.], November 22, 1894.

10. "Chances for a policewoman," *The Washington Times* [D.C.], November 25, 1894.

11. "Lily visits the Police Court," *The Washington Times* [D.C.], December 4, 1894.

12. "Lily won't wield a Billy," *The Washington Times* [D.C.], January 25, 1895.

13. "Woman's World," *Los Angeles Herald*, February 2, 1895.

14. "Reform Forces Combine," *Washington Times* [D.C.], December 5, 1894.

15. "Female Police!" (Ad) *Kansas City Journal* [Mo.], May 8, 1895.

16. "She Would Wear a Star," *Kansas City Journal* [Mo.], November 21, 1897.

17. "Women as Policemen," *The Salt Lake Herald*, November 23, 1897.

18. "A Woman's College in the Bible," *The Courier* [Lincoln, Nebraska], August 18, 1900.

19. "Norfolk to have a Female Police Officer," *The Times* [Richmond, Va.], December 5, 1902.

20. "Women Police Wanted by Matrons of New York Society," *The San Francisco Call*, April 4, 1905.

21. "Wants Women on the Force," *The Sun* [NY, NY], March 7, 1906.

22. "Lady Cops to Tell Men to G'Wan Now!" *The Evening World* [NY, NY], March 8, 1906.

23. "Women Cops if she has her way," *The Minneapolis Journal*, May 7, 1906.

24. "The Policewoman," *The Seattle Star*, May 16, 1906.

25. "Want women to serve as Police." *The Maui News* [Hi.], May 26, 1906.

26. Owen Langdon, "If there were Women Police," *The Rising Son* [Kansas City, Mo.], May 31, 1906.

27. "Policewomen of Bayonne," *The Sun* [NY, NY], March 31, 1907; "She Still Insists on Policewomen," *New York Times*, March 31, 1907, pt. 2, p. 11.

28. "She wants to be a Policewoman," *Richmond Planet* [Va.], December 5, 1908.

29. Ethel Lloyd Patterson. "Policewoman would Prevent Race Suicide," *The Evening World* [NY, NY], February 3, 1909.

30. "Women Police to Patrol Parks and 'Teach' Youths," *Los Angeles Herald*, April 7, 1909.

31. "Her weak point," *The Salt Lake Tribune*, May 10, 1906; and Ad. *Alexandria Gazette* [Virginia], January 13, 1909.

32. "Toledo to have Women Police," *Bisbee Daily Review*, April 21, 1907.

33. "The Policewoman." *Los Angeles Herald*, February 21, 1908.

34. "A Fair Force," *The Jasper News* [Mo.], April 2, 1908.

35. "For Policewomen." *New York Tribune*, September 26, 1908.

36. Higgins, "Historical...," op. cit., p. 823.

37. "Wives and mothers," *Los Angeles Herald*, March 13, 1909.

38. "Conservation," *Los Angeles Herald*, May 25, 1910.

39. No title, *The Roanoke Daily Times* [Va.], September 4, 1896.

40. "The First Policewoman," *The Los Angeles Herald*, September 20, 1896.

41. "A Constable in Petticoats," *The Hocking Sentinel* [Logan, Ohio], August 19, 1897.

42. "A Woman Constable," *The Guthrie Daily Leader* [Ok.], August 1, 1897.

43. "She Wears a Star," *The Broad Ax* [Salt Lake City], May 9, 1899.

44. "A Honolulu Belle," *Crittenden Press* [Marion, Ky.], August 10, 1899.

45. No title, *Austin's Hawaiian Weekly* [Honolulu], October 21, 1899.

46. "Her many duties," *New York Tribune*, June 17, 1901.

47. "Woman Police Sergeant," *Willmar Tribune* [Minnesota], July 17, 1901.

48. "Portland has a Lady Cop," *The Spokane Press* [Washington], January 14, 1907.

49. "America's First Policewoman Sports Dainty Kerchief Instead of Club," *Seattle Star*, December 7, 1907.

50. "Policewoman," *Los Angeles Herald*, January 20, 1909; and "Girl Threatens Suit for Breach of Promise," *Los Angeles Herald*, February 4, 1909.

51. "Woman in Chicago to do Police Duty," *Los Angeles Herald*, May 13, 1909; and "What Some Women are Doing," *San Francisco Call*, August 7, 1909.

52. "Some supervision of Baby Farms is Public Necessity," *The Seattle Star*, September 25, 1909; and "Many Girls Robbed, says Seattle's Policewoman," *The Seattle Star*, December 28, 1909.

53. "Engage in Many Lines of Work," *Los Angeles Herald*, July 17, 1909.

54. "Western Women as Police Officer," *Survey* 29 (December 21, 1912): 345–47; and Lois Higgins. Historical Background of Policewomen's Service," *Journal of Criminal Law and Criminology* 41 (March/April 1951): 822–833.

55. "Woman Made a Detective," *New York Times*, March 2, 1912, p.5; and "The First Mu-

nicipal Woman Detective in the World," *New York Times*, March 3, 1912, sec, 5, p. 1.
56. *Ibid.*

Chapter 3

1. Maud Darwin, "Policewomen: Their Work in America," *The Nineteenth Century and After* 75 (June 1914): p. 1372; and Lois Higgins, "The Policewoman," *Police* 3 (Nov/Dec 1958): 66; and Albert R. Roberts, "Police Social Workers: A History," *Social Work* 21 (July 1976): 295; and "Policewomen for Honolulu," *Honolulu Star-Bulletin*, December 9, 1912.
2. "Prison Reform Worker Scores Methods of Los Angeles Police," *Los Angeles Herald*, February 11, 1910; and "Criminal Lawyer says Police Usurp Their Powers," *Los Angeles Herald*, February 16, 1910.
3. "Around Town," *Los Angeles Herald*, March 15, 1910; and "Prison Reformer Busy," *Los Angeles Herald*, April 30, 1910.
4. "Urge Appointment of Woman Officer," *Los Angeles Herald*, June 9, 1910.
5. "Woman Policeman is Favored by Commission," *Los Angeles Herald*, June 14, 1910.
6. Lois Higgins, "Historical Background of Policewomen's Service," *Journal of Criminal Law and Criminology* 41 (March/April 1951): 825.
7. Bertha H. Smith, "The Policewoman," *Good Housekeeping* 52 (March 1911): 296; and Lois Higgins, "Historical...." op. cit., p. 824; and "Los Angeles Secures First Policewoman," *Los Angeles Herald*, September 14, 1910.
8. Bertha H. Smith, op. cit., pp. 296–298.
9. "First Woman Policeman," *Los Angeles Times*, September 13, 1910, pt. 2, p. 9; and "First Police Woman is on Their Trail," *Los Angeles Times*, September 14, 1910, pt. 2, p. 1; and "New Police Officer Assumes her Duties," *Los Angeles Herald*, September 14, 1910.
10. "Help is Sought by Policewoman," *Los Angeles Herald*, October 30, 1910.
11. Alice Stebbins Wells, "Women on the Police Force," *American City* 8 (April 1913): 401; and Los Higgins, "Historical..." op. cit., p. 824.
12. Maud Darwin, op. cit., p. 1372; Lois Higgins, "Historical..." op. cit., p. 825; and "Western Women as Police Officers," *Survey* 29 (December 21, 1912): 346.
13. August Vollmer, "Meet the Lady Cop," *Survey* 63 (March 15, 1930): 702.
14. Wikipedia, accessed online November 5, 2012.
15. "Current Comment," *The Seattle Republican*, March 11, 1910.

16. "Work of the Policewomen of Chicago," *The Red Cloud Chief* [Red Cloud, Nebraska], September 1, 1910.
17. "Policewoman is a Sphinx." *The Jackson Herald* [Wyoming], August 18, 1910.
18. "Better be good or maybe policewoman will get you," *Omaha Daily Bee*, May 6, 1911.
19. "Chicago's Policewoman," *New York Tribune*, October 29, 1911.
20. "New York's First Policewoman," *Valentine Democrat* [Valentine, Nebraska], February 1, 1912.
21. "Athletic Woman is a Deputy Constable," *San Francisco Call*, April 27, 1912.
22. "Sacramento may have Policewoman," *San Francisco Call*, March 14, 1910.
23. "Would Teach Girls Self-Defense Art," *The Washington Times* [D.C.], July 11, 1910.
24. "No Maryland Women Police," *New York Tribune*, July 12, 1910.
25. "Fight White Slave Trade," *Bemidji Daily Pioneer* [Minnesota], January 26, 1911.
26. Anna Howard Shaw, "We need Women Police if Proper Protection is Expected," *Nassau County Leader*, March 2, 1911.
27. "Wants Women on Police," *New York Times*, July 23, 1909, p. 1; and "To 'Mother' the Criminal," *New York Times*, July 24, 1909, p. 6.
28. "She'd Have Women Police," *New York Times*, January 25, 1911, p. 7.
29. "Boston Police Force is Weak," *The Evening Standard* [Ogden City, Utah], May 3, 1911.
30. "Women's Interests, *The Seattle Republican*, February 3, 1911.
31. Nixola Greeley-Smith, "Holds the Mirror up to Women," *The Evening World* [NY, NY], May 4, 1911.
32. "Why not Women Police," *The Tacoma Times*, April 29, 1911.
33. "The Lady and her Star," *The Bee* [Earlington, Kentucky], August 29, 1911; and "Woman Policeman Gives Views on Duty of Society," *The Arizona Republican*, September 3, 1911.
34. "Woman on Police Force," *Sausalito News*, September 2, 1911.
35. "Police Woman to Cover State on Lecture Tour," *San Francisco Call*, February 20, 1912.
36. "Man Loses his Vocational Monopolies," *San Francisco Call*, March 3, 1912.
37. "Policewoman has Advice for Girls," *San Francisco Call*, March 19, 1912.
38. "Policewomen Requested," *San Francisco Call*, April 27, 1912.
39. "Women Police Officers Needed in City, says Mrs. Alice S. Wells," *San Francisco Call*,

March 21, 1912; and "Y.W.C.A. holds Vesper Service," *San Francisco Call*, June 30, 1912.

40. "Chicago, in Despair, May Try Police-woman," *San Francisco Call*, April 5, 1912.

41. "Seattle Gets Police Women," *San Francisco Call*, July 11, 1912.

42. "Policewoman is Appointed," *San Francisco Call*, August 18, 1912.

43. Owings, op. cit., pp. 124–25.

44. *Ibid.*, p. 144.

45. "Western Women as Police Officers," op. cit., p. 346.

46. "The Police-Woman is Marching On," op. cit., p. 403.

47. No title, *The Day Book* [Chicago], September 16, 1912; and "Police Woman Eschews Club," *San Francisco Call*, September 28, 1912.

48. "Policewomen in Conference," *San Francisco Call*, October 26, 1912; and "Officers Chosen by Policewomen," *San Francisco Call*, October 27, 1912.

49. "Social Reformers ask Women Police for Washington," *The Washington Times* [D.C.], November 12, 1912.

50. "Women Police and Their Work," *The Washington Times* [D.C.], November 17, 1912.

51. "Women Police in District will be urged by Woman," *The Washington Times* [D.C.], November 17, 1912.

52. "Policewomen in Quaker City," *New York Tribune*, November 21, 1912.

53. "Policewoman of Los Angeles Here," *San Francisco Call*, November 21, 1912; and "Policewomen Help in the Los Angeles Juvenile Work," *Omaha Daily Bee*, December 5, 1912.

54. "Policewomen for Honolulu," *Honolulu Star-Bulletin*, December 9, 1912.

55. "Women Police to Solve White Slave Problem," *The Evening World* [NY, NY], December 17, 1912.

56. "The First Policewoman," *The Sun* [NY, NY], December 19, 1912.

57. "Urges Policewomen on Every City Force," *New York Tribune*, December 19, 1912.

58. "Let Women do the Work," *San Francisco Call*, March 1, 1913.

59. "Mrs. Belmont Urges Need of Police-women," *New York Tribune*, March 6, 1913.

60. "Many More Women Want Women Police," *The Sun* [NY, NY], April 4, 1913.

61. "Patrol Women Will Walk Los Angeles Beats," *San Francisco Call*, April 29, 1913.

62. "Charter in Way of Policewoman," *San Francisco Call*, May 24, 1913.

63. No title, *The Tacoma Times*, May 6, 1913.

64. "Policewoman got Fired for Efficiency, but She's Back on the Job," *The Day Book* [Chicago], May 31, 1913.

65. Darwin, op. cit., p. 1375.

66. "Denver Court Reinstates Woman Police Officer," *El Paso Herald*, July 8, 1913; and "Denver's Policewoman quits," *New York Times*, August 6, 1913, p. 7.

67. "Women Police not Needed at Coney," *New York Tribune*, June 20, 1913.

68. "Policewoman's salary less than police-man's," *San Francisco Call*, June 22, 1913.

69. Marguerite Mooers Marshall, "First Policewoman's First Job is to Settle a Domestic Quarrel," *The Evening World* [NY, NY], June 23, 1913.

70. "Oakland Women May Wear Stars," *San Francisco Call*, June 27, 1913.

71. "Women Apply for Police Positions," *San Francisco Call*, June 28, 1913.

72. "Club Women to be not as of Old," *San Francisco Call*, June 30, 1913.

73. "Civil Service Board Wants Information," *San Francisco Call*, July 1, 1913; and "Macphee and Taylor Dismissed from Force," *San Francisco Call*, July 8, 1913.

74. "Women to Patrol Beach," *San Francisco Call*, July 8, 1913; "No Club for Policewoman," *New York Tribune*, July 10, 1913.

75. "Irish Opposes Oakland's Plan of Police-women," *San Francisco Call*, July 13, 1913.

76. Arthur J. Brinton, "Now we Have With Us the Lady Cop," *The Ogden Standard* [Utah], July 17, 1913.

77. "22 Women line up for jobs on Police Force," *San Francisco Call*, July 30, 1913.

78. "Asbury Park's First Policewoman on the Job." *The Day Book* [Chicago], August 2, 1913.

79. "Now we've got Policewomen on the Force," *The Day Book* [Chicago], August 2, 1913.

80. "Chicago's New Policewomen Start Work Today," *The Day Book* [Chicago], August 5, 1913.

81. "Policewoman Chases Masher," *San Francisco Call*, August 7, 1913.

82. "Chicago's Policewomen," *The Washington Herald* [D.C.], August 8, 1913.

83. "Tears cost policewoman case," San Francisco Call, August 9, 1913.

84. Darwin, op. cit., p. 1376; Owings, op. cit., pp. 130–131; and Roberts, op. cit., p. 295.

85. "Asks for Women Police," *New York Times*, July 8, 1913, p. 2; "Names Policewomen for Chicago," *New York Times*, August 2, 1913, p. 5; and "Detectives Show New Policewomen Tamest Chicago," *Chicago Tribune*, August 6, 1913, p. 1.

86. "The Police-Woman is Marching On," *American City* 9 (November 1913): 403.

87. "Chicago Rejoices in Policewomen," *New York Times*, August 6, 1913, p. 7.

88. *Ibid.*

89. "Policewomen in Chicago," *Literary Digest* 47 (August 23, 1913): 271.

90. "Told Annoyer to Beat It," *New York Times*, August 7, 1913, p. 1; and "Policewomen Make Arrest," *New York Times*, August 8, 1913, p. 1.

91. "Women Police Withdrawn," *New York Times*, March 4, 1914, p. 1.

92. "Policewomen to Wrestle," *New York Times*, March 8, 1914, sec. 3, p. 5.

93. Julia Murdock, "Sylvester Favors Women Policemen," *The Washington Times* [D.C.], August 8, 1913.

94. "Policewomen? No, Social Service Inspectors," *San Francisco Call*, August 8, 1913.

95. "Outline Qualifications for New Policewomen," *San Francisco Call*, August 14, 1913.

96. "Women Protective Officers," *San Francisco Call*, August 15, 1913.

97. "Policewomen to Await New Title," *San Francisco Call*, August 16, 1913.

98. "3 Policewomen will be appointed Monday," *San Francisco Call*, September 26, 1913; and "See Copper Watch Coppette; Watch Coppette Cop Jobette," *San Francisco Call*, September 29, 1913.

99. "Two Coppettes Named by Board; Pick Third Later," *San Francisco Call*, September 30, 1913; and "Stuffed Dummy? No," *San Francisco Call*, October 2, 1913.

100. Ad, *San Francisco Call*, October 2, 1913.

101. "America's Second Policewoman Tells of Her Job as a Copper," *The Ogden Standard* [Utah], October 11, 1913, magazine.

102. "Policewoman after Congress," *San Francisco Call*, October 29, 1913.

103. "Copettes sworn, but what they'll do Puzzles Chief," *San Francisco Call*, October 21, 1913.

104. Mary Ashe Miller, "Few thrills for Copettes," *San Francisco Call*, October 31, 1913; and "Coppettes to Watch Mrs. Mary Vaughn," *San Francisco Call*, November 1, 1913.

105. "Guard of Coppettes for Mrs. Pankhurst," *San Francisco Call*, November 1, 1913.

106. Mrs. H. J. Platts, "Mrs. H. J. Platts will devote much of time to City Probation Work in Alameda," *San Francisco Call*, November 25, 1913.

107. "Muscular Coppette drags Fighter off Car; Lands him in jail," *San Francisco Call*, December 26, 1913.

108. "Chief of Chicago's Policewomen," *Tensas Gazette* [St. Joseph, Louisiana], January 16, 1914.

109. "Suffragists tell Mayor they're ready to be Policewomen," *The Evening World* [NY, NY], January 29, 1914.

110. "Bill for New York Policewomen," *New York Times*, January 28, 1914, p. 1.

111. "Hear Officer Alice Wells," *New York Times*, March 12, 1914, p. 3; and "Kills Policewomen Bill," *New York Times*, March 14, 1914, p. 1.

112. "Want Policewomen on the City's Force," *New York Times*, October 28, 1916, p. 4.

113. "She's a Policewoman now," *The Appeal* [St. Paul, Minn.], January 31, 1914; and "Negro Woman on Seattle's Force," *The Kansas City Sun* [Mo.], February 14, 1914.

114. Nixola Greeley-Smith, "Says policewomen will rid streets of mashers who pester young girls," *The Day Book* [Chicago], February 10, 1914.

115. Jane Whitaker, "Policewomen prove little improvement over the brutal man coppers." *The Day Book* [Chicago], February 27, 1914.

116. "Policewomen can't handle disorderly persons of own sex," *Omaha Daily Bee*, March 5, 1914.

117. No title, *San Francisco Call*, March 14, 1914.

118. "Chicago Policewomen receiving instruction in shooting revolvers," *The Evening Herald* [NY, NY], March 23, 1914.

119. "Question: where do policewomen conceal pistols?" *The Evening World* [NY, NY], March 24, 1914.

120. "Premier Policewoman packs pistol in her handbag," *New York Tribune*, March 26, 1914.

121. David Edgar Rice, "Why Women would rather be arrested by men," *Omaha Daily Bee*, March 29, 1914, pt. 2.

122. "Policewomen can shoot straight," *The Ogden Standard* [Utah], April 8, 1914; and "Arming the Policewomen of Chicago," *Mountain Advocate* [Barbourville, Ky.], April 17, 1914.

123. Darwin, op. cit., p.1376.

124. "Jersey Policewoman Quits," *New York Times*, July 8, 1912, p. 20.

125. Owings, op. cit., pp. 136–37; and Sabina Marshall, "Development of the Policewoman's Movement in Cleveland, Ohio," *Journal of Social Hygiene* 11 (April 1925): 194–201.

126. "Week's events in brief paragraphs," *Sausalito News*, May 6, 1914.

127. "Tale of old Tahiti photoplay at Imperial," *San Francisco Call*, February 3, 1913; Internet Movie Database, accessed November 8, 1914; "Rip-roaring comedy," *Sausalito News*, October 17, 1914; and Ad, *Medford Mail Tribune* [Oregon], October 31, 1914.

128. "Diana Dillpickles," *The Tacoma Times* [Wash.], September 30, 1914; and "Impressionable," *Sausalito News*, January 2, 1915.

129. "City has policewoman who knows her business, *Evening Public Ledger* [Philadelphia], January 12, 1915.

130. "Against the Copettes," *The Day Book* [Chicago], January 16, 1915.

131. "Chicago copette with pistol puts end to riot," *Tensas Gazette* [St. Joseph, Louisiana], February 26, 1915.

132. "Bill for New York City policewomen," *New York Tribune*, April 4, 1915.

133. "Policewomen voted as joke on New York," *The Sun* [NY, NY], April 21, 1915.

134. Marguerite Mooers Marshall. "Enter the copperette to jolt Jersey violators of law with night stickette." The Evening World [NY, NY], March 6, 1915.

135. "Policewomen no longer a joke says officer," *The Evening Herald* [Albuquerque], May 18, 1915.

136. "America's first policewoman explains need of her profession," *The Washington Times* [D.C.], May 18, 1915.

137. "Policewomen fail to impress chiefs," *New York Tribune*, May 27, 1915.

138. Mrs. Marshall McLean, "New York one of the few big cities without policewomen," *The Sun* [NY, NY], May 30, 1915.

139. "Policewomen will bar all of modern dances," *The Washington Times* [D.C.], July 31, 1915; "Paterson's Policewoman," *The Evening Herald* [Klamath Falls, Oregon], August 12, 1915.

140. "First head of policewomen," *Tensas Gazette* [St. Joseph, Louisiana], August 6, 1915.

141. "City officials give opinions on the value of policewomen," *The Sun* [NY, NY], September 19, 1915.

142. "A Police-Woman's Record in Topeka," *Survey* 34 (September 25, 1915): 571

143. "You'd better make your eyes behave," *The Ogden Standard* [Utah], October 23, 1915.

144. Ruth Dunbar, "The solution of the girl question is in trade unionism, which teaches how to think, says a feminine bobby," *New York Tribune*, November 4, 1915.

145. "Views differ about a policewoman here," *University Missourian* [Columbia, Mo.], November 18, 1915.

146. "Policewoman captures minister," *El Paso Herald*, December 27, 1915.

147. "Big field for policewoman," *Hopkinsville Kentuckian*, February 1, 1916.

148. "Skirted coppers get 'em." *The Tacoma Times*, November 11, 1916.

149. "Commission government," *Sausalito News*, June 3, 1916.

150. Mary Sumner Boyd, "Women defenders in time of peace," *Honolulu Star-Bulletin*, July 3, 1917.

151. Roberts, op. cit., p. 295; and Darwin, op. cit., p. 1371

152. Louise de Koven Bowen, "Women Police," *Survey* 30 (April 12, 1913): 64.

153. "The Police-Woman is Marching On," *American City* 9 (November 1913): 403.

154. Valeria H. Parker, "A Policewoman's Life," *Woman Citizen* 9 (June 28, 1924): 16.

155. Hutzel, "The Policewoman," op. cit., p. 104; Roberts, op. cit., p. 295; and Elmer D. Graper, *American Police Administration*, New York: Macmillan, 1921, p. 228.

156. Darwin, op. cit., p. 1371.

157. "Western Women as Police Officers," *Survey* 29 (December 21, 1912): 345–46; and "Women Police Meet," *New York Times*, October 27, 1912, p. 1.

158. "Western Women as Police Officers," op. cit., p. 346.

159. Darwin, op. cit., p. 1375; Owings, op. cit., p. 38; and Higgins, "Historical..." op. cit., p. 827.

160. Helen D. Pigeon, "Policewomen in the United States," op. cit., p. 373.

161. Owings, op. cit., pp. 38, 191; Higgins, "Historical..." op. cit., p. 831; and Graper, op. cit., p. 233.

162. Owings, op. cit., pp. 105, 192–93.

163. Buwalda, op. cit., p. 290; and Horne, op. cit., p. 33.

Chapter 4

1. Robert Haldane, *The People's Force*, Melbourne, Australia: Melbourne University Press, 1986, pp. 162–63.

2. *Ibid.*, p. 163; and G. M. O'Brien, *The Australian Police Forces*, Melbourne, Australia: Oxford University Press, 1960, pp. 173–74.

3. Maud Darwin, "Policewomen: Their Work in America," *The Nineteenth Century and After* 75 (June 1914): 1377; Bonnie Reilly Schmidt, "Women on the Force," *Canada's History* 91, no. 4 (August/September) 2011;

John Mackie, "Pounding the Beat," *The Vancouver Sun*, June 25, 2012, p. D6; Jana G. Pruden, "100 years of women on the beat," *Calgary Herald*, September 29, 2012, p. A22.

4. John Carrier, *The Campaign for the Employment of Women as Police Officers*, Aldershot, England: Avebury, 1988, p. 2; and Darwin, op. cit., p. 1377.

5. Constance Tite, "Policewomen: Their Work in Germany," *The Nineteenth Century and After* 75 (June 1914): 1378–82; and Erika S. Fairchild, "Women police in Weimar," *Law and Society Review* 21, no. 3 (1987): 375–402.

6. Chloe Owings, *Women Police*, Montclair, NJ: Patterson Smith, 1969, p. 86, reprint of 1925 ed.

7. Darwin, op. cit., p. 1377.

8. Carrier, op. cit., p. 1.

9. Mary S. Allen, *The Pioneer Policewoman*, London: Chatto and Windus, 1925, pp. 8–9; Carrier, op. cit., pp. 3, 7; and Owings, op. cit., pp. 3–4, 6.

10. "The treatment of women at police stations," *The Times* (London), February 22, 1913, p. 8.

11. "Policewomen," *The Times* (London), March 30, 1914, p. 11.

12. "A woman police officer," *The Times* (London), June 20, 1914, p. 5.

13. "Police women," *The Times* (London), June 20, 1914, p. 5.

14. "Policewomen," *Journal of the American Institute of Criminal Law and Criminology* 5 (November 1914): 607–609.

15. "Women police service in England," *Survey* 38 (September 1, 1917): 491; H. M. Walbrook, "Women police and their work," *The Nineteenth Century and After* 85 (February 1919): 377: and Carrier, op.cit., p. 7.

16. Allen, op. cit., pp. 11–12; Carrier, op. cit., pp. 11–14; and Louise Creighton, "Women police," *Fortnightly Review* 114 (July 1920): 109–110.

17. Carrier, op. cit., p. 12.

18. Walbrook, op. cit., pp. 378–382.

19. Carrier, op. cit., pp. 19, 24, 28, 46–47; Creighton, op. cit., pp. 110–12; and Owings, op. cit., pp. 23–24.

20. Carrier, op. cit., pp. 24–26, 44.

21. "Women's war work," *The Times* (London), May 21, 1915, p. 5; and "The women police," *The Times* (London), April 17, 1917, p. 9.

22. Carrier, op. cit., p. 10; Owings, op. cit., pp. 10–11; and Allen, op. cit., pp. 12–13.

23. Allen, op. cit., p. 14; and Owings, op. cit., p. 11.

24. Allen, op. cit., pp. 27, 30, 32–33; and Owings, op. cit., p. 12.

25. Owings, op. cit., p. 13.

26. Allen, op. cit., p. 15; and Owings, op. cit., p. 13.

27. Carrier, op. cit., pp. 19, 30; and "Brighton women police," *The Times* (London), March 27, 1915, p. 5.

28. Carrier, op. cit., p. 15; and "The Policewoman," *The Times* (London), October 11, 1916, p. 10.

29. Allen, op. cit., pp. 18–22, 41.

30. *Ibid.*, pp. 42, 46–49.

31. *Ibid.*, pp. 58, 60–62, 71–73.

32. *Ibid.*, p. 81.

33. *Ibid.*, pp. 84–85, 95.

34. "Women police service in England," *Survey* 38 (September 1, 1917): 491.

Chapter 5

1. Chloe Owings, *Women Police*, Montclair, NJ: Patterson Smith, 1969, reprint of 1925 ed., p. 119; and Eleonore L. Hutzel, "The Policewoman," *Annals of the American Academy of Political and Social Science* 146 (November 1929): 105.

2. Owings, op. cit., pp. 121–122; Hutzel, "The Policewoman," op. cit., p. 105.

3. Hutzel, "The Policewoman," op. cit., 105.

4. Owings, op. cit., p. 256.

5. *Ibid.*, pp. 285–287; and Frances Drewry McMullen, "The Policewoman's Beat," *The Woman's Journal* 14 (March 1929): 8–9.

6. "The Policewomen of Indianapolis and their new Methods," *Literary Digest* 69 (April 23, 1921): 41–43; and Mina Van Winkle, "The Policewoman," *Survey* 52 (September 15, 1924): 630.

7. Owings, op. cit., 125–29; "She quits Boston Police," *New York Times*, February 1, 1922, p. 19; and Van Winkle, "The Policewoman," op. cit., p. 630.

8. John A. Brandenburger, "Effective Work of Policewomen," *American City* 28 (March 1923): 259; and Owings, op. cit., pp. 168–70.

9. Owings, op. cit., pp. 131–32.

10. *Ibid.*, pp. 138–43.

11. *Ibid.*, p. 167.

12. *Ibid.*, pp. 145–47.

13. "Women Police of Detroit," *New York Times*, March 13, 1921, sec. 9, p. 4.

14. Hutzel, "The Policewoman," op. cit., pp. 107, 111.

15. "Ossining Hires a Policewoman," *New York Times*, September 20, 1917, p. 4.

16. "Boardwalk 'copess' to watch for winks," *Evening Public Ledger* [Philadelphia], May 18, 1917.

17. "Palmist wrong; arrested," *The Washington Times*, May 30, 1917.

18. "Flirts with policewoman; cured? We should cackle!" *The Washington Herald*, May 19, 1917.

19. Marguerite Mooers Marshall, "Policewomen for New York to replace war-called men the latest patriotic effort." *The Evening World* [NY,NY], June 12, 1917.

20. Nixola Greeley-Smith, "Says New York needs many like her to protect girls and rebuff maskers." *The Evening World* [NY, NY], June 14, 1917.

21. "Policewomen necessary in well regulated community," *El Paso Herald*, July 1917.

22. Bill Price, "More women to aid police in need here, appeal says," *The Washington Times*, October 12, 1917.

23. "Mothers of girls told of dangers by policewoman," *The Washington Times*, October 14, 1917.

24. "Heads policewomen," *Tensas Gazette* [St. Joseph, Louisiana], November 23, 1917.

25. "12 armed women soon to be added to police force," *New York Tribune*, May 21, 1918.

26. "First D. C. policewoman tells of her spy hunt," *The Washington Times*, July 23, 1918.

27. "New policewomen here do not awe *Herald*'s reporter a bit," *The Evening Herald* [Albuquerque], August 8, 1918.

28. "Items of interest," *Dakota County Herald* [Dakota City, Nebraska], September 12, 1918.

29. "Don't call a cop; El Paso has new copette on job." *El Paso Herald*, March 24, 1919.

30. "Fair officer now bosses traffic on District's streets," *The Washington Times* [D.C.], November 1, 1918.

31. "Thirty policewomen for Washington," *The Broad Ax* [Salt Lake City], December 28, 1918.

32. "Woman cop at Union Station watches for fair flirters," *The Washington Herald*, May 4, 1919.

33. Hannah Mitchell, "Lady cops in Washington are efficient," *New York Tribune*, May 4, 1919.

34. "Mrs. Herbert H. Votaw," *New York Tribune*, May 4, 1919.

35. "These are the policewomen of the national capitol," *New York Tribune*, September 7, 1919.

36. Owings, op. cit., pp. 176–87.

37. Alice Ward Smith, "Colored Policewomen of Washington," *Southern Workman* 51 (March 1922): 136; and "Fix Policewomen's Dress," *New York Times*, September 18, 1923, p. 9.

38. Albert R. Roberts, "Police Social Workers: A History," *Social Work* 21 (July 1976): 295.

39. Mina Van Winkle, "Municipal Policewomen…" op. cit., pp. 93–94.

40. Owings, op. cit., pp. x, xi.

41. Helen D. Pigeon, "Senate Bill 1750," *Woman Citizen* 10 (February 1926): 30; and Helen D. Pigeon, "The Policewoman's Due," *Woman Citizen* 11 (August 1926): 33.

42. Owings, op. cit., pp. 156–57.

43. "Women to Sweep New York Streets," *New York Times*, August 18, 1918, p. 3.

44. "Widow is named a Police Deputy," *New York Times*, January 29, 1918, pp. 1, 11.

45. "Women's Auxiliary for Police Reserve," *New York Times*, May 10, 1918, p. 11.

46. "Brooklyn Women in Police Reserve," *New York Times*, May 30, 1918, p. 9; and "Duties of Women Police, *New York Times*, July 28, 1918, sec. 3, p. 3.

47. "Will add 12 Women to Regular Police," *New York Times*, May 21, 1918, p. 24; and "Six Policewomen put on the Force," *New York Times*, August 16, 1918, p. 16.

48. "Policewomen for New York," *The North Platte Semi-Weekly* [Nebraska], August 23, 1918.

49. "Six policewomen just appointed are to be armed," *New York Tribune*, August 18, 1918.

50. "Four new policewomen appointed to city force," *New York Tribune*, August 30, 1918.

51. Elene Foster. On the beat with a lady cop," *New York Tribune*, September 22, 1918.

52. "Ten new policewomen appointed by Enright," *New York Tribune*, May 28, 1919.

53. Ellen O'Grady. "Experience endorses our police women," *New York Tribune*, September 7, 1919.

54. "She-cop marries fellow detective," *The Washington Times* [D.C.], September 18, 1919.

55. "Women police reserves well trained now to meet any emergency city may face," *The Sun* [NY, NY], September 8, 1918.

56. "How New York's policewomen spot the German spies," *The Washington Times*, September 15, 1918 American Week Section.

57. Felicia Shpritzer, op. cit., p. 57; Mary E. Hamilton, *The Policewoman: Her Service and Ideals*, New York: Frederick A. Stokes, 1924, pp. 20–21; and Van Winkle, "The Policewoman," p. 629.

58. O'Grady, op. cit., p. 60.

59. Owings, op. cit., p. 229.

60. "Women's Precinct needs are shown," *New York Times*, May 8, 1921, sec 2, p. 6; and Mary Hamilton, Op. cit., pp. 58–61.

61. *Ibid.*; and Carol Bird, "Policewomen's School," *New York Times*, July 31, 1921, sec. 7, p. 3.

62. "Petition Enright to appoint 15 Women on Police Force," *New York Times*, August 14, 1923, p. 1; and "Enright advises Women," *New York Times*, November 10, 1922, p. 19.

63. "To Head Women Police," *New York Times*, March 13, 1924, p. 28; and "Women Police grapple with the Masher Evil," *New York Times*, March 23, 1924, sec. 9, p. 11.

64. "He Hugged a Policewoman," *New York Times*, May 1, 1925, p. 11.

65. "Bureau for Policewomen," *New York Times*, November 2, 1924, p. 25.

66. "Trainer of Policewomen in New York to get Ideas," *New York Times*, April 27, 1924, sec. 9, p. 11.

67. "A 'Mother' of disillusioned Girls in New York City," *Literary Digest* 80 (March 15, 1924): 56, 58; and Bird, op. cit., p. 3.

68. Mary Hamilton, "The Policewoman..." op. cit., pp. 4, 5, 7.

69. *Ibid.*, pp. 7–11, 35.

70. *Ibid.*, pp. 58–61.

71. *Ibid.*, pp. 69, 72, 179, 181, 183, 199.

72. "100 More Policewomen asked in a Campaign Covering City," *New York Times*, March 3, 1925, p. 21; "100 More Policewomen advocated for City," *New York Times*, April 29, 1925, p. 6; and "Enright's Last Acts give 12 Promotions," *New York Times*, December 31, 1925, p. 1.

73. "175 in Motor Squad sent to foot duty," *New York Times*, January 23, 1926, p. 17; and "First Policewoman to Leave Force," *New York Times*, January 27, 1926, p. 25.

74. "Policewomen want chance to rise to Sergeant's Rank," *New York Times*, January 29, 1927, p. 1; and "Women on the Force," *New York Times*, February 22, 1927, p. 18.

75. "Policewomen to Wear Uniforms as Matrons," *New York Times*, July 20, 1928, p. 10.

76. "More Policewomen are urged for City," *New York Times*, January 27, 1929, p. 19.

77. "Women Police Head Demoted by Whalen in Birth Clinic Raid," *New York Times*, May 12, 1929, pp. 1, 15; and "For Woman in Police Job," *New York Times*, May 25, 1929, p. 16.

78. Lily Lykes Rowe. "Appropriation for women police squad under fire," *New York Tribune*, September 7, 1919.

79. *Ibid.*

80. "Policewomen in Washington decide not to unionize," *New York Tribune*, October 5, 1919.

81. "Many girls saved by policewomen," *The Sun* [NY, NY], October 10, 1919.

82. "Negress new D.C. copette," *The Washington Times*, August 19, 1920.

83. "Men here flirt — but girlies coax 'em to, says Mrs. Van Winkle," *The Washington Times* [D.C.], October 11, 1920.

84. "4 mashers nabbed after they picked up leader of copettes," *The Washington Times*, October 19, 1920.

85. "45 classic beauties needed on cop force — doll babies barred," *The Washington Times*, May 19, 1921.

86. "Personality test compulsory for D.C. lady coppers," *The Washington Times* [D.C.], June 14, 1921.

87. "Seek woman cop for duty on force at Washington," *The Evening Herald* [NY, NY], August 19, 1922.

88. "Gotham's woman traffic cops in action," *The Morning Tulsa Daily World*, December 11, 1921.

89. Helen D. Pigeon, "Policewomen and Public Recreation," *American City* 37 (October 1927): 448; and Louis Brownlow, "The Policewoman and the Woman Criminal," *National Municipal Review* 16 (July 1927): 467–68.

90. Willard Johnson, "A Municipal Mother," *Sunset* 62 (April 1929): 25.

91. Hutzel, "The Policewoman," op. cit., p. 104; and Helen D. Pigeon, "Woman's Era in the Police Department," *Annals of the American Academy of Political and Social Science* 143 (May 1929): 254.

92. "The functions and Organization of a Police Unit doing Protective and Preventive Work with Women and Children," *Public Personnel Studies* 5 (December 1927): 246–47, 259.

93. Katharine Bement Davis, "The Police Woman," *Woman Citizen* 10 (May 30, 1925): 14; and Edith Abbott, "Training for the Policewoman's Job," *Woman Citizen* 10 (April 1926): 30.

94. McMullen, op. cit., pp. 7–9.

95. Hutzel, "The Policewoman," op. cit., pp. 112–13.

96. Owings, op. cit., pp. 215–16.97.

97. August Vollmer, "Meet the Lady Cop," *Survey* 63 (March 15, 1930): 703; and Irma Wann Buwalda, "The Policewoman — Yesterday, Today and Tomorrow," *Journal of Social Hygiene* 31 (May 1945): 290.

98. Horne, op. cit., p. 67.

99. "Women Police at Odds," *New York Times*, April 9, 1921, p. 24.

100. Buwalda, op. cit., p. 291.

101. Albert R. Roberts, "Police Social Workers: A History," *Social Work* 21 (July 1976): 297.

Chapter 6

1. "Feminists ban talk on household Science," *New York Times*, June 6, 1926, sec. 2, p. 6.

2. "League declares for women police," *New York Times*, September 16, 1923, p. 3.

3. League of Nations, Advisory Commission for the Protection and Welfare of Children and Young People, Traffic in Women and Children Committee, *The Employment of Women in the Police*, Geneva: League of Nations, 1927, pp. 1–3.

4. *Ibid.*, pp. 2, 5, 8, 12.

5. Chloe Owings, *Women Police*, Montclair, NJ; Patterson Smith, 1969, pp. 69–70, reprint of 1925 edition.

6. League of Nations, op.cit., pp. 5–11.

7. Erika S. Fairchild, "Women police in Weimar," *Law and Society Review* 21, no. 3 (1987): 383–86.

8. *Ibid.*, p. 386.

9. *Ibid.*, pp. 382, 386–90.

10. *Ibid.*, pp. 391–94.

11. *Ibid.*, pp. 378–79.

12. *Ibid.*, pp. 380, 395.

13. Stanislawa Paleolog, *The Women Police of Poland 1925 to 1939*, London: Association for Moral and Social Hygiene, 1957, pp. 10, 12, 16.

14. *Ibid.*, pp. 17–23, 52.

15. *Ibid.*, pp. 23m 115, 143.

16. Owings, op. cit., pp. 14, 17.

17. D. O. G. Peto, "The status of the policewoman," *Spectator* 123 (December 13, 1919): 806.

18. D. O. G. Peto, "The policewoman of the future," *Spectator* 125 (September 11, 1920): 329–30, and Peto, op. cit., p.805.

19. Louise Creighton, "Women police," *Fortnightly Review* 114 (July, 1920): 113–14.

20. Owings. op. cit., p. 29; and John Carrier. *The Campaign for the Employment of Women as Police Officers*, Aldershot, England: Avebury, 1988, pp. 82–84.

21. Mary S. Allen, *The Pioneer Policewoman*, London: Chatto and Windus, 1925, pp. 127–128; Carrier, op. cit., p. 85.

22. Allen, op. cit., pp. 131, 176–79; Carrier, op. cit., p. 89.

23. Carrier, op. cit., pp. 98–100.

24. Allen, op. cit., pp. 133–34, 145, 148, 151.

25. *Ibid.*, pp. 161, 165, 167.

26. "Ideals of the women police," *The Times*, May 25, 1920, p. 12.

27. Allen, op. cit., pp. 221, 245.

28. *Ibid.*, pp. 184–186, 200–204, 209.

29. *Ibid.*, pp. 130–131.

30. Carrier, op. cit., pp. 87, 116.

31. Lilian Wyles, *A Woman of Scotland Yard*, London: Faber and Faber, 1952, pp. 12–15, 17, 21, 23, 28–29.

32. *Ibid.*, pp. 30–31, 43–44, 48.

33. *Ibid.*, pp. 51–56.

34. *Ibid.*, pp. 51, 74–75.

35. *Ibid.*, pp. 86–87.

36. *Ibid.*, pp. 99–101.

37. *Ibid.*, pp. 102–03, 110, 118–120.

38. Owings, op. cit., p. 32; Mina Van Winkle, "The Policewoman," *Survey* 52 (September 15, 1924): 629; Allen, op. cit., p. 180; and "Women police too costly," *New York Times*, February 14, 1922, p. 8.

39. "The 'perfect lady' in politics," *The Times* (London), March 10, 1922, p. 9; and "Home Office vote," *The Times* (London), June 30, 1922, p. 19.

40. "Women police," *The Times* (London), December 14, 1922, p. 12; Wyles, op. cit., pp. 109–10; and Allen, op. cit., p. 180.

41. "Future of women police," *The Times* (London), February 1, 1923, p. 7; "Children first," *The Times* (London), July 13, 1923, p. 13; Van Winkle, op. cit., p. 629; and Allen, op. cit., p. 182.

42. Carrier, op. cit., pp. 168–69.

43. Owings, op. cit., pp. 36–37.

44. *Ibid.*, pp. 37–39.

45. "Women police," *The Times* (London), December 3, 1929, p. 11; and "Man arrested by policewoman," *The Times* (London), July 3, 1929, p. 10.

46. H. Alker Tripp, "Women police," *The Nineteenth Century and After* 107 (June 1930): 815–824.

Chapter 7

1. United States, Women's Bureau, *The Outlook for Women in Police Work*, Bulletin of the Women's Bureau, no. 231, Washington, D.C.: GPO, 1949, p. 4.

2. August Vollmer, "Meet the lady cop," *Survey* 63 (March 15, 1930): 702.

3. Eleonore L. Hutzel, *The Policewoman's Handbook*, New York: Columbia University Press, 1933, p. 1.

4. *Ibid.*, pp. 1–3.

5. *Ibid.*, pp. 4–5, 8, 21, 58.

6. Citizens' Police Committee, *Chicago Po-*

lice Problems, Chicago: University of Chicago Press, 1931, pp. 175–176m 186.

7. Josephine Nelson, "On the policewoman's beat," *Independent Woman* 15 (May 1936): 138–39.

8. *Ibid.*, p. 139.

9. "Unsung policewomen and crime prevention," *Los Angeles Times*, November 12, 1934, sec. 2, p. 5.

10. Joseph Kluchesky, "Policewomen," *American City* 52 (July, 1937): 17.

11. "155 women police to carry pistols," *New York Times*, December 12, 1934, p. 25; "City policewomen to wear uniforms," *New York Times*, January 14, 1935, p. 17; "Policewomen in review," *New York Times*, May 28, 1935, p. 27; and "Women make good on pickpocket squad," *New York Times*, September 25, 1935, p. 9.

12. Lowell Brentano, "Lady cops," *Forum and Century* 101 (April 1939): 223, 226–27.

13. United States, Women's Bureau, op. cit., pp. 3–4, 7, 14–15.

14. "More cities employ policewomen," *American City* 63 (February 1948): 17.

15. "Good Housekeeping finds out what a policewomen does," *Good Housekeeping* 113 (December 1941): 26–27.

16. Albert R. Roberts, "Police social workers: a history," *Social Work* 21 (July 1976): 297.

17. "Policing as a career for young women," *Education for Victory* 2 (October 1, 1943): 11.

18. Karl Detzer, "Detroit's lady cops," *American Mercury* 54 (March 1942): 345–50.

19. *Ibid.*, pp. 346–50.

20. Brenda Warner Rotzoll, "Anna Mae Davis, founder of policewomen's group," *Chicago Sun-Times*, May 30, 2003, p. 70.

21. Stanley Frank, "Some cops have lovely legs," *Saturday Evening Post* 222 (December 24, 1949): 11, 13.

22. *Ibid.*, p. 39.

23. *Ibid.*, pp. 39–40.

24. Felicia Shpritzer, "A case for the promotion of policewomen in the city of New York," *Police* 5 (July/August 1961): 58.

25. United States, The National Advisory Police Committee on Social Protection of the Federal Security Agency, *Techniques of Law Enforcement in the use of policewomen with special reference to social Protection*. Washington, D.C.: Federal Security Agency, Office of Community War Services, Social Protection Division, 1945, pp. 8, 10, 57–59, 62.

26. Lois Higgins, "Women police service," *Journal of Criminal Law and Criminology* 41 (May 1950): 102–3; and Lois Higgins, "Histor-ical background of policewomen's service," *Journal of Criminal Law and Criminology* 41 (March/April 1951): 829.

27. Evabel Tenny, "Women's work in law enforcement," *Journal of Criminal Law and Criminology* 44 (July 1953): 241–43.

28. Thomas C. Edwards, "Social protection — a workable plan," *Journal of Social Hygiene* 38 (December 1952): 379.

29. O. W. Wilson, *Police Administration*, 2nd ed. New York: McGraw-Hill, 1963, pp. 290, 334.

30. Peter Horne, *Women in law enforcement* 2nd ed. Springfield, Ill.: Charles C. Thomas, 1980, p. 68.

31. Ashley Halsey, Jr., "The lady cops of the dope squad," *Saturday Evening Post* 229 (March 30, 1957): 102.

32. Gledhill Cameron, "Detective Kitty Barney, *Colliers* 134 (November 26, 1954): 32, 34, 37.

33. Will Chasen, "New York's finest (female div.)," *New York Times Magazine*, November 20, 1955, p. 26.

34. Frederic Sondern, Jr., "Crime-busters in skirts," *Reader's Digest* 71 (November 1957): 222–23.

35. "The lady is a cop," *Look* 20 (March 6, 1956): 48–50, 52.

36. "More cities hire policewomen," *American City* 65 (March 1950): 17.

37. James M. Owens, "Policewoman in the line," *Police* 3 (September/October 1958): 21.

38. Susan E. Martin, *Breaking and Entering: policewomen on patrol.* Berkeley: University of California Press, 1980, p24; Roi Dianne Townsey, "Black women in American policing," *Journal of Criminal Justice* 10, no. 6 (1982): 460; Catherine Milton. *Women in policing.* Washington, D.C.: Police Foundation, 1972, p. 16; and Esther J. Koening, "An overview of attitudes toward women in law Enforcement," *Public Administration Review* 38 (May 1978): 269.

39. "Police women hailed," *New York Times*, September 29, 1958, p. 29.

40. Koening, op. cit., p. 269.

41. Shpritzer, op. cit., pp. 57–59.

42. "No longer men or women," *U.S. News and World Report* 77 (August 19, 1974): 46.

43. William H. Honan, "Felicia Shpritzer dies at 87," *New York Times*, December 31, 2000.

44. Alice Fleming, *New on the beat*. New York: Coward, McCann and Geoghegan, 1975, pp. 32–33.

45. "Policewoman recalls contempt from

others," *Columbus Ledger-Enquirer* (GA), March 8, 1998, p. C3.

46. George Hesselberg, "Pioneering policewoman Mary Ostrander, 60, dies," *Wisconsin State Journal* (Madison), September 21, 1994.

47. Milton, op. cit., pp. 8–9.

48. Susan Martin, *Breaking and entering..*, op. cit., p. 110.

49. *Ibid.*, pp. 35–37.

50. Fleming, op. cit., p. 19; and Virginia Armat, "Policewomen in action," *Saturday Evening Post* 247 (July 1975): 84.

51. *Ibid.*

Chapter 8

1. "The absurdity of policewomen," *Saturday Review of Politics, Literature, Science and Art* 151 (April 18, 1931): 558.

2. "Women in Scotland Yard," *New York Times*, August 16, 1933, p. 12; and Lilian Wyles, *A Woman at Scotland Yard*. London: Faber and Faber, 1952, p. 126.

3. "Women police," *The Times* (London), July 24, 1934, p. 16; and "Mobile women police suggested," *The Times* (London), October 17, 1935, p. 20.

4. Josephine Nelson, "On the policewoman's beat," *Independent Woman* 15 (May 1936): 138, 154.

5. "Women police," *The Times* (London), August 6, 1940, p. 5; "Points from other replies," *The Times* (London), February 24, 1944, p. 8; and "Women police wanted," *The Times* (London), April 13, 1946, p. 2.

6. John Carrier, *The Campaign for the Employment of Women as Police Officers*. Aldershot, England: Avebury, 1988, p. 257.

7. Wyles, op. cit., p. 56.

8. "2,000 women in police force," *The Times* (London), February 1, 1954, p. 2.

9. "P.C. 119 will be on duty," *The Times* (London), December 24, 1956, p. 9.

10. Catherine Milton, *Women in policing*. Washington, D.C.: Police Foundation, 1972, pp. 9–10.

11. Patricia Coleman, "A lot of the time is spent just helping people," *The Times* (London), February 19, 1969, p. 11.

12. Peter Horne, *Women in Law Enforcement 2nd ed.* Springfield, Ill.: Charles C. Thomas, 1980, p. 14.

13. "China has first policewomen," *New York Times*, September 27, 1933, p. 3; and Nelson, op. cit., p. 154.

14. Robert Haldane, *The People's Force*. Melbourne, Australia: Melbourne University Press,

1986, pp. 191, 226, 288; and G. M. O'Brien, *The Australian Police Forces*. Melbourne, Australia: Oxford University Press, 1960, pp. 176–77.

15. Nelson, op. cit., p. 154.

16. Amarjit Mahajan, *Indian Policewomen*. New Delhi: Deep and Deep, 1982, pp. 39–41.

17. *Ibid.*, pp. 44, 50.

18. "This day in history," *Hamilton Spectator*, March 23, 2012, p. A6.

19. Karl Sepkowski, "Lois Beckett was pioneering policewoman," *The Toronto Star*, August 23, 1998; and Barbara M. Freeman, *The Satellite Sex; The Media and Women's Issues in Canada 1966–1971*, Waterloo: Wilfrid Laurier University Press, 2001, p. 105.

20. "Berlin policewomen," *Life* 24 (April 12, 1948): 75–76, 79.

21. Horne, op. cit., pp. 12–13.

22. Tekena Tamund. *The Police in Modern Nigeria 1861–1965*. Ibadan, Nigeria: Ibadan University Press, 1970, pp 135–137.

23. G. Ochi Ogbuaku, "Ladies on the force," *National Business Woman* 35 (November 1956): 22.

24. Tamund, op. cit., pp. 138–139.

25. "A word with a Brazilian policewoman," *Americas* 9 (July 1957): 26–27.

26. Horne, op. cit., p. 17; and Milton, op. cit., p. 10.

27. Horne, op. cit., p. 16.

Chapter 9

1. Patrick V. Murphy, *Commissioner*. New York: Simon and Schuster, 1977, pp. 248–250.

2. David Burnham, "More women join ranks of nation's police forces," *New York Times*, June 6, 1972, pp. 1, 32.

3. Sonia Nazario, "Force to be reckoned with," *Los Angeles Times*, June 5, 1993, p. A12.

4. C. J. Flammang, *Police Juvenile Enforcement*. Springfield, Ill.: Charles C. Thomas, 1972, pp. 198–99.

5. Gary R. Perlstein, "Policewomen and policemen," *Police Chief* 39 (March 1972): 74, 83.

6. Alana Baranick, "Jean F. Clayton, 77, blazed trail for policewomen," *Cleveland Plain Dealer*, July 11, 2000, p. 7B.

7. "The women in blue," *Time* 99 (May 1, 1972): 60.

8. "The female fuzz," *Newsweek* 80 (October 23, 1972): 117

9. Alice Fleming, *New on the Beat*. New York: Coward, McCann and Geoghegan, 1975, pp. 206–08.

10. Joseph F. Sullivan, "Women as police

must stand tall," *New York Times*, August 6, 1972, pp. 59, 74.

11. Catherine Milton, *Women in Policing*. Washington, D.C.: Police Foundation, 1972, pp. 10, 13, 16, 17, 63.

12. Susan Martin, *Breaking and Entering: Policewomen on Patrol*. Berkeley: University of California Press, 1980, pp. 26–27; and "No longer men or women," *U.S. News and World Report* 77 (August 19, 1974): 45.

13. Roi Dianne Townsey, "Black women in American policing," *Journal of Criminal Justice* 10, no. 6 (1982): 457–60; "More women police assigned to patrol duty, study reports," *Justice Assistance News* 3 (March 1982): 4; and Bruce L. Berg, "Defeminization of women in law enforcement: a new twist in the traditional police personality," *Journal of Police Science and Administration* 14, no. 4 (December 1986): 314.

14. Peter Horne, *Women in law enforcement* 2nd ed. Springfield, Ill.: Charles C. Thomas, 1980, pp. 35, 37–38, 46–47, 69; and Berg, op. cit., p. 314.

15. "President's safety is now often a woman's work," *New York Times*, July 6, 1993, p. A7.

16. Milton, op. cit., pp. 17, 18, 54.

17. *Ibid.*, p. 67; Virginia Armat, "Policewomen in action," *Saturday Evening Post* 247 (July 1975): 87; and "No longer men or women," op. cit., p. 46.

18. Michele Keller, "UC Irvine chooses new female police chief," *Daily Bruin*, October 19, 1992, p. 1.

19. "No longer men or women," op. cit., pp. 45–46.

20. Milton, op. cit., pp. 17, 19.

21. Berg, op. cit., p. 315.

22. Marlene W. Lehtinen, "Sexism in police departments," *Trial* 12 (December 1976): 52, 54.

23. Armat, op. cit., p. 49.

24. Susan Martin, *Breaking and Entering...*, op. cit., pp. 46–47, 91, 93.

25. Armat, op. cit., p. 48.

26. Milton, op. cit., p. 25; Armat, op. cit., p. 48; and Robert L. O'Block, "The emerging role of the female detective," *Police Chief* 47 (May 1980): 54.

27. Fleming, op. cit., p. 24; and Armat, op. cit., p. 87.

28. Susan Martin, *Breaking and Entering...*, op. cit., p. 111; "Policewomen succeed in tough world of streets," *New York Times*, January 27, 1974, p. 38; and Lehtinen, op. cit., p. 54.

29. Susan Martin, *Breaking and Entering...*, op. cit., pp. 111–12.

30. Peter B. Bloch, *Policewomen on Patrol: Final Report*. Washington, D.C.: Police Foundation, 1974, pp. 1–2, 11.

31. *Ibid.*, pp. 11–12.

32. *Ibid.*, p. 5; and "Policewomen as policewomen," *Society* 11 (January/February 1974): 10.

33. Bloch, op. cit., pp. 7, 47–48; "Equal guardians of the law," *Society* 11 (September/October 1974): 10.

34. Fleming, op. cit., p. 23.

35. Jude T. Walsh, "Some questions in re: policewomen on patrol," *Police Chief* 42 (July 1975): 20–22.

36. Lewis J. Sherman, "An evaluation of policewomen on patrol in a suburban police department," *Journal of Police Science and Administration* 3, no. 4 (December 1975): 434–37.

37. Ted Morgan, "Women make good cops," *New York Times Magazine*, November 3, 1974, p. 18.

38. James A. Davis, "Perspectives of policewomen in Texas and Oklahoma," *Journal of Police Science and Administration* 12, no. 4 (December 1984): 395.

39. Merry Morash, "Evaluating women on patrol," *Evaluation Review* 10 (April 1986): 231, 247–49.

40. "Men outperform women as police, study asserts," *New York Times*, July 31, 1978, p. A10.

41. Horne, op. cit., p. 104.

42. "Philadelphia police ordered to give women 25% of jobs," *New York Times*, September 6, 1979, p. A16; and "Philadelphia consents to placing of women in 30% of police jobs," *New York Times*, July 16, 1980, p. A19.

43. Department of the California Highway Patrol. *Women Traffic Officer Project: Final Report*. Sacramento: Department of California Highway Patrol, 1976, pp. 3–4, 7, 11, 14, 33, 59, 106.

44. *Ibid.*, pp. 8, 47, 51, 106.

45. Esther J. Koening, "An overview of attitudes toward women in law enforcement," *Public Administration Review* 38 (May 1978):271.

46. Marilyn Koral Elias, "The urban cop," *Ms* 12 (June 1984): 17.

47. Bill Berry, "Do women make good cops?" *Ebony* 36 (February 1981): 105; Fleming, op. cit., p. 22; Armat, op. cit., p. 86; and Horne, op. cit., pp. 98, 103.

48. Horne, op. cit., pp. 98, 103.

49. "No longer men or women," op. cit., p.46; Claudia Dreifus, "Why two women cops were convicted of cowardice," *Ms* 9 (April

1981): 57; Susan Martin, *Breaking and Entering...*, op. cit., 45; and Townsey, op. cit., pp. 465–66.

50. Martin Waldron, "An all-female class is planned for Jersey State Police Academy," *New York Times*, September 13, 1979, pp. A1, B4.

51. Anthony Marro, "Blacks and women to be hired for Louisiana police-fire jobs." *New York Times*, June 30, 1977, p. A14.

52. "Los Angeles police agree to set minority hiring goals," *New York Times*, November 21, 1980, p. A16.

53. Susan Martin, *On the Move: The Status of Women in Policing*. Washington, D.C.: Police Foundation, 1990, pp. xii, 56, 66–72.

54. Robert Pear, "Justice Dept. presses drive on quotas," *New York Times*, April 3, 1985, p. A16.

55. Joann McGeorge, "A comparison of attitudes between men and women police officers," *Criminal Justice Review* 1 (Fall 1976): 26, 31.

56. Robert E. Hindman, "A survey related to use of female law enforcement officers," *Police Chief* 42 (April 1975): 58–59.

57. Susan Martin, "Policewomen and policewomen: occupational role dilemmas and choices of female Officers," *Journal of Police Science and Administration* 7, no. 3 (September 1979): 317–21.

58. Robert J. Homant, "Police perceptions of spouse abuse," *Journal of Criminal Justice* 13, no. 1 (1985): 29, 40, 42.

59. Leslie Kay Lord. "A comparison of male and female peace officers' stereotypic perceptions of women and women peace officers," *Journal of Police Science and Administration* 14, no. 2 (June 1986): 85, 87, 89–80.

60. Ralph A. Weisheit, "Women in the state police," *Journal of Police Science and Administration* 15, no. 2 (June 1987): 137–42.

61. Ruth E. Masters, "A woman corrections professor and a woman reserve officer's view," *Police Chief* 50 (January 1983): 62.

62. Kenneth W. Kerber, "Citizen attitudes regarding the competence of female police officers," *Journal of Police Science and Administration* 5, no. 3 (September 1977): 337–38.

63. *Ibid.*, pp. 339–43.

64. Susan Martin, "Policewomen...," op. cit., pp. 319, 321–23.

65. Robert J. Homant, "The impact of policewomen on community attitudes toward police," *Journal of Police Science and Administration* 11, no. 1 (March 1983): 17–18.

66. Karin Winnard, "Policewomen and the people they serve," *Police Chief* 53 (August 1986): 62–63.

67. Daniel B. Kennedy, "Attitudes of abused women toward male and female police officers," *Criminal Justice and Behavior* 10, no. 4 (December 1983): 391, 396, 399.

68. Berry, op. cit., p. 105.

69. "Nude model gets job back with NYC police," *Jet* 68 (April 29, 1985): 24.

70. Susan Reed, "Nicknamed Calamity Jane," *People* 24 (August 12, 1985): 51–52.

71. Walter Shapiro, "Reforming our image of a chief," *Time* 136 (November 26, 1990): 80–82; and Roberto Suro, "Houston mayor removes female police chief," *New York Times*, February 18, 1992, p. A20.

72. "Women cops on the beat," *Time* 115 (March 10, 1980): 58.

73. Armat, op. cit., pp. 84–85.

74. "Policewomen say opportunities are improving but slowly," *The Columbian* (Vancouver, WA), May 2, 1996.

75. "Mockler v Multnomah County. Case number 96–35895, date filed March 31, 1998, downloaded from web July 26, 2012.

76. Christina Nifong, "Gender Revolution in Precinct House," *Christian Science Monitor*, May 22, 1996.

77. Kristen Leger, "Public perceptions of female police officers on patrol, *American Journal of Criminal Justice* 21 no 2, (1997): 235–247.

78. Kim Michelle Lersch, "Exploring gender differences in citizen allegations of misconduct," *Women and Criminal Justice* 9 no. 4, (1998): 69–71.

79. "Women recruited at slow rate by nation's law enforcement agencies, report reads," *Jet*, April 26, 1999.

80. Tim R. Sass, Jennifer L. Troyer, "Affirmative action, political representation, unions and female police Employment," *Journal of Labor Research*, 20 (Fall 1999): 574–584.

81. Diana R. Grant, "Perceived gender differences in Policing," *Women and Criminal Justice* 12 no. 1 (2000): 57, 67.

82. Thomas L. Austin, Don Hummer, "What do college students think of policewomen," *Women and Criminal Justice* 10, no. 4, (2000), 1–10.

83. Karla Mantilla, "Male officers worse than females," *Off Our Backs*, April 2001, p. 4.

84. E. A. Harvey, "One of the guys—cops say ability not gender is gauge for policewomen whose numbers are creeping up," *Sunday News* (Lancaster, PA), March 10, 2002, p. E1.

85. "Discrimination against women police rampant," *Women's International Network News* 28 no. 3, (Summer 2002): 64.

86. Al Barker, "Retired police commander sues, charging harassment," *New York Times*, March 24, 2002, p. 47.

87. Peter B. Hoffman, Edward R. Hickey, "Use of force by female officers," *Journal of Criminal Justice* 33 (2005): 145.

88. Cochran, "EEOC — Officer's filing is valid; ex-policewoman says Eagle Lake discriminated against her," *The Ledger* (Lakeland, FL), May 4, 2006.

89. Molly McDonough, "Pregnant pause," *ABA Journal* 92 (August 2006).

90. Richard Seklecki, Rebecca Paynich, "A national survey of female police officers: an overview of findings," *Police Practice and Research* 8, no. 1, (March 2007): 17–26.

91. Calvin Wesley Haba, Robert A. Sarver III, Rhonda Dobbs, Mary B. Sarver, "Attitudes of college students toward women in policing," *Women and Criminal Justice* 19, no. 3 (2009): 235.

92. Gary Cordner, Annmarie Cordner, "Stuck on a Plateau? Obstacles to recruitment, selection, and retention of women police," *Police Quarterly* 14, no. 3 (2011): 207–210, 220.

93. Cara Rabe-Hemp, Dawn Beichner, "An analysis of advertisements: a lens for viewing the social exclusion of women in police imagery," *Women and Criminal Justice* 21 (2011): 63, 69, 76.

Chapter 10

1. Ted Morgan, "Women make good cops," *New York Times Magazine*, November 3, 1974, p. 18.

2. Carol Fischberg, "Copping in," *Ms* 3 (May 1975): 21.

3. Susan Martin, *Breaking and Entering...*, op. cit., pp. 126–28, 133, 143.

4. Horne, op. cit., p. 51.

5. *Ibid.*, pp. 116–117.

6. Maureen Kempton, "All we want for Christmas is our jobs back," *Ms* 4 (December 1975): 69.

7. Anthony Vastola, "Women in policing," *Police Chief* 44 (January 1977): 62–69.

8. Susan Martin, *On the Move...*, op. cit., pp. 141–44.

9. Peggy E. Triplett, "Women in policing," *Police Chief* 43 (December 1976): 47–49.

10. Joan Abramson, "Sizing up the job — a not-so-pacific tale," *Ms* 4 (January 1976): 21.

11. Claudia Dreifus, "Why two women cops were convicted of cowardice, *Ms* 9 (April 1981): 58, 63.

12. *Ibid.*, pp, 57–58, 63–64.

13. "Women cops on the beat," *Time* 115 (March 10, 1980): 58.

14. Townsey, op. cit., pp. 461, 466.

15. Lynne Duke, "Law enforcers grapple with diversity," *Washington Post*, January 27, 1993, pp. A1, A12.

16. Sally Gross, "Women becoming cops," *Police Chief* 51 (January 1984): 32.

17. Carol Ann Martin, "Women police and stress," *Police Chief* 50 (March 1983): 108.

18. Judie Ann Wexler, "Sources of stress among women police officers," *Journal of Police Science and Administration* 11 (March 1983): 46–49.

19. *Ibid.*, pp. 49–52.

20. "Officer, forced to quit, gets new job with city," *New York Times*, July 22, 1984, p. A16.

21. Susan Martin, *On the Move...*, op. cit., pp. xvi, 139.

22. *Ibid.*, pp. 79, 144–46, 149.

23. Dennis Hevesi, "Sex discrimination complaints against the police are upheld," *New York Times*, November 26, 1991, p. B3.

24. "Ruling finds harassment of female officer," *New York Times*, December 17, 1991, p. B7.

25. Susan Bouman Paolino, "My dream of enforcing the law became a nightmare," *Los Angeles Times*, August 18, 1991, p. M6; and Henry Weinstein, "Court finds bias against women deputies," *Los Angeles Times*, July 24, 1991, pp. B1, B7.

26. Patt Morrison, "Female officers unwelcome — but doing fine," *Los Angeles Times*, July 12, 1991, pp. A1, A27-A29.

27. "Officers tell of bias on Fairfax County," *Washington Post*, June 4, 1992, pp. A1, A18; and Patricia Davis, "Complaints of sexism detailed," *Washington Post*, August 3, 1992, p. B1.

28. Koening, op. cit., p. 269.

29. Horne, op. cit., pp. 127–28.

30. Susan Martin, "Sexual politics in the workplace: the interactional world of policewomen," *Symbolic Interaction* 1, no. 2 (Spring 1978): 51, 56–57.

31. Lin Farley, *Sexual Shakedown*, New York: McGraw-Hill, 1978, pp. 54–55.

32. Susan Martin, *On the Move...*, op. cit., pp. 140–146.

33. "Jury awards $900,000 to black female officer in Detroit police case," *Jet* 72 (April 27, 1987): 33.

34. "Three awarded $2.7 million in a sexual harassment suit," *New York Times*, November 12, 1990, p. B8.

35. Jeffrey Higginbotham, "Sexual harass-

ment in the police station," *FBI Law Enforcement Bulletin* 57 (September 1988): 26–27.

36. "Court criticizes police department in a sex case," *New York Times*, July 29, 1992, p. B3.

37. Joseph P. Fried, "Transfer linked to harassment, police say," *New York Times*, October 17, 1992, p. 28.

38. Roxanna Kopetman, "Long Beach policewomen call sexual harassment endemic," *Los Angeles Times*, September 28, 1991, p. B3.

39. *Ibid.*; and N. F. Mendoza, "Crossing the thin blue line," *Los Angeles Times*, May 11, 1993, pp. F1, F7.

40. "Officers of the law should know better," *Los Angeles Times*, February 1, 1991, p. B6.

41. Faye Fiore, "Sheriff's Dept, concedes on 2 sex bias suits," *Los Angeles Times*, December 4, 1992, pp. A1, A36.

42. Shelby Grad, "Irvine orders probe of police sex charges," *Los Angeles Times*, June 24, 1993, p. B8.

43. "Officer's suit says she was raped, then fired," *Los Angeles Times*, December 18, 1992, p. B3.

44. Karen Klabin, "Lewd conduct," *LA Weekly* 15 (March 5, 1993): 14, 16.

45. *Ibid.*; and Sonia Nazario, "Force to be reckoned with," *Los Angeles Times*, June 5, 1993, p. A12.

46. Klabin, op. cit., pp. 14, 16.

47. Dan Weikel, "Sexual harassment suit filed against police, *Los Angeles Times*, September 25, 1992, p. A35; and Nancy Wride, "Women alleging sex harassment cite reprisal fear," *Los Angeles Times*, September 28, 1992, pp. A3, A13.

48. Nancy Wride, "Police chief named in harassment suit to retire," *Los Angeles Times*, October 15, 1992, pp. A3, A29.

49. Nancy Wride, "Newport Beach police chief, aide put on leave over rape allegations," *Los Angeles Times*, October 16, 1992, pp. A3, A36.

50. Nancy Wride, "Police officials sue Newport Beach over harassment inquiry," *Los Angeles Times*, November 13, 1992, pp. A3, A34.

51. Dan Weikel, "4 more women to join suit against police," *Los Angeles Times*, December 2, 1992, pp. A3, A28.

52. Jodi Wilgoren, "Inquiry finds merit in sex harassment suit," *Los Angeles Times*, December 16, 1992, pp. A3, A31.

53. "Face it squarely — deal with it," *Los Angeles Times*, December 17, 1992, p. B6.

54. Dan Weikel, "Police chief fired in Newport Beach," *Los Angeles Times*, December 23, 1992, pp. A3, A22; and "Moving to right a

wrong," *Los Angeles Times*, December 24, 1992, p. B6.

55. Dan Weikel, "Campbell calls firing part of a conspiracy," *Los Angeles Times*, December 24, 1992, pp. A3, A16.

56. Jodi Wilgoren, "Newport Beach won't pay fired officers' legal costs," *Los Angeles Times*, January 29, 1993, p. A29; "Newport Beach settles 4 harassment cases," *Los Angeles Times*, February 4, 1993, p. A17; and Jodi Wilgoren, "Newport Beach settles with fired police chief, captain," *Los Angeles Times*, June 11, 1993, p. B8.

57. Timothy Egan, "New faces, and new roles, for the police," *New York Times*, April 25, 1991, p. B10; and Zsuzsanna Adler, "Hill Street clues," *Personnel Management* 22 (August 1990): 30.

58. Louise Saul, "Women are still scarce as police officers," *New York Times*, April 8, 1990, sec. 12, pp. 1, 6.

59. Susan Martin, *On the Move...*, op. cit., pp. xi, 25–30, 121, 134; and Horne, op. cit., p. 200.

60. Susan Martin, *On the Move...*, op. cit., pp. 25–30, 121, 134.

61. Frederic Muir, "Council sets goat of 44% female LAPD in 8 years," *Los Angeles Times*, September 10, 1992, pp. A1, A23.

62. Nazario, op. cit., pp. A1, A12.

63. "Female quota set for LAPD," *Los Angeles Times*, September 20, 1992, p. M4.

64. Nazario, op. cit., pp. A1, A12.

65. Pauline Repard, "Policewoman gains settlement; Chula Vista to pay $45,000 for alleged sexual Harassment," *San Diego Union-Tribune*, February 2, 1994.

66. Ronnie Greene, "Jury: former policewoman was harassed," *Miami Herald*, December 15, 1994.

67. "Dallas policewomen say 80% harassed," *Austin American-Statesman* (TX), August 10, 1997, p. B6.

68. Paul H. Johnson, "Town, officer settle harassment suit, *The Hartford Courant* (CT), April 30, 1998.

69. Alexandra Marks, "Women face blue wall of resistance," *Christian Science Monitor*, August 18, 1999.

70. Mary Thierry Texeira, "Who protects and serves me?" *Gender and Society* 16, no. 4 (2002): 524–29.

71. Ian Ith, "Ex-policewoman awarded $225,000 to settle lawsuit," *Seattle Times*, February 5, 2003, p. B3.

72. Jennifer Sullivan, "Lawsuit alleges Seattle police assaulted teen during jaywalking arrest," *Seattle Times*, August 18, 2010.

73. "Officers win harassment case," *Long Beach Press Telegram*, June 3, 2003, p. A1.

74. Sue Carter Collins, "Sexual harassment and police discipline," *Policing: An International Journal of Police Strategies and Management* 27, no. 4 (2004): 512–538.

75. *Ibid.*

76. Kimberly A. Lonsway and Angela M. Alipio, "Sex Discrimination Lawsuits in Law Enforcement," *Women and Criminal Justice* 18, no. 4 (2007): 63–65.

Chapter 11

1. "Yard to end separate police-force for women," *The Times* (London), September 23, 1972, p. 2; and Horne, op. cit., pp. 10–12.

2. "Policewomen barred," *The Times* (London), December 20, 1971, p. 2.

3. "Arresting beauty," *Daily Telegraph*, September 14, 1979, p. 3.

4. "Police cover-up," The Times (London), November 29, 1977, p. 3.

5. Peter Evans, "Women shoulder increasing part of burden," *The Times* (London), November 10, 1977, p. 4.

6. Adler, op. cit., p. 33.

7. "Hooliganism danger to woman PCs," *The Times* (London), September 8, 1977, p. 3.

8. "Police chief advises politicians to shun violent rallies," *The Times* (London), September 28, 1977, p. 2.

9. "Women officers may appeal over police reform," *The Times* (London), January 27, 1978, p. 2.

10. Peter Evans, "Women in the police," *The Times* (London), February 2, 1978, p. 14.

11. Alan Hamilton, "Recruitment of women no answer to fall in police manpower," *The Times* (London), April 27, 1978, p. 6.

12. "Equal opportunities on the beat," *The Times* (London), April 27, 1978, p. 19.

13. Pauline C. Low, "Policewomen and equality," *British Journal of Criminology* 29, no. 1 (Winter 1989): 79–80.

14. Robert Chesshyre, "Softly, softly," *New Statesman and Society* 2 (November 24, 1989): 20–21.

15. "Woman police chief attacks bias in force," *The Times* (London), May 13, 1986, p. 3.

16. Roger Graef. *Talking Blues*. London: Collins Harvill, 1989, pp. 195, 203, 208, 211, 212, 383, 384.

17. Horne, op. cit., p. 119.

18. Stewart Tendler, "Yard investigates case of the reluctant 'w,'" *The Times* (London), January 12, 1992, p. 7.

19. Craig Seton, "Police compensate woman barred from detective work," *The Times* (London), April 8, 1992, p. 3.

20. Stewart Tendler, "Police chief says women officers suffer bias," *The Times* (London), March 25, 1992, p. 3.

21. Ronald Faux, "Halford tells of years of misery," *The Times* (London), June 2, 1992, p. 3; Ronald Faux, "Halford drops sex bias case for £142,000," *The Times* (London), July 22, 1992, p. 1; Ronald Faux, "Halford work files altered," *The Times* (London), June 4, 1992, p. 5; "Halford trap claim," *The Times* (London), June 15, 1992, p. 2; and Ronald Faux, "Police chief attacks Halford's victory claims as farcical," *The Times* (London), July 23, 1992, p. 5.

22. Horne, op. cit., p.18.

23. *Ibid.*, pp. 20–22.

24. Horne, op. cit., p. 19.

25. Ming S. Singer, "Sex differences in the perception of male and female police officers in New Zealand," *Journal of Psychology* 119 (January 1985): 54, 57.

26. Brigitte Stampe, "Women in the Danish police service," *Police Chief* 58 (June 1991): 15–16.

27. Mahajan, op. cit., pp. 41, 42, 52, 67.

28. *Ibid.*, pp. 89–91, 117–20, 143, 149, 150, 179.

29. Shamim Aleem, *Women in Indian police.* New Delhi: Sterling, 1991, pp. vii, 4, 12, 16, 17, 32.

30. Shamim Aleem, *Women police and social change.* New Delhi: Ashish, 1991, pp. 13–14, 18, 74.

31. Stella R. Quah, *Friends in blue: the police and the public in Singapore.* Singapore: Oxford University Press, 1988, p. 104.

32. David Clark Scott, "New Mexican police squad combats corruption as it pursues polluters," *Christian Science Monitor*, February 9, 1993, p. 7.

33. Marlies E. Ott, "Effects of the male-female ratio at work," *Psychology of Women Quarterly* 13 (March 1989): 43, 49.

34. "Jordan's policewomen see better times ahead," *Toronto Star*, March 13, 1993, p. J5.

35. Dahlia Moore, "Gender traits and identities in a masculine organization: the Israeli Police Force," *Journal of Social Psychology* 139 (February 1999).

36. Erella Shadmi, "Female Police Officers in Israel: Patterns of Integration and Discrimination," *Feminist Issues*, fall 1993, pp.25–27, 31, 37.

37. David J. King, "Separate but Equal: The Introduction and Integration of Policewomen

in the Bermuda Police 1961–2002," *Police Practice and Research* 6, no. 3, (July 2005): 215, 219–20.

38. Sara Nelson, "Constructing and Negotiating Gender in Women's Police Stations in Brazil," *Latin American Perspectives* 23 (1996): 131–139; and Celia MacDowell Santos, "Engendering the Police: Women's Police Stations and Feminism in Sao Paulo," *Latin American Perspective* 39, no. 3, (October 2004): 29–30, 38–39, 50.

39. Mangai Natarajan, "Towards Equality," *Women and Criminal Justice* 8, no. 2 (1996): 3–4, 6–7.

40. "Policewomen learn methods to handle discrimination," *The Times of India* (Bombay), February 22, 2002.

41. S. Seethalakshmi, "State Policewomen a Frustrated Lot," *The Times of India* (Bombay), August 16, 2003.

42. Shujaat Bukhari, "Quit jobs, Militants tell Muslim Policewomen," *The Hindu* (Madras), January 21, 2003.

43. Chitra V. Ramani, "Policewomen face discrimination," The *Hindu* (Madras), December 2, 2006.

44. "New in Moroccan Capital: Policewomen on Patrol," *The Orlando Sentinel*, March 4, 1998, p. A24.

45. S. Monk, "Policewomen just as Physical as the Men," *The Courier Mail* (Brisbane), July 2, 1998, p. 4.

46. Misha Schubert, "Policewoman nets $125,000 in Sex Harassment Case," *The Australian*, June 2, 1998, p. 3.

47. Liz Porter, "Police pay out on Harassment," *Fairfax Digital* (Australia), May 18, 2003.

48. "Just don't complain. Policewomen told to Ignore Sex Harassment," *Daily Telegraph* (Sydney), January 12, 2007.

49. Tim Prenzler, Jenny Fleming and Amanda L. King, "Gender Equality in Australian and New Zealand Policing," *International Journal of Police Science and Management* 12, no. 4, (2010): 588.

50. Pauline Amos-Wilson, "The Women in Blue," *Women in Management Review* 14, no. 4 (1999): 129–30.

51. Andrea Mandel-Campbell, "The Swans don't bite," *U.S. News & World Report*, November 1, 1999.

52. "Iranian Policewomen back on job — 215 graduates to serve alongside men," *Seattle Times*, October 5, 2003.

53. "Iran: Police Commander says Policewomen Necessary for Society," *Irna New Agency* (Tehran, Iran), February 4, 2003.

54. "Afghan Policewomen," *Pittsburgh Post-Gazette*, January 1, 2003, p. A4.

55. Karine G. Barzegar, "Pioneering Afghan Policewomen: Female Recruits Overcome Security, Religious Concerns," *The Columbian* (Vancouver, WA), September 22, 2003, p. A3.

56. Nasrat Shoaib, "Taliban Kill Afghanistan's most high-profile Policewoman," *Agence France-Presse*, September 28, 2008.

57. "For Afghan Policewomen, Sex Abuse is a job hazard," National Public Radio show *All Things Considered*, March 8, 2012.

58. "Policewomen Discriminated against, study finds," *The Jakarta Post* (Indonesia), October 4, 2006.

59. Tina Susman, "Policewomen lose their guns — weapons will be redistributed to men," *The Grand Rapids Press* (MI), December 12, 2007.

60. Tina Susman, "Iraqi Officials let Policewomen keep guns," *Greenwich Time* (CT), January 1, 2008.

61. Jenan Hussein, "Women join ranks of Iraq's Police," *The Miami Herald*, January 27, 2009.

62. "Street Heroines," *Economist*, February 28, 2004.

63. Kim Rahn, "Policewomen less appreciated," *Korea Times*, October 20, 2006.

64. Tagheed El Khodary, "Under robe and veil, crossing boundaries as Policewomen," *New York Times*, January 18, 2008, p. A4.

65. "Working in a Man's World: Women in the Fiji Police Force," *World of Work* no. 65 (April, 2009): 14–15.

66. Staci Strobl, "The Women's Police Directorate in Bahrain," *International Criminal Justice Review* 18 (March 2008): 39–40, 47, 51.

67. Staci Strobl, "Progressive or Neo-Traditional? Policewomen in Gulf Cooperation Council (GCC) Countries," *Feminist Formations* 22, no. 3 (2010): 53–54.

68. Kubra Gultekin, Ellen C. Leichtman, and Carole G. Garrison, "Gender Issues and the Women of the Turkish National Police," *Police Practice and Research* 11 (October 2010): 426–30.

69. Geraldine Bedell, "When Bigotry is part of the job," *The Independent on Sunday* (London, UK), December 12, 1993, p. 8.

70. Hester Lacey, "Real Lives," *The Independent* (London UK), March 21, 1999.

71. Vikram Dodd, "Met's £1m Hate Campaign Payout," *The Guardian* (UK), June 6, 2000.

72. Stewart Tendler, "Policewomen impris-

oned by a Macho Culture," *The Times* (London), February 7, 1994.

73. Paul Wilkinson, "Policewoman wins huge payout in Sex Harassment Case," *The Times* (London), September 18, 1996.

74. Stewart Tendler, "Policewoman wins fight over Work Sex Gibes," *The Times* (London), November 11, 1997.

75. "£300,000 payout for Policewoman," *The Independent* (London, UK), May 14, 1998.

76. Kevin C. Gaston, Jackie A. Alexander, "Women in the Police: Factors Influencing Managerial Advancement," *Women in Management Review* 12, no. 2 (1997): 47, 50.

77. Ruaridh Nicoll, "Policewomen Backed over Sexist Ruling," *The Guardian* (London UK), May 23, 1998.

78. "Ex-police Inspector wins Discrimination fight against force," *The Birmingham Post* (UK), September 5, 1998.

79. "Met pays £150,000 to ex-policewoman," *Greater London, Kent and Surrey Counties Publication* (UK), December 6, 2000.

80. Jane Simpson, "Revealed, the force is biased against its Policewomen," *The Mail on Sunday* (UK), March 19, 2006.

81. Gavin Dick, and Beverley Metcalfe, "The Progress of Female Police Officers," *International Journal of Public Sector Management* 20 no. 2 (2007): 81–100.

82. Ben Quinn, "Do Women make better riot Police?" *Christian Science Monitor*, August 27, 2009.

83. "A Canadian first," *Maclean's*, December 12, 1994.

84. Rae Corelli, "Aiming for respect," *Maclean's*, April 10, 1995; Katherine Bell, "Male colleagues harassed her, ex-mountie says," *Vancouver Sun*, September 8, 1993, p. 19.

85. Carmelina Prete, "Policewomen face harassment, cop says; senior female officer from Newfoundland tells conference of 'tremendous pressure to conform,'" *Hamilton Spectator*, September 26, 2000, p. A11.

86. "Greatest Mancatchers Alive," *The Times* (Moncton, New Brunswick), July 4, 2011, p. C9.

87. Bonnie Reilly Schmidt, "Women on the Force," *Canada's History* 91, no. 4 (September-October 2011).

88. Vivian Luk, "I broke. I completely broke," *The Province* (Vancouver, BC), November 9, 2011, p. A3.

89. "Sexual Harassment allegations at the RCMP," CBC Television show: *The National*, November 8, 2011.

90. Vivian Luk, "RCMP operates as 'old boys' culture," *The Province* (Vancouver, BC), November 10, 2011, p. A8.

91. Terri Theodore, and Keven Drews, "Run like your hair is one fire," *The Canadian Press*, November 10, 2011.

92. Gary Mason, "Dozens of female RCMP officers seek justice through class-action lawsuit," *The Globe and Mail* (Toronto), January 21, 2012, p. S1.

93. Tobi Cohen, "Top Mountie outlines plan to address harassment in RCMP," *Calgary Herald*, February 1, 2012, p. A8.

94. Barbara D. Janusz, "Mounting pressure," *Herizons* (Summer 2012): 17.

95. James Keller, "Federal government issues denial in one of several RCMP harassment lawsuits," *The Canadian Press*, October 23, 2012.

96. Douglas Quan, "RCMP audit reveals bias against women," *The Ottawa Citizen*, November 21, 2012, p. A4.

97. Jennifer Brown, "European Policewomen: a comparative research perspective," *International Journal of the Sociology of Law* 25 (1997): 3–6.

98. Stans de Haas, Greetje Timmerman, and Mechtild Hoing, "Sexual harassment and health among male and Female police officers," *Journal of Occupational Health Psychology* 14, no. 4 (2009): 390.

Bibliography

Abbott, Edith, "Training for the Police-woman's Job," *Woman Citizen* 10 (April 1926): 30.

Abramson, Joan, "Sizing up the Job — A not-so-pacific Tale," *Ms* 4 (January 1976): 21.

"Absurdity of Policewomen, The," *Saturday Reviews of Politics, Literature, Science and Arts* 151 (April 18, 1931): 558.

"Additional Minneapolis News," *St. Paul Daily Globe*, March 8, 1887.

Ad, *Alexandria Gazette* (VA), January 13, 1909.

Ad, *San Francisco Call*, October 2, 1913.

Ad, *Medford Mail Tribune* (Oregon), October 31, 1914.

"Adjourned Sine Die," *St. Paul Daily Globe*, July 22, 1886.

Adler, Zsuzsanna, "Hill Street Clues," *Personnel Management* 22 (August 1990): 28–33.

"Afghan policewomen," *Pittsburgh Post-Gazette*, January 1, 2003, p. A4.

"Against the copettes," *The Day Book* (Chicago), January 16, 1915.

Aleem, Shamim, *Women in Indian Police*, New Delhi: Sterling, 1991.

Aleem, Shamim, *Women Police and Social Change*, New Delhi: Ashish, 1991.

Allen, Mary S., *The Pioneer Policewoman*, London: Chatto and Windus, 1925.

"America's first Policewoman explains need of her profession," *The Washington Times* (DC), May 18, 1915.

"America's first Policewoman sports dainty kerchief instead of club," *The Seattle Star*, December 7, 1907.

"America's second policewoman tells of her job as a copper," *The Ogden Standard* (Utah), October 11, 1913, magazine.

Amos-Wilson, Pauline, "The women in blue," *Women in Management Review* 14, no. 4 (1999): 128–35.

"And now the Matron," *St. Paul Daily Globe*, October 29, 1891.

"Answers to Queries," *San Francisco Call*, August 2, 1910.

Armat, Virginia, "Policewomen in Action," *Saturday Evening Post* 247 (July 1975): 48–49ff.

"Arming the policewomen of Chicago," *Mountain Advocate* (Barbourville, KY), April 17, 1914.

"Army in the West, The," *Los Angeles Herald*, January 18, 1896.

"Around town," *Los Angeles Herald*, March 15, 1910.

"Arresting Beauty," *Daily Telegraph*, September 14, 1979, p. 3.

"Asbury Park's first policewoman on the job," *The Day Book* (Chicago), August 2, 1913.

"Asks for Women Police," *New York Times*, July 8, 1913, p. 2.

"Athletic woman is a deputy constable," *San Francisco Call*, April 27, 1912.

Austin, Thomas L., and Don Hummer, "What do college students think of policewomen?" *Women and Criminal Justice* 10, no. 4 (2000): 1–24.

Baker, Al, "Retired police commander sues, charging harassment," *New York Times*, March 24, 2002, p. 47.

Baranick, Alana, "Jean F. Clayton, 77,

blazed trail for policewomen," *The Plain Dealer* (Cleveland) July 11, 2000, p. 7B.

Barzegar, Karine G., "Pioneering Afghan policewomen; female recruits overcome security, religious Concerns," *The Columbian* (Vancouver, WA), September 22, 2003, p. A3.

Bedell, Geraldine, "Where bigotry is part of the job," *The Independent on Sunday* (London, UK), December 12, 1993, p. 8.

Bell, Katherine, "Male Colleagues Harassed Her, Ex-Mountie Says," *Vancouver Sun*, September 8, 1993, p. A4.

Berg, Bruce L., "Defeminization of Women in Law Enforcement: A New Twist in the Traditional Police Personality," *Journal of Police Science and Administration* 14, no. 4 (December 1986): 314–19.

"Berlin Policewomen," *Life* 24 (April 12, 1948): 75–76ff.

Berry, Bill, "Do Women Make Good Cops?" *Ebony* 36 (February 1981): 104–06ff.

"Better be good or maybe policewoman will get you," *Omaha Daily Bee*, May 6, 1911.

"Big field for policewoman," *Hopkinsville Kentuckian*, February 1, 1916.

"Bill for New York City Policewomen," *New York Tribune*, April 4, 1915.

"Bill for New York Policewomen," *New York Times*, January 28, 1914, p. 1.

Bird, Carol, "Policewomen's School," *New York Times*, July 31, 1921, sec. 7, p. 3.

Bloch, Peter B., *Policewomen on Patrol: Final Report*, Washington, D.C.: Police Foundation, 1974.

"Boardwalk 'cop-ess' to watch for winks," *Evening Public Ledger* (Philadelphia) May 18, 1917.

"Boston police force is weak," *The Evening Standard* (Ogden City, UT), May 3, 1911.

Bowen, Louise de Koven, "Women Police," *Survey* 30 (April 12, 1913): 64–65.

Boyd, Mary Sumner, "Women defenders in time of peace," *Honolulu Star-Bulletin*, July 3, 1917.

Brandenburger, John A., "Effective Work of Policewomen," *American City* 28 (March 1923): 259–60.

Brentano, Lowell, "Lady Cops," *Forum and Century* 101 (April 1939): 223–27.

"Brighton Women Police," *The Times* (London), March 27, 1915, p. 5.

Brinton, Arthur J., "Now we have with us the lady cop," *The Ogden Standard* (Utah), July 17, 1913.

"Brooklyn Police Matrons," *The Sun* (New York), July 12, 1887.

"Brooklyn Police Matrons," *The Evening World* (New York), March 12, 1892.

"Brooklyn Women in Police Reserve," *New York Times*, May 30, 1918, p. 9.

Brown, Jennifer, "European policewomen: a comparative research perspective," *International Journal of the Sociology of Law* 25 (1997): 1–19.

Brownlow, Louis, "The Policewoman and the Woman Criminal," *National Municipal Review* 16 (July 1927): 467–68.

Bukhari, Shujaat, "Quit jobs, militants tell Muslim policewomen," *The Hindu* (Madras, India), January 21, 2003.

"Bureau for Policewomen," *New York Times*, November 2, 1924, p. 25.

Burnham, David, "More Women Join Ranks of Nation's Police Forces," *New York Times*, June 6, 1972, pp. 1, 32.

Buwalda, Imra Wann, "The Policewoman — Yesterday, Today and Tomorrow," *Journal of Social Hygiene* 31 (May 1945): 290–293.

California, Department of the California Highway Patrol, *Women Traffic Officer Project: Final Report*. Sacramento: Department of California Highway Patrol, 1976.

Cameron, Gledhill, "Detective Kitty Barney," *Colliers* 134 (November 26, 1954): 32ff.

"A Canadian first," *Maclean's*, December 12, 1994.

"Captains opposed to Police Matrons," *New York Tribune*, February 10, 1883.

Carrier, John, *The Campaign for the Employment of Women as Police Officers*, Aldershot, England: Avebury, 1988.

"Chances for a Policewoman," *The Washington Times* (DC), November 25, 1894.

"Charter in way of policewoman," *San Francisco Call*, May 24, 1913.

Chasen, Will, "New York's Finest (Female Div.)," *New York Times Magazine*, November 20, 1955, p. 26.

Chesshyre, Robert, "Softly Softly," *New*

Statesman and Society 2 (November 24, 1989): 20–21.

"Chicago copette with pistol puts end to riot," *Tensas Gazette* (St. Joseph, LA), February 26, 1915.

"Chicago, in despair, may try Police-women," *San Francisco Call*, April 5, 1912.

"Chicago Policewomen receiving instruction in shooting revolvers," *The Evening Herald* (New York), March 23, 1914.

"Chicago Rejoices in Policewomen," *New York Times*, August 6, 1913, p. 7.

"Chicago's new policewomen start work today," *The Day Book* (Chicago), August 5, 1913.

"Chicago's Policewoman," *New York Tribune*, October 29, 1911.

"Chicago's Policewomen, *The Washington Herald* (DC), August 8, 1913.

"Chief of Chicago's Policewomen," *Tensas Gazette* (St. Joseph, LA), January 16, 1914.

"Children First," *The Times* (London), July 13, 1923, p. 13.

"China Has First Policewomen," *New York Times*, September 27, 1933, p. 3.

Citizens' Police Committee, *Chicago Police Problems*, Chicago: University of Chicago Press, 1931.

"City and Suburban News," *New York Times*, October 24, 1891, p. 3.

"City has policewoman who knows her business," *Evening Public Ledger* (Philadelphia), January 12, 1915.

"City officials give opinions on the value of policewomen," *The Sun* (New York), September 19, 1915.

"City Policewomen to Wear Uniforms," *New York Times*, January 14, 1935, p. 17.

"Civil service board wants information," *San Francisco Call*, July 1, 1913.

"Cleveland Women Win," *Los Angeles Herald*, April 22, 1894.

"Club women to be not as of old," *San Francisco Call*, June 30, 1913.

Cochran, Joy, "EEOC — officer's filing is valid; ex-policewoman says Eagle Lake discriminated against her," *The Ledger* (Lakeland, FL), May 4, 2006.

Cohen, Tobi, "Top Mountie outlines plan to address harassment in RCMP," *Calgary Herald*, February 1, 2012, p. A8.

Coleman, Patricia, "A lot of Time is Spent Just Helping People," *The Times* (London), February 19, 1969, p. 11.

Collins, Sue Carter, "Sexual harassment and police discipline," *Policing: An International Journal of Police Strategies and Management*, 27, no. 4 (2004): 512–538.

"Concerned for their Sex," *Los Angeles Herald*, February 15, 1894.

"Commission government," *Sausalito News*, June 3, 1916.

"Conservation," *Los Angeles Herald*, May 25, 1910.

"A Constable in Petticoats," *The Hocking Sentinel* (Logan, OH), August 19, 1897.

"Copettes sworn, but what they'll do puzzles chief," *San Francisco Call*, October 21, 1913.

"Coppettes to watch Mrs. Mary Vaughn," *San Francisco Call*, November 1, 1913.

Cordner, Gary, and Annmarie Cordner, "Stuck on a Plateau? Obstacles to recruitment, selection, and retention of women police," *Police Quarterly*, 14, no. 3 (2011): 207–226.

Corelli, Rae, "Aiming for respect," *Maclean's*, April 10, 1995.

"Court Criticizes Police Department in a Sex Case," *New York Times*, July 29, 1992, p. B3.

Creighton, Louise, "Women Police," *Fortnightly Review* 114 (July 1920): 109–17.

"Criminal lawyer says police usurp their powers," *Los Angeles Herald*, February 16, 1910.

Critchley, T. A., *A History of Police in England and Wales*, rev. ed., London: Constable, 1978.

"Current comment," *The Seattle Republican*, March 11, 1910.

"Dallas policewomen say 80% harassed," *Austin American-Statesman* (TX), August 10, 1997, p. B6.

Darwin, Maud, "Policewomen: Their Work in America," *The Nineteenth Century and After* 75 (June 1914): 1371–77.

Davis, James A., "Perspectives of Policewomen in Texas and Oklahoma," *Journal of Police Science and Administration* 12, no. 4 (December 1984): 395–403.

Davis, Katharine Bement, "The Police Woman" *Woman Citizen* 10 (May 30, 1925): 14.

Davis, Patricia, "Complaints of Sexism Detailed," *Washington Post*, August 3, 1992, pp. B1, B5.

De Haas, Greetje Timmerman, and Mechtild Hoing, "Sexual harassment and health among male and female Police officers," *Journal of Occupational Health Psychology* 14, no. 4 (2009): 390–401.

"Denver court reinstates woman police officer," *El Paso Herald*, July 8, 1913.

"Denver's Policewoman Quits," *New York Times*, August 6, 1913, p. 7.

"Detectives Show New Policewomen Tamest Chicago," *Chicago Tribune*, August 6, 1913, pp. 1, 2.

Detzer, Karl, "Detroit's Lady Cops," *American Mercury* 54 (March 1942): 345–51.

"Diana Dillpickles" (comic strip), *The Tacoma Times*, September 30, 1914.

Dick, Gavin, and Beverley Metcalfe, "The progress of female police officers," *International Journal of Public Sector Management* 20, no. 2 (2007): 81–100.

"Discrimination against women police rampant," *Women's International Network News* 28, no. 3 (Summer 2002): 64.

Dodd, Vikram, "Met's £1m hate campaign payout," *The Guardian* (UK), June 6, 2000.

"Don't call her a cop; El Paso has new copette on job," *El Paso Herald*, March 24, 1919.

Dreifus, Claudia, "Why Two Women Cops Were Convicted of Cowardice," *Ms.* 9 (April 1981): 57–58.

Duke, Lynne, "Law Enforcers Grapple with Diversity," *Washington Post*, January 27, 1993, pp. A1, A12.

Dunbar, Ruth, "The solution of the girl question is a trade unionism, which teaches how to think, says feminine lobby," *New York Tribune*, November 4, 1915.

"Duties of Women Police," *New York Times*, July 28, 1918, sec. 3, p. 3.

Editorial, *The Sun*, (New York), May 5, 1882.

Editorial, *Sacramento Daily Union*, May 17, 1882.

Edwards, Thomas C., "Social Protection — A Workable Plan," *Journal of Social Hygiene* 38 (December 1952): 373–81.

Egan, Timothy, "New Faces and New Roles, for the Police," *New York Times*, April 25, 1991, pp. A1, B10.

Elias, Marilyn Koral, "The Urban Cop," *Ms.* 12 (June 1984): 17.

"Engage in many lines of work," *Los Angeles Herald*, July 17, 1909.

"Enright Advises Women," *New York Times*, November 10, 1992, p. 19.

"Enright's Last Acts Give 12 Promotions," *New York Times*, December 31, 1925, p. 1.

"Equal Guardians of the Law," *Society* 11 (September/October 1974): 8, 10.

"Equal Opportunities on the Beat," *The Times* (London), April 27, 1978, p. 19.

Evans, Peter, "Women in the Police," *The Times* (London), February 2, 1976, p. 14.

Evans, Peter, "Women Shoulder Increasing Part of Burden," *The Times* (London), November 10, 1977, p. 4.

"Ex-police inspector wins discrimination fight against force," *The Birmingham Post* (UK), September 5, 1998.

"Face It Squarely — Deal with It," *Los Angeles Times*, December 17, 1992, p. B6.

"A fair force," *The Jasper News* (MO), April 2, 1908.

"Fair officer now bosses traffic on District's streets," *The Washington Times* (DC), November 1, 1918.

Fairchild, Erika S., "Women Police in Weimar," *Law and Society Review* 21, no. 3 (1987): 375–402.

Farley, Lin, *Sexual Shakedown*, New York: McGraw-Hill, 1978.

Faux, Ronald, "Halford Drops Sex Bias Case for £142,000," *The Times* (London), July 22, 1992, p. 1.

Faux, Ronald, "Halford Tells of Years of Misery," *The Times* (London), June 2, 1992, p. 3.

Faux, Ronald, "Halford Work Files Altered," *The Times* (London), June 4, 1992, p. 5.

Faux, Ronald, "Police Chief Attacks Halford's Victory Claims as Farcical," *The Times* (London), July 23, 1992, p. 5.

"Female Fuzz, The," *Newsweek* 80 (October 23, 1972): 117.

"Female Police," *Kansas City Journal* (MO), May 8, 1895.

"Female Police Officer, The," *St. Paul Daily Globe*, September 18, 1887.

"Female Quota Set for LAPD," *Los Angeles Times*, September 20, 1992, p. M4.

"Feminists Ban Talk on Household Science," *New York Times*, June 6, 1926, sec. 2, p. 6.

"15-Year Police Matron," *Kansas City Journal* (MO), January 2, 1898.

"Fight white slave trade," *Bemidji Daily Pioneer* (MN), January 26, 1911.

Fiore, Faye, "Sheriff's Dept. Concedes on 2 Sex Bias Suits," *Los Angeles Times*, December 4, 1992, pp. A1, A36.

"First D.C. policewoman tells of her spy hunt," *The Washington Times* (DC), July 23, 1918.

"First head of policewomen," *Tensas Gazette* (St. Joseph LA), August 6, 1915.

"First Municipal Women Detective in the World, The," *New York Times*, March 3, 1912, pt. 5, p. 1.

"First Police Woman Is on Their Trail," *Los Angeles Times*, September 14, 1910, pt. 2, p. 1.

"First Policewoman, The," *The Herald* (Los Angeles), September 20, 1896.

"First Policewoman, The," *The Sun* (New York), December 19, 1912.

"First Policewoman to Leave Force," *New York Times*, January 27, 1926, p. 25.

"First Woman 'Policeman,'" *Los Angeles Times*, September 13, 1910, pt. 2, p. 9.

Fischberg, Carole, "Copping In," *Ms.* 3 (May 1975): 21.

"Fix Policewomen's Dress," *New York Times*, September 18, 1923, p. 9.

Flammang, C. J., *Police Juvenile Enforcement*, Springfield, IL: Charles C. Thomas, 1972.

Fleming, Alice, *New on the Beat*, New York: Coward, McCann and Geoghegan, 1975.

"Flirts with policewoman; cured? We should cackle," *The Washington Herald* (DC), May 19, 1917.

"For Afghan policewomen, sex abuse is a job hazard," *National Public Radio* (show: *All Things Considered*), March 8, 2012.

"For Policewomen," *New York Tribune*, September 26, 1908.

"For the Ladies," *The Forest Republican* (Tionesta, PA), June 28, 1882.

"For Woman in Police Job," *New York Times*, May 25, 1929, p. 16.

"45 classic beauties needed on cop force; doll babies barred," *The Washington Times* (DC), May 19, 1921.

Fosdick, Raymond B., *American Police Systems*, Montclair, NJ: Patterson Smith, 1972, reprint 1920 ed.

Foster, Elene, "On the beat with a lady cop," *New York Tribune*, September 22, 1918.

"Four mashers nabbed after they picked up leader of copettes," *The Washington Times* (DC), October 19, 1920.

"Four new policewomen appointed to city force," *New York Tribune*, August 30, 1918.

Frank, Stanley, "Some Cops Have Lovely Legs," *Saturday Evening Post* 222 (December 24, 1949): 11–13

Freeman, Barbara M., *The Satellite Sex: The Media and Women's Issues in Canada 1966–1971*, Waterloo: Wilfrid Laurier University Press, 2001.

Fried, Joseph P., "Transfer Linked to Harassment, Police Cay," *New York Times*, October 17, 1992, p. 28.

"Functions and Organization of a Police Unit Doing Protective and Preventive Work with Women and Children," *Public Personnel Studies* 5 (December 1927): 245–74.

"Future of Women Police, *The Times* (London), February 1, 1923, p. 7.

Gaston, Kevin C., and Jackie A. Alexander, "Women in the police: factors influencing managerial Advancement," *Women in Management Review* 12, no. 2 (1997): 47–55.

"A Girl Burglar's Sentence," *The Sun* (New York), July 15, 1882.

"Girl threatens suit for breach of promise," *Los Angeles Herald*, February 4, 1909.

"Good Housekeeping Finds Out What a Policewoman Does," *Good Housekeeping* 113 (December 1941): 26–27.

"Gotham's woman traffic cops in action," *The Morning Tulsa Daily World*, December 11, 1921.

Grad, Shelby, "Irvine Orders Probe of Police Sex Charges," *Los Angeles Times*, June 24, 1993, p. B8.

Graef, Roger, *Talking Blues*, London: Collins Harvill, 1989.

Grant, Diana R., "Perceived gender differences in policing," *Women and Criminal Justice* 12, no. 1 (2000): 53–74.

Graper, Elmer D., *American Police Administration*, New York: Macmillan, 1921.

"Greatest mancatchers alive," *The Times* (Moncton, NB), July 4, 2011, p. C9.

Greeley-Smith, Nixola, "Holds the mirror up to women," *The Evening World* (New York), May 4, 1911.

Greeley-Smith, Nixola, "Says more policewomen will rid streets of mashers who pester young girls," *The Day Book* (Chicago), February 10, 1914.

Greeley-Smith, Nixola, "Says New York needs many like her to protect girls and rebuff mashers," *The Evening World* (New York), June 14, 1917.

Greene, Ronnie, "Jury: former policewoman was harassed," *Miami Herald*, December 15, 1994.

Gross, Sally, "Women Becoming Cops," *Police Chief* 51 (January 1984): 32–35.

"Guard of coppettes for Mrs. Pankhurst," *San Francisco Call*, November 1, 1913.

Gultekin, Ellen C. Leichtman, and Carole G. Garrison, "Gender issues and the women of the Turkish National Police," *Police Practice and Research* 11 (October 2010): 423–436.

Haba, Calvin Wesley, Robert A. Sarver III, Rhonda Dobbs, and Mary B. Sarver, "Attitudes of college Students toward women in policing," *Women and Criminal Justice* 19, no. 3 (2009): 235–50.

Haldane, Robert, *The People's Force*, Melbourne, Australia: Melbourne University Press, 1986.

"Halford Trap Claim," *The Times* (London), June 15, 1992, p. 2.

Halsey, Ashley Jr., "The Lady Cops of the Dope Squad," *Saturday Evening Post* 229 (March 30, 1957): 36–37.

Hamilton, Alan, "Recruitment of Women No Answer to fall in Police Manpower," *The Times* (London), April 27, 1978, p. 6.

Hamilton, Mary E., *The Policewoman: Her Service and Ideals*, New York: Frederick A. Stokes, 1924.

Hamilton, Mary E., "Woman's Place in the Police Department," *American City* 32 (February 1925): 194–95.

Harvey, E. A., "One of the guys—cops say ability not gender is gauge for policewomen whose numbers are creeping up," *Sunday News* (Lancaster, PA), March 10, 2002, p. G1.

"He Hugged a Policewoman," *New York Times*, May 1, 1925, p. 11.

"Heads policewomen," *Tensas Gazette* (St. Joseph, LA), November 23, 1917.

"Hear Officer Alice Wells," *New York Times*, March 12, 1914, p. 3.

"Help is sought by Policewoman," *Los Angeles Herald*, October 30, 1910.

"Her Many Duties," *New York Tribune*, June 17, 1901.

"Her weak point," *The Salt Lake Tribune*, May 10, 1906.

Herman, M., *Prisoners' Rights Sourcebook*, New York: Clark Boardman, 1973.

Hesselberg, George, "Pioneering policewoman Mary Ostrander, 60, dies," *Wisconsin State Journal* (Madison), September 21, 1994.

Hevesi, Dennis, "Sex Discrimination Complaints against the Police Are Upheld," *New York Times*, November 26, 1991, p. B3.

Higginbotham, Jeffrey, "Sexual Harassment in the Police Station," *FBI Law Enforcement Bulletin* 57 (September 1988): 22–29.

Higgins, Lois, "Historical Background of Policewomen's Service," *Journal of Criminal Law and Criminology* 41 (March/April 1951): 822–33.

Higgins, Lois, "The Policewoman," *Police* 3 (November/December 1958): 66–67.

Higgins, Lois, "Women Police Service," *Journal of Criminal Law and Criminology* 41 (May 1950): 101–106.

Hindman, Robert E. "A Survey Related to use of Female Law Enforcement Officers," *Police Chief* 42 (April 1975): 58–59.

"History of the Police Matron," *The Evening World* (New York), October 22, 1892.

Hoffman, Peter B., and Edward R. Hickey, "Use of force by female officers," *Journal of Criminal Justice* 33 (2005): 145–151.

Homant, Robert J., "The Impact of Policewomen on Community Attitudes toward Police," *Journal of Police Science and Administration*, 11, no. 1 (March 1983): 16–22.

Homant, Robert J., "Police Perception of Spouse Abuse," *Journal of Criminal Justice* 13, no. 1 (1985): 29–47.

"Home Office Vote," *The Times* (London), June 30, 1922, p. 19.

Honan, William H., "Felicia Shpritzer dies at 87," *New York Times*, December 31, 2000.

"A Honolulu Belle," *Crittenden Press* (Marion, KY), August 10, 1899.

"Hooliganism Danger to Woman PCs," *The Times* (London), September 8, 1977, p. 3.

Horne, Peter, *Women in Law Enforcement*, 2nd ed., Springfield, IL: Charles C. Thomas, 1980.

"How New York's Policewomen spot the German spies," *The Washington Times* (DC), September 15, 1918, American Wk. Sec.

"How Women Prisoners Fare at the Central Station," *The St. Paul Globe*, March 30, 1902.

Hussein, Jenan, "Women join ranks of Iraq's police," *The Miami Herald*, January 27, 2009.

Hutzel, Eleonore L., "The Policewoman," *Annals of the American Academy of Political and Social Science* 146 (November 1929): 104–114.

Hutzel, Eleonore L., *The Policewoman's Handbook*, New York: Columbia University Press, 1933.

"Ideals of the Women Police," *The Times* (London), May 25, 1920, p. 12.

"Impressionable," *Sausalito News*, January 2, 1915.

"In the World of Women," *Evening Capital Journal* (Salem, OR), April 28, 1890.

"Iran: police commander says policewomen necessary for society," *Irna News Agency* (Tehran, Iran), February 4, 2003.

"Iranian policewomen back on job — 215 graduates to serve alongside men," *Seattle Times*, October 5, 2003, p. A24.

"Irish opposes Oakland's plan of policewomen," *San Francisco Call*, July 13, 1913.

"Items of interest," *Dakota County Herald* (Dakota City, NE), September 12, 1918.

Ith, Ian, "Ex-policewoman awarded $225,000 to settle lawsuit," *The Seattle Times*, February 5, 2003, p. B3.

Janusz, Barbara D., "Mounting pressure, *Herizons* (Summer 2012): 16–19.

"Jersey Policewoman Quits," *New York Times*, July 8, 1914, p. 20.

Johnson, Paul H., "Town, officer settle harassment suit," *The Hartford Courant*, April 30, 1998, p. B3.

Johnson, Willard, "A Municipal Mother," *Sunset* 62 (April 1929): 25.

Jordan, Modeste H., "Twenty-Four Hours with the Police Matron in the St. Louis Four Courts," *The St. Louis Republican*, January 26, 1902, magazine sec.

"Jordan's policewomen see better times ahead," *Toronto Star*, March 13, 1993, p. J5.

"Jury Awards $900,000 to Black Female Officer in Detroit Police case," *Jet* 72 (April 27, 1987): 33.

"Just don't complain. Policewomen told to ignore sex harassment," *Daily Telegraph* (Sydney, Australia), January 12, 2007.

Keller, James, "Federal government issues denial in one of several RCMP harassment lawsuits," *The Canadian Press*, October 23, 2012.

Keller, Michele, "UC Irvine Chooses new Female Police Chief," *Daily Bruin*, October 19, 1992, p. 1.

Kempton, Maureen, "All we Want for Christmas is our Jobs Back," *Ms.* 4 (December 1975): 68–69.

Kennedy, Daniel B., "Attitudes of Abused Women toward Male and Female Police Officers," *Criminal Justice and Behavior* 10, no. 4 (December 1983): 391–405.

Kerber, Kenneth W., "Citizen Attitudes Regarding the Competence of Female Police Officers," *Journal of Police Science and Administration* 5, no. 3 (September 1977): 337–47.

Khodary, Tagheed el, "Under robe and veil, crossing boundaries as policewomen," *New York Times*, January 18, 2008, p. A4.

"Kills Policewomen Bill," *New York Times*, March 14, 1914, p. 1.

King, David J., "Separate but equal: the introduction and integration of policewomen in the Bermuda Police 1961–2002," *Police Practice and Research* 6, no. 3 (July 2005): 215–233.

Klabin, Karen, "Lewd Conduct," *LA Weekly* 15 (March 5, 1993): 14, 16.

Kluchesky, Joseph, "Policewomen," *American City* 52 (July 1937): 17.

Koening, Esther J., "Attitudes toward Policewomen: A Study of Interrelationships and Determinants," *Journal of Police Science and Administration* 9, no. 4 (December 1981): 463–74.

Koening, Esther J., "An Overview of Attitudes toward Women in Law Enforcement," *Public Administration Review* 38 (May 1978): 267–75.

Kopetman, Roxana, "Long Beach Policewomen Call Sexual Harassment Endemic," *Los Angeles Times*, September 28, 1991, p. B3.

Lacy, Hester, "Real lives," *The Independent* (London UK), March 21, 1999.

"Ladies of Temperance," *St. Paul Daily Globe*, July 31, 1886.

"Lady and her star, The," *The Bee* (Earlington, KY), August 29, 1911.

"Lady Cops to tell men to g'wan now," *The Evening World* (New York), March 8, 1906.

"Lady is a Cop, The, "Look 20 (March 6, 1956): 48–53.

"League Declares for Women Police," New York Times, September 16, 1923, p. 3.

League of Nations. Advisory Commission for the Protection and Welfare of Children and Young People. Traffic in Women and Children Committee. *The Employment of Women in the Police*, Geneva: League of Nations, 1927.

Leger, Kristen, "Public perceptions of female police officers on patrol," *American Journal of Criminal Justice* 21, no. 2 (1997): 231–249.

Lehtinen, Marlene W., "Sexism in Police Departments," *Trial* 12 (December 1976): 52.

Lersch, Kim Michelle, "Exploring gender differences in citizen allegations of misconduct," *Women and Criminal Justice* 9, no. 4 (1998): 69–79.

"Let women do the work," *San Francisco Call*, March 1, 1913.

"Life of Police Matrons," *New York Tribune*, May 13, 1904.

"Lily Pines for a Billy," *The Washington Times* (DC), November 21, 1894.

"Lily visits the Police Court," *The Washington Times*, (DC), December 4, 1894.

"Lily won't wield a Billy," *The Washington Times* (DC), January 25, 1895.

Lonsway, Kimberly A., and Angela M. Alipio, "Sex discrimination lawsuits in law enforcement," *Women and Criminal Justice* 18, no. 4 (2007): 63–103.

Lord, Lesli Kay, "A Comparison of Male and Female Peace Officers' Stereotypic Perceptions of Women and Women Peace Officers," *Journal of Police Science and Administration* 14, no. 2 (June 1986): 83–97.

"Los Angeles Police Agree to set Minority Hiring Goads," *New York Times*, November 21, 1980, p. A16.

"Los Angeles secures first Policewoman, *Los Angeles Herald*, September 13, 1910.

"Low-Down Journalism," *Los Angeles Daily Herald*, August 31, 1888.

Low, Pauline C., "Policewomen and Equality," *British Journal of Criminology* 29, no. 1 (Winter 1989): 79–80.

Luk, Vivian, "I broke. I completely broke," *The Province* (Vancouver BC), November 9, 2011, p. A3.

Luk, Vivian, "RCMP operates as 'old boys' culture," *The Province* (Vancouver BC) November 10, 2011, p. A8.

Mackie, John, "Pounding the beat," *Vancouver Sun* (BC), June 25, 2012, p. D6.

"Macphee and Taylor dismissed from force," *San Francisco Call*, July 8, 1913.

McGeorge, Joann, "A Comparison of Attitudes Between Men and Women Police Officers," *Criminal Justice Review* 1 (Fall 1976): 21–33.

McMullen, Frances Drewry, "The Policewoman's Beat," *The Woman's Journal* 14 (March 1929): 7–9.

Mahajan, Amarjit, *Indian Policewomen*, New Delhi: Deep and Deep, 1982.

"Making a Prison Cheerful," *Daily Globe* (St. Paul, MN), March 24, 1878.

"Man Arrested by Policewoman," *The Times* (London), July 3, 1929, p. 10.

"Man loses his vocational monopolies," *San Francisco Call*, March 3, 1912.

Mandel-Campbell, Andrea, "The swans don't bite," *U.S. News & World Report*, November 1, 1999.

Mantilla, Karla, "Male officers worse than females," *Off Our Backs*, April 2001, p. 4.

"Many girls robbed, says Seattle's Policewoman," *The Seattle Star*, December 28, 1909.

"Many girls saved by policewomen," *The Sun* (New York), October 10, 1919.

"Many more women want women police," *The Sun* (New York), April 4, 1913.

Marks, Alexandra, "Women face blue wall of resistance," *Christian Science Monitor*, August 18, 1999.

Marro, Anthony, "Blacks and Women to be Hired for Louisiana Police-Fire Jobs," *New York Times*, June 30, 1977, p. A14.

Marshall, Marguerite Mooers, "Enter the copperette to jolt Jersey violators of law with night stickette," *The Evening World* (New York), March 6, 1915.

Marshall, Marguerite Mooers, "First policewoman's first job is to settle a domestic quarrel," *The Evening World* (New York), June 23, 1913.

Marshall, Marguerite Mooers, "Policewomen for New York to replace war-called men the latest patriotic effort," *The Evening World* (New York), June 12, 1917.

Marshall, Sabina, "Development of the Policewoman's Movement in Cleveland, Ohio," *Journal of Social Hygiene* 11 (April 1925): 193–209.

Martin, Carol Ann, "Women Police and Stress, *Police Chief* 50 (March 1983): 107–09.

Martin, Susan, *Breaking and Entering: Policewomen on Patrol*, Berkeley: University of California Press, 1980.

Martin, Susan, *On the Move: The Status of Women in Policing*, Washington, DC: Police Foundation, 1990.

Martin, Susan, "Policewomen and Policewomen: Occupational Role Dilemmas and Choices of Female Officers," *Journal of Police Science and Administration* 7, no. 3 (September 1979): 314–23.

Martin, Susan, "Sexual Politics in the Workplace: The Interactional World of Policewomen," *Symbolic Interaction* 1, no. 2 (Spring 1978): 44–60.

Mason, Gary, "Dozens of female RCMP officers seek justice through class-action lawsuit," *The Globe and Mail* (Toronto), January 21, 2012, p. S1.

Masters, Ruth E., "A Woman Corrections Professor and a Woman Reserve Officer's View," *Police Chief* 50 (January 1983): 61–66.

"Matron on Duty, The," *St. Paul Daily Globe*, March 23, 1890.

"Matrons at the City Jail," *Omaha Daily Bee*, September 12, 1900.

"Matrons in Police Stations," *New York Tribune*, May 30, 1888.

"Matrons may not be Matrons," *New York Times*, June 28, 1899, p. 5.

McDonough, Molly, "Pregnant pause," *ABA Journal* 92 (August 2006).

McLean, Mrs. Marshall, "New York one of few big cities without policewomen," *The Sun* (New York), May 30, 1915.

"Men here flirt — but girlies coax em to, says Mrs. Van Winkle," *The Washington Times* (DC), October 11, 1920.

"Men outperform Women as Police, Study Asserts," *New York Times*, July 31, 1978, p. A10.

Mendoza, N. F., "Crossing the Thin Blue Line," *Los Angeles Times*, May 11, 1993, pp. F1, F7.

"Met pays £150,000 to ex-policewoman," *Greater London, Kent and Surrey Counties Publication* (UK), December 6, 2000.

Miller, Mary Ashe, "Few thrills for copettes," *San Francisco Call*, October 31, 1913.

Milton, Catherine, *Women in Policing*," Washington, DC: Police Foundation, 1972.

"Minneapolis Globules," *St. Paul Daily Globe*, July 24, 1888.

Mitchell, Hannah, "Lady cops in Washington are efficient," *New York Tribune*, May 4, 1919.

"Mobile Women Police Suggested," *The Times* (London), October 17, 1935, p. 20.

Mockler v. Multnomah County, Case number 96–35895, downloaded from web, July 26, 1912.

"Money for Matrons," *Pittsburg Dispatch*, December 10, 1889.

Monk, S., "Policewomen just as physical as the men," *The Courier Mail* (Brisbane), July 2, 1998, p. 4.

Moore, Dahlia, "Gender traits and identities in a masculine organization: the Israeli police force," *Journal of Social Psychology* 39 (February 1999).

Morash, Merry, "Evaluating Women on Patrol," *Evaluation Review* 10 (April 1986): 230–55.

"More Cities Employ Policewomen," *American City* 63 (February 1948): 17.

"More Cities Hire Policewomen," *American City* 65 (March 1950): 17.

"More Policewomen are Urged for City," *New York Times*, January 27, 1929, p. 19.

"More Women Police Assigned to Patrol Duty, Study Reports," *Justice Assistance News* 3 (March 1982): 1, 4.

"More Women Police Needed," *The Times* (London), March 11, 1944, p. 2.

Morgan, Ted, "Women Make Good Cops," *New York Times Magazine*, November 3, 1974, p. 18.

Morrison, Patt, "Female Officers Unwelcome—but Doing Fine," *Los Angeles Times*, July 12, 1991, pp. A1, A27-A29.

"'Mother' of Disillusioned Girls in New York City, A," *Literary Digest* 80 (March 15, 1924): 56, 58.

"Mothers of girls told of dangers by policewoman," *The Washington Times*, October 14, 1917.

"Moving to Right a Wrong," *Los Angeles Times*, December 24, 1992, p. B6.

"Mrs. Belmont urges need of policewomen," *New York Tribune*, March 6, 1913.

"Mrs. Herbert H. Votaw," *New York Tribune*, May 4, 1919.

"Mrs. Sarah B. Schaeffer," *The Minneapolis Journal*, January 16, 1901.

Muir, Frederick, "Council sets Goal of 44% Female LAPD in 8 Years," *Los Angeles Times*, September 10, 1992, pp. A1, A23.

Murdock, Julia, "Sylvester favors women policemen," *The Washington Times* (DC), August 8, 1913.

Murphy, Patrick V., *Commissioner*, New York: Simon and Schuster, 1977.

"Muscular coppette drags fighter off car; lands him in jail," *San Francisco Call*, December 26, 1913.

"Names Policewomen for Chicago," *New York Times*, August 2, 1913, p. 5.

Natarajan, Mangai, "Towards equality," *Women and Criminal Justice* 8, no. 2 (1996): 1–18.

Nazario, Sonia, "Force to be Reckoned with," *Los Angeles Times*, June 5, 1993, pp. A1, A12.

"Needed Police Reform, A," *New York Times*, March 23, 1890, p. 20.

"Negress new D.C. copette," *The Washington Times* (DC), August 19, 1920.

"Negro woman on Seattle's force," *The Kansas City Sun* (MO), February 14, 1914.

"Nellie Bly," *The Norfolk Virginian*, April 11, 1895.

Nelson, Josephine, "On the Policewoman's Beat," *Independent Woman* 15 (May 1936): 138–40.

Nelson, Sara, "Constructing and negotiating gender in women's police stations in Brazil," *Latin American Perspectives* 23 (1996): 131–148.

"New Honors for Women," *San Francisco Call*, September 17, 1911.

"New police officer assumes her duties," *Los Angeles Herald*, September 14, 1910.

"New Policewomen here do not awe Herald's reporter a bit," *The Evening Herald* (Albuquerque), August 8, 1918.

"New York's first Policewoman," *Valentine Democrat* (Valentine, NE), February 1, 1912.

"Newport Beach Settles 4 Harassment Cases," *Los Angeles Times*, February 4, 1993, p. A17.

Nicholl, Ruaridh, "Policewoman backed over sexist ruling," *The Guardian* (UK), May 23, 1998.

Nifong, Christina, "Gender revolution in precinct house," *Christian Science Monitor*, May 22, 1996.

"No club for policewoman," *New York Tribune*, July 10, 1913.

"No Longer Men or Women," *U.S. News and World Report* 77 (August 19, 1974): 45–46.

"No Maryland women Police," *New York Tribune*, July 12, 1910.

"No Police Matrons," *National Republican* (Washington, DC), February 5, 1888.

"No Police Matrons yet," *New York Times*, August 13, 1890, p. 8.

No Title, *Western Reserve Chronicle* (Warren, Ohio), September 7, 1870.

No Title, *The Anderson Intelligencer*, (Anderson, SC), June 23, 1881.

No Title, *Daily Alta California*, March 15, 1886.

No Title, *St. Paul Daily Globe*, April 14, 1887.

No Title, *Sausalito News*, May 3, 1888.

No Title, *New York Tribune*, May 30, 1888.

No Title, *Omaha Daily Bee*, June 5, 1888.

No title, *New York Tribune*, October 23, 1888.

No Title, *Albuquerque Daily Citizen*, April 7, 1899.

No Title, *The Roanoke Daily Times* (VA), September 4, 1896.

No Title, *Austin's Hawaiian Weekly* (Honolulu), October 21, 1899.

No Title, *The Day Book* (Chicago), September 16, 1912.

No Title, *The Tacoma Times*, May 6, 1913.

No Title, *San Francisco Call*, March 14, 1914.

"Norfolk to have a female police officer," *The Times* (Richmond, VA), December 5, 1902.

"Now in Moroccan capital: policewomen on patrol," *The Orlando Sentinel*, March 4, 1998, p. A24.

"Now we've got policewomen on the force," *The Day Book* (Chicago), August 2, 1913.

"Nude Model gets Job back with NYC Police," *Jet* 68 (April 29, 1985): 24.

"Oakland women may wear stars," *San Francisco Call*, June 27, 1913.

O'Block, Robert L., "The Emerging Role of the Female Detective," *Police Chief* 47 (May 1980): 54–55, 69.

O'Brien, G. M., *The Australian Police Forces*, Melbourne, Australia: Oxford University Press, 1960.

"Officer Forced to Quit, gets new Job with City," *New York Times*, July 22, 1984, p. A16.

"Officers chosen by Policewomen," *San Francisco Call*, October 27, 1912.

"Officers of the Law should know Better," *Los Angeles Times*, February 1, 1991, p. B6.

"Officer's Suit says she was Raped, then Fired," *Los Angeles Times*, December 18, 1992, p. B3.

"Officers tell of Bias on Fairfax County," *Washington Post*, June 4, 1992, pp. A1, A18.

"Officers win harassment case," *Long Beach Press Telegram*, June 3, 2003, p. A1.

Ogbuaku, G. Ochi, "Ladies on the Force," *National Business Woman* 35 (November 1956): 22.

O'Grady, Ellen A., "Experience endorses our police women," *New York Tribune*, September 7, 1919.

O'Grady, Ellen A., "Policewomen and their Work," *American City* 20 (January 1919): 59–60.

"100 more policewomen advocated for City," *New York Times*, April 29, 1925, p. 6.

"100 More Policewomen asked in a Campaign Covering City," *New York Times*, March 3, 1925, p. 21.

"155 Women Police to Carry Pistols," *New York Times*, December 12, 1934, p. 25.

"175 in Motor Squad sent to Foot Duty," *New York Times*, January 23, 1926, p. 17

"Ordinance No. 123," *Los Angeles Daily Herald*, June 10, 1889.

"Ossining Hires a Policewoman," *New York Times*, September 20, 1927, p. 4.

Ott, E. Marlies, "Effects of the Male-Female Ratio at Work," *Psychology of Women Quarterly* 13 (March 1989): 41–57.

"Out of a Good Job," *Kansas City Daily Journal* (MO), July 3, 1896.

"Outline qualifications for new policewomen," *San Francisco Call*, August 14, 1913.

Owen, Langdon, "If there were Women Police," *The Rising Son* (Kansas City, MO), May 31, 1906.

Owens, James M., "Policewoman in the Line," *Police* 3 (September/October 1958): 21–22.

Owings, Chloe, *Women Police*, Montclair, NJ: Patterson Smith, 1969, reprint of 1925 ed.

Owings, Chloe, "Women Police," *Journal of Social Hygiene* 11 (January 1925): 38–45.

Paleolog, Stanislawa, *The Women Police of Poland 1925 to 1939*, London: Association for Moral and Social Hygiene, 1957.

"Palmist wrong; arrested," *The Washington Times* (DC), May 30, 1917.

Paolino, Susan Bouman, "My Dream of Enforcing the Law became a Nightmare," *Los Angeles Times*, August 18, 1991, pp. M3, M6.

Parker, Valeria H., "A Policewoman's Life," *Woman Citizen* 9 (June 28, 1924): 16–17.

"Patrol women will walk Los Angeles beats," *San Francisco Call*, April 29, 1913.

"Paterson's policewoman," *The Evening Herald* (Klamath Falls, OR), August 12, 1915.

Patterson, Ethel Lloyd, "Policewoman would prevent race suicide," *The Evening World* (New York), February 3, 1909.

"P.C. 119 will be on Duty," *The Times* (London), December 24, 1956, p. 9.

Pear, Robert, "Justice Dept. presses drive on Quotas," *New York Times*, April 3, 1985, p. A16.

"Perfect Lady in Politics, The," *The Times* (London), March 10, 1922, p. 9.

Perlstein, Gary R. "Policewomen and Policemen," *Police Chief* 39 (March 1972): 72–74.

"Personality test compulsory for D.C. lady coppers," *The Washington Times* (DC), June 14, 1921.

"Petition Enright to appoint 15 women on Police Force," *New York Times*, August 14, 1923, p. 1.

Peto, D. O. G., "The Policewoman of the Future," *Spectator* 125 (September 11, 1920): 329–30.

Peto, D. O. G., "The Status of the Policewoman," *Spectator* 123 (December 13, 1919): 805–06.

"Philadelphia Consents to Placing of Women in 30% of Police Jobs," *New York Times*, July 16, 1980, p. A19.

"Philadelphia Police Ordered to give Women 25% of Jobs," *New York Times*, September 6, 1979, p. A16.

Pigeon, Helen D., "The Policewoman's due," *Woman Citizen* 11 (August 1926): 33.

Pigeon, Helen D., "Policewomen and Public Recreation," *American City* 37 (October 1927): 448–50.

Pigeon, Helen D., "Policewomen in the United States, *Journal of the American Institute of Criminal Law and Criminology* 18 (November 1017): 372–77.

Pigeon, Helen D., "Senate Bill 1750," *Woman Citizen* 10 (February 1926): 30.

Pigeon, Helen D., "Woman's era in the Police Department," *Annals of the American Academy of Political and Social Science* 143 (May 1929): 249–54.

Platts, H. J., "Mrs. H. J. Platts will devote much of time to city probation work in Alameda," *San Francisco Call*, November 25, 1913.

"Points from other Replies," *The Times* (London), February 24, 1944, p. 8.

"Police," *Evening Star* (Washington, DC), November 30, 1889.

"Police Chief advises Politicians to shun Violent Rallies," *The Times* (London), September 28, 1977, p. 2.

"Police Commission," *Los Angeles Daily Herald*, August 2, 1888.

"Police Cover-Up," *The Times* (London), November 29, 1977, p. 3.

"Police Matron Many Years," *The Jackson Herald* (MO), May 5, 1904.

"Police Matrons," *St. Paul Daily Globe*, August 7, 1887.

"Police Matrons," *Harper's Weekly* 34 (August 30, 1890): 675.

"Police Matrons," *The Sun* (New York), August 2, 1890.

"Police Matrons," *New York Times*, August 3, 1890, p. 4.

"Police Matrons," *New York Times*, October 1, 1890, p. 4.

"Police Matrons," *The Sun* (New York), December 28, 1890.

"Police Matrons at Last," *The Evening World* (New York), March 21, 1891.

"Police Matrons begin Work," *New York Times*, October 6, 1891, p. 9.

"Police Matrons Divide Work," *Los Angeles Herald*, July 30, 1906.

"Police Matrons in New Uniforms," *New York Tribune*, October 17, 1899.

"Police Matrons Needed," *New York Times*, December 25, 1890, p. 8.

"Police Matrons on Duty," *Pittsburg Dispatch*, June 3, 1889.

"Police Matrons Wanted," *The Sun* (New York), March 3, 1882.

"Police Matron's Work, The," *St. Paul Daily Globe*, June 26, 1888.

"Police Report," *The Courier* (Lincoln, NE), May 11, 1901.

"Police woman eschews club," *San Francisco Call*, September 28, 1912.

"A Police Woman in Prospect," *The Washington Times* (DC), November 21, 1894.

"Police Woman to cover state on lecture tour," *San Francisco Call*, February 20, 1912.

"Policewoman, The," *The Seattle Star*, May 16, 1906.

"Policewoman, The," *Los Angeles Herald*, February 21, 1908.

"Policewoman," *Los Angeles Herald*, January 20, 1909.

"Policewoman, The," *The Times* (London), October 11, 1916, p. 10.

"Policewoman after Congress," *San Francisco Call*, October 29, 1913.

"Policewoman captures minister," *El Paso Herald*, December 27, 1915.

"Policewoman chases masher," *San Francisco Call*, August 7, 1913.

"Policewoman got fired for efficiency, but she's back on the job," *The Day Book* (Chicago), May 31, 1913.

"Policewoman has advice for girls," *San Francisco Call*, March 19, 1912.

"Policewoman is a sphinx," *The Jackson Herald* (WY), August 18, 1910.

"Policewoman is appointed," *San Francisco Call*, August 18, 1912.

"Police-Woman is Marching on, The," *American City* 9 (November 1913): 403.

"Policewoman of Los Angeles here," *San Francisco Call*, November 21, 1912.

"Policewoman on Trial, A," *Survey* 48 (April 15, 1922): 69–70.

"Policewoman recalls contempt from others," *Columbus Ledger-Enquirer* (GA), March 8, 1998, p. C3.

"Police-Woman's Record in Topeka, A," *Survey* 34 (September 25, 1915): 571.

"Policewoman's salary less than policeman's," *San Francisco Call*, June 22, 1913.

"Policewoman will bar all of modern dances," *The Washington Times* (DC), July 31, 1915.

"Police Women," *The Times* (London), June 20, 1914, p. 5.

"Police Women Hailed," *New York Times*, September 29, 1958, p. 29.

"Policewomen," *Journal of the American Institute of Criminal Law and Criminology* 5 (November 1914): 606–09.

"Policewomen," *New York Times*, March 31, 1880, p. 4.

"Policewomen," *The Times* (London), March 30, 1914, p. 11.

"Policewomen as Policewomen," *Society* 11 (January/February 1974): 7–10.

"Policewomen Barred," *The Times* (London), December 20, 1971, p. 2.

"Policewomen can shoot straight," *The Ogden Standard* (Utah), April 8, 1914.

"Policewomen can't handle disorderly persons of own sex," *Omaha Daily Bee*, March 5, 1914.

"Policewomen discriminated against, study finds," *The Jakarta Post* (Indonesia), October 4, 2006.

"Policewomen fail to impress chiefs," *New York Tribune*, May 27, 1915.

"Policewomen for Honolulu," *Honolulu Star-Bulletin*, December 9, 1912.

"Policewomen for New York," *The North Platte Semi-Weekly* (Nebraska), August 23, 1918.

"Policewomen held in the Los Angeles juvenile work," *Omaha Daily Bee*, December 5, 1912.

"Policewomen in Chicago," *Literary Digest* 47 (August 23, 1913): 271.

"Policewomen in conference," *San Francisco Call*, October 26, 1912.

"Policewomen in Quaker city," *New York Tribune*, November 21, 1912.

"Policewomen in Review," *New York Times*, May 28, 1935, p. 27.

"Policewomen in Washington decide not to unionize," *New York Tribune*, October 5, 1919.

"Policewomen learn methods to handle discrimination," *The Times of India* (Bombay), February 22, 2002

"Policewomen make Arrest," *New York Times*, August 8, 1913, p. 1.

"Policewomen necessary in well regulated community," *El Paso Herald*, July 14, 1917.

"Policewomen no longer a joke says officer," *The Evening Herald* (Albuquerque), May 18, 1915.

"Policewomen? No, social service inspectors," *San Francisco Call*, August 8, 1913.

"Policewomen of Indianapolis and their new Methods, The," *Literary Digest* 69 (April 23, 1921): 41–43.

"Policewomen of Bayonne," *The Sun* (New York), March 31, 1907.

"Policewomen requested," *San Francisco Call*, April 27, 1912.

"Policewomen say opportunities are improving, but slowly," *The Columbian* (Vancouver WA), May 2, 1996.

"Policewomen succeed in tough World of Streets," *New York Times*, January 27, 1974, p. 38.

"Policewomen to await new title," *San Francisco Call*, August 16, 1913.

"Policewomen to wear Uniforms as Matrons," *New York Times*, July 20, 1928, p. 10.

"Policewomen to Wrestle," *New York Times*, March 8, 1914, sec. 3, p. 5.

"Policewomen voted as joke on New York," *The Sun* (New York), April 21, 1915.

"Policewomen want change to rise to Sergeant's Rank," *New York Times*, January 29, 1927, p. 1.

"'Policing' as a Career for Young Women," *Education for Victory* 2 (October 1, 1943): 11.

"A Population Puzzle," *Daily Alta California*, June 6, 1888.

Porter, Liz, "Police pay out on harassment," *Fairfax Digital* (Australia), May 18, 2003.

"Portland has a Lady Cop," *The Spokane Press* (WA), January 14, 1907.

"£300,000 payout for policewoman," *The Independent* (London UK), May 14, 1998.

"Premier Policewoman packs pistol in her handbag," *New York Tribune*, March 26, 1914.

Prenzler, Tim, Jenny Fleming, Amanda L. King, "Gender equality in Australian and New Zealand Policing," *International Journal of Police Science and Management* 12 no 4 (2010): 584–595.

"President's safety is now often a Woman's work," *New York Times*, July 6, 1993, p. A7.

Prete, Carmelina, "Policewomen face harassment, cop says: senior female officer from Newfoundland tells conference of 'tremendous pressure to conform,'" *Hamilton Spectator* (Ontario), September 26, 2000, p. A11.

Price, Bill, "More women to aid police is need here, appeal says," *The Washington Times* (DC), October 12, 1917.

"Prison Notes," *Los Angeles Herald*, November 28, 1895.

"Prison reform worker scores methods of Los Angeles Police," *Los Angeles Herald*, February 11, 1910.

"Prison reformer busy," *Los Angeles Herald*, April 30, 1910.

Pruden, Jana G., "100 years on the beat," *Calgary Herald*, September 29, 2012.

Public Affairs Information Service 1915, New York: PAIS, 1915.

Quah, Stella R., *Friends in Blue: The Police and the Public in Singapore*, Singapore: Oxford University Press, 1988.

Quan, Douglas, "RCMP audit reveals bias against women," *The Ottawa Citizen* (Ontario), November 21, 2012, p. A4.

"Question of Police Matrons, The," *The Sun* (New York), December 29, 1890.

"Question: where do policewomen conceal pistols?" *The Evening World* (New York), March 24, 1914.

Quinn, Ben, "Do women make better riot

police?" *Christian Science Monitor*, August 22, 2009.

"Quite Natural," *The Carbon Advocate* (Leighton, PA), July 13, 1889.

Rabe-Hemp, Cara, Dawn Beichner, "An analysis of advertisements: a lens for viewing the social Exclusion of women in police imagery," *Women and Criminal Justice* 21 (2011): 63–81.

Rahn, Kim, "Policewomen less appreciated," *Korea Times* (Seoul), October 20, 2006.

Ramani, Chitra V., "Policewomen face discrimination," *The Hindu* (Madras, India), December 2, 2006.

Reed, Susan, "Nicknamed 'Calamity Jane,'" *People* 24 (August 12, 1985): 51–52.

"Reform forces combine," *Washington Times* (DC), December 5, 1894.

Repard, Pauline, "Policewoman gains settlement; Chula Vista to pay $45,000 for alleged sexual harassment," *San Diego Union-Tribune*, February 2, 1994.

"Result hard to Reach, A," *New York Times*, December 10, 1889, p. 9.

Rice, David Edgar, "Why women would rather be arrested by men," *Omaha Daily Bee*, March 29, 1914, pt. 2.

"Rip-roaring comedy," *Sausalito News*, October 17, 1914.

Roberts, Albert R., "Police Social Workers: A History," *Social Work* 21 (July 1976): 294–99.

Rotzoll, Brenda Warner, "Anna Mae Davis, founder of policewomen's group," *Chicago Sun-Times*, May 30, 2003, p. 70.

Rowe, Lily Lykes, "Appropriation for women on police squad under fire," *New York Tribune*, September 7, 1919.

"Ruling finds Harassment of Female Officer," *The Times* (London), December 17, 1991, p. B7.

"Russell Sage Police Matron's Friend," *New York Tribune*, March 21, 1901.

"Sacramento may have Policewoman," *San Francisco Call*, March 14, 1910.

"Salary increase made," *San Francisco Call*, December 6, 1910.

Santos, Celia MacDowell, "En-gendering the police: women's police stations and feminism in Sao Paulo," *Latin American Research Review* 39, no. 3 (October 2004): 29–55.

Sass, Tim R., and Jennifer L. Troyer, "Affirmative action, political representations, unions and female police employment," *Journal of Labor Research* 20 (Fall 1999): 571–87.

Saul, Louise, "Women are still scarce as Police Officers," *The Times* (London), April 8, 1990, sec. 12, pp. 1, 6, 7.

Schmidt, Bonnie Reilly, "Women on the force," *Canada's History* 91 no 4 (August/September 2011).

Schubert, Misha, "Policewoman nets $125,000 in sex harassment case," *The Australian*, June 2, 1998.

Scott, David Clark, "New Mexican Police Squad combats Corruption as it pursues Polluters," *Christian Science Monitor*, February 9, 1993, p. 7.

"See copper watch coppette, watch coppette cop jobette," *San Francisco Call*, September 29, 1913.

Seethalakshmi, S., "State policewomen a frustrated lot," *The Times of India* (Bombay), August 16, 2003.

"Seeing how it is Oneself," *St. Paul Daily Globe*, March 17, 1889.

"Seattle gets police women," *San Francisco Call*, July 11, 1912.

"Seek woman cop for duty on force at Washington," *The Evening World* (New York), August 19, 1922.

Seklecki, Richard, Rebecca Paynich, "A national survey of female police officers: an overview of Findings," *Police Practice and Research* 8 no 1 (March 2007): 17–30.

Sepkowski, Karl, "Lois Beckett was pioneering policewoman," *Toronto Star*, August 23, 1998.

Seton, Craig, "Police compensate Woman barred from Detective Work," *The Times* (London), April 8, 1992, p. 3.

"Sexual harassment allegations at the RCMP," *CBC Television* (show: *The National*), November 8, 2011.

Shadmi, Erella, "Female police officers in Israel: pattern of integration and discrimination," *Feminist Issues* (Fall 1993): 23–44.

Shapiro, Walter, "Reforming our image of

a Chief," *Time* 136 (November 26, 1990): 80–82.

Shaw, Anna Howard, "We need women police if proper protection is expected." *Nassau County Leader*, March 2, 1911.

"She-cop married fellow detective," *The Washington Times* (DC), September 18, 1919.

"She quits Boston Police," *New York Times*, February 1, 1922, p. 19.

"She still insists on Policewomen," *New York Times*, March 31, 1907, pt. 2, p. 11.

"She wants to be a Policewoman," *Richmond Planet* (VA), December 5, 1908.

"She wears a star," *The Broad Ax* (Salt Lake City), May 9, 1899.

"She would wear a Star," *Kansas City Journal* (MO), November 21, 1897.

"She'd have Women Police," *New York Times*, January 25, 1911, p. 7.

"She's a Policewoman now," *The Appeal* (St. Paul, MN), January 31, 1914.

Sherman, Lewis J., "An evaluation of Policewomen on Patrol in a Suburban Police Department," *Journal of Police Science and Administration* 3, no. 4 (December 1975): 434–38.

Shoaib, Nasrat, "Taliban kill Afghanistan's most high profile policewoman. *Agence France-Presse*, September 28, 2008.

Shpritzer, Felicia, "A Case for the Promotion of Policewomen in the City of New York," *Police* 5 (July/August 1961): 57–50.

Simpson, Jane, "Revealed, the force is biased against its policewomen," *The Mail on Sunday* (UK), March 19, 2006.

Singer, Ming S., "Sex Differences in the Perception of Male and Female Police Officers in New Zealand," *Journal of Psychology* 119 (January 1985): 53–57.

"Six policewomen just appointed are to be armed," *New York Tribune*, August 16, 1918.

"Six Policewomen put on the Force," *New York Times*, August 16, 1918, p. 16.

"Skirted coppers get 'em," *The Tacoma Times*, November 11, 1916.

Smith, Alice Ward, "Colored Policewomen of Washington," *Southern Workman* 51 (March 1922): 135–6.

Smith, Bertha H., "The Policewoman," *Good Housekeeping* 52 (March 1911): 296–98.

"Social reformers ask women police for Washington," *The Washington Times* (DC), November 12, 1912.

"Some supervision of baby farms is public necessity," *The Seattle Star*, September 25, 1909.

Sondern, Frederic, Jr., "Crime-Busters in Skirts," *Reader's Digest* 71 (November 1957): 222–25.

Stampe, Birgitte, "Women in the Danish Police Service," *Police Chief* 58 (June 1991): 15–16.

"Station-House Matrons," *New York Times*, March 3, 1882, p. 3.

"Street heroines," *Economist*, February 28, 2004.

Strobl, Staci, "Progressive or neo-traditional? Policewomen in Gulf Cooperation Council (GCC) Countries," *Feminist Formations* 22, no. 3 (2010): 51–74.

Strobl, Staci, "The Women's Police Directorate in Bahrain," *International Criminal Justice Review* 18 (March 2008): 39–58.

"Stuffed dummy? No," *San Francisco Call*, October 2, 1913.

"Suffragists tell mayor they're ready to be policewomen," *The Evening World* (New York), January 29, 1914.

Sullivan, Jennifer, "Lawsuit alleges Seattle police assaulted teen during jaywalking arrest," *Seattle Times*, August 18, 2010.

Sullivan, Joseph F., "Women as Police Must Stand Tall," *New York Times*, August 6, 1972, pp. 59, 74.

Suro, Roberto, "Houston Mayor removes Female Police Chief," *New York Times*, February 18, 1992, p. A20.

Susman, Tina, "Iraqi officials let policewomen keep guns," *Greenwich Time* (CT), January 1, 2008.

Susman, Tina, "Policewomen lose their guns—weapons will be redistributed to men," *The Grand Rapids Press* (MI), December 12, 2007.

"Tale of old Tahiti photoplay at Imperial," *San Francisco Call*, February 3, 1913.

Tamund, Tekena, *The Police in Modern*

Nigeria 1861–1965, Ibadan, Nigeria: Ibadan University Press, 1970.

"Tears cost policewoman case," *San Francisco Call*, August 9, 1913.

"Ten new policewomen appointed by Enright," *New York Times*, May 28, 1919.

Tendler, Stewart, "Police Chief says Women Officers suffer Bias," *The Times* (London), March 25, 1922, p. 3.

Tendler, Stewart, "Policewomen imprisoned by a macho culture," *The Times* (London), February 7, 1994.

Tendler, Stewart, "Policewoman wins fight over work sex gibes," *The Times* (London), November 11, 1997.

Tendler, Stewart, "Yard Investigates case of the reluctant 'W,'" *The Times* (London), January 12, 1992, p. 7.

Tenny, Evabel, "Women's Work in Law Enforcement," *Journal of Criminal Law and Criminology* 44 (July 1953): 239–46.

Texeira, Mary Thierry, "Who protects and serves me?" *Gender and Society* 16, no. 4 (2002): 524–545.

"That Matron Matter," *Fort Worth Gazette*, February 12, 1895.

Theodore, Terri, Keven Drews, "Run like your hair is on fire," *The Canadian Press*, November 10, 2011.

"These are the policewomen of the national capitol," *New York Tribune*, September 7, 1919.

"Thirty policewomen for Washington," *The Broad Ax* (Salt Lake City), December 28, 1918.

"This day in history," *Hamilton Spectator* (Ontario), March 23, 2012, p. A6.

"Three Awarded $2.7 Million in a Sexual Harassment Suit," *New York Times*, November 12, 1990, p. B8.

"3 Policewomen will be appointed Monday," *San Francisco Call*, September 26, 1913.

Tite, Constance, "Policewomen: Their Work in Germany," *The Nineteenth Century and After* 75 (June 1914): 1378–83.

"To awaken an interest," *Los Angeles Herald*, January 19, 1896.

"To Head Women Police," *New York Times*, March 13, 1924, p. 28.

"To 'Mother' the Criminal," *New York Times*, July 24, 1909, p. 6.

"Told Annoyer to 'Beat It,'" *New York Times*, August 7, 1913, p. 1.

"Toledo to have Women Police, *Bisbee Daily Review*, April 21, 1907.

"Tombs, The," *New York Times*, January 16, 1870, p. 3.

Townsey, Roi Dianne, "Black Women in American Policing," *Journal of Criminal Justice* 10, no. 6 (1982): 455–68.

"Trainer of Policewomen in New York to get Ideas," *New York Times*, April 27, 1924, sec. 9, p. 11.

"Treatment of Women at Police Stations, The," *The Times* (London), February 22, 1913, p. 8.

Triplett, Peggy E., "Women in Policing," *Police Chief* 43 (December 1976): 46–49.

Tripp, H. Alker, "Women Police," *The Nineteenth Century and After* 107 (June 1930): 815–24.

"12 armed women soon to be added to police force," *New York Tribune*, May 21, 1918.

"22 women line up for jobs on police force," *San Francisco Call*, July 30, 1913.

"Two coppettes named by board; pick third later," *San Francisco Call*, September 30, 1913.

"2,000 Women in Police Force," *The Times* (London), February 1, 1954, p. 2.

United States. The National Advisory Police Committee on Social Protection of the Federal Security Agency, *Techniques of Law Enforcement in the Use of Policewomen with Special Reference To Social Protection*, Washington, DC: Federal Security Agency, Office of Community War Services, Social Protection Division, 1945.

United States, Women's Bureau, "The Outlook for Women in Police Work," *Bulletin of the Women's Bureau*, no. 231, Washington, DC: GPO, 1949.

"Unsung Policewomen and Crime Prevention," *Los Angeles Times*, November 12, 1934, sec. 2, p. 5.

"Urge appointment of woman officer," *Los Angeles Herald*, June 9, 1910.

"Urges Policewomen on every city force," *New York Tribune*, December 19, 1912.

Van Winkle, Mina, "Municipal Police-women — Their Duties and Opportuni-ties," *American City* 25 (August 1921): 93–96.

Van Winkle, Mina, "The Policewoman," *Survey* 52 (September 15, 1924): 629–31.

Vastola, Anthony, "Women in Policing," *Police Chief* 44 (January 1977): 62–69.

"Views differ about a policewoman here," *University Missourian* (Columbia, MO), November 18, 1915.

Vollmer, August, "Meet the Lady Cop," *Survey* 63 (March 15, 1930): 702–03.

Walbrook, H. M., "Women Police and their Work," *The Nineteenth Century and After* 85 (February 1919): 377–82.

Waldron, Martin, "An All-Female Class is planned for Jersey State Police Academy, *New York Times*, September 13, 1979, pp. A1, B4.

Walsh, Jude T., "Some Questions in Re: Po-licewomen on Patrol," *Police Chief* 42 (July 1975): 20–22.

"Want Policewomen on the City's Force," *New York Times*, October 28, 1916, p. 4.

"Want Time to Consider," *Evening World* (New York), August 6, 1890.

"Want to be Police Matrons," *New York Times*, May 21, 1891, p. 10.

"Want Women to serve as Police," *The Maui News*, May 26, 1906.

"Wants Women on Police," *New York Times*, July 23, 1909, p. 1.

"Wants Women on the force," *The Sun* (New York), March 7, 1906.

"Weeks' events in brief paragraphs," *Sausalito News*, May 16, 1914.

Weikel, Dan, "Campbell Calls Firing part of a Conspiracy," *Los Angeles Times*, De-cember 24, 1992, pp. A3, A16.

Weikel, Dan, "4 more Women to join suit against Police, *Los Angeles Times*, De-cember 2, 1992, pp. A3, A28.

Weikel, Dan, "Police Chief fired in New-port Beach," *Los Angeles Times*, Decem-ber 23, 1992, pp. A3, A22.

Weikel, Dan, "Sexual Harassment suit filed against Police," *Los Angeles Times*, Sep-tember 25, 1992, p. A35.

Weinstein, Henry, "Court finds Bias against Women Deputies," *Los Angeles Times*, July 24, 1991, pp. B1, B7.

Weisheit, Ralph A., "Women in the State Police," *Journal of Police Science and Ad-ministration* 15, no. 2 (June 1987): 137–44.

Wells, Alice Stebbins, "Women on the Po-lice Force," *American City* 8 (April 1913): 401.

Wells, Barbara, "The Feminine Arm of the Law," *Independent Woman* 27 (February 1948): 34–36.

"Western Policewomen," *The Washington Herald* (DC), August 16, 1909.

"Western Women as Police Officers," *Sur-vey* 29 (December 21, 1912): 345–47.

Wexler, Judie Gaffin, "Sources of Stress among Women Police Officers," *Journal of Police Science and Administration* 11 (March 1983): 46–53.

"What some Women are doing," *San Fran-cisco Call*, August 7, 1909.

Whitaker, Jane, "Policewomen prove little improvement over the brutal men cop-pers," *The Day Book* (Chicago), Febru-ary 27, 1914.

"Why not women police," *The Tacoma Times*, April 29, 1911.

"Why Women may Win," *Pittsburg Dis-patch*, November 1, 1889.

"Widow is Named a Police Deputy," *New York Times*, January 29, 1918, pp. 1, 11.

Wilgoren, Jodi, "Inquiry finds merit in Sex Harassment Suit," *Los Angeles Times*, December 16, 1992, pp. A3, A31.

Wilgoren, Jodi, "Newport Beach settles with fired Police Chief, Captain," *Los Angeles Times*, June 11, 1993, p. B8.

Wilgoren, Jodi, "Newport Beach won't pay fired Officers' Legal Costs," *Los Angeles Times*, January 29, 1993, p. A29.

Wilkinson, Paul, "Policewoman wins huge payout in sex harassment case," *The Times* (London), September 18, 1996.

"Will add 12 Women to Regular Police," *New York Times*, May 21, 1918, p. 24.

"Will Begin Today," *Kansas City Daily Journal* (MO), February 5, 1896.

Wilson, O. W., *Police Administration*, 2nd ed., New York: McGraw-Hill, 1963.

Winnard, Karin, "Policewomen and the People they Serve," *Police Chief* 53 (Au-gust 1986): 62–63.

"Wish to be Police Matrons," *The Evening World* (New York), May 20, 1891.

"Wives and mothers," *Los Angeles Herald*, March 13, 1909.

"A Woman Constable," *The Guthrie Daily Leader* (OK), August 1, 1897.

"Woman cop at Union Station watches for fair flirters," *The Washington Herald* (DC), May 4, 1919.

"Woman in Chicago to do police duty," *Los Angeles Herald*, May 13, 1909.

"Woman made a Detective," *New York Times*, March 2, 1912, p. 5.

"Woman Officers may appeal over Police Reform, *The Times* (London), January 27, 1978, p. 2.

"Woman on police force," *Sausalito News*, September 2, 1911.

"Woman Police Chief attacks bias in Force," *The Times* (London), May 13, 1986, p. 3.

"Woman Police head demoted by Whalen in Birth Clinic Raid," *New York Times*, May 12, 1929, pp. 1, 15.

"Woman Police Officer, A," *The Times* (London), June 12, 1914, p. 5.

"Woman Police Sergeant," *Willmar Tribune* (MN), July 17, 1901.

"Woman Policeman gives views on duty of society," *The Arizona Republican*, September 3, 1911.

"Woman Policeman Is Favored by Commission," *Los Angeles Herald*, June 14, 1910.

"A Woman's College in the Bible," *The Courier* (Lincoln, NE) August 18, 1900.

"A Woman's Prison," *The New Northwest* (Portland, OR), August 8, 1878.

"Woman's World," *Los Angeles Herald*, December 31, 1893.

"Woman's World," *Los Angeles Herald*, February 2, 1895.

"Women apply for police positions," *San Francisco Call*, June 28, 1913.

"Women as Policemen," *The Salt Lake Herald*, November 23, 1897.

"Women back the Widow," *The Washington Times* (DC), November 22, 1894.

"Women Cops if she has her way," *The Minneapolis Journal*, May 7, 1906.

"Women Cops on the Beat," *Time* 115 (March 10, 1980): 58.

"Women in Blue, The," *Time* 99 (May 1, 1972): 60.

"Women in Scotland Yard," *New York Times*, August 16, 1933, p. 12.

"Women make good on Pickpocket Squad," *New York Times*, September 25, 1935, p. 9.

"Women on the Force," *New York Times*, February 22, 1927, p. 18.

"Women Police, The, *The Times* (London), April 17, 1917, p. 9.

"Women Police," *The Times* (London), December 14, 1922, p. 12.

"Women Police," *The Times* (London), July 24, 1934, p. 16.

"Women Police," *The Times* (London), December 3, 1929, p. 11.

"Women Police," *The Times* (London): August 6, 1940, p. 5.

"Women Police and their work," *The Washington Times* (DC), November 17, 1912.

"Women Police at Odds," *New York Times*, April 9, 1921, p. 24.

"Women Police grapple with the Masher Evil," *New York Times*, March 23, 1924, sec. pp. 11.

"Women Police in district will be urged by woman," *The Washington Times* (DC), November 17, 1912.

"Women Police Meet," *New York Times*, October 27, 1912, p. 1.

"Women Police not needed at Coney," *New York Tribune*, June 20, 1913.

"Women Police of Detroit," *New York Times*, March 13, 1921, sec. 9, p. 4.

"Women Police Officers needed in city, says Mrs. Alice S. Wells," *San Francisco Call*, March 21, 1912.

"Women Police patrol parks and teach youths," *Los Angeles Herald*, April 7, 1909.

"Women Police Reserves well trained now to meet any emergency city may face," *The Sun* (New York), September 8, 1918.

"Women Police Service in England," *Survey* 38 (September 1, 1917): 490–491.

"Women Police to solve white slave problem," *The Evening World* (New York), December 17, 1912.

"Women Police too Costly," *New York Times*, February 14, 1922, p. 8.

"Women Police Wanted," *The Times* (London), April 13, 1946, p. 2.

"Women Police Wanted by Matrons of New York Society," *The San Francisco Call*, April 4, 1905.

"Women Police Withdrawn," *New York Times*, March 4, 1914, p. 1.

"Women protective officers," *San Francisco Call*, August 15, 1913.

"Women recruited at slow rate by nation's law enforcement agencies, report reveals," *Jet*, April 26, 1999.

"Women to patrol beach," *San Francisco Call*, July 8, 1913.

"Women to Sweep New York Streets," *New York Times*, August 18, 1918, p. 3.

"Women's Auxiliary for Police Reserve," *New York Times*, May 10, 1918, p. 11.

"Women's interests," *The Seattle Republican*, February 3, 1911.

"Women's Police Work to undergo new Study," *New York Times*, July 7, 1929, sec. 8, p. 9.

"Women's Precinct needs are shown," *New York Times*, May 8, 1921, sec. 2, p. 6.

"Women's War Work," *The Times* (London), May 21, 1915, p. 5.

"Word with a Brazilian Policewoman, A," *Americas* 9 (July 1957): 26–27.

"Work of a Police Matron," *Omaha Daily Bee*, September 26, 1909.

"Work of the Policewomen of Chicago," *The Red Cloud Chief* (Red Cloud, NE), September 1, 1910.

"Working in a man's world: women in the Fiji police force," *World of Work* no. 65 (April 2009): 14–15.

"World's Fair Notes," *Los Angeles Herald*, July 1, 1890.

"Would teach girls self-defense art," *The Washington Times* (DC), July 11, 1910.

Wride, Nancy, "Newport Beach Police Chief, Aide put on leave over Rape Allegations," *Los Angeles Times*, October 16, 1992, pp. A3, A36.

Wride, Nancy, "Police Chief named in Harassment suit to Retire," *Los Angeles Times*, October 15, 1992, pp. A3, A29.

Wride, Nancy, "Police Officials sue Newport Beach over Harassment Inquiry," *Los Angeles Times*, November 13, 1992, pp. A3, A34.

Wride, Nancy, "Women alleging Sex Harassment cite Reprisal Fear," *Los Angeles Times*, September 28, 1992, pp. A3, A13.

Wyles, Lilian, *A Woman of Scotland Yard*, London: Faber and Faber, 1952.

"Yard to end separate Police-Force for Women," *The Times* (London), September 23, 1972, p. 2.

"You'd better make your eyes behave," *The Ogden Standard* (Utah), October 23, 1915.

"Y.W.C.A. holds vesper service," *San Francisco Call*, June 30, 1912.

Index

367